Acoustic Phonetics

Acoustic Phonetics

A course of basic readings

edited by D. B. Fry

Cambridge University Press

Cambridge
London   New York   Melbourne

CAMBRIDGE UNIVERSITY PRESS
Cambridge, New York, Melbourne, Madrid, Cape Town, Singapore, São Paulo, Delhi

Cambridge University Press
The Edinburgh Building, Cambridge CB2 8RU, UK

Published in the United States of America by Cambridge University Press, New York

www.cambridge.org
Information on this title: www.cambridge.org/9780521107457

First published 1976
This digitally printed version 2009

A catalogue record for this publication is available from the British Library

Library of Congress Catalogue Card Number: 76–16916

ISBN 978-0-521-21393-6 hardback
ISBN 978-0-521-10745-7 paperback

Contents

Preface 9

Introduction 11

Part One
Acoustics of the Speech Mechanism 19

1 Homer Dudley (1940)
The Carrier Nature of Speech 21

2 James L. Flanagan (1958)
Some Properties of the Glottal Sound Source 31

3 Kenneth N. Stevens and Arthur S. House (1961)
An Acoustical Theory of Vowel Production and Some of its Implications 52

Part Two
Acoustic Analysis of Speech 75

4 W. Koenig, H. K. Dunn and L. Y. Lacy (1946)
The Sound Spectrograph 77

Analysis of Vowel Sounds 92

5 R. S. Paget (1922)
Vowel Resonances 95

6 Gordon E. Peterson and Harold L. Barney (1952)
Control Methods Used in a Study of the Vowels 104

Analysis of Consonant Sounds 123

7 Wiktor Jassem (1962)
The Acoustics of Consonants 124

8 Peter Strevens (1960)
Spectra of Fricative Noise in Human Speech 132

9 George W. Hughes and Morris Halle (1956)
Spectral Properties of Fricative Consonants 151

10 M. Halle, G. W. Hughes and J.-P. A. Radley (1957)
Acoustic Properties of Stop Consonants 162

Part Three
Acoustic Cues in Speech 177

11 Harvey Fletcher (1953)
Effects of Filtering and Masking 179

12 George A. Miller and Patricia E. Nicely (1955)
An Analysis of Perceptual Confusions Among Some English Consonants 184

Speech Synthesis 202

13 Franklin S. Cooper, Alvin M. Liberman and John M. Borst (1951)
The Interconversion of Audible and Visible Patterns as a Basis for Research in the Perception of Speech 204

14 W. Lawrence (1953)
The Synthesis of Speech from Signals Which Have a Low Information Rate 208

Perceptual Experiments 219

15 Pierre C. Delattre, Alvin M. Liberman, Franklin S. Cooper and Louis J. Gerstman (1952)
An Experimental Study of the Acoustic Determinants of Vowel Color; Observations on One- and Two-Formant Vowels Synthesized from Spectrographic Patterns 221

16 Dennis B. Fry, Arthur S. Abramson, Peter D. Eimas and Alvin M. Liberman (1962)
The Identification and Discrimination of Synthetic Vowels 238

17 Franklin S. Cooper, Pierre C. Delattre, Alvin M. Liberman, John M. Borst and Louis J. Gerstman (1952)
Some Experiments on the Perception of Synthetic Speech Sounds 258

18 Pierre C. Delattre, Alvin M. Liberman and Franklin S. Cooper (1955)
Acoustic Loci and Transitional Cues for Consonants 273

19 Katherine S. Harris (1958)
Cues for the Discrimination of American English Fricatives in Spoken Syllables 284

20 J. D. O'Connor, Louis J. Gerstman, A. M. Liberman, Pierre C.
Delattre and Franklin S. Cooper (1957)
Acoustic Cues for the Perception of Initial /w, j, r, l/ in English 298

21 Alvin M. Liberman, Pierre C. Delattre, Franklin S. Cooper and
Louis J. Gerstman (1954)
*The Role of Consonant–Vowel Transitions in the Perception of the Stop
and Nasal Consonants* 315

Perception and Linguistic Categories 332

22 Alvin M. Liberman, Katherine S. Harris, Howard S. Hoffman and
Belver C. Griffith (1957)
*The Discrimination of Speech Sounds Within and Across Phoneme
Boundaries* 333

23 Leigh Lisker and Arthur S. Abramson (1970)
*The Voicing Dimension: Some Experiments in Comparative
Phonetics* 348

Part Four
Investigation of Prosodic Features 353

24 Ilse Lehiste and Gordon E. Peterson (1959)
Vowel Amplitude and Phonemic Stress in American English 355

25 Arthur S. House (1961)
On Vowel Duration in English 369

26 Ilse Lehiste and Gordon E. Peterson (1961)
Some Basic Considerations in the Analysis of Intonation 378

27 Philip Lieberman (1960)
Some Acoustic Correlates of Word Stress in American English 394

28 Dennis B. Fry (1958)
Experiments in the Perception of Stress 401

29 Dennis B. Fry (1965)
The Dependence of Stress Judgments on Vowel Formant Structure 425

30 Kerstin Hadding-Koch and Michael Studdert-Kennedy (1964)
An Experimental Study of Some Intonation Contours 431

Part Five
Speech Synthesis by Rule   443

31 Alvin M. Liberman, Frances Ingemann, Leigh Lisker, Pierre C. Delattre and Franklin S. Cooper (1959)
Minimal Rules for Synthesizing Speech   445

Further Reading   466

Acknowledgements   467

The plates will be found between pp. 254 and 255

Preface

This book of readings is intended primarily for students of linguistics and phonetics, though it may also prove of value as a source book for teachers and research workers in the field. It is concerned exclusively with work in acoustic phonetics, with the methods and results of experimental research and with theoretical viewpoints which have developed in the course of this study. The papers reprinted here cover much of the history of the subject and many of them have been deliberately chosen because they present the rationale of what has been done as well as its results. Without this information it is difficult for students to appreciate the significance of much of the more recent work which rests upon the solid foundation of the research reported in these papers, many of them rightly regarded as 'classics' of the experimental work on speech of the past decades.

Introduction

Whatever knowledge we have at present of linguistics, i.e. about the way in which language works, derives ultimately from observation of people talking and listening to each other. Speech is the primary and universal expression of language. It precedes other forms of expression in the individual and in human communities, with very few exceptions as far as our records go. The study of speech is, therefore, fundamental for our understanding of linguistics.

As ordinary language users, we inevitably regard speech as a unitary activity although it is in fact a complex of many different kinds of activity carried on at a number of different levels. It can be viewed from at least the three standpoints of psychology, physiology and physics. The use of memory stores of words, of grammatical and phonological forms, the organizing of messages at the semantic level and, in fact, most of what we regard as linguistic activity in speech is a matter of psychological functioning. The working of nerves and muscles, broadly the articulatory aspect of speech, is material for physiological study, while the generation, transmission and reception of sound waves are accessible only to the methods of physics.

For the student of linguistics, the interest of work in these three fields lies in the fact that the working of language systems can be traced through related events occurring in sound waves, nerves, muscles, memory and thoughts. The study of these connections is the basic function of the discipline which is generally termed *experimental phonetics* for the good reason that the necessary observations cannot be made in the natural conditions of speech communication, but call for the control of some of the factors which influence speech events, that is, for an experimental situation. Measurement is a basic procedure in this work and since measurement in physics and physiology requires the use of a variety of measuring and registering instruments, the term *instrumental phonetics* is sometimes applied to this kind of research.

The sound waves of speech clearly play a vital part in the communication process. The measurement of sound waves and the examination of the links between the features of speech sound waves and the working of linguistic systems is the task of one specific part of experimental phonetics, *acoustic phonetics*. In this context the word 'acoustic' bears its root meaning of 'related to the sense of hearing', for work in this field is concerned with relating measurable features of speech sound waves with the effect which speech stimuli have on the hearing mechanism and with the perceptual world which results from the transmission of auditory information to the brain. Acoustics in its wider usage refers mainly to the study of the generation and measurement of sound waves, and acoustic phonetics necessarily makes use of the physical methods of acoustics for similar purposes, that is, in order to establish the properties of the sound stimuli which speech presents to the ear. To extend the inquiry to the perceptual effects of these stimuli and their relation to language working, it employs methods which are very largely those of experimental psychology and are described in a number of the papers included in this book.

The mechanisms for generating sounds which are dealt with in acoustics generally have physical properties which are well known or can be established with some certainty. The speech-producing mechanism is altogether another matter, consisting as it does of a part of the human body and operating under the control of the human brain. If it were the case that the physical dimensions, the characteristics and physical constants of the vocal tract could be completely specified for one speaker speaking at a given time, then the acoustic output of the tract at that time could be predicted with certainty, and if the changes in these factors during a stretch of speech were known, then the variations in acoustic output could again be predicted. We are far from knowing these physical characteristics in every detail but there is now a body of acoustical theory which relates what is known of the vocal tract with the main features of the sounds of speech; that is to say we have reasonably firm answers to questions such as what kinds of sound can be produced by the various actions of the speech mechanism, what acoustic principles are involved and what limits can be set to the range of sounds likely to occur in the course of human speech.

The view of the speech mechanism as an acoustic generator which has proved most enlightening and fruitful is that which regards the larynx as producing a 'carrier' wave which is continuously modulated by the action of the articulatory mechanism. The vocal cord tone, or the sound of 'voice', is the factor in speech which makes it most readily audible; it is the modulations or modifications imposed on this tone by the articulations of speech which are principally responsible for its intelligibility. The vocal tract above the larynx acts as a resonating system for the vocal cord tone and it is the characteristics of this resonating or filtering system which are continuously changed by the sequence of articulations. In this theoretical framework, the larynx mechanism is referred to as the 'source' of sound and the wave form which it generates as the 'source function', while the characteristic of the vocal tract is referred to as the 'system' function. During whispered speech, the larynx is still the source of sound but this is now a noise instead of the periodic tone which is present in voiced speech and it is the noise that is modulated by the system. In normal speech, the larynx is not in fact the only source of sound; many consonant articulations result in the setting up of a noise source at some other point in the vocal tract, for example at the teeth ridge, the hard or the soft palate, and this noise generator may be working alone or at the same time as the larynx tone generator (as it is in the case of voiced fricatives, for example).

These basic acoustic principles underlie the production of human speech wherever we find it and are applicable to all natural languages which we know anything about. For this reason papers on these general aspects of speech acoustics have been placed first in this book. They deal with the properties of the larynx as a sound source, the vocal tract as a resonating system and the nature of the noises which are used in speech.

One of the basic tools of acoustic phonetics is acoustic analysis, which commonly deals with the distribution of speech sound energy over the acoustic spectrum in terms of frequency and intensity, and with variations in this distribution with time. The instrument employed to make such an analysis is a sound spectrograph, which is, as its name conveys, a device for drawing spectra. So much of the published work is based on analyses made with a spectrograph of one particular design that it seemed advisable to include in the book a paper describing this machine in some detail. The information obtained through its use is most often presented in the form of a visible pattern in which the passage of time is represented on the horizontal scale, successive frequency bands on the vertical scale and variations of sound intensity with both frequency and time are presented as changes in the darkness of the trace. A number of the papers reprinted include spectrograms of this sort and, where necessary, the conditions in which the analyses are made can be established by reference to the descriptive paper on spectrography by Koenig, Dunn and Lacy (see Reading 4).

Acoustic analysis must obviously be applied to *particular* samples of speech, to utterances by individual speakers using a given language; but the results of the analysis will be *generally* useful, to the extent that they provide a basis for generalizing about sounds occurring in one language or about types of sound which may be found in a variety of languages. The papers on acoustic analysis reprinted here are intended to exemplify the methods most often used and the kind of result which can be looked for. References to acoustic differences between languages which may occur are incidental to this main purpose and no attempt is made to provide a body of information about the sounds of a particular language. Since a great proportion of the acoustic analysis of speech sounds which has been done is concerned with English speech, it is inevitable that material on varieties of this language should loom rather large in the papers included in this book.

Much of the work on acoustic analysis has been devoted to the specification of sound differences operating at the phonological level. Similar methods can be applied with respect to prosodic features, in exploring the acoustic correlates of stress, tone and length in various languages. In order to afford a more coherent picture of this work, papers dealing with this topic are collected in the section on prosodic features.

Whether one is dealing with the phonemic system of a language or with its tone and stress patterns, the basis for acoustic research is always the functional systems of the language, which is to say the results of linguistic analysis. Contrary to a belief which has sometimes been expressed in the course of the history of linguistic studies, these functional systems or functional units cannot be arrived at through acoustic analysis. The reason for this is that the phonological system of a language represents the mode in which the human brain organizes acoustic information and not something which is explicit in the acoustic sphere itself. There must clearly be correspondences between language units and features in the sound waves, and the purpose of acoustic work in linguistics is to discover what these correspondences are; but, for reasons which will be touched on later, the correlations are not and cannot be one-to-one.

The point of departure is therefore the phonemic or stress or tone system of a language as arrived at through linguistic analysis. A range of utterances containing examples of realizations of the various units then forms a body of material for acoustic analysis and the object of this process is to discover regularities in the acoustic data which correspond to the occurrence of given language units. Measurements will be made in several dimensions, principally frequency, intensity and time but often derived quantities such as the rate of change of frequency with time are found to be important. In order that conclusions can be drawn reliably from the measurements it is necessary to look at a large number of samples and the measuring is therefore laborious. It is in this connection that the sound spectrograph has proved so valuable because it provides visible patterns which portray the chief acoustic characteristics of speech sequences, and it is possible, simply by inspection of a large enough number of these, to discover what specific measurements are likely to be the most rewarding. Much of the work described in the papers on acoustic analysis is based on this method.

As soon as modern techniques of acoustic analysis began to be widely used in studying speech, one of the most striking discoveries was that the occurrence of a given language unit was very often marked not by the presence of just one acoustic feature but by several. Furthermore, it was far from certain that all of these acoustic features would recur with every occurrence of the unit; sometimes one feature would be missing or very much weakened, sometimes another, so that the most one could say was that when language unit x occurs in the sequence, there is a strong tendency for features *a*, *b*, *c* and *d* to be present in the acoustic analysis in some combination or other. This effectively disposed of the idea of a one-to-one correspondence between, for example, phonemes and acoustic features, and of the theory that every unit is signalled by some acoustic invariant. The contribution of acoustic analysis to knowledge in this field was now seen to lie in the specification of all the various features which tended to recur and which must presumably provide the basis for the identification of different language units by people listening to speech.

Attention now began to be focused very much on the perception of speech and it became clear that some very complex processing must be involved. If there could be as many as three or four acoustic features recurring with a given unit, were they all important as 'cues' for the identification of the sound? Since some could be missing from the acoustic analysis, presumably not; were some of the cues redundant altogether perhaps, or was there at any rate a difference in the 'weight' of the various cues for identification? Questions of this kind led to an entirely new line of research connected with the acoustics of speech. They could not be answered except by finding some method which would make it possible to separate out the different cues and, if possible, test their effectiveness one at a time. Efforts in this direction had already been made by such means as filtering out frequency bands in the speech signal or masking them by noise. What this technique does in effect is to subtract certain information from the total speech signal and test the influence of this on the identification of different speech sounds. If the speech is transmitted through a low-pass filter which cuts off sharply at 3000 Hz, for example, any cues which depend on frequency information in the band above this will be suppressed. Much of our basic knowledge about speech recognition has come from work of this kind; a classic example of the use of the technique is presented in the paper by Miller and Nicely (see Reading 12).

When this method of subtracting information is used, however, there may well be several cues for a particular sound in what is left, so that we are still dealing with a group of cues and the interactions between them. In order to study the effect of any single cue, it is necessary to have recourse to speech synthesis, that is to the generating of speech-like sounds by the use of electronic circuits or by some other means in conditions where one acoustic feature of the signal can be systematically varied under the control of the experimenter. The sounds manufactured must be 'speech-like' only to the extent necessary for listeners to treat them as if they were speech. It is found in practice that sounds having small resemblance to speech are readily dealt with in this way by ordinary listeners. A speech synthesizer makes it possible to generate a whole series of sound stimuli in which a single acoustic feature is varied systematically over a range of values, while all other aspects of the sound are held constant. The stimuli can then be formed into listening tests, generally random sequences of the stimuli, each one repeated many times, and listeners asked to identify each item in the test as some speech sound or other. The influence of the particular cue on identification is then reflected in variations in the certainty with which a sound is identified either by a group of listeners or by an individual listener who has heard the stimuli many times.

A number of different kinds of speech synthesizer are now in use in various laboratories and in the present phase of research many of these are controlled by means of digital computers. The earliest synthesizer to be used for perceptual experiments was a device for 'replaying' sound spectrograms. The pioneer work in this field was done with this machine by research workers at the Haskins Laboratories and therefore a paper which includes a description of the apparatus is reproduced here, together with a number of other papers from the same research team which report the classical work in this area (see Readings, 13, 15–23).

The method of speech synthesis and perceptual experiment is applicable not only to the study of cues for phonemic distinctions but also to the exploration of cues for differences of tone and stress. Papers describing this work are included in the section on prosodic features.

There remains a great deal which is still unknown about the processes of speech recognition and identification, particularly with regard to the interaction of cues. One method of evaluating progress in this direction is the attempt to formulate rules for synthesizing speech in a given language. The theoretical basis for this is the idea that if we knew all the cues for all phonemic distinctions and all functional differences of tone and stress, and the conditions in which each cue operates, for example in English, we could then write a complete set of rules for synthesizing English, the application of which would result in the production of intelligible English. One of the earlier papers is this field in included to illustrate this extension of the work on speech synthesis and perception.

The material contained in the book is confined to accounts of fundamental research in acoustic phonetics; it does not deal with any of the numerous applications of this research, for example, to the design of speech recognizing machines, to the teaching of languages, to the diagnosis and treatment of pathological conditions involving speech and language. In such areas as these the discoveries recorded in this book are of the utmost importance; so too will be the results of future research in acoustic phonetics. As in many fields, there is continuous interaction between fundamental research and the application of knowledge gained by it. A good example of this is to be found in the work of the Haskins Laboratories, where basic research on speech perception grew out of the practical project of constructing a reading device for the blind. The future direction of work in acoustic phonetics is likely to be connected with work on brain functioning, which is of importance for the field of artificial intelligence and the development of many of the artefacts which lie ahead in the computer age. This will call for experimentation involving the whole of speech programming and processing, including the relations between the acoustic level of speech and operations at the grammatical, syntactical and lexical levels as well as at the phonological.

Part One
Acoustics of the Speech Mechanism

The three papers in the first section present some fundamental acoustic concepts connected with the working of the speech mechanism as a sound generating device. Dudley's paper is the clearest statement in the literature of the carrier nature of speech and is also a good example of the interaction that has taken place between the approach to practical problems and the development of theoretical viewpoints. It was the designing of a speech synthesizer which led him to consider and to formulate the essential functions of the speech mechanism, making explicit the relation between the part played by the larynx tone and by the articulatory movements which occur at syllabic rates.

The acoustical principles involved in the operation of both the sound source in the larynx and the filtering system of the vocal tract form the subject of a considerable body of published work. The two papers included here can provide only samples of the kind of work that has been done and the student is advised to supplement the reading of them by reference to some of the standard works listed in the Further Reading list. Among these, two should be mentioned here; the first is Flanagan's *Speech Analysis, Synthesis and Perception* (1972) which gives a very full technical treatment of the subject but contains a good deal of material which is quite accessible to the student of linguistics. The second is Fant's *Acoustic Theory of Speech Production* (1960). The contribution made by Fant to our knowledge in this field is universally recognized and his book affords the best means of becoming acquainted with his work; it is for this reason that he is not represented in the present collection of papers.

With the modern techniques available for recording, registering and measuring sound, it is possible to specify with a high degree of accuracy the properties of speech sounds produced by the human speech mechanism. It is a matter of much greater difficulty to give a rigorous account of the way in which they are produced. In the papers by Flanagan and by Stevens and House the student is introduced to the standard method of attempting this, which is to set up first a mathematical model and then, if necessary, a physically existing model which represents an approximation to the speech mechanism, to compare the output of such a model with natural speech sounds and to refine the model by successive modifications so as to improve the approximation of its output to natural speech. In these two papers this is done with reference to the glottal sound source and to the vocal tract as a mechanism for producing vowel sounds. The Stevens and House paper deals with the fundamental concept of the *formant* which figures in a considerable proportion of the papers in the book.

1 Homer Dudley

The Carrier Nature of Speech

Excerpt from Homer Dudley, 'The carrier nature of speech', *Bell System Technical Journal*, vol. 19 (1940), pp. 495–513. Copyright 1940, American Telephone and Telegraph Company.

Speech is like a radio wave in that information is transmitted over a suitably chosen carrier. In fact the modern radio broadcast system is but an electrical analogue of man's acoustic broadcast system supplied by nature. Communication by speech consists in a sending by one mind and the receiving by another of a succession of phonetic symbols with some emotional content added. Such material of itself changes gradually at syllabic rates and so is inaudible. Accordingly, an audible sound stream is interposed between the talker's brain and the listener. On this sound stream there is moulded an imprint of the message. The listener receives the moulded sound stream and unravels the imprinted message.

In the past this carrier nature has been obscured by the complexity of speech.[1] However, in developing electrical speech synthesizers copying the human mechanism in principle, it was soon apparent that carrier circuits were being set up. Tracing the carrier idea back to the voice mechanism there was unfolded, a little at a time, the carrier nature of speech. Ultimately the speech mechanism was revealed in its simplest terms as a mechanical sender of acoustic waves analogous to the electrical sender of electromagnetic waves in the form of the radio transmitter. Each of these senders embodies a modulating device for moulding message information on a carrier wave suitable for propagation of energy through a transmission medium between the sending and receiving points.

The carrier elements of speech

This carrier basis of speech will be illustrated by simple speech examples selected to show separately the three carrier elements of speech, namely, the

1. Speech-making processes are here explained in the terms of the carrier engineer to give a clearer insight into the physical nature of speech. The point of view is essentially that of the philologist who associates a message of tongue and lip positions with each sound he hears. This aspect also underlies the gesture theory of speech by Paget and others and the visible speech ideas of Alexander Melville Bell. The author has been assisted in expressing speech fundamentals in carrier engineering terms by numerous associates in the Bell Telephone Laboratories experienced in carrier circuit theory. Acknowledgment is made in particular of the contributions of Mr Lloyd Espenschied.

carrier wave, the message wave and their combining by a modulating mechanism. These illustrations serve the purpose of broad definitions of the carrier elements in speech.

The illustration chosen for the carrier wave of speech is a talker's sustained tone such as the sound *ah*. In the idealized case there is no variation of intensity, spectrum or frequency. This carrier then is audible but contains no information, for information is dynamic,[2] ever changing. The carrier provides the connecting link to the listener's ear over which information can be carried. Thus the talker may pass information over this link by starting and stopping in a prearranged code the vocal tone as in imitating a telegraph buzzer. For transmitting information it is necessary to modulate this carrier with the message to be transmitted.

For the second illustration, message waves are produced as muscular motions in the vocal tract of a 'silent talker' as he goes through all the vocal effort of talking except that he holds his breath. The message is inaudible because the motions are at slow syllabic rates limited by the relatively sluggish muscular actions in the vocal tract. Nevertheless, these motions contain the dynamic speech information, as is proved by their interpretation by lip readers to the extent that visibility permits. Another method of demonstrating the information content of certain of these motions is the artificial injection of a sound stream into the back of the mouth for a 'carrier' whereby intelligible speech can be produced from almost any sound stream (Riesz, 1930; Firestone, 1940). The need of an audible 'carrier' to transmit this inaudible 'message' is obvious.

The final example, to illustrate the modulating mechanism in speech production, is from a person talking in a normal fashion. In this example are present the message and carrier waves of the previous examples, for both are needed if the former is to modulate the latter. However, the mere presence of the carrier and message waves will not make speech, for if they are supplied separately, one by a silent talker and the other by an intoner, no speech is heard but only the audible intoned carrier. Ordinary speech results from a single person producing the message waves and the carrier waves simultaneously in his vocal tract, for then the carrier of speech receives an imprint of the message by modulation.

The speech mechanism as a circuit

The foregoing three illustrations, by segregating the basic elements in speech production reveal the underlying principles. The present paper

2. The information referred to is that in the communication of intelligence. There is, however, static information in the carrier itself. This serves for 'station identification' in radio and may similarly help in telling whether it was Uncle Bill or Aunt Sue who said *ah*.

treats of these elements as functioning parts of a circuit. In Figure 1 is shown a cross-section of the vocal system. The idea to be expressed originates in the talker's brain at the top left. Thence, impulses pass through the nerves to the vocal tract with the complete information of the 'message', that is to say, what carrier should be used, what fundamental frequency if

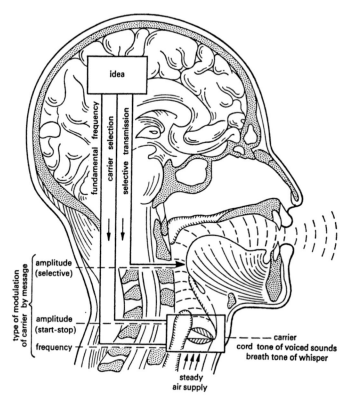

Figure 1 The vocal system as a carrier circuit

the carrier is of the voiced type and what transmission through the vocal tract as a function of frequency. The carrier, whether voiced or unvoiced, is shown for simplicity as arising at the talker's vocal cords. This carrier is modulated to form speech having the complete message imprinted on it preparatory to radiation from the talker's mouth to the ear of the listener, who recognizes the imprinted message.

In discussing the speech mechanism as a circuit, it is clearer to start with a block schematic. Figure 2 has thus been drawn to sketch the basic plan

Homer Dudley 23

of speech synthesizing. As in Figure 1, the idea gives rise to the message which modulates the voice carrier to produce the speech radiated from the talker's mouth. One can follow the path of the message from its inception in the talker's brain to its radiation from his mouth as an imprint on the

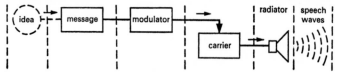

Figure 2 The basic plan of synthesizing speech

issuing sound stream. The progress of the sound stream is also seen from its origin as an oscillatory carrier to its radiation from the talker's mouth carrying the message imprint.[3] The smaller arrow heads indicate direction of flow while the larger ones indicate a modulatory control of the carrier by the message. This modulatory control is exerted on the carrier wave in part as the carrier is generated and in part as it is transmitted after generation.

Relevant carrier theory

The heart of the speech synthesizing circuit of Figure 2 is the part in which the group of waves making up the message modulate the component waves of the carrier. In any one of these modulations, there is the simple carrier

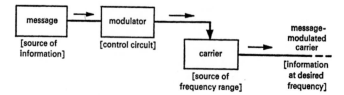

Figure 3 The elements of a carrier sender

process blocked out in Figure 3. Here a message[4] containing the information modulates a carrier determining the frequency range so that the end product in the form of the message-modulated carrier contains the information of the message translated to frequencies in the neighborhood of

3. Here the carrier path is stressed to show the alteration of the carrier sound stream as it proceeds on its way from the point of origin to the point of radiation. This also accords with the importance of the voice carrier which is received and used by the ear, and thus differs from the treatment of the carrier in simple radio broadcast reception.
4. The word 'message' has been substituted for the usual carrier term 'signal' to avoid confusion since the input signal is commonly speech whereas here the output wave is speech. 'Message' seems particularly appropriate with its suggestion of code as in telegraph.

the carrier. In this way the carrier sound stream of speech is imprinted with the message.

The prerequisites of the carrier system sender are, as indicated in Figure 3, first, a carrier wave source; second, a message wave source; and third, a modulating circuit of variable impedance by which the message controls the carrier. The carrier wave is for the simplest case a single sine wave function of time characterized by an amplitude, a frequency and a phase. The message wave as a rule is more complex but may be analysed as the sum of component sine waves each of which is characterized by its own amplitude, frequency and phase. In most carrier circuits the frequency range of the message is below that of the carrier. This is true of speech production.

The function of the modulating circuit is supplying a means for the message wave to modify a characteristic of the carrier. If the carrier wave amplitude is modified by the message wave amplitude the process is known as amplitude modulation; if the carrier wave frequency is so modified the process is called frequency modulation while if the carrier wave phase is so modified the process is called phase modulation. No distinction is made as to whether the modification occurs during or after the generation of the carrier. Modification of the carrier wave characteristics by other than the amplitude of the message need not be considered here. In the voice mechanism significant amplitude and frequency modulations of the carrier occur. Phase modulation takes place also but will not be discussed because the listener's ear is not very sensitive to these phase changes in the carrier.

In attempting to segregate the carrier elements of speech we run into one serious difficulty. In an idealized carrier circuit as shown in Figure 3 connections can be cut between the two energy sources and the modulator so that each boxed element can be studied independently. With the human flesh of the voice mechanism this is no longer feasible; the use of cadavers would help very little because normal energizing is then impossible. The same difficulty often appears in electrical modulators as, for example, within a modulating vacuum tube where a grid voltage modulates a plate current. In such a case of common parts it is necessary to discuss the action of each of the three elements in the presence of the other two.

With this carrier theory review as a background we are in a position to analyse the three elements making up the carrier transmitting system of the human voice. While the picture presented is oversimplified in details the principles hold and aid in applying carrier methodology to explain the mechanism of speech.

The voice carrier

In electrical circuits the carrier is obtained from an oscillatory energy source. The same holds for speech. In the electrical circuit the oscillatory waves a.c. are ordinarily generated from a supply of d.c. energy.[5] The same is true in speech with the compressed air in the lungs furnishing the steady supply. Confusion must be avoided, for in speech the conversion of steady to oscillatory energy is often described as 'modulation'. Here this conversion of energy form will be considered as an oscillatory action so that the term modulation can be reserved for the low-frequency syllabic control of this oscillatory energy to produce the desired speech. Oscillatory then will refer to automatic natural responses while modulatory will refer to forced responses which are controlled volitionally. This distinction is consistent with carrier terminology.

In the simplest electrical modulating circuits the carrier is a sine wave although this is not true of the damped wave carriers of multi-frequency type once commonly used in spark wave radio telegraphy. The carrier wave in speech is not a simple sine wave. Such a sound would be like a whistle and so too limited for the rich flexibility of speech. Instead the voice carrier is a compound tone having a multiplicity of components of different frequencies which together cover the audible range fairly completely. While these components may be considered as a multiplicity of separate carriers it is simpler to think of the ensemble as a single complex carrier; so this terminology has been used in the earlier carrier illustration and elsewhere in this paper.

Aside from this compound nature of the voice carrier, the voice has two distinct types of carrier, one for voiced and one for unvoiced sounds. Some sounds such as [z] have both types present at the same time but this case may be treated as the superposition of one carrier on the other. For voiced sounds the carrier is the vocal cord tone, an acoustic wave produced by the vibration of the vocal cords consisting of a fundamental frequency component and the upper harmonics thereof. These decrease in amplitude with increasing frequency. For unvoiced sounds the carrier is the breath tone, a complex tone resulting from a constriction formed somewhere in the vocal tract through which the breath is forced turbulently to produce a continuous spectrum of frequency components in the audible range.

These carrier waves must be dissociated from any effects of resonant vocal chambers, for such characterize the speech message rather than the carrier. Furthermore, these carrier waves must be mentally pictured as sustained indefinitely with the starting and stopping of them also characteriz-

5. In the usual electrical circuit the carrier is cut off by turning off the output but leaving the carrier oscillator energized as, for example, in voice frequency telegraphy. In the voice mechanism, however, the oscillator is stopped at the source. The difference between the electrical on-off switching and the start-stop switching of speech is not fundamental but results from the use of the most suitable action in each case in view of the conditions prevailing.

ing the message wave. Pauses for breath, due to incidental human limitations, do not invalidate the fundamental theory.

The speech message

Since a sustained voice carrier has no dynamic flow of information there is need for a source of message waves and a modulating mechanism for imprinting the message on the carrier. Conversely, any variation from the sustained carrier infers the presence of a message wave moulding the carrier. The message consists of those articulating, phonating and inflecting motions of the vocal parts which imprint the information on the carrier sound stream. The importance of the message waves cannot be stressed too much. Any impairment of them is an impairment of the message.

The message waves include the motions producing speech changes at infra-syllabic rates, such as the effect of anger when a talker may be high pitched for many minutes. When the carrier is thus altered over a long period of time the question arises whether to use a long- or short-term value of the carrier. The answer may well be the same as in the analogous radio problem. If weather causes a carrier frequency to be slightly high all day, this higher value is taken as the normal carrier in studying short-term effects such as the degree of modulation. But in long-term studies of carrier stability the deviations from the mean represent a frequency modulation which is observed as a 'message' effect.

Due to the inseparability of the message wave motion and its associated wave of impedance change in the modulating mechanism there may be confusion in distinguishing between the modulating elements and the source of the message waves. The rule followed here is simple. From the standpoint of the human flesh lining the vocal tract, the message source is internal, the modulating elements, external. The message consists of those muscular motions (or pressures or displacements) in the vocal tract which are present in the 'silent talker' and are volitional in nature. This definition excludes the oscillatory motions which make up the carrier. The modulating elements are acoustic in nature since the carrier starts as a sound stream and ends as a modulated sound stream.

There are three important variations of the voice carrier and so three types of message and of associated modulation. These variations are: first, selecting the carrier; second, setting the fundamental frequency of the voiced carrier; and third, controlling the selective transmission of the vocal tract.[6] The message waves in the three cases will be discussed with the

6. A fourth message characteristic prescribes the intensity of the speech. This message may be included in the carrier selection if the carrier is selected for intensity as well as type. The matter of intensity is passed over rather lightly here because a comparison is being developed between the human and electrical speech synthesizers with the final intensity in the latter under control of an amplifier setting.

corresponding modulation reserved for consideration under the next heading.

Selecting the carrier appears as a simple start-stop message, complicated somewhat by the presence of two types of carrier and by locating the constriction for the unvoiced type at several places in the vocal tract. We may think of a start-stop type of message for each point where constrictions are formed, including the vocal cords for the voiced type of carrier. A constriction message may be plotted as the opening between vocal parts at the constriction with critical values for the onset of audible carrier. The constrictions are to a certain extent independent. Thus with the vocal cords vibrating, a constriction from the tongue tip to the upper teeth may also be formed, as in making the [z] sound. Again, in whispering, there may be simultaneous constrictions, both of the unvoiced type, one at the vocal cords and one in the mouth. As the voice has two distinct types of carrier, the vocal cord tone and the breath tone, the selection sets up one of four carrier conditions at any instant: no carrier; vocal cord tone only; breath tone only; or a combination of vocal cord tone and breath tone. This start-stop message resembles the on-off type of telegraph where switching controlled by other muscular motions sets up speech information in another code, that of telegraph. As mentioned earlier a communication system can be made with the vocal system by starting and stopping a voice carrier in a vocal imitation of a telegraph buzzer. While this would be a clumsy way of communicating information it marks the start-stop control of the voice carrier as a speech message and not part of the voice carrier. Another check is that the 'silent talker' does form such constrictions.

The second type of message wave specifies the fundamental frequency with any related voice changes for the voiced type of carrier. This message, in a mechanical form, may be the time variation of the tension of the vocal cords. As the frequency of each upper harmonic is changed in the same ratio as the fundamental frequency, a single parameter suffices for all of the carrier components. The unvoiced carrier has no message of this type impressed since the unvoiced sounds are not characterized by pitch.

The third and final type of message wave controls the selective transmission in the vocal tract. By comparison, the first two types of message are simple, with the selecting of carriers ideally changing all components of the carrier by the same amplitude factor and the fundamental frequency control changing them by a uniform frequency factor. The vocal transmission, however, results from a multi-resonance condition with more than one degree of freedom. There follows a selective amplitude modulation with some carrier components decreasing in amplitude at the same instant that others are increasing. Maximum transmission occurs when a component coincides with an overall resonance, minimum transmission when it coincides with an anti-resonance and intermediate transmission for other cases. The voice message for transmission appears in mechanical form as the displacements of lips, teeth, tongue, etc., with as many such displacements considered as are needed for adequately expressing the speech content. This infers finding the simplest lumped impedance structure equivalent to the distributed impedance structure of the vocal tract to the necessary degree of approximation.

All these mechanical displacements of vocal parts that together constitute the voice message lead to corresponding displacements of air in the vocal system, resulting in a set of air waves that likewise contain all the information of speech. These airborne message waves, however, are at syllabic rates and so below the frequency range of audibility.

The voice modulators

The three voice modulators associated with the three speech messages are the mechanisms of selecting the carrier, setting the fundamental frequency and controlling the selective transmission. The mechanism for starting and stopping a voice carrier is simple. Assume a sustained carrier of either the voiced or unvoiced type. It can be stopped by opening the constriction at which it is formed. This alters the acoustic impedance of the opening which is then the modulating element in this case.

The modulating mechanism for controlling the fundamental frequency appears in the vibrating portions of air at the glottis. The exact mechanism is of no importance here so long as the message wave at the vocal cords finds means for altering the fundamental frequency under the control of the will.[7] This is a case of frequency modulation of multiple carriers harmonically related.

The modulating mechanism for controlling the transmission through the vocal tract as a function of frequency consists of the masses and stiffnesses of air chambers and openings in the vocal tract. These are varied under control of the message in the form of muscular displacements of vocal tract parts. There is a more complicated modulation in the vocal tract than in the usual electrical circuit for amplitude modulation because the varying impedances are reactive in the voice mechanism but resistive in the electrical circuit and also because several independent modulator elements are used in the voice mechanism as against either a single one or a group functioning as a unit in the simple electrical modulator. The reactive nature of the vocal impedances leads to the selective control of the amplitudes of the various harmonics of the voice carrier. The amplitude modulation of

7. For a simplified theory of the larynx vibration see Wegel (1930). The analogy of the larynx to a vacuum tube oscillator is described in an abstract (Wegel, 1929).

each carrier component by the combined message waves produces an output containing the carrier and sideband frequencies.

References

FIRESTONE, F. A. (1940), 'An artificial larynx for speaking and choral singing by one person', *J. acoust. Soc. Amer.*, vol. 11, p. 357.

RIESZ, R. R. (1930), 'Description and demonstration of an artificial larynx', *J. acoust. Soc. Amer.*, vol. 1, p. 273.

WEGEL, R. L. (1929), 'Theory of vibration of the larynx' (abstract), *J. acoust. Soc. Amer.*, vol. 1, p. 33.

WEGEL, R. L. (1930), 'Theory of vibration of the larynx', *Bell Syst. tech. J.*, vol. 9 p. 207.

2 James L. Flanagan

Some Properties of the Glottal Sound Source

James L. Flanagan, 'Some properties of the glottal sound source', *Journal of Speech and Hearing Research*, vol. 1 (1958), pp. 99–111.

Recent researches have demonstrated the usefulness of electrical analog techniques in studying the physics of speech production (Dunn, 1950; House, 1957; House and Stevens, 1956; Stevens and House, 1955; Stevens, Kasowski and Fant, 1953). Related techniques have also been found rewarding in the electrical synthesis of speech (Fant, 1953), and in schemes for reducing the channel capacity necessary to transmit speech (Flanagan and House, 1956). Basic to such an approach is an electrical system whose transmission properties are similar to the acoustical properties of the vocal tract. In the analog, electrical voltages usually are made analogous to sound pressures and electrical currents analogous to acoustic volume velocities. The electrical elements of the analog are manipulated to simulate the configurations of the vocal system.

Having derived an electrical model that possesses the appropriate transmission properties (this is usually done from measurements on X-rays of the vocal tract), it is of considerable importance to know how the analog should be excited. Ideally the excitation of the model should be exactly analogous to the excitation of the human vocal tract, and this of course requires a knowledge of the properties of the vocal excitation. Acoustic measurements on the sources of excitation within the vocal tract, however, are very difficult to make. Consequently, the excitation of existing analogs usually has been arrived at largely on empirical grounds. Such determination frequently leaves something to be desired since it often is difficult to localize accurately certain inadequacies in the simulation. An attempt has been made, therefore, to determine quantitatively some of the properties of the vocal excitation for voiced sounds.

To establish a frame of reference for the dimensions that must be considered, a highly schematized diagram of the lower respiratory system of an adult male is shown in Figure 1. The diagram essentially represents a median-plane section, perpendicular to an anterior–posterior line, through the glottis and trachea.

The voiced sounds of speech are produced by exciting the tract with the glottal or vocal fold source. The vibrating folds act as a variable valve that allows quasi-periodic pulses of air to escape from the lungs into the tract. These air 'puffs' produce an impulsive excitation of the acoustical conduit constituting the vocal tract. If it were possible to determine the waveform of the volume flow through the glottis, and the equivalent acoustic impedance of the glottis, then it should be possible to make an electrical source which generates a current similar to the glottal volume flow, and

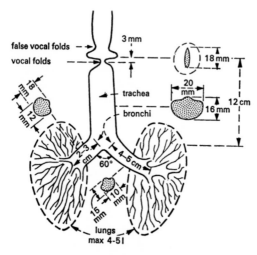

Figure 1 Simplified schematic diagram of lower respiratory system of adult male

which has an electrical impedance analogous to the acoustic impedance of the glottal source. Because the phase spectrum of speech usually is of secondary importance to intelligibility, the next best analogous source would be a periodic one whose amplitude spectrum (but not necessarily waveform) has the same shape as that of the glottal volume velocity function, and whose internal impedance is of an appropriate value. It is of consequence, therefore, to establish some of the properties of the glottal volume flow, its amplitude spectrum, and the acoustic impedance of the glottis.

To a first approximation the glottis might be considered as an orifice separating two relatively large tubes (corresponding crudely to the trachea and vocal tract, respectively) as shown in Figure 2. As a start, the simple relations for steady incompressible flow through such an orifice might be considered.

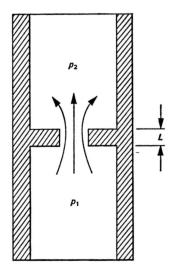

Figure 2 Idealization of the glottis as an orifice separating two relatively large tubes

Steady flow through an orifice

Let the pressures on the subglottic and supraglottic sides of the orifice be P_1 and P_2, respectively. Let the particle velocity of the air in the orifice be U, and the area of the orifice be A. If the cross-sectional areas of the adjacent tubes are much larger than A, variations in the pressures P_1 and P_2 caused by flow through the orifice are very small, and P_1 and P_2 can be assumed to remain sensibly constant. Also, if the velocity of air in the tubes is very small compared with the velocity in the orifice, the kinetic energy of the air in the tubes may be neglected. Further, if the dimensions of the orifice are small compared with the wavelength of an acoustic disturbance in the medium, and if the mean flow velocity is much smaller than the speed of sound, an acoustic disturbance is known essentially instantaneously throughout the vicinity of the orifice. In such a case it is reasonably valid to assume conditions of incompressibility. In addition, let it be assumed that the distribution of velocity is uniform over the orifice and that there is no viscous dissipation. Under these assumptions, the kinetic energy per-unit-volume possessed by the air in the orifice is developed by the pressure difference $(P_1 - P_2)$, and is

$$(P_1 - P_2) = \frac{\rho U^2}{2}, \hspace{3cm} 1$$

where ρ is the density of the air. Rewriting **1** yields for the particle velocity

$$U = \left[\frac{2(P_1 - P_2)}{\rho}\right]^{\frac{1}{2}}. \qquad\qquad 2$$

If the resistance of the orifice, R, is defined as the ratio of pressure drop $(P_1 - P_2)$ to volume flow (UA), then

$$R = \frac{\rho U}{2A} = \frac{\rho Q}{2A^2}, \qquad\qquad 3$$

where $Q = UA$ is the volume velocity.

In practical situations, considerable variation actually exists in the distribution of particle velocity over the orifice, and the assumption of uniform velocity distribution is not particularly good. To determine the volume discharge at the orifice precisely it is necessary to integrate the particle velocity over the orifice area, and this requires a knowledge of the velocity profile. However, the converging flow establishes a contraction of the jet at a short distance downstream at the so-called *vena contracta*, and at this cross-section the streamlines are essentially straight and parallel, and the velocity distribution uniform. If A_c and U_c are the area and particle velocity at the *vena contracta*, then the volume flow is $A_c U_c$. If A and A_c are related by an empirically determined contraction coefficient, δ_c, so that

$$A_c = \delta_c A, \qquad\qquad 4$$

and if $U_c \approx U$, then **3** might be modified and written more accurately as

$$R = \frac{\rho Q}{2} (\delta_c A)^2. \qquad\qquad 5$$

In a similar vein, the pressure-to-kinetic energy conversion in the orifice can never be accomplished without some viscous loss, and the particle velocity is actually somewhat less than that given by **2**. If a simple relation of the form **5** is to be used to approximate the resistance of an orifice, it is customary practice to introduce an empirically determined velocity coefficient, δ_v, to account for viscous loss, so that **2** is modified to

$$U = \delta_v \left[2\left(\frac{P_1 - P_2}{\rho}\right)\right]^{\frac{1}{2}}, \qquad\qquad 6$$

and **5** is revised to

$$R = \frac{\rho Q}{2(\delta_v \delta_c A)^2} = \frac{\rho Q}{2(\delta A)^2}, \qquad\qquad 7$$

where $\delta = \delta_c \delta_v$ is an empirical flow coefficient for the orifice.

The coefficient δ is dependent upon Reynolds' number, but for orifices of dimensions comparable to the glottis, and for flows reasonably representative of vocal flows, δ is of the order of 0·8.

If the area of the orifice and the velocity of flow are sufficiently small, the discharge actually may be governed by viscous laws rather than by the kinetic energy of the issuing particles. An expression such as 7, therefore, may not be very precise for small flow velocity and orifice area. A formula for orifice resistance, valid also for small values of velocity and area, should include a term to account for the 'low velocity' resistance. To a first approximation, the expression might have a form that is some linear combination of kinetic and viscous terms, such as

$$R = R_v + k \left(\frac{\rho Q}{2A^2} \right),\qquad\qquad 8$$

where R_v is a viscous resistance and k is a constant. For steady laminar flow in smooth tubes, the Hagen–Poiseuille law shows R_v to be proportional to the kinematic coefficient of viscosity and the length of the conducting passage, and inversely proportional to a function of the cross-sectional area.

Flow resistance of the glottal orifice

Both Wegel (1930) and van den Berg, Zantema and Doornenbal Jr (1957) have made steady flow measurements on models of the human larynx, and have obtained empirical formulas for the resistance of the glottal orifice. The two experimentally derived formulas, while differing in form, yield results that are essentially similar. The measurements of van den Berg *et al.*, however, are the more extensive and were made on an actual plaster cast model of a normal larynx. In van den Berg's model the glottis was idealized as a rectangular slit whose length was maintained constant at 18 mm. Changes in the area of the orifice were made by changing the width, w, of the slit, as shown in Figure 3. Van den Berg gives the resistance of the glottis to steady flow as

$$R = \frac{12\mu L}{lw^3} + 0·875 \frac{\rho Q}{2l^2 w^2},\qquad\qquad 9$$

where μ is the coefficient of viscosity, L is the thickness of the glottis and l is the length of the glottal slit. Van den Berg says that expression 9 holds well for $0·1 \leqslant w \leqslant 2·0$ mm, for subglottic pressures up to 64 cm H_2O at small widths, and for volume velocities up to 2000 cm³/s at large widths.

Since R is the ratio of subglottic pressure to glottal volume flow, it is possible, if values of subglottic pressure and glottal area are given, to deduce from 9 corresponding values of glottal volume flow for steady flow conditions. The question now arises as to how precisely expression **9**, or the more approximate expression **7**, holds in the case of non-steady flow, occasioned primarily by changes in the glottal area with time. It is apparent that if the inertial and compliant effects of the medium could be neglected,

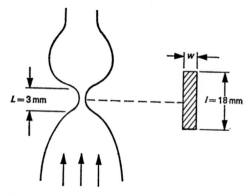

Figure 3 Model of human larynx used in steady flow measurements (see van den Berg, Zantema and Doornenbal Jr, 1957)

the foregoing relations also could be applied in the time-varying situation. If the orifice were made to execute some periodic variation in area, it might be asked at what frequency does the mass reactance of the fluid passing the orifice become appreciable. To get a very rough idea of this value, the case may be considered where the area is made to execute a step function, so that

$$A(t) = \begin{cases} 0, t \uparrow < \uparrow 0 \\ A, t \uparrow > \uparrow 0. \end{cases} \qquad\qquad \textbf{10}$$

An estimate can be made of the time required for the flow to build up to the steady-state value when a constant pressure difference is maintained across the orifice. Referring to the simple diagram in Figure 2, the mass of the air plug in the orifice is assumed to be $\rho A L_e$, where

$$L_e = (L + 0 \cdot 8 \sqrt{A})$$

is the effective thickness of the orifice taking into account an 'end effect' for the air plug. It is further assumed that the pressure difference acts to accelerate the air plug only over the distance L_e. The equation of motion for the plug is, therefore,

$$\rho L_e \frac{dU(t)}{dt} + (P_2 - P_1) = 0. \qquad\qquad \textbf{11}$$

From **10**, $U(t) = 0$ for $t = 0$, and the solution for **11** is

$$U(t) = \frac{(P_1 - P_2)}{\rho L_e} t, \qquad\qquad 12$$

which essentially is valid only for positive values of t near to zero. An estimate of the rise-time of the flow may be made by assuming $U(t)$ to increase linearly until the ideal steady-state value

$$U_0 = \left[2\left(\frac{P_1 - P_2}{\rho}\right) \right]^{\frac{1}{2}}$$

is reached. The time required to accomplish this build-up is, therefore,

$$T = \frac{2L_e}{U_0}. \qquad\qquad 13$$

This time is somewhat less than the actual rise-time since the fluid acceleration does not remain constant, but drops off as the steady-state velocity is reached. Even so, T serves as a reasonable measure of minimum rise-time.

It might be assumed, somewhat arbitrarily, that an orifice area variation whose period is at least of an order of magnitude greater than T is sufficiently slow so that the fluctuations in volume flow may be considered as a series of consecutively established steady states. If such an assumption is tenable, then the previous relations for steady flow may be applied in cases where the variations in area take place in times greater than $10T$. This says in other words, that the acoustic mass reactance of the orifice is relatively small compared with its resistance, and the 'static' relations between orifice area, pressure differential and volume flow may be used just as the static characteristic curves for a vacuum tube are used in dynamic applications. An additional piece of experimental evidence lends confidence to the foregoing assumption. Westervelt and McAuliffe (1950) have found that the acoustic mass reactance of an orifice in the presence of a d.c. through flow is decreased to about one third of its value in the absence of through flow for particle velocities in excess of about 300 cm/s. This means that the acoustic inertance of the orifice is appreciably less than $\rho L_e / A$ in the presence of such through flow.

Expression **13** can be evaluated in terms of typical glottal dimensions and subglottic pressure. The following values may be taken as typical for an adult male during normal conversational speech: the thickness L of the glottal orifice is approximately 3 mm; the mean glottal area is approximately 6 mm^2; the subglottic pressure $(P_1 - P_2)$ is of the order of 8 cm H_2O. Using these values in **13** yields

$$T \approx 0\cdot3 \text{ ms}, \quad \text{and} \quad 0\cdot1T \approx 330 \text{ Hz}. \qquad\qquad 14$$

For such conditions and for variations in glottal area of frequency less than about 300 Hz, it appears reasonable to consider the glottal flow as a series of consecutively established steady rates, and to evaluate the time-varying glottal resistance from the steady flow relation 9, or from the more approximate relation 7. It can also be seen from 13 that T is inversely proportional to the square root of the subglottic pressure. The value of $0.1T$ in 14, therefore, would be increased to about 470 Hz if the subglottic pressure were doubled, and decreased to about 230 Hz if the pressure were halved. Happily, the subglottic pressure and the minimum produceable sound pressure level are essentially monotonically increasing functions of vocal pitch.

Proceeding under the assumption that the rationale for applying the steady flow relations to the time-varying case is sufficiently valid, relation 9 shows that for small glottal areas, where the flow is controlled mainly by the viscous term, Q is essentially proportional to $(P_1 - P_2)A^3$. Similarly, for large glottal openings, where the flow is determined chiefly by the kinetic term, Q is essentially proportional to $A\sqrt{(P_1 - P_2)}$. Van den Berg has pointed out that the leading and trailing edges of the volume velocity waveform are more steep than those of the area function, and it is to be expected that the glottis will generate more intense higher harmonics than those computed from an harmonic analysis of $A(t)$. One facet of the problem under consideration is the relative importance of this 'sharpening' effect.

Since it is desired to determine the volume velocity waveform, given the glottal area function and the subglottic pressure, van den Berg's formula 9 has been used to make a plot of Q v. A, with $P_s = (P_1 - P_2)$ as a parameter. This plot is shown in Figure 4. It is now proposed that Figure 4 be used to deduce waveforms of glottal volume velocity from existing data on glottal area and subglottic pressure, and that Fourier analyses be made of the area and volume velocity functions to obtain their amplitude spectra.

Subglottic pressure during phonation

Several investigators have made measurements of mean subglottic pressure during phonation, and have reported data in the literature (Curry, 1940; Gutzmann, 1909; Judson and Weaver, 1942). Most of the data, however, have been obtained on subjects who could not phonate normally, for example, subjects with fistulas in the trachea. Probably the best measurements to date on a normal subject have been made by van den Berg (1956) using both a direct and an indirect technique in which catheters were inserted in the glottis and œsophagus. Van den Berg made measurements of subglottic pressure over an intensity range beginning with the lowest intensity that the subject could sustain (liminal intensity) and increasing in

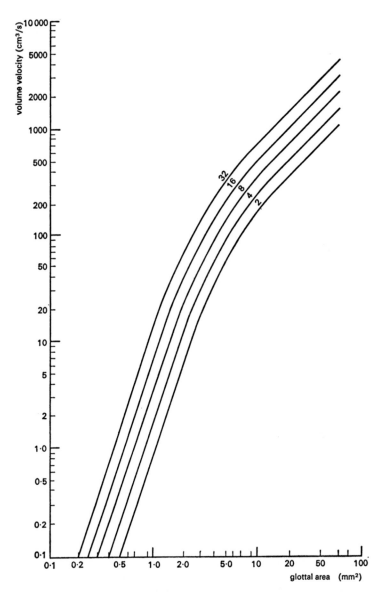

Figure 4 Relation between glottal volume velocity and glottal area for different values of subglottic pressure, P_s, measured in cm H_2O

five dB steps to the loudest level at which the subject could phonate. The pitch range covered in the measurements began with the lowest-pitched chest voice and ranged upward to falsetto. Van den Berg's data have been taken, therefore, and averaged to obtain representative values of subglottic pressure as a function of intensity and pitch for a male voice. These values, over the ranges of interest, are given in Table 1.

Table 1 Relations between pitch, sound pressure level and mean subglottic pressure, adapted and averaged from data reported by van den Berg (1956)

Pitch (Hz)	Liminal spl[a] (dB)[b]	Subglottic pressure, cm H_2O^c (dB)			
		+0	+5	+10	+15
97	56	4	7	9	—
145	57	6	7	10	—
218	62	9	11	14	19
274	67	12	21	26	29

[a] Liminal sound pressure level measured 25 cm in front of the mouth
[b] dB re 0·0002 dyn/cm²
[c] Sound pressure level relative to liminal sound pressure level

In the earlier discussion, it was assumed that subglottic pressure remains essentially constant within the duration of an appreciable number of vocal periods. Since the trachea and vocal tract are not infinitely large reservoirs, and since they are coupled acoustically, the subglottic pressure is subject to variation about its mean value. Van den Berg *et al.* (1957) have made calculations of the magnitude of this variation and estimate it to be less than 5 per cent of the mean subglottic pressure. A qualitative notion of the relative magnitudes of mean subglottic pressure and acoustic sound pressure in the tract can be had by realizing that the peak acoustic pressure at the mouth of a speaker producing a very loud sound usually is less than about 10^2 dynes/cm², while a typical mean subglottic pressure is of the order of 10^4 dynes/cm². For first-order approximation, therefore, the assumption of constant subglottic pressure during the production of voiced sounds seems reasonably valid and realistic, and this assumption will be made in using Figure 4 and Table 1 to relate area and volume flow.

Glottal area and volume flow during phonation
Several years ago a technique was developed at the Bell Laboratories for making high-speed motion pictures of the vibrations of the vocal folds

(Farnsworth, 1940). This technique has since been used by a number of investigators, and a substantial amount of data is available in the literature on the area of the glottal port during voicing. Among these works is a comprehensive study of internal laryngeal activity by Fletcher (1950). Because of his measurements of sound pressure levels concomitant with the photography, his glottal area data have been used to deduce waveforms of volume velocity.

Fletcher took high-speed pictures (4000 frames/s) for three normal subjects: two male and one female. The subjects were instructed to produce the vowel [æ] under four different conditions:

1 At the lowest pitch and intensity possible, consistent with sustaining the vowel sound;
2 At the same pitch as 1, but with the intensity increased to the highest level possible without altering the vowel;
3 At the lowest intensity possible but with the pitch approximately one octave above 1;
4 At the same pitch as 3 and at the highest intensity possible without altering the vowel.

Measurements were made of the intensity differences between conditions 1 and 2 and between 3 and 4. The values of pitch and intensity difference for Fletcher's male subjects (A and B) are shown in Table 2. To

Table 2 Pitch and intensity data, adapted from Fletcher (1950), for two adult males phonating the vowel [æ] under four different conditions

	Pitch (Hz)				Intensity difference (dB)	
Subject	1	2	3	4	2−1	4−3
A	125	125	250	235	7	16
B	111	111	222	250	5	17

determine continuous functions representing typical cycles of the glottal area for these conditions, smooth curves with continuity of slope were drawn through the data points.[1]

1. Fletcher's data constitute samples of glottal area obtained at a rate of 4000 times/s. For the present analysis continuous area functions are desired. The argument for drawing smooth curves with continuity of slope through the area samples is as follows:

Using the data in Table 1, values were estimated for the subglottic pressures corresponding to the conditions under which Fletcher's male subjects phonated. These estimated values are recorded in Table 3.

Table 3 Estimated subglottic pressures for the four conditions (see Table 2) under which male subjects A and B phonated

	Subglottic pressure (cm H_2O)			
Subject	*1*	*2*	*3*	*4*
A	4	8	10	20
B	4	7	9	24

With the pressure data of Table 3, the glottal area functions from Fletcher, and the relation plotted in Figure 4, corresponding cycles of glottal volume flow were determined for subjects A and B (male). The plotted area and velocity functions for these two subjects are shown in Figures 5 and 6. The area functions for the female subject also were plotted but are not reproduced here. The volume flow functions for this subject were not determined because data on subglottic pressure were not available for the female.

It is apparent from these plots that the leading and trailing edges of the velocity function are slightly more steep than those of the area function. As already pointed out, the volume velocity is approximately proportional to the third power of the area for small values of glottal area, and is more nearly proportional to the first power of the area for large glottal openings. It may also be noted that in most of the low intensity cases complete closure of the glottis is not attained, while in the higher intensity cases complete closure usually is attained.

An IBM 650 digital computer was programmed to make a Fourier series analysis of each of the area and velocity functions. In the analysis each function was sampled at every five degrees of the argument, resulting in effective sampling rates for the various conditions as shown in Table 4. The amplitudes and phases of 35 harmonic components were computed for each function, and the calculated series reproduced the original functions within the maximum errors shown in Table 5. The harmonic amplitude spectrum for each function was computed in terms of dB relative to the

---

the vocal folds are massive elements; the laryngeal muscles can exert only a finite force; therefore, the acceleration of the folds must be finite, and their velocity and displacement must be continuous functions of time.

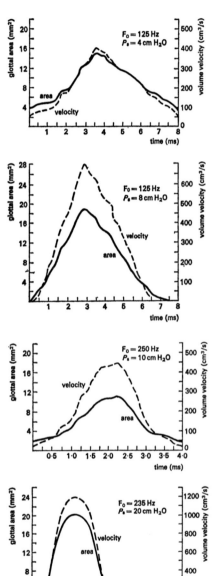

Figure 5 Typical cycles of the glottal area and volume velocity functions for male subject A phonating under four different conditions of pitch (F_0) and intensity

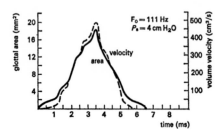

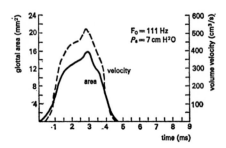

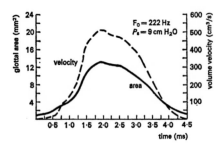

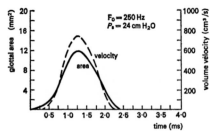

Figure 6 Typical cycles of the glottal area and volume velocity functions for male subject B phonating under four different conditions of pitch (F_0) and intensity

amplitude of the fundamental component. The computed amplitude spectra are plotted in Figures 7 and 8.

In most of the cases, the spectral graphs show that in terms of dB the spectra for the area and volume velocity functions do not differ greatly. The

Table 4 Effective sampling rates for harmonic analysis of the glottal area and volume velocity functions for the four conditions under which male subjects A and B phonated

| Subject | Samples per second | | | |
	1	2	3	4
A	9000	9000	18000	16900
B	8000	8000	16000	18000

Table 5 Maximum errors in the computed series for the area and velocity functions. 1–4 represent the conditions under which male subjects A and B phonated

Subject	1	2	3	4
area function (mm^2)				
A	0·007	0·008	0·011	0·003
B	0·036	0·004	0·010	0·0001
volume velocity function (cm^3/s)				
A	0·18	0·36	0·21	1·27
B	0·23	0·33	0·41	0·08

'sharpening' effect that tends to make the higher harmonics of the velocity function more intense than those of the area function is, for the most part, only slightly discernible. This is particularly true for the low intensity, low pitch cases. It is less true for the high intensity, high pitch cases where the disparity between the area and velocity functions is, in general, more noticeable. Considering the effectiveness of low frequency components in masking higher ones, and considering also the spectral distributions of energy for vocalic sounds, the differences between the area and velocity spectra probably are not greatly significant in terms of perception. To the extent that prior assumptions are valid, and barring the cases of extremely

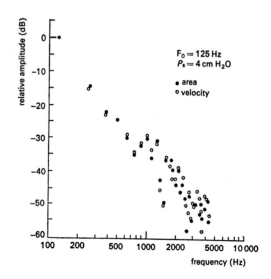

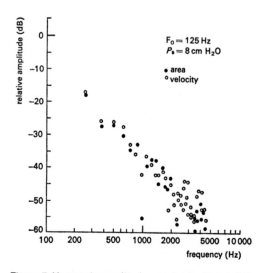

Figure 7 Harmonic amplitude spectra for the glottal area and volume velocity functions shown in Figure 5

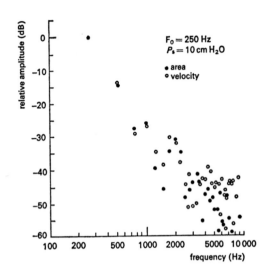

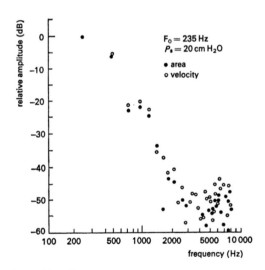

Figure 7 *cont.*

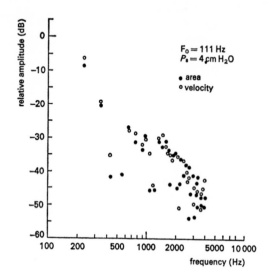

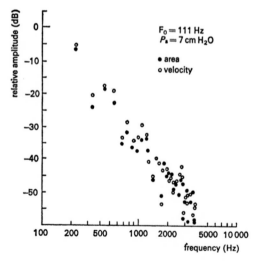

Figure 8 Harmonic amplitude spectra for the glottal area and volume velocity functions shown in Figure 6

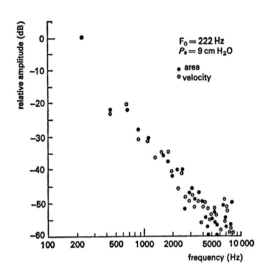

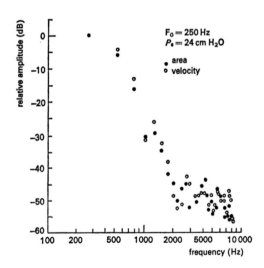

Figure 8 *cont.*

high pitch and intensity, the spectra indicate (as have already the time functions in Figures 5 and 6), that the area function is a fairly reasonable representation of the volume flow.

If a straight line were fitted to the spectral envelopes, the best fit would have a slope of the order of -10 to -12 dB/octave. To a rough approximation, therefore, the amplitudes of the spectral components vary inversely with frequency, or harmonic number, raised to the power $1 \cdot 7$ to $2 \cdot 0$. (This relation was also found to apply to the area data for the female speaker.) In most of the low pitch cases a straight line fits the spectral envelopes relatively well. In the high pitch cases, however, the fit to a straight line is fairly good at the low frequency end of the spectrum, but the high frequency end is, in general, more intense than is indicated by a simple -10 to -12 dB/octave line.

It is tempting, in the light of the foregoing data, to digress and speculate on the physical correlates of voice quality. For phonation under essentially the same conditions, the two male subjects (A and B) have amplitude spectra that are quite similar. Their waveforms of glottal area and velocity, however, differ considerably in shape. It may be expected, consequently, that the phase spectra of their glottal functions also differ. Examination of the computed phase spectra (not reproduced here) shows this to be the case. Despite the way in which Helmholtz has been repeatedly interpreted (or rather misinterpreted), it is clear that man is not completely 'phase-deaf'. It seems conceivable, therefore, that one important correlate of voice quality might be the phase spectrum of the glottal source.

The implication is not that glottal 'phase' is the entire story; most assuredly other factors contribute to voice quality. Characteristic patterns of pitch inflection and stress can serve to label a given voice, as can 'residual' nasal coupling and characteristic damping of vocal resonances. Nevertheless, the phase spectrum of the glottal source could play a significant role. Considerable psychoacoustic experimentation appears to be needed before a satisfactory quantification of voice quality can be formulated.

References

CURRY, R. O. L. (1940), *The Mechanism of the Human Voice*, Longman.

DUNN, H. K. (1950), 'The calculation of vowel resonances and an electrical vocal tract', *J. acoust. Soc. Amer.*, vol. 22, pp. 740–53.

FANT, C. G. M. (1953), 'Speech communication research', *Ingen. Vetensk. Akad.*, vol. 24, pp. 331–7, Stockholm.

FARNSWORTH, D. W. (1940), 'High-speed motion pictures of the human vocal cords', *Bell Labs. Record*, vol. 18, pp. 203–8.

FLANAGAN, J. L., and HOUSE, A. S. (1956), 'Development and testing of a formant-coding speech compression system', *J. acoust. Soc. Amer.*, vol. 28, pp. 1099–1106.

FLETCHER, W. W. (1950), *A Study of Internal Laryngeal Activity in Relation to Voca: Intensity*, Ph.D. thesis, Northwestern University.

GUTZMANN, H. (1909) *Physiologie der Stimme und Sprache*, Vieweg und Sohn, Braunschweig.

HOUSE, A. S. (1957), 'Analog studies of nasal consonants', *JSHD*, vol. 22, pp. 190–204.

HOUSE, A. S., and STEVENS, K. N. (1956), 'Analog studies of the nasalization of vowels', *JSHD*, vol. 21, pp. 218–32.

JUDSON, L. S., and WEAVER, A. T. (1942), *Voice Science*, F. S. Crofts & Co., New York.

OLSON, H. F. (1947), *Elements of Acoustical Engineering*, 2nd edn, Van Nostrand.

STEVENS, K. N., and HOUSE, A. S. (1955), 'Development of a quantitative description of vowel articulation', *J. acoust. Soc. Amer.*, vol. 27, pp. 484–93.

STEVENS, K. N., KASOWSKI, S., and FANT, C. G. M. (1953), 'An electrical analog of the vocal tract', *J. acoust. Soc. Amer.*, vol. 25, pp. 734–42.

VAN DEN BERG, J. W. (1956), 'Direct and indirect determination of the mean subglottic pressure', *Folia Phoniatr.*, vol. 8, pp. 1–24.

VAN DEN BERG, J. W., ZANTEMA, J. T., and DOORNENBAL, P., Jr (1957), 'On the air resistance and the Bernoulli effect of the human larynx', *J. acoust. Soc. Amer.*, vol. 29, pp. 626–31.

WEGEL, R. L. (1930), 'Theory of vibration of the larynx', *Bell Syst. tech. J.*, vol. 9 pp. 207–27.

WESTERVELT, P. J., and MCAULIFFE, C. E. (1950), 'Differential resistance and reactance of sharp-edged, circular orifices', *Quarterly report*, Acoustics Laboratory, MIT, July–September, pp. 15–16.

3 Kenneth N. Stevens and Arthur S. House

An Acoustical Theory of Vowel Production and Some of its Implications

Kenneth N. Stevens and Arthur S. House, 'An acoustical theory of vowel production and some of its implications', *Journal of Speech and Hearing Research*, vol. 4 (1961) pp. 303–20.

It is 20 years since the publication of the monograph on the vowel by Chiba and Kajiyama (1941) – a work that introduces and epitomizes the modern era in the study of speech production and perception. The past two decades have seen a continuous advance in the understanding of the mechanism of speech sound generation, as exemplified by the publication of Fant's treatise (1960). The fruits of the experimental and theoretical progress, however, have not been universally appreciated and applied. The time may be ripe, therefore, for a concise yet rigorous exposition of current concepts of speech production. The remarks that follow represent an attempt to provide such an exposition of an acoustical theory of vowel production, and to point out its relevance to and compatibility with certain known characteristics of speech.

Theory of vowel production

Vowel sounds are produced by acoustic excitation of the vocal tract by a source at the glottis. The vocal tract is viewed as an acoustic circuit, and the acoustic disturbances in this circuit are usually described in terms of sound pressures and volume velocities of vibration of the air at various points in the circuit. In all cases of present interest, the cross-sectional dimensions of the vocal tract may be considered to be small compared with a wavelength. This means that only plane acoustic waves propagate in the vocal tract, and that the sound pressure and volume velocity measured in the vocal tract are functions of only one spatial dimension – the distance measured along the vocal tract from the glottis.

For those who prefer to think in terms of electric rather than acoustic circuits, the following analogous quantities should be noted: sound pressure p is analogous to voltage; volume velocity U is analogous to current. Acoustic impedance is defined by $Z = p/U$, where p and U are complex amplitudes, following the usual conventions of electric current theory.[1]

When one end of an acoustic tube such as the vocal tract is open, the effect of this open end on the sound in the tube can be represented by a

1. See for example, E. A. Guillemin (1953).

radiation impedance. At low frequencies this radiation impedance may be represented by a resistance $\rho c/A$ in parallel with a small acoustic mass $M_r \approx 0\cdot4(\rho/\sqrt{A})$, where A is the cross-sectional area, ρ is the density of air, and c is the velocity of sound. In the study of speech sounds, the experimenter usually is interested in the sound pressure p_r measured at some distance r from the mouth. If $U_0(j\omega)$ represents the Fourier spectrum of the volume velocity at the mouth opening, where ω is the radian frequency, then at low frequencies (below, say, 5000 Hz) the relation that describes the radiation of sound from the mouth $R(j\omega)$ is approximately that for a 'simple source' (Morse, 1948, p. 312):

$$R(j\omega) = p_r(j\omega)/U_0(j\omega) = j\omega\rho/4\pi r. \qquad\qquad \textbf{1}$$

Of particular interest is the factor of ω in the numerator, indicating a radiation characteristic $p_r(j\omega)/U_0(j\omega)$ that rises at 6 dB per octave.

In Figure 1 is shown a schematized midsagittal section through the vocal tract during the production of a vowel. The excitation of the tract is a quasi-periodic series of pulses of air that pass through the glottis during the open

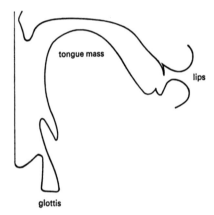

tongue mass

lips

glottis

Figure 1 Schematized midsagittal section through the vocal tract during the production of a vowel. Adapted from Wendahl (1957)

phases of the vocal-fold vibratory cycle. A typical waveform of the volume velocity as a function of time is shown in Figure 2, along with its corresponding Fourier spectrum. The dashed curve describes the envelope of the line spectrum. The slope of the spectrum envelope at low frequencies is derived from Fourier analysis of quasi-triangular waveforms. The general shape of the volume velocity waveform is not unlike that of the waveform of the area of the glottis opening as a function of time (Flanagan, 1958).

The duration and shape of the pulses shown in Figure 2 are similar to that derived from study of the larynx in action (Sonesson, 1960; Timcke *et al.*, 1958). It can be demonstrated that this volume velocity waveform $U_s(t)$ is relatively independent of the vocal-tract configuration (van den Berg,

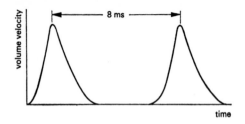

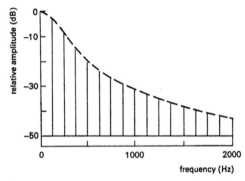

Figure 2

1954; 1955a), that is, is more or less independent of the acoustic impedance looking into the vocal tract from the glottis, and consequently the internal impedance of the volume velocity source can be considered to be high. The Fourier spectrum of U_s, assuming a periodic waveform, is a line spectrum with components at multiples of the fundamental frequency. At frequencies above about 250 Hz (for a typical male voice) the magnitude of these components decreases with increasing frequency at a rate of about 12 dB per octave, that is, the spectrum 'envelope' of $U_s(j\omega)$ is roughly proportional to ω^{-2}. Below 250 Hz, the downward slope of the spectrum envelope is less steep. This low-frequency behavior of the spectrum envelope is predicted from Fourier analysis of triangular waveforms of the type shown in Figure 2.

The shape of the spectrum shown in Figure 2 is typical of the glottal output for conversational speech. The slope of the spectrum envelope at high frequencies can deviate from that of Figure 2 as vocal effort is changed (Licklider *et al.*, 1955). Furthermore, irregularities are present in the spectrum shape (Flanagan, 1958; Miller, 1959), particularly when the spectrum of a single glottal pulse is considered.

As a result of the excitation at the glottis, a volume velocity $U_0(t)$ exists at the mouth opening. If $U_0(j\omega)$ is the Fourier spectrum of the output volume velocity, and $U_s(j\omega)$ the spectrum of the input volume velocity, then a transfer ratio $T(j\omega) = U_0(j\omega)/U_s(j\omega)$ can be defined. In general this transfer function is characterized by a number of resonances or poles, and varies markedly as the configuration of the vocal tract changes.

The above remarks may be summarized by saying that the Fourier spectrum of the sound pressure p_r measured at a distance from the lips during vowel production may be considered as the product of three terms

$$p_r(j\omega) = U_s(j\omega)T(j\omega)R(j\omega), \qquad\qquad 2$$

where $R(j\omega)$ is a factor that accounts for radiation from the lips as given in 1. Each term in this product has a phase and an amplitude, each of which is a function of frequency. Usually the experimenter is concerned only with the amplitude spectrum, in which case the magnitude of each term in the product is taken. In general, $U_s(j\omega)$ and $R(j\omega)$ are independent of the articulatory configurations, whereas $T(j\omega)$ is highly dependent upon the vocal-tract shape, and thus varies considerably from vowel to vowel.

Lumped-circuit approximation

A rough approximation to $T(j\omega)$ may be obtained if the vocal tract is viewed as a lumped circuit, that is, if the dimensions of the vocal tract are considered to be small compared with a wavelength in the frequency range of interest. Figure 1 shows a typical configuration for which this approximation is valid at low frequencies. The assumption of lumped-circuit elements is not unreasonable, since at 300 Hz the wavelength is about 100 cm and the length of the vocal tract for an average male is about 17 cm. An equivalent circuit for this configuration is shown in Figure 3, together with a plot of the transfer ratio (in dB) as a function of frequency. The volume of the tract is represented by C, and the narrow mouth opening (including the radiation impedance) by M. In the ideal lossless case, there is no resistance R in the circuit, and the transfer ratio for this circuit tends to infinity at frequency $F_1 = 1/\{2\pi\sqrt{(MC)}\}$. Small amounts of dissipation always are present, however, and consequently the transfer ratio will have a finite peak at approximately the same frequency. The figure shows curves for the theoretical lossless case and for the case in which the dissipation is typical of that found in the vocal tract.

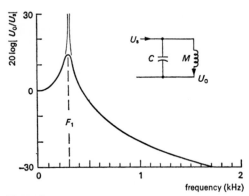

Figure 3

A typical value for the volume V of the tract between lips and glottis is about 50 cm^3, so that $C = V/\rho c^2 = 3 \cdot 5 \times 10^{-5}$ cm^5/dyne. For this particular configuration the length l of the mouth opening is about 2 cm and has an average cross-sectional area A of about 0·3 cm^2, so that

$$M = \rho l/A = 8 \cdot 0 \times 10^{-3} \text{ gm/cm}^4.$$

Thus $F_1 \approx 300$ Hz, a value near the observed frequency of the lowest resonance for the vowel /u/ as spoken by male voices.

If a small amount of dissipation is included in the equivalent circuit of Figure 3, it can be shown from linear circuit theory that the transfer function can be written

$$T_1(j\omega) = \frac{U_0(j\omega)}{U_s(j\omega)} = \frac{s_1 . s_1^*}{(j\omega - s_1)(j\omega - s_1^*)}, \qquad \mathbf{3}$$

where $s_1 = \sigma_1 + j\omega_1$, $s_1^* = \sigma_1 - j\omega_1$, $\omega_1 = 2\pi F_1$ and σ_1 is a constant that depends on the amount of dissipation. When the amount of dissipation is small, $\sigma_1 \uparrow \ll \uparrow \omega_1$ and the half-power bandwidth of the resonance is σ_1/π Hz. The complex numbers s_1 and s_1^* are often called the *poles* of the transfer function. Under the assumption $\sigma_1 \uparrow \ll \uparrow \omega_1$, the magnitude of the transfer function is

$$|T_1(j\omega)| = \left| \frac{U_0(j\omega)}{U_s(j\omega)} \right|$$

$$\approx \frac{\omega_1^2}{(\omega + \omega_1)\{(\omega - \omega_1)^2 + \sigma_1^2\}^{\frac{1}{2}}} .$$

This relation was used to plot the transfer ratio in Figure 3

The transfer function of the vocal-tract configuration represented by the equivalent circuit in Figure 3 can be described in any of three equivalent ways: the volume of the tract and the length and area of the lip opening (together with an appropriate damping constant) can be specified; the values of C and M (and the resistance) in the equivalent circuit can be specified; or the resonant frequency ω_1 and the damping constant σ_1 can be specified. From any one of these specifications the entire resonance curve in Figure 3 can be described at all frequencies for which the approximations stated above are valid. If the previous statement that the spectrum envelope of the source and the radiation characteristic are relatively invariant is accepted, then it can be asserted that specification of the resonant frequency and bandwidth (or damping constant) permits the construction of the entire spectrum envelope for the vowel. This conclusion will be of particular significance when more complicated models for the vocal tract are discussed.

A one-resonator approximation to the vocal tract is rather unrealistic since it is valid only for frequencies below about 300 Hz. A vocal-tract model consisting of more than one resonator would be valid over a frequency range for which *each* resonator is small compared to the wavelength. A representation of the vocal tract by two resonators, which might be valid up to a frequency of about 1000 Hz, is shown in Figure 4 along

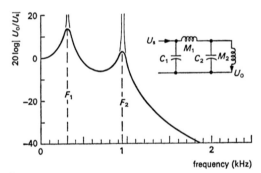

Figure 4

with a plot of the transfer function. Transfer ratios for the lossless case and the slightly dissipative case are shown (see Figure 3). The transfer function is now the product of two terms of the type shown in equations 3 and 4. In this case, the transfer function exhibits two resonances; each resonant frequency is dependent upon the volumes of both resonators and on the dimensions of both constrictions in the model. The extent to which a given resonance is affiliated with a particular cavity depends upon the amount of coupling between the cavities, that is, upon the sizes of the constrictions. For vocal-tract configurations appropriate to vowel production, it is generally not valid to assign resonant frequencies exclusively to particular cavities (Chiba and Kajiyama, 1941, p. 93; Dunn, 1950; Fant, 1960, p. 284).

Transmission-line description

A more general description of the vocal tract that is accurate over a wide frequency range considers the tract as a distributed system or transmission line in which one-dimensional plane waves propagate. In order to explicate this approach it is convenient first to consider a vocal-tract configuration in which the cross-sectional area is constant and in which the radiation impedance is negligible. This provides a uniform acoustic tube driven at one

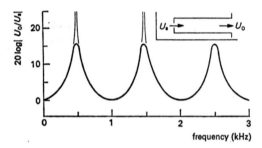

Figure 5 A plot of the magnitude of the transfer ratio (in dB) as a function of frequency for a distributed (transmission line) representation of an acoustic tube

end by a volume velocity U_s and terminated in a short circuit through which volume velocity U_0 flows. The situation is illustrated in Figure 5; the tube is 17 cm long. The curve has infinite peaks at resonant frequencies for the ideal lossless case, and peaks of finite amplitude for the slightly dissipative case. The half-power bandwidth of all resonances was assumed to be 100 Hz. The articulation of the schwa vowel is similar to this uniform configuration.

   Transmission-line theory must be used to compute the transfer function for the uniform configuration, whereas lumped-circuit theory was adequate in the situation where the dimensions of the configuration were small compared with a wavelength. When an acoustic tube is considered as a transmission line, the acoustic disturbances in the tube are viewed as being composed of plane sound waves propagating in both directions. Such a tube has, in theory, an infinite number of resonances, rather than just one resonance as was the case for the simple resonator in Figure 3. The contribution of each resonance to the transfer function of the tube has the same form as that given in equations 3 and 4. To account for all the resonances it is necessary to take the product of an infinite number of factors like $T_1(j\omega)$ in equations 3 or 4. Each factor is characterized, however, by a different pair of poles, that is, by a different resonant frequency and a different damping constant. Thus

$$T(j\omega) = \frac{U_0}{U_s}$$

$$= \left\{ \frac{s_1 \cdot s_1^*}{(j\omega - s_1)(j\omega - s_1^*)} \right\} \left\{ \frac{s_2 \cdot s_2^*}{(j\omega - s_2)(j\omega - s_2^*)} \right\} \cdots \left\{ \frac{s_n \cdot s_n}{(j\omega - s_n)(j\omega - s_n^*)} \right\} \cdots, \qquad 5$$

where $s_n = \sigma_n + j\omega_n$.

In the case of the uniform-tube model of the vocal tract, if end effects are neglected, the various resonant frequencies $f_n = \omega_n/2\pi$ are odd multiples of a lowest natural frequency, that is, the resonances for the familiar situation of a pipe open at one end and closed at the other. In this case, therefore, $\omega_n = (2n+1)\omega_1$, where n is an integer. The lowest natural frequency $\omega_1/2\pi$ occurs when the length l of the tube is one-quarter wavelength. Since the wavelength λ is given by $\lambda = c/f$, where f is the frequency and c is the velocity of propagation of sound, then

$$\omega_n = (2n+1)\frac{\pi c}{2l},$$

or $\quad f_n = (2n+1)\frac{c}{4l}.$

For the case of a uniform vocal tract of length 17 cm, the resonant frequencies occur at about 500, 1500, 2500, ... Hz.

A plot of the magnitude of the transfer function in decibels (similar to the plot in Figure 3 for a single resonance) for the uniform tube of length 17 cm can be constructed by *adding* together an infinite number of curves each similar to that in Figure 3, with resonant frequencies at 500, 1500, 2500, ... Hz. The result of such a construction, assuming resonance bandwidths of 100 Hz, is shown in Figure 5. The important features of this plot are that the value of $|T(j\omega)|$ is the same at each resonant frequency, and that $|T(j\omega)|$ is approximately unity at zero frequency and at frequencies midway between the resonant frequencies, that is, at 1000, 2000, 3000, ... Hz in this case.

The uniform tube is an idealized configuration that may not occur precisely in practice. Several conclusions may be drawn from a discussion of the properties of this configuration, however, and these conclusions will apply, in general, to other configurations.

1 The transfer function $T(j\omega)$ is characterized by an infinite number of resonances; on the average, these resonances occur every $c/2l$ Hz (or approximately every 1000 Hz for male voices).

2 Lengthening the vocal tract tends to lower the frequencies of all resonances; shortening the tract increases the frequencies of all resonances.

In order to study resonant frequencies for a particular vowel configuration for which the cross-sectional area of the vocal tract is not uniform, the configuration can be visualized as a perturbation of the uniform tube. (It is assumed throughout the discussion that there is no coupling to the nasal cavities.) Starting with the uniform tube with resonant frequencies at, say, 500, 1500, 2500, . . . Hz, the shape is distorted gradually until the configuration approaches that of the vowel under study. As this perturbation process is carried out, the resonant frequencies gradually shift their positions and in the limit settle at new values. The number of resonances and their average spacing will not change, however, if the vocal-tract length does not change. For a configuration appropriate for the production of /ɑ/, for example, typical values of the resonant frequencies are 800, 1200, 2500, etc. (House *et al.*, 1960). Thus, for a general vowel configuration, equation 5 can still be used to specify the vocal-tract transfer function, but the values of ω_n and σ_n must be selected to correspond to the resonant frequencies and bandwidths for that particular configuration. The values of ω_1, ω_2, . . . for a particular vocal-tract configuration may be viewed as the natural frequencies of free vibration for that configuration, and they are the same, independent of how the system is excited. Once the values of the resonant frequencies and bandwidths are known, then these values can be used in equation 5 to compute the *entire* transfer function $T(j\omega) = U_0/U_s$ for *all frequencies*.

The relations between the configuration of the vocal tract and the resonant frequencies and bandwidths have been the subject of study for many years (Chiba and Kajiyama, 1941; Delattre, 1951; Dunn, 1950; Fant, 1960; Stevens and House, 1955; van den Berg, 1955a). When the cross-sectional area of the vocal tract is known at all points along its length, calculations of the resonant frequencies can be made, but such calculations are complex, and, therefore, computational aids such as electrical analog devices and digital computers have been used to establish the relations (Dunn, 1950; Fant, 1960; Stevens and House, 1955). While it is not the purpose of this paper to discuss these relations in detail, one general relation will, however, be noted since it has a bearing on the ensuing discussion. This relation is the following: the frequency of the first resonance tends to decrease as the cross-sectional area at some point along the vocal tract decreases, that is, as the vocal tract becomes more constricted (except when the constriction occurs within a few centimeters of the glottis). This result has been discussed in quantitative terms elsewhere (Stevens and House, 1955), but can easily be verified if reference is made to the analog circuits shown in Figures 3 or 4, which are reasonably valid representations of the acoustic behavior of the vocal tract at low frequencies. In these circuits a vocal-tract constriction is represented by an acoustic mass M whose magnitude is inversely proportional to the cross-sectional area of the constriction. In the case of Figure 3, therefore, M becomes larger as the area of the constriction decreases, and thus the frequency of the first resonance $F_1 = 1/\{2\pi\sqrt{(MC)}\}$ decreases. In the case of Figure 4, which corresponds to a two-cavity idealization of the vocal-tract configuration, it can be shown that the frequency F_1 of the first resonance decreases as M_2 becomes large, and also decreases as M_1 becomes large, provided the constriction with which M_1 is associated is not too close to the glottis. An increase in M_1 corresponds to a decrease in the cross-sectional area of the constriction separating the two cavities, whereas an increase in M_2 corresponds to a decrease in the cross-sectional area of the anterior end of the vocal tract.

Properties of the spectrum envelope

It has been shown in equation 2 above that the spectrum of the sound pressure p_r measured at a distance r in front of the lips is the product of three terms (or the sum of three terms if each is expressed in decibels): a source spectrum $U_s(j\omega)$, a radiation characteristic $R(j\omega)$, and a transfer function $T(j\omega)$. The first two terms are both almost independent of the articulatory configuration, while the last is dependent on the configuration and is characterized by a number of resonances or poles. The spectrum envelope of a vowel can be constructed, therefore, simply by adding to the $20.\log |U_0/U_s|$ curve of Figure 5 the spectrum envelope of U_s which has a form similar to that shown in the lower part of Figure 2, plus the radiation characteristic, which rises at 6 dB/octave in the frequency range of interest. An overall vowel spectrum envelope constructed in this way for the uniform vocal-tract configuration is shown in Figure 6. For a glottal excitation of fixed frequency the spectrum actually is a line spectrum, the spacing between components being equal to the fundamental frequency.

When the vocal-tract configuration differs from the uniform-tube idealization, the frequencies of the resonances and hence the frequencies at which there are peaks in the spectrum envelope, shift to positions different from those shown in Figure 6. If the frequencies and bandwidths of the resonances for the new configuration are known, then the transfer function

$T(j\omega)$ can be computed using equation **5** in the manner discussed above, and the entire spectrum envelope can again be constructed by adding to $T(j\omega)$ (in decibels) the radiation characteristic and the spectrum envelope of the source. This procedure has been used to construct the three spectrum envelope curves shown in Figure 7. In order to simplify the calculations, the half-power bandwidths of all resonances again were assumed to

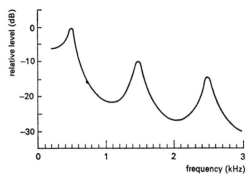

Figure 6

be 100 Hz, a value that is not greatly different from the bandwidths of the first three resonances for spoken vowels (Bogert, 1953; House and Stevens, 1958; Lewis, 1936). The three curves correspond roughly to the spectrum envelopes for /i/, /ɑ/ and /u/.

The curves in Figures 6 and 7 demonstrate that the relative amplitudes of the spectral peaks vary markedly depending on the frequencies of the resonances. Consider, for example, spectra (a) and (c) in Figure 7, in which the frequencies of the first and third resonances are roughly the same but the second resonance is at 2200 Hz in one case and 1000 Hz in the other. The amplitude of the third spectral peak is about 24 dB higher in spectrum (a) than in spectrum (c) as a result of the difference in the frequencies of the second resonances.

The fact that the amplitudes of the spectral peaks in vowel spectra are predictable when the resonant frequencies are known has been discussed in some detail by Fant (1956). From theoretical considerations, Fant predicted the amplitudes of the first three spectral peaks of selected vowels and showed that these calculated levels were in good agreement with previously reported measurements of the average levels of the spectral peaks of spoken English and Swedish vowels.

Some insight into the causes for the changes in the amplitudes of the spectral peaks with changes in the resonant frequencies can be gained from re-examination of the transfer function for the two-resonator approxi-

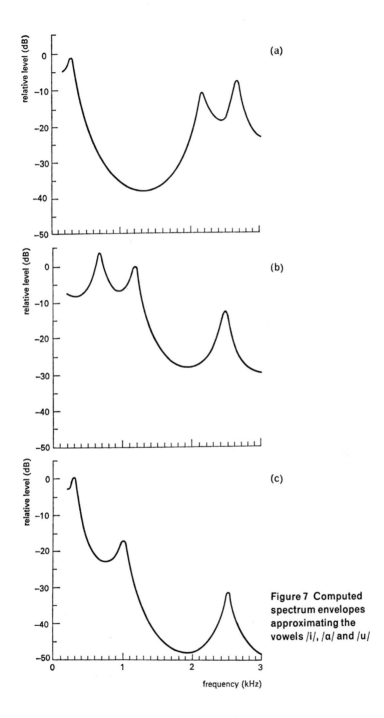

Figure 7 Computed spectrum envelopes approximating the vowels /i/, /ɑ/ and /u/

mation of the vocal tract. It is recalled that the transfer function in Figure 4 was constructed by adding two simple resonance curves of the type shown in Figure 3. In that example the resonant frequency for one component curve was 300 Hz and the resonant frequency for the other was 950 Hz. If now the frequency F_2 of the second resonance is shifted upwards while the first resonant frequency F_1 is held fixed, then the amplitude of the second peak in the composite curve will decrease. Likewise, if F_2 is held fixed while F_1 is shifted upwards, then the amplitude of the second peak in the composite curve will increase. There will be concomitant changes in the amplitude of the first resonance peak in both these cases, but these changes will be relatively small. Although the amplitude relations just noted are discussed with reference to the vocal-tract transfer function, the same relations apply to the overall spectrum envelope, since the source spectrum envelope and the radiation characteristic that are added to the transfer function to obtain the overall spectrum envelope are independent of changes in the transfer function. Furthermore, these relations apply not only to the two-resonator model but also to the more exact transmission-line model, for which the transfer function is constructed by the addition of many resonance curves.

Calculations of levels of resonance

Up to this point it has been assumed tacitly that the spectra under discussion were characterized by resonances, each of which gives rise to a separate peak or prominence at the resonance frequency. When resonant frequencies are sufficiently close, however, they are not necessarily identical with the frequencies of the peaks in the spectrum. For example, when two resonances with bandwidths of about 100 Hz are about 100 Hz apart, the spectrum envelope may show only one prominence; the frequency of the peak will be somewhere between the two resonant frequencies. In the discussion that follows, the levels of the resonances will be defined to be the levels of the spectral envelope at the frequencies of the resonances (rather than at the spectral peaks).

The quantitative relations among the levels of the three lowest resonances for a range of values of the frequencies of the first two resonances can be calculated by means of the relations discussed above. Such calculations have been carried out by means of a digital computer, and are depicted by the contour plots shown in Figures 8 and 9. Along any one contour the level of a particular resonance remains constant at the indicated value. In Figure 8, the dashed contours represent loci of constant amplitude of the first resonance, while the other contours represent corresponding loci for the second resonance; the contours in Figure 9 pertain to the third resonance. In both figures the amplitude levels are given in decibels relative to the level of the first resonance when $F_1 = 500$ Hz, $F_2 = 1500$ Hz, $F_3 = 2500$ Hz, etc.

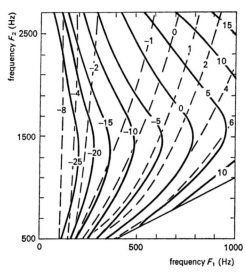

Figure 8 Computed isoamplitude contours of the first resonance peak (dashed curves) and second resonance peak (solid curves) for vowel spectrum envelopes as a function of the frequencies of the first and second resonances

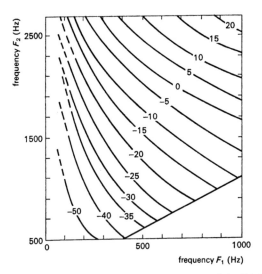

Figure 9 Computed isoamplitude contours of the third resonance peak for vowel spectrum envelopes as a function of the frequencies of the first two resonances

The following constraints were applied to the generation of the data in Figures 8 and 9. The bandwidths of all resonances were 100 Hz. The spectrum envelope of the glottal output was that shown in Figure 2, and the overall level of the excitation was held constant. The third and higher resonances were held constant at 2500 Hz, 3500 Hz, 4500 Hz, etc., except that $F_3 = F_2 + 500$ Hz when F_2 exceeded 2000 Hz and $F_4 = F_3 + 500$ Hz when F_3 exceeded 3000 Hz.

The use of the contours is made clear by considering the spectrum envelope associated with the uniform tube, as shown in Figure 6. If the level of the first resonance at 500 Hz is the zero dB reference, then the level of the second resonance is about −9·5 dB and that of the third resonance is about −15 dB. In Figure 8, the intersection of $F_1 = 500$ Hz and $F_2 = 1500$ Hz gives levels of zero dB and about −9·5 dB, respectively; the same operation in Figure 9 provides a level of about −15 dB for the third resonance. Similarly the relative levels of the resonances of the three samples in Figure 7 may be read from the contours.

In general the contour plots indicate that the level of a given resonance is influenced strongly by the frequencies of the lower resonances. Thus the level of the second resonance at a given frequency drops sharply when the frequency of the first resonance is decreased; similarly the level of the third resonance is influenced strongly by the frequencies of both the first and second resonances. If the frequencies of two resonances are close together, the levels of both are relatively high, as when F_2 is below 1500 Hz and F_1 is above 500 Hz, or when F_2 is above 2000 Hz and F_3 is only 500 Hz higher.

Since the contours in Figures 8 and 9 assume that the bandwidths of the various resonances are always 100 Hz, a word must be said about the effect of variations from this value. If the bandwidth B of a given resonance differs from 100 Hz, then $20 . \log_{10}(100/B)$ should be added to the level read from Figure 8 or 9 for that resonance. For example, if the bandwidth of the second resonance of the vowel shown in Figure 6 is narrowed to 70 Hz, the correction to be applied is +3 dB, and hence the level of the second resonance becomes −6·5 dB instead of −9·5 dB.

Some implications of the theory

A number of measurements pertaining to amplitudes and spectra of speech sounds have been reported in the literature. In particular, studies have been made of frequencies and amplitudes of vowel formants, amplitude relations and formant transitions within syllables, and relative intensities of vowels and consonants. In general, acoustic data of this type have not been organized within a cohesive theoretical framework, except in the technical monograph by Fant which appeared recently (1960). The acoustical theory of vowel production outlined above provides such a framework for the discussion of amplitude relations in syllabic nuclei.

Relative intensities of vowels

It has long been recognized that different vowels generated with the same vocal effort have different overall levels (Black, 1949; Fairbanks *et al.*, 1950; Sacia and Beck, 1926). The range of overall levels for the common vowels of American English is roughly 4 to 5 dB, with /i/ and /u/ having the lowest levels and /æ/, /ɑ/, and /ɔ/ the highest levels.

An attempt to relate these data to articulation was made by Fairbanks (1950), who postulated that vowel intensity should be correlated with the anterior opening of the vocal conduit, and demonstrated such a correlation between two sets of published data. Figure 8 shows that the overall intensity of a vowel is determined largely by the frequency of the first vowel resonance since the level of that resonance is always greater than that of higher resonances. But the frequency of the first resonance is closely related to the size of the mouth opening (see Stevens and House, 1955), and, therefore, the positive correlation described by Fairbanks can be considered to be a consequence of the acoustical theory.

Quantitative prediction of the overall vowel intensities can be made from the contours of Figure 8. The procedure is first to find the relative levels of the first two resonance peaks, knowing the frequencies of these resonances. For resonance bandwidths of 100 Hz, the relative levels given in the contours are identical to the contributions of the individual resonances to the overall vowel intensity. If, however, the bandwidth B of a resonance is different from 100 Hz, a correction of $10 . \log_{10}(100/B)$ must be added to determine the contribution of that resonance to the overall vowel intensity.[2] The overall relative intensity of the vowel is obtained by summing the contributions of the first two resonances (the contribution of higher resonances will be very small and can be neglected).

Typical calculations for four vowels are shown in Table 1. The values of resonant frequencies and bandwidths represent means for three male talkers who generated the vowels in a large number of consonant contexts. The measurements were made with the aid of a digital computer using spectrum matching techniques, and refer to spectral samples appearing centrally in the temporal course of the vowel (House *et al.*, 1960). The computed values of relative intensity in the right-hand column of the table compare well to previously published measurements of vowel intensity, the range from /u/

2. The correction factor to determine the contribution of a resonance to overall intensity is different from the correction used to find the level of the resonance peak. The overall intensity is determined by the area under the spectrum envelope, and is a function, therefore, both of the height of the resonance peak and of its width.

Table 1 Calculation of the overall relative intensities of four vowels. The assumptions regarding higher formants and glottal spectrum are the same as those used in constructing Figures 8 and 9

Vowel	A^a (Hz)	B^b (dB)	C^c (Hz)	D^d (dB)	E^e (dB)	F^f (dB)
i	$F_1 = 300$	− 1·9	50	3·0	1·1	1·3
	$F_2 = 2260$	−11·0	120	−0·8	−11·8	
æ	$F_1 = 730$	2·0	100	—	2·0	3·8
	$F_2 = 1650$	− 1·0	100	—	− 1·0	
ɑ	$F_1 = 720$	4·2	130	−1·1	3·1	5·6
	$F_2 = 1190$	1·0	80	1·0	2·0	
u	$F_1 = 320$	− 1·1	60	2·2	1·1	1·2
	$F_2 = 1110$	−16·0	100	—	−16·0	

[a] Average frequencies of the first and second vowel resonances (House et al., 1960)
[b] Relative levels of resonance peaks, derived from Figure 8
[c] Half-power bandwidths of resonances (House et al., 1960)
[d] Corrections $10. \log_{10}(100/B)$ to account for deviation of bandwidths from 100 Hz
[e] Relative contributions of resonances to overall intensity of vowel
[f] Relative intensity of vowels

to /ɑ/ being 4·4 dB. For example, from the data of Sacia and Beck (1926) a list of these four vowels in order of intensity ('average peak power') would be /u,i,æ,ɑ/, with 4·8 dB difference between the extreme vowels; other experimenters report similar data (Black 1949; Fairbanks et al., 1950).

Amplitude relations within the syllable

The motoric description of speech production espoused by Stetson (1951) defines the so-called releasing and arresting actions of consonants (or of other muscular activity) to constitute the boundaries of the syllable. In a symmetric consonant-vowel-consonant (CVC) syllable, the initial C that releases the syllable is characterized by a vocal-tract constriction that gradually (or abruptly) increases in size, while the final C that arrests the syllable is characterized by a gradual (or abrupt) decrease in the size of a constriction in the vocal tract. During the temporal course of this activity, the vocal tract may be excited by one or more acoustic sources, but typically the central portion of the syllable is characterized by glottal excitation or voice. It has already been noted above that the frequency of the first resonance decreases as the vocal tract becomes more constricted. The amplitude relations depicted in Figure 8 demonstrate, moreover, that the amplitude of the first resonance peak – and consequently the overall amplitude of the vowel – decreases as F_1 decreases. The rate of decrease becomes more rapid as F_1 falls below 300 Hz, that is, as F_1 assumes values associated with vocal-tract configurations more appropriate to consonant production than vowel production (Stevens and House, 1957). In other words, during the course of a typical CVC syllable the acoustical theory predicts that, while the source excitation remains constant, the overall intensity will build up to a maximum value in a central (vocalic) portion and then decrease.

Stetson (1951, p. 179), has reported data on amplitude fluctuations within the syllable obtained by simultaneous kymographic and spectrographic recordings. These data, together with descriptions of the typical form of oscillographic and graphic level records (see Fairbanks *et al.*, 1950; House and Fairbanks, 1953), demonstrate that the syllable is characterized by an intensity maximum reached during the central portion of the vowel. The acoustical theory of vowel production, therefore, is compatible both with the motoric point of view regarding syllable production and with the classical statements of inherent and relative sonority and syllabic peaks of prominence (Jones, 1956). Hence the so-called 'undulation of prominence' (p. 55) that is perceived by the hearer is a reflection both of the acoustic end-product and of the articulatory events responsible for it.

Spectrum balance in the vowel

While the overall vowel intensities discussed above are related primarily to changes in the first vocal-tract resonance, Figures 8 and 9 also demonstrate wide variations in the levels of the second and third resonance peaks as a function of the frequencies of the first two resonances. The variation in the levels of resonance peaks within the vowels of actual speech is well known (Peterson and Barney, 1952), but the dependence of these variations on articulation was not explained adequately until recently (Fant, 1956).

The fact that rigorous relations obtain among the levels of the resonance peaks, the frequencies of the resonances, and the articulatory configuration, has a bearing on the formulation of theories of vowel perception. The lack of independence among these factors makes it inappropriate to hypothesize that the perception of a vowel is attributable to any one of them to the exclusion of the others. Independent manipulation of these characteristics in experiments using synthetic speech is to be questioned if the results are to be generalized to explain the perception of natural speech.

The attempts made in the past to characterize a vowel in terms of the frequency locations of spectral prominences have focused attention on an aspect of the physical event that may not be clearly observable (Ladefoged, 1960), particularly when two resonances are closely spaced in frequency, a resonance has a broad bandwidth, or the amplitude of a resonance is very low. The theoretical discussions above indicate, however, that the presence of a resonance may be signalled not only by spectral prominences, but also by amplitude relations within the spectrum envelope. In the spectrum of a vowel /u/, for example, the third resonance is often below the dynamic range of the measuring equipment, while the first two resonances are sometimes not manifested as separate spectral prominences. When it is understood, however, that a low amplitude third resonance is a consequence of low-frequency first and second resonances the spectrogram is easily interpreted.

On defining the formant

The discussions above suggest the need for more precise definitions of some of the traditional terms used by linguists, phoneticians and other students of speech. One such term, conspicuous because of its almost complete absence in this paper to this point, is the word *formant*.

In the literature the term formant has been used principally to indicate a concentration of spectral energy in a narrow frequency region of a speech signal. Furthermore, it generally has been applied only to those portions of the speech signal called voiced, that is, characterized by glottal excitation. When sound spectrograms (intensity–frequency–time displays) are made on an instrument using a broad (300 Hz) analysing filter, the formant structure of continuous speech is displayed as a number of more-or-less horizontal 'bars' (Potter, *et al.*, 1947). For any given vocalic sound a number of formants may occur in the frequency range 0 to 4000 Hz, but attention is usually focused on the lowest two or three.

When the term formant was proposed originally, it was used to designate a natural frequency (*charakteristischer Ton*) of the vocal cavities, and a so-called inharmonic theory of vowel production was implied (Hermann, 1894; 1895). Subsequently the term was adopted by the advocates of another theory of production – the harmonic theory – and used to designate the center frequency in a 'tonal domain' contributing to the character of the particular vowel (Stumpf, 1926).

A typical description of a formant was given by Joos (1948): 'The frequencies corresponding to the centers of the two principal peaks of the [spectrum] profile ... are called formant 1 and formant 2, respectively.' Potter and Steinberg (1950), on the other hand, attempted to specify the measurement procedures used in their investigations as follows: ' ... we suspect that the ear deals with something akin to effective pitch centers of loudness of the energy concentrations. For our initial work we have adopted as an approximation of such a center, a weighted average of the frequencies of the formant components.'

The problem of defining the formant was confused further by the attempts of investigators to specify variant and invariant formants in speech spectra.

Sovijärvi (1939), for example, reported finding seven variable and eleven fixed formants and attempted to relate each of them to a cavity resonator in the vocal system. More recently, Ochiai and Fukumura (1953), in an investigation of voice quality, have discussed the probable role of invariant formants. These investigators have complicated the terminological situation still further by using formant to refer to spectral concentration that is manifested when the vowel spectra of a number of subjects are summed graphically.

In view of this historical resumé, the common usage of the term formant leaves several questions unanswered. Should the word be applied to energy concentrations in consonant spectra? If so, is it permissible to apply it to both voiced and voiceless consonants? It is appropriate to refer to the various energy concentrations in the spectrum of a nasalized vowel or a nasal consonant as formants? How can the frequency of a formant be measured precisely? And so on . . .

It has been recognized (Fant, 1960; Flanagan and House, 1956; Heinz and Stevens, 1961) that the acoustical theory of speech production can provide a precise definition for the term formant. Following Hermann (1894), it is proposed that a formant be interpreted as a normal mode of vibration of the vocal tract, and formant frequency be defined as the frequency of such a normal mode of vibration. The term formant is applied to the vocal tract in a manner similar to the way in which *pole* is used to characterize an electric network, and implies, therefore, a complex number consisting of a real part (proportional to the formant bandwidth) and an imaginary part (the formant frequency).

This definition of formant means that the vocal tract has formants regardless of its excitation. During the production of certain sounds (notably the vowels) the formants are manifested in the acoustic output as maxima in the spectra. When the formants are reasonably well separated in frequency, and when their bandwidths are not abnormally wide, the frequencies of the spectral maxima are good measures of the formant frequencies. During the production of other sounds (particularly certain consonants) certain normal modes are only weakly excited and will not be immediately apparent in the output spectra. It can be argued, however, that since the vocal tract executes continuous motions during the production of syllables, the formant frequencies are continuous functions of time (Fant, 1952).

Defining the formant in terms of articulation raises certain problems of measurement, since usually only the acoustic signal is available for analysis. Traditional spectrographic procedures for measuring formant frequencies of vowels can often lead to reliable data, however, providing that the constraints imposed by the acoustical theory are kept in mind. A more powerful technique should take into account the effect of a given formant on the entire spectrum shape. Such techniques are under development and will provide data relative to consonant as well as vowel production (Fant, 1960; Fujimura, 1960; Heinz and Stevens, 1961; House *et al.*, 1960; Mathews *et al.*, 1961). It is interesting to note that, as early as 1936, Lewis (1936) used a technique of matching simple resonance curves to vowel spectra in the vicinity of spectral maxima, thus applying to his measurements some of the constraints imposed by the acoustic theory.

Summary

A contemporary acoustical theory of vowel production is outlined and certain implications of the theory are discussed. The theory considers a vowel sound to be the result of excitation of a linear acoustic system by a quasi-periodic volume velocity source. The transfer function of the acoustic system is completely described by a number of poles whose frequency locations depend on the vocal-tract configuration. It is shown that the theory is compatible with data relevant to the overall intensity of vowels, amplitude relations within syllables, and questions of balance in the vowel spectrum. Finally it is proposed that the traditional term *formant* be restricted to mean a normal mode of vibration of the vocal system.

References

BLACK, J. W. (1949), 'Natural frequency, duration, and intensity of vowels in reading', *JSHD*, vol. 14, pp. 216–21.

BOGERT, B. P. (1953), 'On the bandwidth of vowel formants', *J. acoust. Soc. Amer.*, vol. 25, pp. 791–2.

CHIBA, T., and KAJIYAMA, M. (1941), *The Vowel, Its Nature and Structure*, Tokyo-Kaiseikan, Tokyo.

DELATTRE, P. (1951), 'The physiological interpretation of sound spectrograms', *Mod. Lang. Assn Publ.*, vol. 66, pp. 864–75.

DUNN, H. K. (1950), 'The calculation of vowel resonances, and an electrical vocal tract', *J. acoust. Soc. Amer.*, vol. 22, pp. 740–53.

FAIRBANKS, G. (1950), 'A physiological correlative of vowel intensity', *Speech Mongr.*, vol. 17, pp. 390–95.

FAIRBANKS, G., HOUSE, A. S., and STEVENS, E. L. (1950), 'An experimental study of vowel intensities', *J. acoust. Soc. Amer.*, vol. 22, pp. 457–9.

FANT, C. G. M. (1952), 'Transmission properties of the vocal tract with application to the acoustic specification of phonemes', *Tech. Rep.*, vol. 12, January, Acoustics Laboratory, MIT.

FANT, C. G. M. (1956), 'On the predictability of formant levels and spectrum envelope from formant frequencies', in M. Halle *et al.*, *For Roman Jakobson*, Mouton, The Hague, pp. 109–20.

FANT, C. G. M. (1960), *Acoustic Theory of Speech Production*, Mouton, The Hague.

FLANAGAN, J. L. (1958), 'Some properties of the glottal sound source', *JSHR.*, vol. 1, pp. 99–111. Reprinted here, pp. 31–51.

FLANAGAN, J. L., and HOUSE, A. S. (1956), 'Development and testing of a formant-coding speech compression system', *J. acoust. Soc. Amer.*, vol. 28, pp. 1099–1106.

FUJIMURA, O. (1961), 'Spectrum matching of nasal consonants', *J. acoust. Soc. Amer.*, vol. 32, p. 1517, Abstract: 'Analysis of nasal consonants', *Quart. Prog. Rep.* 60, 15 January, pp. 184–8, Res. Lab. Electronics, MIT.

GUILLEMIN, E. A. (1953), *Introductory Circuit Theory*, Wiley.

HEINZ, J. M., and STEVENS, K. N. (1961), 'On the properties of voiceless fricative consonants', *J. acoust. Soc. Amer.*, vol. 33, pp. 589–96.

HERMANN, L. (1894), 'Nachtrag zur Untersuchung der Vokalkurven', *Arch. ges. Physiol.*, vol. 58, pp. 264–79.

HERMANN, L. (1895), 'Weitere Untersuchungen über das Wesen der Vokale', *Arch. ges. Physiol.*, vol. 61, pp. 169–204.

HOUSE, A. S., and FAIRBANKS, G. (1953), 'The influence of consonant environment upon the secondary acoustical characteristics of vowels', *J. acoust. Soc. Amer.*, vol. 25, pp. 105–13.

HOUSE, A. S., and STEVENS, K. N., (1958), 'Estimation of formant band widths from measurements of transient response of the vocal tract', *J. Speech Hearing Res.*, vol. 1, pp. 309–15.

HOUSE, A. S., STEVENS, K. N., and FUJISAKI, H. (1960), 'Automatic measurement of the formants of vowels in diverse consonantal environments', *J. acoust. Soc. Amer.*, vol. 32, p. 1517.

JONES, D. (1956), *An Outline of English Phonetics*, 8th edn, Dutton, New York.

JOOS, M. (1948), *Acoustic phonetics*, Language Monograph, no. 23.

LADEFOGED, P. (1960), 'Spectrographic determination of vowel quality', *J. acoust. Soc. Amer.*, vol. 32, pp. 918–19.

LEWIS, D. (1936), 'Vocal resonance', *J. acoust. Soc. Amer.*, vol. 8, pp. 91–9.

LICKLIDER, J. C. R., HAWLEY, M. E., and WALKLING, R. A. (1955), 'Influences of variations in speech intensity and other factors upon the speech spectrum', *J. acoust. Soc. Amer.*, vol. 27, p. 207.

MATHEWS, M. V., MILLER, J. E., and DAVID, E. E., Jr (1961), 'Pitch synchronous analysis of voiced sounds', *J. acoust. Soc. Amer.*, vol. 33, pp. 179–86.

MILLER, R. L. (1959), 'Nature of the vocal cord wave', *J. acoust. Soc. Amer.*, vol. 31, pp. 667–77.

MORSE, P. M. (1948), *Vibration and Sound*, 2nd edn, McGraw-Hill.

OCHIAI, Y., and FUKUMURA, T. (1953), 'Timbre study of vocalic voices', *Mem. Fac. Engng. Nagoya*, vol. 5, no, 2, pp. 253–80.

PETERSON, G. E., and BARNEY, H. L. (1952), 'Control methods used in a study of the vowels', *J. acoust. Soc. Amer.*, vol. 24, pp. 175–84. Reprinted here, pp. 104–22.

POTTER, R. K., KOPP, G. A., and GREEN, H. C. (1947), *Visible Speech*, Van Nostrand.

POTTER, R. K., and STEINBERG, J. C. (1950), 'Toward the specification of speech', *J. acoust. Soc. Amer.*, vol. 22, pp. 807–20.

SACIA, C. F., and BECK, C. J. (1926), 'The power of fundamental speech sounds', *Bell Syst. tech. J.*, vol. 5, pp. 393–403.

SONESSON, B. (1960), 'On the anatomy and vibratory pattern of the human vocal folds', *Acta Otolaryng.*, suppl. 156, pp. 7–80.

SOVIJÄRVI, A. (1939), 'Die wechselnden und festen Formanten der Vokale, erklärt durch Spektrogramme und Röntgenogramme der Finnischen Vokale', *Proc. Third Int. Congr. Phonet. Sci.*, pp. 407–20.

STETSON, R. H. (1951), *Motor Phonetics; A Study of Speech Movements in Action*, 2nd edn, North-Holland, Amsterdam.

STEVENS, K. N., and HOUSE, A. S. (1955), 'Development of a quantitative description of vowel articulation', *J. acoust. Soc. Amer.*, vol. 27, pp. 484–93.

STEVENS, K. N., and HOUSE, A. S. (1956), 'Studies of formant transitions using a vocal tract analog', *J. acoust. Soc. Amer.*, vol. 28, pp. 578–85.

STUMPF, C. (1926), *Die Sprachlaute*, Springer, Berlin.

TIMCKE, R., VON LEIDEN, H., and MOORE, P. (1958), 'Laryngeal vibrations: measurements of the glottic wave. Part I: the normal vibratory cycle', *Arch. Otolaryng.*, vol. 68, pp. 1–19.

VAN DEN BERG, J. W. (1954), 'Über die Koppelung bei der Stimmbildung', *Z. Phonet. USW*, vol. 8, pp. 281–93.

VAN DEN BERG, J. W. (1955a), 'Calculations on a model of the vocal tract for vowel /i/ (meat) and on the larynx', *J. acoust. Soc. Amer.*, vol. 27, pp. 332–8.

VAN DEN BERG, J. W. (1955b), 'Transmission of the vocal cavities', *J. acoust. Soc. Amer.*, vol. 27, pp. 161–8.

WENDAHL, R. W. (1957), 'Vowel formant frequencies and vocal cavity dimensions' Ph.D. thesis, University of Iowa.

Part Two
Acoustic Analysis of Speech

During any stretch of natural speech the conditions in the larynx and the vocal tract are changing continuously; the period of the opening and closing of the vocal folds varies literally from cycle to cycle and the articulators are in movement all the time, never maintaining the same configuration for much more than one tenth of a second. Hence the main characteristic of the acoustic output of the speech mechanism is its variation with time and any technique for examining this output has to provide a means of following this variation if it is to be really useful. One of the reasons for the very widespread use of sound spectrography in acoustic phonetics is that, in its most commonly used form, it does this.

An equally important matter, of course, is what measurements or quantities one is to follow the variations of. The wave-form of speech sounds, that is, the record of air-particle displacement in the path of the wave, contains within itself all the available information about the sound, and if it is registered in suitable conditions it provides an accurate record of time variations in speech. This information is not very easily accessible, however, until it has been broken down in some way and hence it is usual to subject the sound to some stages of acoustic analysis. The choice of analytical operations has been greatly influenced by our view of the action of the human hearing mechanism. The ear is generally looked upon as being basically a harmonic analyser, which is to say that when it is presented with a complex sound, it analyses it into the various harmonics, or at least narrow frequency bands, of which it is composed and the impression which the brain receives of the sound is largely determined by the relative amounts of sound energy carried in successive harmonics or bands throughout the whole of the frequency range. The acoustic analyser now most often used for speech is the sound spectrograph, a device which registers the amount of acoustic energy in successive harmonics or frequency bands when a sound is put into it and displays as a visible pattern the variations in this spectral distribution of energy with time.

The analysis is carried out by means of filtering circuits and it can be arranged that the filter covers a very narrow or a wider band of frequencies; in other words, the whole frequency range can be split up into narrow slices or into broader ones. The sound spectrograph which is commercially available provides two adjustments of the filter bandwidth, one of 45 Hz and the other of 300 Hz. If the first is used, the machine records the amount of acoustic energy present in successive bands 45 Hz wide and will, for example, register the strength of each harmonic in a complex periodic sound (provided the fundamental does not have a very low value). When the filter bandwidth is 300 Hz all the energy within bands of this width is added together so that if a periodic sound were analysed, the energy of several harmonics would be summed in each band, unless the fundamental were very high. Such filters are resonance circuits and are subject to the laws which govern the performance of resonators. If a resonator is sharply tuned, it will continue to 'ring' after energy has ceased to be applied to it; consequently it will be capable of discriminating between two inputs which are separated by a small distance in frequency but will not be able to distinguish inputs which are separated by a small time interval. In the spectrograph, then, if we choose to inspect narrow frequency slices, we have to put up with comparatively broad time slices, and vice versa. With the 45 Hz bandwidth, the apparatus will not register events in time separated by less than about 20 ms, while with the filter bandwidth at 300 Hz, it will take note of events which are more than 3–4 ms apart. In the study of speech, time discrimination tends to be important but both the narrow and the wide filter bandwidth have been found useful in the analysis of speech inputs.

A number of the papers in this book include spectrograms made with a commercially produced sound spectrograph whose design is similar to that of the prototype described in the paper by Koenig, Dunn and Lacy (Reading 4). The three-dimensional patterns portray an acoustic analysis covering the frequency range from about 80 to 8000 Hz for samples of speech lasting up to 2·4 s. Differences in intensity are registered by differences in the darkness of the trace and it should be noted that in the process the range of intensities in the sound input to the machine is very much compressed. The paper on which the patterns are traced will permit variations equivalent to a range of not more than about 12 dB, which is considerably less than the variation in sound intensity which one may expect in a speech sample. However, in addition to the three-dimensional pattern, the sound spectrograph will provide a 'section', that is the spectrum of a small time segment of a sound, in which the dynamic range is much greater, allowing for variations in intensity up to about 30 dB.

Koenig, Dunn and Lacy give a full account of the first sound spectrograph together with some of the considerations which influenced its design and their paper is a most useful basis for the understanding of the working of this indispensable item of equipment in the phonetics laboratory.

4 W. Koenig, H. K. Dunn and L. Y. Lacy

The Sound Spectrograph

Excerpt from W. Koenig, H. K. Dunn and L. Y. Lacy, 'The sound spectrograph', *Journal of the Acoustical Society of America*, vol. 18 (1946), pp. 21–32.

In many fields of research it is necessary to analyse complex waves. If these waves are steady in time, the analysis presents no particular difficulties. If, however, the wave is complex in its frequency composition and also varies rapidly in time, the problem is very difficult. Numerous methods have been employed in the past to try to show changing energy–frequency distribution; several examples have appeared in the pages of this journal. Figure 1, for instance, shows a series of harmonic analyses of the successive periods of a vowel sound (Steinberg, 1934). The dotted lines mark the regions of resonance which change continuously throughout the production of the sound. By performing this operation on a whole sentence, an effort was made, as shown in Figure 2 taken from the same paper, to represent the time variations in the energy–frequency distributions. Here the frequencies of the various resonant regions are represented by the solid lines and their relative amplitudes are roughly indicated by the widths of the lines. The generation of this graph represented a formidable amount of time and labour.

Plate 1 shows another representation of a changing wave form (Potter, 1930). This is an oscillogram of a series of 11 steady tones sent over a radio channel and received through a bank of narrow band filters whose outputs were commutated at the rate of $12\frac{1}{2}$ times per second. A slight gap was left between cycles, as marked at the bottom of Plate 1. A single cycle is included in the section marked A. The successive cycles show varying profiles, due to the fact that the frequency response of the radio channel was continually changed by selective fading. Similar pictures would have been obtained if a varying signal such as speech had been impressed on the bank of filters without the radio link. Instead of making oscillograms, however, the output was at that time displayed on a cathode-ray tube. The changing profiles of these patterns portrayed the changing energy frequency distribution in speech. An attempt was made to learn to recognize these word patterns, but with little success.

Plate 2 shows another device for portraying a complex wave (Schuck and Young, 1943). Here a kind of three-dimensional model was developed by analysing the amplitude of each harmonic component of a piano note as a function of time, plotting the results on cards, and cutting out the profiles.

Still another method is illustrated in Figure 3. Here the frequency range was divided into ten bands (Dudley, 1939) by means of band filters. The

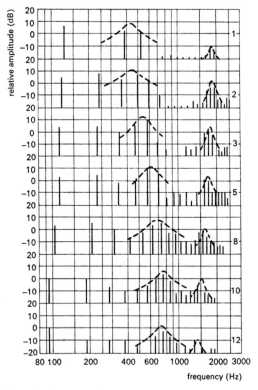

Figure 1 A series of harmonic analyses of successive periods of the vowel in the word 'out'

output of each band was rectified and recorded with a string oscillograph, so that each oscillogram shows the variation of amplitude with time. Despite the rather small number of bands, a kind of speech pattern can be discerned in this array of oscillograms.

Plate 3 shows this process carried further. These are solid models built up of oscillograms of about 200 overlapping frequency bands, cut out in profile and stacked side by side. The words are 'visual telephony for the deaf'. In the upper model only the high peaks in the speech are prominent.

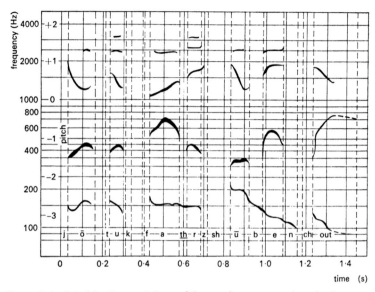

Figure 2 A plot of the time variations of the vocal resonances in a short
sentence, compiled from a series of analyses like those in Figure 1

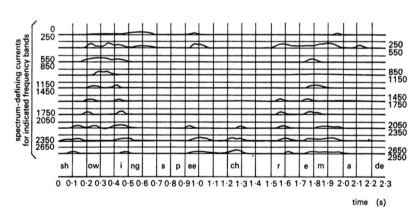

Figure 3 Another method of illustrating the energy–frequency–time
distribution in speech

In the lower model the level differences among the various regions have been equalized by electrical compression which will be explained subsequently. Of particular interest in these models is the sharpness of the wave front which appears at the beginning of some of the words. It can be seen from these models that in speech the energy–frequency distribution is very complex and changes form rapidly with time.

The production of solid models, while useful for particular purposes, is hardly a practical method for everyday needs. Furthermore, it is difficult to portray the results usefully in a two-dimensional picture. If, however, we substitute for the third dimension in these models a system of varying shades of grey or black with the highest amplitudes represented by dark areas and the lowest amplitudes by light areas on a flat surface, then we have a method which can be rapid and convenient. This is the method of the sound spectrograph.

General plan and first model of the sound spectrograph

Figure 4 shows in highly schematic fashion the basic method of the sound spectrograph, as originally proposed by Mr R. K. Potter (1946). It is necessary, first, to have a means of recording the sound in such a form that it can be reproduced over and over. The means shown here is a magnetic tape, mounted on a rotating disk. In recording, some predistortion of the signal may be desirable and is therefore indicated in connection with the recording amplifier. With speech, for example, it has been found advan-

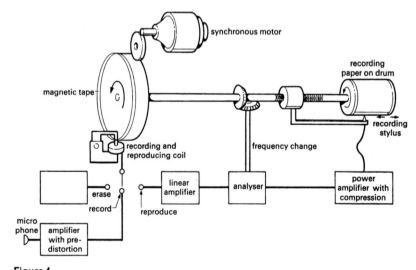

Figure 4

tageous to raise the amplitude of the higher frequencies by about 6 dB per octave in order to equalize the representation of the different energy regions.

Second, a means of analysing must be provided. Most convenient is the heterodyne type of analyser employing a fixed band pass filter, with a variable oscillator and modulator system by which any portion of the sound spectrum can be brought within the frequency range of the filter.

Finally, the output of the analyser must be recorded in synchronism with the reproduced sound. The simplest method is by means of a drum, on the same shaft with the magnetic tape, carrying a recording medium which should be capable of showing gradations of density depending on the intensity of the analyser output. Each time the drum revolves, the stylus which marks the paper is moved laterally a small distance, and the oscillator frequency is changed slightly. Thus a picture is built up which has time as one coordinate and frequency as the other, with intensity shown by the density or darkness of the record. It may be necessary or desirable to distort the amplitudes in the analyser output, depending on the recording medium used and the use to be made of the spectrograms. This function is indicated in the figure by the compression in the last amplifier.

The first spectrograph set up in the laboratory differed in some particulars from the arrangement shown in Figure 4. Instead of a recording drum on the same shaft with the magnetic tape, use was made of a machine built for radio facsimile reception, which happened to be available. This device had a cam-driven arm sweeping a stylus across a strip of conducting paper. The paper had a light-colored surface which became progressively darker as the current passing through it increased. Each sweep of the arm was started by a synchronizing signal which in this case came from a contact connected to the disk carrying the magnetic tape. The paper was automatically advanced 0·01 inch between sweeps. The machine had to be modified to the extent of slowing down the motion and providing a new cam to make the motion more uniform.

For the analysing portion of the system, use was made of another piece of available equipment, namely an ERPI heterodyne analyser. No mechanical connection was provided between the analyser and the magnetic tape or the recording system, so the frequency had to be shifted by hand after each sweep of the recording arm. In the beginning, the output of the analyser was rectified and a thyratron threshold arrangement was employed ahead of the recorder, so that it printed only when the analyser output rose above a predetermined level, and there were no gradations in density. When it was found that intensity could be shown by the density or blackness of the record, the threshold was dispensed with: but because of the small range of currents required for printing the full density range of the paper, it was necessary to compress the signal. This was done with a sort of partial automatic volume control arrangement, and adjustments were made until a 35 dB signal level range was discovered, with what looked to the eye like even density steps on the paper for even dB changes of level.

A sample spectrogram of speech made with this arrangement is shown in Plate 4. The coordinates of time and frequency are indicated. The analysing band width was 200 Hz, with the band being shifted (by hand) 50 Hz for each new sweep of the recording arm. The sentence shown is a familiar one, containing most of the vowel sounds. The most gratifying feature of these early spectrograms was the clear indication of the almost continual shifting in frequency of the dark bars which represent the vocal resonances. It would take weeks or months of harmonic analysis from oscillograms to obtain the same information. Considerable consonant detail may be seen as well. Predistortion, to the extent of raising the higher frequencies by 6 dB per octave was used in making this spectrogram.

While pitch inflection is not shown in Plate 4, it may be brought out by two methods. If the analysing band is made narrow enough, the separate voice harmonics appear and their rise and fall with pitch can be seen. The other method is to permit the beats between harmonics in a wide band to register, producing characteristic striations vertically across the pattern. Both of these effects will be illustrated subsequently.

The work with this experimental equipment was carried out before our entry into the war. Because of its military interest it was given official rating as a war project and a self-contained model was developed which is described in the next section.

Present model

A photograph of the present model portable sound spectrograph is shown in Plate 5 with the equipment set up as in operation. The recorder unit is at the right, the amplifier-analyser is at the left with associated control circuits mounted on a panel attached above it, and the power supply is on the lower shelf of the table. The units are interconnected by means of flexible cords and connectors so they can be transported separately. This spectrograph, although basically the same as the early model described above, differs considerably in mechanical and operational details.

The recorder unit, which serves as the magnetic tape recorder as well as the spectrograph pattern recorder, is built around a modified commercial two-speed turntable of the type used for disk recording. The signals to be analysed are recorded on a length of vicalloy magnetic tape $\frac{1}{4}$ inch wide and between 2 and 3 mils thick, mounted against a shoulder in a step turned on the lower edge of the 13 inch turntable platter. About one third of the tape projects below the platter rim. Precise machining of the step is necessary to prevent eccentricity or wrinkling of the tape. The ends of the tape are sheared diagonally at about 45°, to a length which will provide a 2 or 3 mil butt joint when the tape is mounted. The joint is slanted so that the overhanging sharp pointed edge of the tape trails as the turntable rotates. When the tape is cut and mounted carefully, the joint is hardly noticeable in the patterns. The tape is held to the platter rim by a serving of heavy linen thread wrapped around the upper two thirds of the tape and cemented in place by several coats of clear lacquer. The turntable is rim-driven by a synchronous motor through friction drive idlers at 25 r.p.m. for recording and 78 r.p.m. for analysis.

Two sets of magnetic pole pieces, one for recording (or reproducing) and another for erasing, are mounted on the bed of the machine so that the overhanging edge of the tape passes between their faces. The recording pole faces are about 40 mils square and are mounted with a pivot and spring so that their inside edges will just pass in a shearing fashion when the tape is removed. In order to ensure good contact with the tape at the shearing edges, the pole faces are initially machined at a slight angle (2 or 3 degrees to the tape) to reduce the time for 'running in' to a good fit. Very small misalignments of the pole faces may cause a decided loss of high frequency response. As shown in Plate 6, the erasing pole pieces are placed about one inch ahead of the recording pole pieces; their pole faces are slightly wider than the recording pole faces so that erasing will be effective even if there is a small relative misalignment of the two sets of pole pieces. Between the two sets of pole pieces may be seen a spreader with which they may be lifted out of contact with the tape for safety during shipment or handling of the turntable. An oil-saturated wick placed ahead of the pole pieces serves to clean and lubricate the tape as it rotates.

The superstructure mounted above the turntable (Plate 5) serves as the spectrogram pattern recorder. In addition to the conventional cutting head carriage and lead screw, a 4 inch diameter metal drum, mounted on a shaft parallel to and below the lead screw, is driven through 1:1 spiral gears from a vertical extension of the turntable shaft. A flexible stainless steel stylus about 10 mils in diameter is mounted on an insulating block fastened to the cutting head carriage, which can be lowered to or raised from the recording position manually. An automatic paper index mounted on the drum shaft indicates the position for placing the lap in the facsimile paper so that the beginning of the sound sample recorded on the tape will coincide with the leading edge of the paper.

· The schematic diagram in Figure 5 shows the various elements of the spectrograph used in the recording condition. The signal amplifier and the biasing and erasing oscillator are in the amplifier-analyser unit. The signal amplifier is used also for reproducing and the oscillator forms a part of the carrier oscillator for analysis of the recorded signals. Switch contacts for

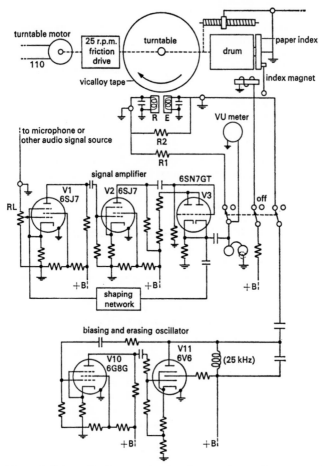

Figure 5 Schematic diagram showing the spectrograph components arranged for recording a sample on the tape

making the change from the 'record' to the 'reproduce' condition, however, are left out of the schematics to make them more straightforward.

A microphone or other signal source is connected to the amplifier input, and the recording level, which can be read on the VU meter, is adjusted by means of the RL potentiometer. Shaping networks are provided in the feedback circuit so that the relative levels of high and low frequencies in the signal may be changed if desired. The low impedance output of the amplifier is connected to the recording coil R through a high resistance R1 which gives essentially constant recording current for equal voltages over the frequency range of the input signal. Erasing current of 25 Hz is supplied to the erase coil E by the biasing and erasing oscillator. Some of this current is also applied as a bias to the recording coil R through the resistor R2. Small tuning condensers across the recording and erasing coils raise the effective coil impedance at 25 Hz but have little effect in the voice frequency range. These condensers also serve to reduce oscillator switching transients which otherwise tend to magnetize the tape so strongly that complete erasure is difficult.

The turntable and tape are driven at 25 r.p.m. which permits recording a sample of 2·4 s duration at a linear tape speed of approximately 16 inches per second. Continuous recording and erasing are effected as long as the switch is in the recording position. The erasing coil, since it is just ahead of the recording coil, erases signals which were recorded 2·4 s earlier. When the 'record-reproduce' switch is thrown to the right, erasing and recording are simultaneously stopped, thereby capturing the last 2·4 s of signal on the loop of tape, after which it may be reproduced over and over.

The paper index magnet is energized in the recording position, and the paper index rotates frictionally with the drum until the index magnet armature engages a pin projecting on the side of the paper index, causing it to remain in a fixed position. When the index magnet is released at the end of a recorded sample, the paper index is free to rotate with the drum again. The paper index then indicates the position on the drum corresponding to the end of the sample recorded on the tape. Since the drum is directly geared to the turntable on which the tape is mounted, the above relationship will remain fixed and the facsimile paper can be placed on the drum so that the end of the paper coincides exactly with the end of the recorded sample. After a desired sample has been recorded, the turntable is stopped and a pre-cut sheet of electrically sensitive paper is secured to the drum by means of rolling springs.

The turntable is then speeded up to 78 r.p.m. by shifting idler pulleys in the friction drive. It should be pointed out that, although the signal sounds unnatural when speeded up approximately 3 to 1 by this shift, its wave form is unaltered. The effect is merely to divide the reproducing time approximately by 3 and multiply all of the frequency components of the recorded signal by the same factor. This operation converts the original frequency range of approximately 100 to 3500 Hz to about 300 to 10 500 Hz. Since it is very difficult to vary a narrow band pass filter over this range for analysis, a heterodyning process is used with a fixed band filter.

Figure 6 shows the various circuits of the spectrograph in the reproducing condition. Starting at the upper left of the diagram, the signal is picked up from the magnetic tape by the reproducing coil R. A small equalizing condenser in shunt resonates the coil at about 12 000 Hz to keep the high frequency response from falling off. This provides an overall frequency response which is essentially flat when the sample has been recorded without pre-equalization.

The reproducing coil works into the R L potentiometer which is used to adjust the level of the reproduced signal to a suitable value. The three-stage

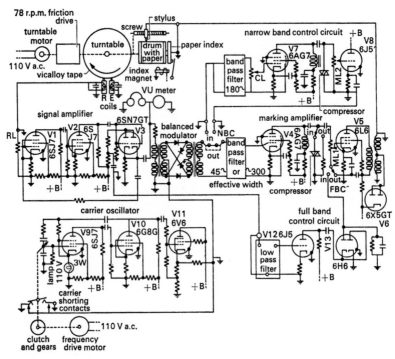

Figure 6 Schematic diagram showing the spectrograph components arranged for reproducing and analysing the recorded signal

feedback signal amplifier has a resistive feedback network to provide a flat frequency response with a voltage gain of about 100 times while reproducing.

The output of the signal amplifier is impressed on the balanced copper oxide modulator. Carrier is supplied to the modulator by the R-C carrier oscillator through the cathode follower amplifier stage V11. As the carrier frequency is slowly shifted by the frequency drive motor from approximately 22 500 Hz to 12 000 Hz, the lower sideband output of the modulator is swept slowly across the fixed band filter connected to its output. The normal sweep rate is such that the turntable makes approximately two hundred revolutions in the time required for the frequency to change from the highest to the lowest value. Since the stylus advances about 10 mils for each revolution of the turntable, the resulting spectrogram is approximately 2 inches wide for the 3500 Hz frequency range. The carrier shorting contacts, which are operated from a cam on the condenser drive shaft, switch the carrier current on and off to define the high and low frequency boundaries of the spectrograms.

Either of two filter widths may be selected by a switch which selects one of two values of mutual capacity between the anti-resonant sections of the

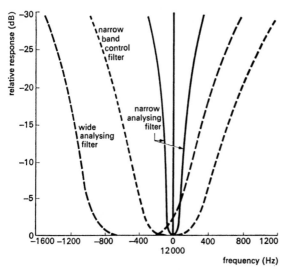

Figure 7 The characteristics of the several filters used in the spectrograph

band pass filter. The characteristics of the two filters are shown in Figure 7. It will be noted that the mid band frequency of the wide analysing filter is lower than that of the narrow filter. With this particular filter structure, changing the pass band is accomplished by shifting the lower cut-off; the upper (theoretical) cut-off remains the same. These curves show the actual pass bands of the filters; the effective widths are about one third of the indicated widths, because the frequencies of the speeded-up reproduced signal are spread apart by a factor equal to the speed-up ratio, namely about 3:1. As pointed out previously, this does not alter the wave shape of the signal but spreads out frequencies and reduces time, with a net effect of speeding up the analysis by a factor of three.

W. Koenig, H. K. Dunn and L. Y. Lacy 87

The output of the analysing filter is impressed directly on a two-stage amplifier which has enough gain to raise the rather low voltage to a value sufficiently high to mark the facsimile paper. The output of the amplifier is not rectified, but is connected to the stylus through a step-up transformer having a turns ratio of about 1:2. Under some conditions a very high signal may reach the grid of the final marking amplifier stage. If the stylus is not lowered to load the amplifier, very high positive peak voltages tend to appear across the output transformer secondary. The biased diode (V6) is shunted across a portion of the high winding to limit the peak voltage to a value which will not damage the transformer insulation. When the stylus is on the paper, the normal range of marking voltages does not exceed the bias voltage and the diode has no effect. A rather small transformer with ordinary insulation will safely withstand the voltages with the diode protection.

In this connection it may be noted that the process of recording on the paper generates a considerable amount of smoke. A blower is therefore incorporated in the recorder unit to draw the smoke through a charcoal filter. The hinged plastic shield which may be seen in Plate 5 directs the smoke into a slot in the top of the recorder box.

The marking range of the paper is limited to about 21 dB. A 70 V signal on the stylus will make a barely visible mark and about 300 V will mark the paper full black at the linear paper speed of approximately 16 inches per second. Since for some applications it is desirable to show components of speech which cover a range of 30 to 40 dB, it is necessary to apply a compressing action to the marking amplifier to reduce the signal range to the limited range of the facsimile paper. One kind of compressing action is secured by shunting across a high impedance point a non-linear compressing resistor (thyrite) whose voltage varies as the 3rd or 4th root of the current through it. This form of compression operates directly on the wave shape, and there is no time constant involved. It produces a rather uniform gradation of blackness on the recording paper over a 35 or 40 dB range of signal intensity and brings out low level detail in the signal being analysed. However, the compressing action when secured in this manner tends to degrade the frequency resolution of the filter. Better definition has been secured by the use of control circuits which accomplish compression in a different manner.

Two control circuits are provided as shown in Figure 6. The narrow band control circuit is used with the narrow (45 Hz) analysing filter and the full band control circuit is used ordinarily with the wide (300 Hz) filter. The narrow band control circuit is a series arrangement which may be switched in ahead of the 45 Hz analysing filter. It includes a control filter whose characteristic is shown in Figure 7. Its pass-band is about 180 Hz (effective) surrounding the pass-band of the narrow analysing filter. A compressor having the same characteristics as the one described above is inserted in the control circuit amplifier. Since the compressing action takes place ahead of the analysing filter, the frequency resolution of the analysing filter is not impaired as it is when the compressing action is placed after it. Compression at this point is permissible because the control filter passes such a narrow band that no important modulation products generated by the compressor fall in the pass-band of the analysing filter. Various degrees of control can be obtained by changing the working level of the compressor by means of the gain controls provided.

The full band control circuit, ordinarily but not necessarily used with the 300 Hz analysing filter, is a shunt arrangement. The low pass filter passes the entire frequency spectrum of the signal which is then amplified and rectified with a time constant of 2 ms. The filtered or smoothed d.c. output of the rectifier is applied as a bias to the marking amplifier grid thereby controlling its gain. This arrangement serves to control the gain after the analysing filter by the spectrum ahead of the filter. The direction of control is to reduce gain for higher spectrum energy.

The effect of these control circuits on the spectrograms will be illustrated in the next section.

Returning to the photograph, Plate 5, the location of the various items mentioned above is as follows. The panel attached above the amplifier-analyser unit houses the control circuits, which were added relatively recently. The two left-hand dials regulate the degree of narrow band control and the right-hand dial the degree of full band control. The switch on this panel selects the type of control – 'full band', 'narrow band', 'compressor (in the marking amplifier) in' and 'compressor out'.

The main panel has two attenuators at the upper left, one for controlling the recording level, the other for the reproducing level, both levels being read on the VU meter in the center. The next knob is the recording-reproducing switch, and the next the filter selecting switch. To the left of the VU meter is the predistortion selector, and to the right is the dial for resetting the carrier oscillator at the beginning of each pattern. This dial returns the rotating condenser plates to their starting position; a small motor inside the panel then drives them slowly back through a friction clutch.

Just below the VU meter is a gear shift lever by means of which the rate of frequency sweep can be changed so as to make the patterns 4 inches high instead of 2 inches. The two buttons at the bottom permit reading the carrier and marking voltages, respectively, on the meter.

The power supply unit provides filament and plate voltages to the rest of the equipment. It is highly regulated and operates at 280 V from 110 V a.c. power.

Spectrograms of speech

Plate 7A shows one kind of spectrogram produced by the later models of the sound spectrograph. The well-known sentence which appears in this spectrogram has been used for testing and illustrative purposes because it contains monosyllabic words with a variety of resonance patterns. The frequency scale of the spectrogram is linear and covers 3500 Hz as shown by the scale at the left. The time scale is also linear and covers 2·4 s (in the illustrations the spectrograms have been trimmed at the ends). They have also been photographically reduced; in the originals the vertical height is 2 inches and the length is 12·5 inches, making the time scale slightly over 5 inches per second.

This spectrogram shows a great deal more detail than the ones in Plate 8; it was made with a much narrower analysing filter – about 45 Hz wide at the 3 dB points. With this filter the individual harmonics of the voiced sounds can be clearly distinguished. The traces curve up and down as the pitch of the voice is varied in normal speech. The wider the spacing between harmonics, the higher the pitch at any particular instant. In the word 'shall' for instance, the pitch first rose and then fell. If the words are spoken in a monotone, the harmonic traces remain level and equidistant as shown in Plate 7B. If the words are spoken in a whisper, the spectrogram appears as in 7C. It will be noted that the distribution of dark and light areas is closely similar in all three spectrograms. These dark areas indicate the regions of maximum energy – in other words the vocal resonances. In the whispered words the vowels and consonants all have the same fuzzy texture with no harmonics present. The same texture appears in normal speech in unvoiced sounds such as the 'sh' sounds in 7A.

These spectrograms were made with the compressor in the marking amplifier. The gradations of black produced by various signal intensities are shown in the upper right-hand corner. Since the last two steps are nearly alike in blackness, the range is somewhere between 35 and 40 dB.

The effect of widening the analysing filter can be seen in Plate 8. These are spectrograms of a rather high pitched female voice. The filter used in Plate 8A was twice as wide as that in the previous illustration, that is, 90 Hz. In 8B the filter width was 180 Hz, and the harmonics of this high pitched voice are still clearly resolved. In 8C and 8D the filter widths were 300 and 475 Hz, respectively; the words are 'you will make that line send'. With these wide filters the individual harmonics tend to merge and only the resonant areas can be clearly resolved. The first word in these illustrations shows clearly that the trend of the resonant areas may be opposite from that of the voice pitch. It is evident that the pitch is rising in this first word but the frequency of resonance is rapidly falling so that each harmonic in turn is reinforced momentarily, producing a step effect which is somewhat undesirable for visible speech purposes. With a lower pitched voice such as is illustrated in Plate 9, the resonance areas tend to form smooth dark bands as soon as the filter becomes wide enough so as not to resolve the individual harmonics. The filter widths in this figure are the same as in Plate 8. With most male voices a filter about 200 Hz wide would be adequate to smooth the resonance bands. A 300 Hz width has been adopted as a compromise, and is adequate for most voices.

In Plate 9 it will be noted that there is a distinct pattern of vertical striations in the voiced sounds. This pattern is caused by the fact that more than one harmonic is passed by the analysing filter. It is well known that two or more frequencies separated by equal intervals will produce beats at the interval frequency. In the case of speech, this frequency of course is the voice pitch. Each vertical striation represents the crest of a beat, and the separation between crests can be seen to vary as the pitch changes. In Plate 8, where the pitch is very high, the vertical striations are so close together as to be barely distinguishable. Incidentally these vertical striations sometimes persist unbroken across the whole frequency range, which is probably due to the particular kind of phase relations resulting from the mechanism of phonation. Sometimes there are phase reversals in the striations, however; this subject would make an interesting study in itself and probably throw light on the voicing mechanism.

References

DUDLEY, H. (1959), 'Remaking speech', *J. acoust. Soc. Amer.*, vol. 11, pp. 169–77.
POTTER, R. K. (1930), 'Transmission characteristics of a short-wave telephone circuit', *Proc. I.R.E.*, vol. 18, pp. 581–648.
SCHUCK, O. H., and YOUNG, R. W. (1943), 'Observations on the vibrations of piano strings', *J. acoust. Soc. Amer.*, vol. 15, pp. 1–11.
STEINBERG, J. C. (1934), 'Application of sound measuring instruments to the study of phonetic problems', *J. acoust. Soc. Amer.*, vol. 6, pp. 16–24.

Analysis of Vowel Sounds

The two following papers on the analysis of vowel sounds give a good deal of information about the vowels of British and American English and, what is more important, illustrate a number of points of principle. Between the dates of their publication there is a period of thirty years, the methods described in them are different in almost every respect and yet there is no serious disagreement between the results they report, given the real difference in the material studied.

One of the threads running through the papers collected in this book is the fundamental fact that the acoustics of speech sounds is of interest only for the light that it can throw on the working of language systems. In this context the acoustic analyser which really concerns us is the ear and it has already been pointed out that the design of the sound spectrograph owes a good deal to what we know about the functioning of the ear. Paget's paper (Reading 5) reports the frequencies of Formant 1 and Formant 2 for his own set of British English vowel sounds, arrived at through his analysis of them by ear alone.

The ability to discriminate among vowel sounds is shared by all language users and we can be certain that this ability rests in part on the effects of formant frequencies (see for example pp. 238–257). To establish and to label formant frequency ranges, however, is possible only for someone with a considerable degree of aptitude and with musical training. The circumstances in which Paget carried out the task may be of more than anecdotal interest. He was obliged to remain in bed for some time during convalescence from an illness and it occurred to him to occupy himself in this way. As he did not possess absolute pitch, he needed some reference pitch and he adopted for the purpose the pitch of the sound given out when he tapped his forehead with his finger. Having established this pitch by reference to a musical instrument, he was able thereafter to note the pitch of the formants of the various vowels by exercising his very acute sense of relative pitch and to calculate their frequency ranges. Among the important facts which he recorded, in addition to the formant frequencies themselves, were the relations between tongue configuration and formant frequency, the influence of fundamental frequency on formant ranges, the differences between spoken and sung vowels and the fact that the recognition of vowel sounds probably depended on relative formant pitch rather than absolute. While he did categorically assign Formant 1 to the back resonator and Formant 2 to the front resonator and even spoke of them as being independent (a formulation contrary to present acoustical theory, which states that formant frequencies are a function of the whole vocal tract) he did, on the other hand, say that any conformation of the throat and mouth cavities which gave the same formants would give the same vowel sound and he demonstrated the effect upon vowel sounds of artificially extending the length of the vocal tract.

The paper by Peterson and Barney (Reading 6) gives an account of the use of the sound spectrograph in a survey of American English vowel sounds. The samples were obtained from a total of seventy-six speakers, including men, women and children, and the recognition of the vowels was checked by reference to a group of seventy adult listeners. The data published in the paper include the mean fundamental frequency, the mean frequencies and intensity levels for the first three formants for men, for women and for children.

Both the source of the data and the collecting of them are so different in the Paget and the Peterson and Barney work that it would have been no surprise if the results had been substantially different. One set refers to the speech of a single speaker of British English, recorded in the early

Table 1

	Formant 1 (Hz)			Formant 2 (Hz)		
	Paget	*Wells*	*Peterson and Barney*	*Paget*	*Wells*	*Peterson and Barney*
iː	340	300	270	2400	2300	2290
i	360	360	390	2300	2100	1990
e	540	570	530	1930	1970	1840
a	720	750	660	1820	1750	1720
aː	790	680	730	1250	1100	1090
o	720	600		1150	900	
oː	550	450	570	910	740	840
u	360	380	440	960	950	1020
uː	380	300	300	720	940	870
ʌ	760	720	640	1450	1240	1190
əː	480	580	490	1530	1380	1350

1920s, the other set is for a large group of speakers of American English in the 1950s and yet the values for Formants 1 and 2 for the vowels which correspond in the two systems are remarkably close. More recent data for a group of thirty-two British English speakers has been collected by Wells (1962) and in Table 1 the mean frequencies of Formants 1 and 2 from all three sources are set out for comparison. In the case of the Paget data, the values given are the mid-points of his ranges and for Peterson and Barney, the means for male speakers.

References

WELLS, J. C. (1962), *A Study of the Formants of the Pure Vowels of British English*, MA thesis, University of London, unpublished.

5 R. S. Paget

Vowel Resonances

R. S. Paget, *Vowel resonances*, International Phonetic Association, 1922

When the various vowel sounds are breathed – either in or out – *without* sounding the vocal chords, each one appears, when analysed by ear, to consist almost entirely of a characteristic combination of two component sounds. The two components are each more or less constant for each breathed vowel sound. They consist of an upper series of notes, ranging – in the case of the writer's own voice (bass) – from about ♯ d″ (608 ∿)[1] to e‴ (2579 ∿), and a lower series ranging from ♯ d′ (304 ∿) to ♯ a″ (912 ∿).

The upper series of notes, which are much more clearly audible than the lower series when the vowel sound is breathed, are similar to notes made when the mouth is, as it were, prepared for whistling, and the breath is drawn in or out without allowing the whistle actually to 'speak'. The upper series of notes may conveniently be referred to as *front resonances*.

Any given note of the whistle or front series can readily be produced with wide variations in the degree of opening of the mouth, and the pitch of the notes (except the lower notes of the series) appears to depend primarily on the extent to which the tongue is raised or lowered to or from the palate and moved forward or back immediately behind the lower teeth, i.e. on the capacity of the front cavity, the pitch being raised as the tongue itself is raised and moved forward and vice versa. In the lower notes – below ♯ g (812 ∿) – the control is presumably due in part to the movement of the back of the tongue.

The methods found most effective for sounding this series are as follows:

From about a′ (430 ∿) to a‴ (1722 ∿) – by tapping the front of the front upper teeth with the butt end of a pencil.

Above 1722 ∿ – by drawing the breath rapidly in and out.

The lower series, on the other hand, appear to be more directly controlled by the degree of constriction of the front opening of the lower or back cavity (either by the tongue or lips), and to depend – at all events in many cases – on the area and length of this opening, like the note of a Helmholz resonator of fixed volume, i.e. the note becomes lower as the opening becomes smaller and longer and vice versa.

1. That is, 608 complete vibrations per second.

The lower series will for convenience, be referred to as *back resonances*.

Dealing first with the front resonances, if the attempt is made to breathe a scale of these notes both up and down *with the mouth wide open*, i.e. *not* in a whistling posture, it is found (in the writer's own case) that the series can be continued down to ♯ g″ (812 ∽) – corresponding to the vowel ɑ in its cardinal form – without reducing the mouth opening, but that below this frequency it is difficult to form the note without shaping the *lips* as for whistling. In other words the front part of the tongue having been lowered to its limit, further lowering of the upper resonance note requires the cooperation of the back of the tongue *and* a protrusion of the lips.

Similarly, if the scale be taken to its upper limit, it is found that above e‴″ (2579 ∽) it is difficult to produce a breathed front resonance note with the lips and tongue in a vowel posture. (It is, however, possible, by rounding the lips and bringing the tongue forward into a consonant position, to produce still higher resonance notes.)

It will be seen later that the whole series of observed front resonances (except those of the o² and u sounds) actually lie within the limits within which a complete range of front resonance notes may be produced apparently *independently of* the area for the opening of the jaw and lips.

It is not suggested that in this series the area of the mouth opening has *no* effect on the pitch, but rather that within the range mentioned, any effect due to variation in the opening of the jaw and lips is automatically compensated for by a slight adjustment of the tongue. Thus, if while breathing a complete scale of front resonance notes with the mouth open, the opening is intermittently closed by a stopper with a fixed orifice, such as to reduce the lower resonator note by eight to ten semi-tones, the note is only lowered by from one to five semi-tones, the lowering being least for the upper notes, and increasing towards the lower notes of the scale.

In the accompanying chart,[3] the various vowel sounds, which are represented by the letters of the International Phonetic Association, are plotted so as to show the characteristic ranges of front and back resonator notes observed in the case of the writer's own voice, when the various vowels are breathed. The range of the front and back resonator notes shown in each case represent the range over which the writer's own vowel sounds were found to vary – at different trials, and in different positions in connected speech – without producing any appreciable difference in the vowel sound.

2. First part of the English diphthong.
3. The broken vertical line at 645/683 for ei (hay) represents a faint additional component.

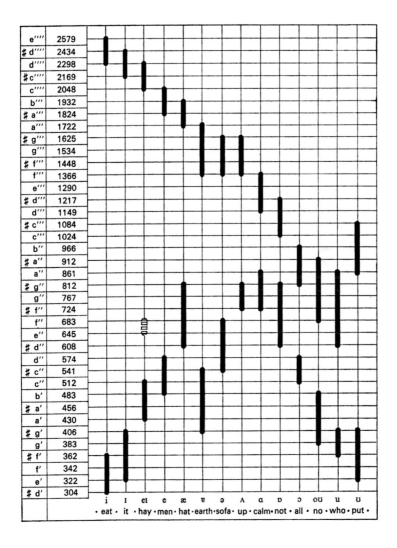

The vowels are arranged in such order as to form as nearly as possible a descending series of front notes and a continuous (rising and falling) progression of back resonator notes. In oʊ, ɪ and eɪ the first part of these diphthong sounds is referred to in each case.

In the case of the back resonator notes, the area of the opening made by the tongue or lips *appears* to be the principal factor, and the compensation, if any (which may be supposed to be due to adjustment of the soft parts of the back of the mouth cavity and pharynx), must operate similarly to preserve the correct relation between the capacity of the mouth cavity (considered as a Helmholz resonator) and the area and length of the mouth opening (whether produced by the lips or tongue) to give the desired back resonator note.

The back resonator notes (as for example ♯ d″ (301 ∿) which characterizes the vowel i as in *eat*) are most easily identified by tapping with a pencil the skin of the throat, on a line between the ear and the larynx. They can also be recognized by using the glottal stop, i.e. by making a tapping sound by the sudden release of breath by the glottis – but this method equally emphasises the front resonance.

Another method by which one or other, or in some cases both, of the front and back resonator components can be made clearly audible is by clapping the hands in front of the mouth, so as to drive a sudden jet of air into the mouth and produce resonance. The best method of doing this is to hold say, the left hand with thumb and first finger widely extended and palm up, immediately against the chin, so that the palm is on a level with the under lip. By clapping gently with the right hand (with the fingers held close together and in line with the fingers of the left hand) on the palm of the left hand, a jet of air is driven sharply into the mouth with but little spurious noise, and a relatively pure resonance effect is produced in the mouth cavity.

This method is not feasible for detecting high notes, say of frequency 1400 and upwards – i.e. for the front vowels – as the clapping is liable to give faint characteristic notes of these frequencies, which may be mistaken for the resonance of upper notes in the mouth cavity. (In its more developed form this clapping device has been heard as a solo instrument on the music-hall stage.)

From the series of front and back resonator notes observed, it appears possible to make an exclusively acoustic classification of the vowel sounds, since, though different vowel sounds may have similar or overlapping ranges of either front resonance notes or of back resonance notes, they appear always to differ as to the other component in each case.

Thus ɐ (*earth*), ə (*sofa*) and ʌ (*up*), may all have the same front note (at about 1534), but their back resonator notes are at about 456, 574, and 812 respectively. Again, ə (*sofa*) and ɑ (*calm*), can both be produced with front resonances at about 1366, but their back resonator notes are at about 574 and 812 respectively.

Similarly, ʊ (*put*), oʊ (*no*), and ɔ (*all*) may be produced with identical front resonances at 912, but their back resonator notes form an ascending series.

Turning to the back resonator notes, we find that i (*eat*), ɪ (*it*), and ʊ (*put*) may each be produced with the same back resonator note at about 322; and oʊ (*no*), eɪ (*hay*), ɐ (*earth*), and e (*men*) with a common back resonator note at 483, but in each case the front notes are different. In point of fact, when any of these series of vowels are breathed *in succession*, both series of notes appear to be changed.

It is possible, though not easy, by adjusting the front note (by the elevation or depression of the tongue) and the back note (by the mouth opening) to bring the two series together into unison. The meeting point (in the writer's own voice) is at about 724, and the vowel sound resulting turns out to be a hollow and unpleasant variety of ɔ (*awe*) – the lack of character of the sound being presumably due to lack of harmonics. It may be noted that the meeting point found lies about midway between the two components of the true ɔ of the breathed series.

Vowel sounds spoken and sung

When a larynx tone is superadded to the breathed vowel, the effects become more complex and more difficult to analyse by ear.

If a chromatic scale be sung to the vowel sound of the French y (as in *tu*) the front note 2048 can be clearly heard as a constant component of each sound in the scale. The same constancy of the front resonance and *also* of the back resonator note was found in the case of a deep-toned ɐ (*earth*) whose front note 1534 and back resonator note 406 remained unchanged through the chromatic scale; in this case the back resonator note was observed by flicking the throat between the ear and larynx while singing the chromatic scale. In the case of the high front resonance notes, therefore, it appears that these are unaffected by the pitch of the larynx note to which they are spoken or sung.

A different result is found, however, in the case of the vowels with lower front resonances. Thus, if a chromatic scale be sung to the vowel sound ɑ (*calm*), beginning, say at ♯ G 102 – with a front resonance note at d‴ 1149, this note is found to fluctuate as the larynx note is varied, thus:

Larynx note	Front resonance note
♯ G 102	d‴ 1149
A 108	♯ d‴ 1217
♯ A 114	d‴ 1149
B 121	♯ d‴ 1217
c 128	d‴ 1149
♯ c 135	♯ d‴ 1217
d 144	d‴ 1149

though the back resonator note, at about 724, appeared to remain constant.

R. S. Paget 99

In the same way, taking the vowel sound oʊ (*no*) (first part), a chromatic scale gave the following front resonance notes:

Larynx note	Front resonance note
♯ G 102	♯ f″ 724
A 108	g″ 767
♯ A 114	♯ g″ 812
B 121	♯ f″ 724 + ♯ a″ 912
c 128	g″ 767
♯ c 135	f″ 683 or a″ 861
d 144	♯ f″ 724
♯ d 152	♯ g″ 812
e 161	a″ 861
f 171	f″ 683
♯ f 181	♯ f″ 724
g 192	g″ 767

the back resonator note remaining constant at 406.

It will be seen, therefore, that in the case of this vowel sound the front resonance note varied from f″ 683 to ♯ a″ 912, i.e. over the whole range found for this vowel in the breathed series, when the fundamental larynx note was varied by semi-tones from ♯ G 102 to g 192.

With a vowel sound of 1366 front resonance note and 406 back resonator note – forming a slightly advanced u – it was found that, on singing a chromatic scale from ♯ C 68 to ♯ c′ 271, the front resonance remained constant at 1366, but that, as the larynx note was further raised, the front resonance note became affected thus:

Larynx note	Front resonance note
♯ c′ 271	f‴ 1366
d′ 287	♯ f‴ 1448
♯ d′ 304	g‴ 1534

Similarly, in the case of a vowel sound of front resonance 1024 and back resonance 304,[4] when a chromatic scale was sung from ♯ G 51, the front resonance note was constant up to a larynx note of ♯ G 102, after which the following front resonance notes were observed:

4. That is, a very forward variety of u.

Larynx note	Front resonance note
♯G 102	c″ 1024
A 108	♯c″ 1084
♯A 114	c″ 1024
B 121	♯c″ 1084
c 128	c″ 1024
♯c 135	♯c″ 1084
d 144	c″ 1024
♯d 152	♯c″ 1084
e 161	d″ 1149

It thus appears that, when the larynx note and front resonance note are widely separated, the front resonance is constant – possibly because it can then always approximate to some higher harmonic of the larynx note – but that as they approach one another, within two or three octaves, the front resonance becomes variable and adjusts itself to the nearest harmonic of the larynx note.

That a front resonance note does naturally tend to be affected by a note produced by the larynx, is easily shown by whistling and singing together. The two operations are mechanically quite distinct, so that, for example, an ascending scale may be sung, and a descending scale whistled simultaneously, but the natural effect is for the larynx note to dominate the front resonance note, and for the latter to rise and fall proportionately to the former.

On the other hand, the front and back resonance notes appear to be independent of one another. This can be illustrated by the clapping method, namely, by placing the mouth in the position for sounding the vowel u (*who*), for example, and then gradually increasing the mouth opening and lowering the tongue so as to produce two scales in contrary motion. The characteristic ranges and actual notes observed all refer to one voice (the writer's), and indicate the extremely unstable character of the vowel sounds, even in a single voice.

It is probable that much greater ranges would be found if additional voices were examined in the same way, and that, in recognizing vowel sounds, the ear is guided more by the relative pitch of the different characteristics than by their absolute pitch. Since it appears that the vowel quality is dependent on the natural resonance frequencies of the front and back resonator note series respectively, it should follow that *any* conformation of the mouth and throat cavities which gives the same pair of front and back resonator notes respectively, should give the same vowel sound – and this actually appears to be the case so far as present observations have gone.

It is also possible to convert vowels formed normally by the mouth and throat into other identifiable vowels by *adding* artificially to the front resonance cavity. Thus a plasticine resonator was made about 70 mm long with a wide mouthpiece about 27 mm diameter – to fix against the open mouth of the operator – and with a lateral orifice of about 7 mm diameter, and of such interior capacity as to give a natural resonance of 1024 with both orifices open. When the extra resonator was applied during the breathing or voicing of various vowels, the following effects were observed:

ɑ (*calm*) became rather like ɔ (*awe*)
æ (*hat*) became rather like ɑ (*calm*)
ʌ (*up*) became a sound between ɐ and o
ɒ (*not*) became ɔ (*awe*)
oʊ (*no*) became u (*who*)
i (*he*) became rather like French y (*tu*)
eɪ (*hay*) became rather like French ø (*peu*)
ɐ (*earth*) became u (*who*)

In summary, it would appear that all the writer's English vowel sounds, when breathed, are mainly characterized by two components, a front (whistle-like) note and a back resonator note, each of which may, in most cases at all events, vary over from two to five semi-tones, without producing very material difference in the vowel effect.

The pitch of the front notes – except the notes below ♯g″ 812 – is primarily controlled, for any one lip position, by the position of the tongue, being higher as the tongue is raised and pushed forward towards the teeth; while the pitch of the back resonance notes is primarily controlled by the degree of opening of the orifice formed by the lips or by the tongue against the palate – being lower as the orifice is reduced and vice versa. The front resonance notes below 812 require the cooperation of the lips.

It follows that vowels of low back resonance, such as u, i, ɪ, cannot be produced with an open orifice of lips or tongue against palate, since an open orifice raises the back resonator note. Nor can vowels with high back resonance, such as ʌ, ɒ, ɑ, be produced with a small orifice, since this lowers the back resonator note.

The two series are quite independent, and are due to the *resonance frequencies* of the mouth and throat cavities rather than to the shape of the cavities.

Certain vowels sounds have front and back components whose ranges overlap; when these vowels are sounded in succession, their components are different, but when the attempt is made to produce the different vowels with the *same* components, they are distinguished in practice by differences of emphasis and of the duration of the vowel sound.

In the case of sung or spoken vowels, it appears that when the larynx note and the characteristic range of the front resonances are widely separated, the front resonance remains constant in spite of changes of pitch of the larynx note, but that as these approach within two or three octaves of one another, the front resonance tends to be dominated by the larynx note, and to adjust itself or 'draw' towards the nearest harmonic of the larynx note that falls within its range. This 'drawing' appears to be a mechanical effect operating on the highly mobile resonating cavity, since the clapping method also gives a harmonic of the larynx note.

The back resonator notes – so far as has been observed – do *not* vary with the larynx note, though they (like the front resonance notes) may also vary over a range of as much as three to five semi-tones (in certain cases) without substantially changing the character of the resultant vowel sound. The back resonator notes cannot in general be heard *as such* when a larynx note is sounded, (though they can be made audible by tapping or clapping during the sounding of a larynx note); but the larynx note is 'coloured' by its passage through the cavities which give rise to the back resonator note.

Every series of sung or spoken vowels is in fact a trio performed by three instruments, a reed and two resonators – soprano and alto – of which the soprano resonator is in close harmonic relation with the reed.

6 Gordon E. Peterson and Harold L. Barney

Control Methods Used in a Study of the Vowels

Gordon E. Peterson and Harold L. Barney, 'Control methods used in a study of the vowels', *Journal of the Acoustical Society of America*, vol. 24 (1952), pp. 175–84.

Introduction

Considerable variation is to be found in the processes of speech production because of their complexity and because they depend upon the past experience of the individual. As in much of human behavior there is a self-correcting, or servomechanism type of feedback involved as the speaker hears his own voice and adjusts his articulatory mechanisms (Lee, 1950).

In the elementary case of a word containing a consonant-vowel-consonant phoneme structure (Bloch, 1948; 1950), a speaker's pronunciation of the vowel within the word will be influenced by his particular dialectal background and his pronunciation of the vowel may differ both in phonetic quality and in measurable characteristics from that produced in the word by speakers with other backgrounds. A listener, likewise, is influenced in his identification of a sound by his past experience.

Variations are observed when a given individual makes repeated utterances of the same phoneme. A very significant property of these variations is that they are not random in a statistical sense, but show trends and sudden breaks or shifts in level, and other types of nonrandom fluctuations (Potter and Steinberg, 1950). Variations likewise appear in the successive identifications by a listener of the same utterance. It is probable that the identification of repeated sounds is also nonrandom but there is little direct evidence in this work to support such a conclusion.

A study of sustained vowels was undertaken to investigate in a general way the relation between the vowel phoneme intended by a speaker and that identified by a listener, and to relate these in turn to acoustical measurements of the formant or energy concentration positions in the speech waves. In the plan of the study certain methods and techniques were employed which aided greatly in the collection of significant data. These methods included randomization of test material and repetitions to obtain sequences of observations for the purpose of checking the measurement procedures and the speaker and listener consistency. The acoustic measurements were made with the sound spectrograph. To minimize measurement errors, a method was used for rapid calibration of the recording and analysing apparatus by means of a complex test tone. Statistical techniques were applied to the results of measurements both of the calibrating signals and of the vowel sounds.

These methods of measurement and analysis have been found to be precise enough to resolve the effects of different dialectal backgrounds and of the nonrandom trends in speakers' utterances. Some aspects of the vowel study will be presented in the following paragraphs to illustrate the usefulness of the methods employed.

Experimental procedures

The plan of the study is illustrated in Figure 1. A list of words (list 1) was presented to the speaker and his utterances of the words were recorded with a magnetic tape recorder. The list contained ten monosyllabic words each beginning with [h] and ending with [d] and differing only in the vowel.

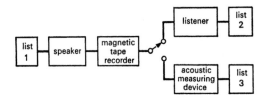

Figure 1 Recording and measuring arrangements for vowel study

The words used were *heed, hid, head, had, hod, hawed, hood, who'd, hud* and *heard*. The order of the words was randomized in each list, and each speaker was asked to pronounce two different lists. The purpose of randomizing the words in the list was to avoid practice effects which would be associated with an unvarying order.

If a given list 1, recorded by a speaker, was played back to a listener and the listener was asked to write down what he heard on a second list (list 2), a comparison of list 1 and list 2 would reveal occasional differences, or disagreements, between speaker and listener. Instead of being played back to a listener, list 1 might be played into an acoustic measuring device and the outputs classified according to the measured properties of the sounds into a list 3. The three lists will differ in some words depending upon the characteristics of the speaker, the listener and the measuring device.

A total of 76 speakers, including 33 men, 28 women and 15 children, each recorded two lists of 10 words, making a total of 1520 recorded words. Two of the speakers were born outside the United States and a few others spoke a foreign language before learning English. Most of the women and children grew up in the Middle Atlantic speech area (Thomas, 1947). The male speakers represented a much broader regional sampling of the United States; the majority of them spoke General American.

The words were randomized and were presented to a group of 70 listeners in a series of 8 sessions. The listening group contained only men and women, and represented much the same dialectal distribution as did the group of speakers, with the exception that a few observers were included who had spoken a foreign language throughout their youth. Thirty-two of the 76 speakers were also among the 70 observers. The 1520 words were also analysed by means of the sound spectrograph (Koenig, Dunn and Lacy, 1946; Kersta, 1948).

Representative spectrograms and sections of these words by a male speaker are shown in Figure 2 of the paper by Potter and Steinberg (1950); a similar list by a female speaker is shown here as Plate 10.[1] In the spectrograms, we see the initial [h] followed by the vowel, and then by the final [d]. There is generally a part of the vowel following the influence of the [h] and preceding the influence of the [d] during which a practically steady state is reached. In this interval, a section is made, as shown to the right of the spectrograms. The sections, portraying frequency on a horizontal scale and amplitude of the voiced harmonics on the vertical side, have been measured with calibrated Plexiglass templates to provide data about the fundamental and formant frequencies and relative formant amplitudes of each of the 1520 recorded sounds.

Listening tests

The 1520 recorded words were presented to the group of 70 adult observers over a high quality loud speaker system in Arnold Auditorium at the Murray Hill Laboratories. The general purpose of these tests was to obtain an aural classification of each vowel to supplement the speaker's classification. In presenting the words to the observers, the procedure was to reproduce at each of 7 sessions, 200 words recorded by 10 speakers. At the eighth session, there remained 5 men's and 1 child's recordings to be presented; to these were added 3 women's and 1 child's recordings which had been given in previous sessions, making again a total of 200 words. The sound level at the observers' positions was approximately 70 dB re 0·0002 dyne/cm^2, and varied over a range of about 3 dB at the different positions.

In selecting the speakers for each of the first 7 sessions, 4 men, 4 women, and 2 children were chosen at random from the respective groups of 33, 28,

1. Key words for the vowel symbols are as follows: [i] heed, [ɪ] hid, [ɛ] head, [æ] had, [ɑ] father, [ɔ] ball, [ʊ] hood, [u] who'd, [ʌ] hud, [ɝ] heard.

and 15. The order of occurrence of the 200 words spoken by the 10 speakers for each session was randomized for presentation to the observers.

Each observer was given a pad containing 200 lines having the 10 words on each line. He was asked to draw a line through the one word in each line that he heard. The observers' seating positions in the auditorium were chosen by a randomizing procedure, and each observer took the same position for each of the 8 sessions, which were given on 8 different days.

The randomizing of the speakers in the listening sessions was designed to facilitate checks of learning effects from one session to another. The randomizing of words in each group of 200 was designed to minimize successful guessing and the learning of a particular speaker's dialect. The seating positions of the listeners were randomized so that it would be possible to determine whether position in the auditorium had an effect on the identification of the sounds.

Discussion of listening test results

The total of 1520 sounds heard by the observers consisted of the 10 vowels, each presented 152 times. The ease with which the observers classified the various vowels varied greatly. Of the 152 [i] sounds, for instance, 143 were unanimously classified by all observers as [i]. Of the 152 sounds which the speakers intended for [ɑ], on the other hand, only 9 were unanimously classified as [ɑ] by the whole jury.

These data are summarized in Figure 2. This figure shows the positions

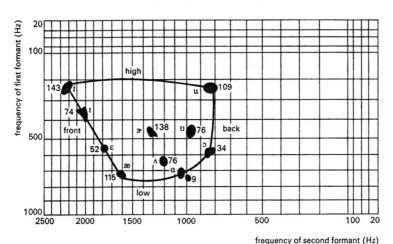

Figure 2 Vowel loop with numbers of sounds unanimously classified by listeners

Gordon E. Peterson and Harold L. Barney 107

of the 10 vowels in a vowel loop in which the frequency of the first formant is plotted against the frequency of the second formant (Potter and Peterson, 1948) on mel scales (Stevens and Volkman, 1940); in this plot the origin is at the upper right. The numbers beside each of the phonetic symbols are the numbers of sounds, out of 152, which were unanimously classified as that particular vowel by the jury. It is of interest in passing that in no case did the jury agree unanimously that a sound was something other than what the speaker intended. Figure 2 shows that [i], [ɝ], [æ], and [u] are generally quite well understood.

To obtain the locations of the small areas shown in Figure 2, the vowels were repeated by a single speaker on twelve different days. A line enclosing all twelve points was drawn for each vowel; the differences in the shapes of these areas probably have little significance.

When the vowels are plotted in the manner shown in Figure 2, they appear in essentially the same positions as those shown in the tongue hump position diagrams which phoneticians have employed for many years (Jones, 1947). The terms *high, front, low, back* refer to the tongue positions in the mouth. The [i], for instance, is made with the tongue hump high and forward, the [u] with the hump high and back, and the [ɑ] and [æ] with the tongue hump low.

It is of interest that when observers disagreed with speakers on the classification of a vowel, the two classifications were nearly always in adjacent positions of the vowel loop of Figure 2. This is illustrated by the data shown in Table 1. This table shows how the observers classified the vowels, as compared with the vowels intended by the speakers. For instance, on all

Table 1 Classifications of vowels by speakers and by listeners.

Vowels intended by speakers	*Vowels as classified by listeners*									
	i	ɪ	ɛ	æ	ɑ	ɔ	ʊ	u	ʌ	ɝ
i	10267	4	6	—	—	3	—	—	—	—
ɪ	6	9549	694	2	1	1	—	—	—	26
ɛ	—	257	9014	949	1	3	—	—	2	51
æ	—	1	300	9919	2	2	—	—	15	39
ɑ	—	1	—	19	8936	1013	69	—	228	7
ɔ	—	—	1	2	590	9534	71	5	62	14
ʊ	—	—	1	1	16	51	9924	96	171	19
u	—	—	1	—	2	—	78	10196	—	2
ʌ	—	1	1	8	540	127	103	—	9476	21
ɝ	—	—	23	6	2	3	—	—	2	10243

the 152 sounds intended as [i] by the speakers, there were 10,267 total votes by all observers that they were [i], 4 votes for [ɪ], 6 votes for [ɛ], and 3 votes for [ɔ]. Of the 152 [ɑ] sounds, there was a large fraction of the sounds on which some of the observers voted for [ɔ]. [ɪ] was taken for [ɛ] a sizable percentage of the time, and [ɝ] was called either [ɪ] or [æ] (adjacent sounds on the vowel loop shown in the preceding Figure 2) quite a large number of times. [ɑ] and [ɔ], and [ʌ] and [ɑ] were also confused to a certain extent. Here again, as in Plate 10, the [i], [ɝ], [æ], and [u] show high intelligibility scores.

It is of considerable interest that the substitutions shown conform to present dialectal trends in American speech rather well (Gray and Wise, 1946), and, in part, to the prevailing vowel shifts observable over long periods of time in most languages (Bloomfield, 1933). The common tendency is continually to shift toward higher vowels in speech, which correspond to smaller mouth openings.

The listener, on the other hand, would tend to make the opposite substitution. This effect is most simply described in terms of the front vowels. If a speaker produces [ɪ] for [ɛ], for example [mɪn] for [mɛn] as currently heard in some American dialects; then such an individual when serving as a listener will be inclined to write *men* when he hears [mɪn]. Thus it is that in the substitutions shown in Table 1, [ɪ] most frequently became [ɛ], and [ɛ] most frequently became [æ]. The explanation of the high intelligibility of [æ] is probably based on this same pattern. It will be noted along the vowel loop that a wide gap appears between [æ] and [ɑ]. The [a] of the Romance languages appears in this region. Since that vowel was present in neither the lists nor the dialects of most of the speakers and observers the [æ] was usually correctly identified.

The [i] and the [u] are the terminal or end positions in the mouth and on the vowel loop toward which the vowels are normally directed in the prevailing process of pronunciation change. In the formation of [i] the tongue is humped higher and farther forward than for any other vowel; in [u] the tongue hump takes the highest posterior position in the mouth and the lips are more rounded than for any other vowel. The vowels [u] and [i] are thus much more difficult to displace, and a greater stability in the organic formation of these sounds would probably be expected, which in turn should mean that these sounds are recognized more consistently by a listener.

The high intelligibility of [ɝ] probably results from the retroflexion which is present to a marked degree only in the formation of this vowel; that is, in addition to the regular humping of the tongue, the edges of the tongue are turned up against the gum ridge or the hard palate. In the acoustical pattern the third formant is markedly lower than for any other vowel.

Thus in both physiological and acoustical phonetics the [ɝ] occupies a singular position among the American vowels.

The very low scores on [ɑ] and [ɔ] in Figure 2 undoubtedly result primarily from the fact that some members of the speaking group and many members of the listening group speak one of the forms of American dialects in which [ɑ] and [ɔ] are not differentiated.

When the individuals' votes on the sounds are analysed, marked differences are seen in the way they classified the sounds. Not only did the total numbers of agreements with the speakers vary, but the proportions of agreements for the various vowels was significantly different. Figure 3 will be used to illustrate this point. If we plot total numbers of disagreements for all tests, rather than agreements, the result is shown by the upper chart. This shows that [ɪ], [ɛ], [ɑ], [ɔ], and [ʌ] had the most disagreements. An 'average' observer would be expected to have a distribution of disagreements similar in proportions to this graph. The middle graph illustrates the distribution of disagreements given by observer number 6. His chief difficulty was in distinguishing between [ɑ] and [ɔ]. This type of distribution is characteristic of several observers. Observer 13, whose distribution of disagreements is plotted on the bottom graph, shows a tendency to confuse [ɪ] and [ɛ] more than the average.

The distributions of disagreements of all 70 observers differ from each other, depending on their language experience, but the differences are generally less extreme than the two examples shown on Figure 3. Thirty-two of the 70 observers were also speakers. In cases where an observer such as 6 was also a speaker, the remainder of the jury generally had more disagreements with his [ɑ] and [ɔ] sounds than with the other sounds he spoke. Thus it appears that if a speaker does not differentiate clearly between a pair of sounds in speaking them, he is unlikely to classify them properly when he hears others speak them. His language experience, as would be expected, influences both his speaking and his hearing of sounds.

Since the listening group was not given a series of training sessions for these tests, learning would be expected in the results of the tests (Fletcher and Galt, 1950). Several pieces of evidence indicate a certain amount of practice effect, but the data are not such as to provide anything more than a very approximate measure of its magnitude.

For one check on practice effect, a ninth test was given the jury, in which all the words having more than 10 disagreements in any of the preceding 8 tests were repeated. There was a total of about 175 such words; to these were added 25 words which had no disagreements, picked at random from the first 8 tests. On the ninth test, 67 words had more disagreements, 109 had less disagreements and 24 had the same number of disagreements as in the preceding tests. The probability of getting this result had there been no

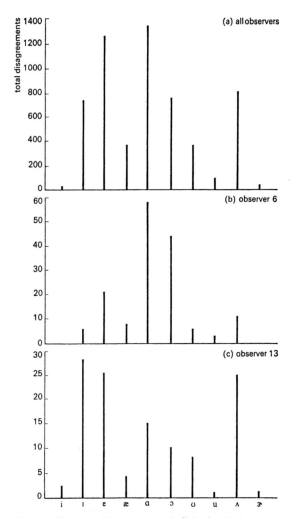

Figure 3 Observer disagreements in listening tests

practice or other effect, but only a random variation of observers' votes, would be about 0·01. When these data are broken down into three groups for the men, women and children speakers, the largest differences in numbers of disagreements for the original and repeated tests was on the childrens' words, indicating a larger practice or learning effect on their sounds. The indicated learning effect on men's and women's speech was nearly the same. When the data are classified according to the vowel sound, the learning effect indicated by the repetitions was least on [i], [ɝ], and [u], and greatest on [ɑ] and [ɔ].

Another indication that there was a practice effect lies in the sequence of total numbers of disagreements by tests. From the second to the seventh test, the total number of disagreements by all observers diminished consistently from test to test, and the first test had considerably more disagreements than the eighth, thus strongly indicating a downward trend. With the speakers randomized in their order of appearance in the eight tests, each test would be expected to have approximately the same number of disagreements. The probability of getting the sequence of numbers of total disagreements which was obtained would be somewhat less than 0·05 if there were no learning trend or other nonrandom effect.

It was also found that the listening position had an effect upon the scores obtained. The observers were arranged in 9 rows in the auditorium, and the listeners in the back 4 rows had a significantly greater number of disagreements with the speakers than did the listeners in the first 5 rows. The effect of a listener's position within an auditorium upon intelligibility has been observed previously and is reported in the literature (Knudsen and Harris, 1950).

Acoustic measurements

Calibrations of equipment

A rapid calibrating technique was developed for checking the overall performance of the recording and analysing systems. This depended on the use of a test tone which had an envelope spectrum that was essentially flat with frequency over the voice band. The circuit used to generate this test tone is shown schematically in Figure 4. It consists essentially of an overloading amplifier and pulse sharpening circuit. The wave shapes which may be observed at several different points in the test tone generator are indicated in Figure 4.

The test tone generator may be driven by an input sine wave signal of any frequency between 50 and 2000 Hz. Figure 5a shows a section of the test tone with a 100 Hz repetition frequency, which had been recorded on magnetic tape in place of the word lists by the speaker, and then played back into the sound spectrograph. The departure from uniform frequency response of the overall systems is indicated by the shape of the envelope enclosing the peaks of the 100 Hz harmonics. With the 100 Hz from the Sound Laboratories' standard frequency oscillator as the drive signal, the frequency calibration of the systems may be checked very readily by comparison of the harmonic spacing on the section with the template scale. The

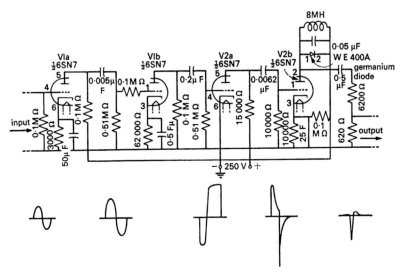

Figure 4 Schematic of calibrating tone generator

amplitude scale in 5a is obtained by inserting a pure tone at the spectrograph in 5 dB increments. The frequency scale for spectrograms may also be calibrated as shown in Figure 5b. The horizontal lines here are representations of the harmonics of the test tone when the test tone generator is driven by a 500 Hz standard frequency. These lines further afford a means of checking the amount of speed irregularity or wow in the overall mechanical system. A calibration of the time scale may be obtained by using the test tone generator with 100 Hz drive and making a broad band spectrogram as shown in Figure 5c. The spacings between vertical striations in this case correspond to one-hundredth of a second intervals.

In the process of recording some of the word lists, it was arranged to substitute the calibrating test tone circuit for the microphone circuit, and record a few seconds of test tone between the lists of words. When the word lists were analysed with the spectrograph, the accompanying test tone sections provided a means of checking the overall frequency response of the recorder and analyser, and the frequency scale of the sectioner.

The effect of speed variations in either the recorder or the sound spectrograph is to change the frequency scale. A series of measurements with the 100 Hz test tone showed that the tape recorder ran approximately one per cent slower when playing back than it did on recording.

The speed variations on the sound spectrograph were measured with the test tone applied directly, and the maximum short time variations were

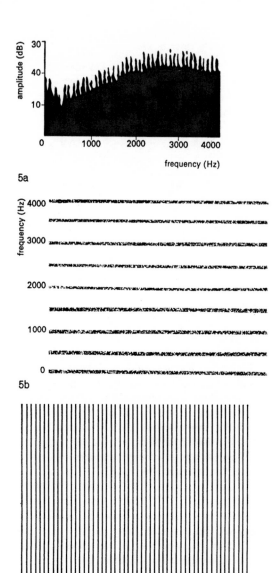

amplitude (dB)

frequency (Hz)

5a

frequency (Hz)

5b

time (s)

5c

Figure 5 Spectrograms and sections of calibrating tone

114 Acoustic Analysis of Speech

found to be ±0·3 per cent. Such direct calibrations of the frequency scale of the spectrograph, during a period of four weeks when most of the spectrographic analysis was done, showed maximum deviations of ±30 Hz at the thirty-first harmonic of the 100 Hz test tone. During that period a control chart[2] of the measurements of the 3100 Hz component of the test tone showed a downward trend of about 10 Hz, which was attributed to changes in the electronic circuit components of the spectrograph. As a result of these calibration tests, it was concluded that the frequency scale of the sound spectrograph could be relied upon as being accurate within ±1 per cent.

Formant measurements

Measurements of both the frequency and the amplitude of the formants were made for the 20 words recorded by each of the 76 speakers. The frequency position of each formant was obtained by estimating a weighted average of the frequencies of the principal components in the formant (see Potter and Steinberg, 1950). When the principal components in the formant were symmetrically distributed about a dominant component, such as the second formant of [ʌ] *hud* in Plate 10, there is little ambiguity in choosing the formant frequency. When the distribution is asymmetrical, however, as in the first formant of [ɜ·] *heard* in Plate 10, the difference between estimated formant frequency and that assigned by the ear may be appreciable.

One of the greatest difficulties in estimating formant frequencies was encountered in those cases where the fundamental frequency was high so that the formant was poorly defined. These factors may account for some, but certainly not all, of the differences discussed later between vowel classification by ear and by measured values of formant frequencies.

Amplitudes were obtained by assigning a value in decibels to the formant peak. In the case of the amplitude measurements it was then necessary to apply a correction for the overall frequency response of the system.

The procedure of making duplicate recordings and analyses of the ten words for each of the speakers provided the basis for essential checks on the reliability of the data.

One method by which the duplicate measured values were used is illustrated by Figure 6. This is a plot of the values for the first formant frequency F_1 of [i] as in *heed*, as spoken by the 28 female subjects. Each point represents, for a single speaker, the value of F_1 measured for the *heed* in the first list, versus the value of F_1 for the *heed* in the second list. If the F_1 for the second list or calling was greater than that for the first calling, the point lies above a 45-degree line; if it is less, the point lies below the 45 degree line.

2. 'ASTM manual on presentation of data', Am. Soc. Testing Materials (Philadelphia, 1945), Appendix B.

The average difference $\bar{R}$ between the paired values of F_1 for the first and second callings, was 17·2 Hz. The estimated standard deviation σ derived from the differences between pairs of F_1 values was 15·3 Hz. The dotted lines in Figure 6 are spaced $\pm 3\,\sigma$ cycles from the 45 degree line through the origin. In case a point falls outside the dotted lines, it is generally because of an erroneous measurement.

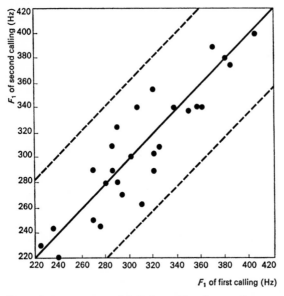

Figure 6 Accuracy-precision chart of first formant frequencies of [i] (heed) as spoken by twenty-eight women

Each of the three formant frequencies for each of the 10 vowels was plotted in this way. There were 760 such points for each formant, or a total of 2280 points plotted on 90 accuracy-precision charts like Figure 6. Of these 2280 points, 118 fell outside the $\pm 3\,\sigma$ limits. On checking back over the measurements, it was found that 88 of the points were incorrect because of gross measurement errors, typographical errors in transcribing the data, or because the section had been made during the influence period of the consonants instead of in the steady state period of the vowel. When corrected, these 88 points were within the $\pm 3\,\sigma$ limits. Of the remaining 30 points which were still outside the limits, 20 were the result of the individuals' having produced pairs of sounds which were unlike phonetically, as shown by the results of the listening tests.

The duplicate measurements may also be used to show that the difference between successive utterances of the same sound by the same individual is much less significant statistically than the difference between utterances of the same sound by different individuals. An analysis of variance of the data in Figure 6 shows that the differences between callings of pairs are not significant. However, the value for the variance ratio when comparing speakers is much larger than that corresponding to a 0·1 per cent probability. In other words, if the measurements shown in Figure 6 for all callings by all speakers were assumed to constitute a body of statistically random data, the probability of having a variance ratio as high as that found when comparing speakers would be less than one in a thousand. Therefore it is assumed that the data are not statistically random, but that there are statistically significant differences between speakers. Since the measurements for pairs of callings were so nearly alike, as contrasted with the measurements on the same sound for different speakers, this indicated that the precision of measurements with the sound spectrograph was sufficient to resolve satisfactorily the differences between the various individuals' pronunciations of the same sounds.

Results of acoustic measurements

In Figure 2, as discussed previously, are plotted areas in the plane of the second formant F_2 versus the first formant F_1. These areas enclose points for several repetitions of the sustained vowels by one of the writers. It is clear that here the vowels may be separated readily, simply by plotting F_2 against F_1; that is, on the F_2–F_1 plane, points for each vowel lie in isolated areas, with no overlapping of adjacent areas, even though there exists the variation of the measured values which we have discussed above.

The variation of the measured data for a group of speakers is much larger than the variation encountered in repetitions with the same speaker, however, as may be shown by the data for F_1 and F_2 for the 76 speakers. In Figure 7 are plotted the points for the second calling by each speaker, with the points identified according to the speaker's word list. The closed loops for each vowel have been drawn arbitrarily to enclose most of the points; the more extreme and isolated points were disregarded so that in general these loops include about 90 per cent of the values. The frequency scales on this and Figure 8 are spaced according to the approximation to an aural scale described by Koenig, which is linear to 1000 Hz and logarithmic above (1949).

Considerable overlapping of areas is indicated, particularly between [ɝ] and [ɛ], [ɝ] and [ʊ], [ʊ] and [u], and [ɑ] and [ɔ]. In the case of the [ɝ] sound it may be easily distinguished from all the others if the third formant frequency is used, as the position of the third formant is very close in frequency to that of the second.

The data of Figure 7 show that the distribution of points in the F_1–F_2 plane is continuous in going from sound to sound; these distributions doubtless represent large differences in the way individuals speak the sounds. The values for F_3 and the relative amplitudes of the formants also

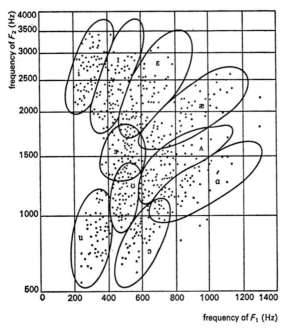

Figure 7 Frequency of second formant v. frequency of first formant for ten vowels by seventy-six speakers

have correspondingly large variations between individuals. Part of the variations are because of the differences between classes of speakers, that is, men, women and children. In general, the children's formants are highest in frequency, the women's intermediate, and the men's formants are lowest in frequency.

These differences may be observed in the averaged formant frequencies given on Table 2. The first formants for the children are seen to be about half an octave higher than those of the men, and the second and third formants are also appreciably higher. The measurements of amplitudes of the formants did not show decided differences between classes of speakers, and so have been averaged all together. The formant amplitudes are all referred to the amplitude of the first formant in [ɔ], when the total phonetic powers

Table 2 Averages of fundamental and formant frequencies and formant amplitudes of vowels by 76 speakers

		i	ɪ	ɛ	æ	ɑ	ɔ	ʊ	u	ʌ	ɝ
fundamental frequencies	M	136	135	130	127	124	129	137	141	130	133
(Hz)	W	235	232	223	210	212	216	232	231	221	218
	Ch	272	269	260	251	256	263	276	274	261	261
formant frequencies (Hz)											
	M	270	390	530	660	730	570	440	300	640	490
F_1	W	310	430	610	860	850	590	470	370	760	500
	Ch	370	530	690	1010	1030	680	560	430	850	560
	M	2290	1990	1840	1720	1090	840	1020	870	1190	1350
F_2	W	2790	2480	2330	2050	1220	920	1160	950	1400	1640
	Ch	3200	2730	2610	2320	1370	1060	1410	1170	1590	1820
	M	3010	2550	2480	2410	2440	2410	2240	2240	2390	1690
F_3	W	3310	3070	2990	2850	2810	2710	2680	2670	2780	1960
	Ch	3730	3600	3570	3320	3170	3180	3310	3260	3360	2160
	L_1	−4	−3	−2	−1	−1	0	−1	−3	−1	−5
formant amplitudes (dB)	L_2	−24	−23	−17	−12	−5	−7	−12	−19	−10	−15
	L_3	−28	−27	−24	−22	−28	−34	−34	−43	−27	−20

of the vowels are corrected so as to be related to each other by the ratios of powers given by Fletcher (1953).

Various methods of correlating the results of the listening tests with the formant measurements have been studied. In terms of the first two formants the nature of the relationship is illustrated in Figure 8. In this figure measurements for all vowels of both callings are plotted in which all members of the listening group agreed with the speaker. Since the values for the men and the children generally lie at the two ends of the distributions for each vowel, the confusion between vowels is well illustrated by their data; thus the measurements for the women speakers have been omitted.

The lines on Figure 8 are the same as the boundaries drawn in Figure 7. As indicated previously, some vowels received 100 per cent agreement much more frequently than others.

The [ɝ] produces extensive overlap in the [ʊ] region in a graph involving only the first two formants. As explained previously, however, the [ɝ] may be isolated from the other vowels readily by means of the third formant.

When only vowels which received 100 per cent recognition are plotted, the scatter and overlap are somewhat reduced over that for all callings. The scatter is greater, however, than might be expected.

If the first and second formant parameters measured from these words well defined their phonetic values; and if the listening tests were an exact means of classifying the words, then the points for each vowel of Figure 8

Gordon E. Peterson and Harold L. Barney 119

should be well separated. Words judged intermediate in phonetic position should fall at intermediate positions in such a plot. In other words, the distributions of measured formant values in these plots do not correspond closely to the distributions of phonetic values.

It is the present belief that the complex acoustical patterns represented by the words are not adequately represented by a single section, but require a more complex portrayal. The initial and final influences often shown in

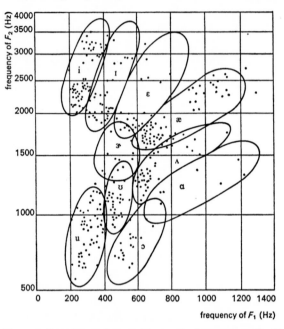

Figure 8 Frequency of second formant *v*. frequency of first formant for vowels spoken by men and children, which were classified unanimously by all listeners

the bar movements of the spectrograms are of importance here (Potter, Kopp and Green, 1947). The evaluation of these changing bar patterns of normal conversational speech is, of course, a problem of major importance in the study of the fundamental information bearing elements of speech.

A further study of the vowel formants is now nearing completion. This study employs sustained vowels, without influences, obtained and measured under controlled conditions. The general objectives are to determine further the most fundamental means of evaluating the formants, and to obtain the relations among the various formants for each of the vowels as produced by different speakers. When this information has been obtained it is anticipated that it will serve as a basis for determining methods of evaluating and relating the changing formants within words as produced by various speakers.

Summary

The results of our work to date on the development of methods for making acoustic and aural measurements on vowel sounds may be summarized as follows:

1 Calibration and measurement techniques have been developed with the sound spectrograph which make possible its use in a detailed study of the variations that appear in a broad sample of speech.
2 Repeated utterances, repeated measurements at various stages in the vowel study, and randomization in test procedures have made possible the application of powerful statistical methods in the analysis of the data.
3 The data, when so analysed, reveal that both the production and the identification of vowel sounds by an individual depend on his previous language experience.
4 It is also found that the production of vowel sounds by an individual is not a random process, i.e. the values of the acoustic measurements of the sounds are not distributed in random order. This is probably true of many other processes involving individuals' subjective responses.
5 Finally, the data show that certain of the vowels are generally better understood than others, possibly because they represent 'limit' positions of the articulatory mechanisms.

Acknowledgements

The work which we have discussed has involved the contributions of a number of people. We should like to acknowledge the guidance of R. K. Potter and J. C. Steinberg in the plan of the experiment, and the contribution of Dr W. A. Shewhart who has assisted in the design and interpretation of the study with respect to the application of statistical methods. We are indebted to Miss M. C. Packer for assistance in statistical analyses of the data. We wish to acknowledge also the assistance given by Anthony Prestigiacomo, George Blake, and Miss E. T. Leddy in the recording and analysis of the sounds and in the preparation of the data.

References

BLOCH, B. (1948), 'A set of postulates for phonemic analysis', *Language*, vol. 24, pp. 3–46.
BLOCH, B. (1950), 'Studies in colloquial Japanese IV : Phonemics', *Language*, vol. 26, p. 88.

BLOOMFIELD, L. (1933), *Language*, Henry Holt, New York, pp. 369–91.

FLETCHER, H. (1953), *Speech and Hearing in Communication*, Van Nostrand, p. 86.

FLETCHER, H., and GALT, R. H. (1950), 'The perception of speech and its relation to telephony', *J. acoust. Soc. Amer.*, vol. 22, pp. 89–151.

GRAY, G. W., and WISE, C. M. (1946), *The Bases of Speech*, Harper & Row, pp. 217–302.

JONES, D. (1947), *An Outline of English Phonetics*, Heffer.

KERSTA, L. G. (1948), 'Amplitude cross-section representation with the sound spectrograph', *J. acoust. Soc. Amer.*, vol. 20, p. 796.

KNUDSEN, V. O., and HARRIS, C. M. (1950), *Acoustical Designing in Architecture*, Wiley, pp. 180–81.

KOENIG, W. (1949), 'A new frequency scale for acoustic measurements', *Bell Labs. Record*, vol. 27, pp. 299–301.

KOENIG, W., DUNN, H. K., and LACY, L. Y. (1946), 'The sound spectrograph', *J. acoust. Soc. Amer.*, vol. 18, pp. 19–49. Excerpt reprinted here, pp. 77–91.

LEE, B. S. (1950), 'Effects of delayed speech feedback', *J. acoust. Soc. Amer.*, vol. 22, pp. 824–6.

POTTER, R. K., KOPP, G. A, and GREEN, H. C. (1947), *Visible Speech*, Van Nostrand.

POTTER, R. K., and PETERSON, G. E. (1948), 'The representation of vowels and their movements', *J. acoust. Soc. Amer.*, vol. 20, pp. 528–35.

POTTER, R. K., and STEINBERG, J. C. (1950), 'Toward the specification of speech', *J. acoust. Soc. Amer.*, vol. 22, p. 807.

STEVENS, S. S., and VOLKMAN, J. (1940), 'The relation of pitch to frequency: a revised scale', *Amer. J. Psychol.*, vol. 53, pp. 329–53.

THOMAS C. K. (1947), *Phonetics of American English*, Ronald Press, New York.

Analysis of Consonant Sounds

The acoustic analysis of consonant sounds presents rather more problems than the analysis of vowels. Many of them are aperiodic and therefore have no harmonic structure; they last on the whole a much shorter time than the vowels, the plosives, in particular, involving very short bursts of noise; and they are often the result of noise generated at different points along the length of the vocal tract so that the filtering effects of the tract are very complex. The four papers included in this section illustrate the use of the sound spectrograph in the analysis of consonants and also bring home the acoustic complexity of many of the sounds. They do not cover in detail the analysis of all classes of consonant sound though the paper by Jassem (Reading 7) does deal with all the types occurring in the Polish sound system. The paper by Strevens (Reading 8) deals with a wide range of fricative noises which are not confined to any one language system and the two following papers give an account of the analysis of the fricatives and stops of the English system. The information contained in these papers is supplemented by those in the later section on perceptual experiments which include data taken from acoustic analysis.

7 Wiktor Jassem

The Acoustics of Consonants

Wiktor Jassem, 'The acoustics of consonants', in A. Sovijärvi and P. Aalto (eds.), *Proceedings of the 4th International Congress of Phonetic Sciences*, Mouton, The Hague, 1962, pp. 50–72.

An oscillographic or a spectrographic display of the speech wave shows the following basic types of events; (a) (near-)periodic, (b) aperiodic, (c) aperiodic superimposed on periodic, and (d) pulse-like. Besides longer stretches of zero energy (corresponding to pauses) there are also gaps of limited duration rarely exceeding 150 ms. In a good spectrogram of a syllable, word or any stretch of connected speech there are points along the time axis at which either of the following phenomena – or both – are discernible: a rapid change from one kind of disturbance to another, e.g. from a periodic to an aperiodic; a maximum of the rate of change of the spectrum envelope. In a curve displaying changes of overall level, such as is produced by a high-speed level recorder or the 'amplitude display' unit (an accessory of the Sonagraph), points along the time axis may be determined at which the rate of change of the overall level (with an integration eliminating the periodicity of the fundamental) is maximum. These points mostly coincide with those named before. Plate 11 shows a spectrogram and the amplitude display of the Polish word /momen'talni/*momentalny*. All the three types of changes are easily seen there. Those particular points at which one or more of the three specified changes occur are *boundaries* between *acoustic segments*. The acoustic segments which have thus been demarcated can be correlated with phonetic units based on the consideration of auditory sensations, articulations and structural linguistic principles. This does not mean that an acoustic segment always corresponds to one phoneme. The segmental acoustic correlate of a phoneme may consist of two or more segments, but the number is always integral and probably never greater than eight. One segment may occasionally correspond to two or even three phonemes, if a single phonetic unit (on the level of perception and/or articulation) has for structural reasons to be interpreted as representing two or three consecutive phonemes (such as the Southern British English vocalic triphthongs). The segmentation of the speech wave, then, reduces a continuous time function to a discrete function. Thus, every particular sound of a syllable or a longer stretch of connected speech can be correlated with one or more segments on a spectrogram, although some cue or cues for its auditory recognition may be contained in a segment which is primarily correlated with an adjoining sound. For instance formant transitions in vowel segments are known to be important cues for the recognition of neighbouring plosives and nasals.[1]

The division between the two classes of elements referred to as vowels and consonants may be based on a purely phonetic description, or else it may be structural, i.e. phonemic. It is often necessary to state clearly whether the terms 'vowel' and 'consonant' are being used with their phonetic or their phonemic implications. The convenient terms 'vocoid' and 'contoid' introduced by K. L. Pike are based on the analysis of articulations without reference to the phonemic status of the speech sounds. Naturally, then, if we deal with speech sounds disregarding their function in any particular language, we can only mean vocoids and contoids, but it may be permissible to use the traditional and widely current terms 'vowels' and 'consonants' instead, provided we make it perfectly clear that those terms are being used without structural implications. We shall here be primarily dealing with consonants as phonetic elements, not as phonemic units.

. Although the correlations between specific auditory features and specific acoustic features are not always simple, certain large classes of speech sounds are found to be represented by segments having quite clearly definable acoustic features in common. We will therefore proceed in our description classifying our material according to traditional distinctions based on articulatory features.

The number of the different consonants occurring in various languages is very large and many of them have not yet been investigated acoustically. We shall here limit ourselves to the consonants occurring in standard Polish. Whilst this is a severe limitation in a general perspective, we hope that at least the most important problems will come under discussion because this language has a well-developed system of consonants. The observations are based on several hundred short utterances (mostly single words) produced by eleven speakers (male and female). The recordings were all made in Poznań, Poland, and the spectrograms were made in the Speech Transmission Laboratory of the Royal Institute of Technology in Stockholm, at the Phonetics Department of the University of Edinburgh, Scotland, and at the Acoustic Phonetics Laboratory of the Polish Academy of Sciences. I wish to thank Dr Gunnar Fant and Mr David Abercrombie for the opportunity of working in their respective institutions.

The nasal consonants. These are represented by periodic segments. They have a distinct formant structure. Below 4 kHz up to seven formants can be

1. On segmentation see Lisker (1957b). More recently see Fant (1960, pp. 207–8) and Peterson and Lehiste (1960).

distinguished. All nasals have one formant near the first harmonic, two around 2 kHz and two (or sometimes one) just above 3 kHz. Although some systematic differences in the exact position of those formants may be observed, e.g. the two above 3 kHz are closer together in the velar than in the others, the four Polish nasals – [m], [n], [ɲ] and [ŋ] – mainly differ in the shape of that part of the spectrum which lies between approximately 0·3 kHz and 1·8 kHz. The labial has a strong formant whose position varies somewhat according to the phonetic context, but is contained between 0·7 and 1·2 kHz. It also has a faint trace of a formant at approximately 0·4 kHz. The dental has two rather weak formants, one at 0·7 and the other at 1·5kHz. The palatal and velar nasals both have one formant only in this region which lies at about 0·8 kHz. They seem to differ chiefly in that the two formants just above 2 kHz tend to be closer together in the palatal than in the velar, whilst the two above 3 kHz are closer together in the velar than in the palatal. Spectrograms and 'sections' of isolated nasals are shown in Plate 12. Not all of the named formants are always visible on spectrograms of complete words (but most can be seen in Plates 25 and 26 ([m]), 35 and 39 ([n]), 24 ([ɲ]) and 14 [ŋ]). Our data on the formants of the labial, dental and palatal nasals are in good agreement with those given by Fant for the three Russian nasals (1960, pp. 139–61). A comparison of Plates 25 and 26 shows how the exact position of the formant around 1 kHz in [m] depends on the neighbouring vowel. The figures also illustrate another important feature common to all nasal consonants – the relative stability of the formants with time. The relations in the F_2 and F_3 transitions of neighbouring vowels are complex and require further study. Only a general and very brief statement can be made here. Next to [m] F_3 is usually negative. The F_3 transition is negative in front vowels and absent in back vowels. Next to the dental, front vowels have no transitions and back vowels have a positive F_2 transition. Both F_2 and F_3 transitions are positive next to [ɲ] except in [i] which has none. F_3 is negative and F_2 positive next to [ŋ] in front vowels. Both are negative or absent in back vowels (see Plates 14 and 18).

The laterals. Acoustically, the laterals resemble the vowels more than any other consonants. If pronounced in isolation or if considered without regard to a neighbouring vowel, a lateral has not yet received a clear acoustic definition which would unambiguously distinguish it from a vowel sound. Probably the positions of the formants, especially the higher ones, relative to each other show some peculiarities. Fant, for instance, points to the clustering of the higher formants (1960, p. 167). Another possibility is a strong anti-resonance below 2 kHz. Plate 13 which represents the sequence [lilalolu] shows that the formant frequencies of a lateral vary largely according to the context. In agreement with the findings of O'Connor, Gerstman, Liberman, Delattre and Cooper (1957), the lowest formant of [l] has been found somewhat higher than that of the nasals, and lies around 0·4 kHz. Our data for the higher formants differ slightly from those given by Lisker (1957a) chiefly in that F_2 and F_3 are closer together in our material than in Lisker's. The greatest separation between F_2 and F_3 in [l] occurs next to [a] and is of the order of 1 kHz. Next to [i] and [u], F_2 and F_3 frequencies differ by about 0·5 kHz. F_2 is contained, according to the neighbouring vowel, between 1·3 and 1·8 kHz. F_4 is approximately 0·5 kHz higher than F_3 and lies near 2·5 kHz next to [u] and at 3·0 or somewhat higher next to front vowels. Next to back vowels, then, F_3 and F_4 of an [l] are relatively low and the transitions of the vowel formants are negative and very rapid (they may be even under 50 ms in duration, see Plate 23).

The flapped and the rolled [r]. Both the flapped and the rolled tip-of-tongue voiced [r] are used in Polish (without phonemic distinction, by the way). Intervocalically a flapped [r] is represented by a single segment, lasting about 20–25 ms, showing considerable reduction of overall level, with some formant-like energy concentration near the fundamental and at 1·5, 2·9 and between 3·5 and 4·0 kHz. Otherwise a flapped [r] consists of two segments, the one just described and another one which has all the features of a neutral, i.e. shwa-like, vowel except that it is usually rather short (20–50 ms). Sometimes, however, this segment exceeds 50 ms (100 is the highest value in our materials) and it then reaches the status of a phonetic shwa. A rolled [r] is an alternating succession of the two kinds of segments. Up to eight segments have been found in naturally pronounced words. An interesting feature of the flapped [r] is that there is a rapid and very marked minus transition of both F_3 and F_4 of the neighbouring vowels. Those transitions are clearly visible in Figure 18. (Good examples of flapped and rolled [r]s also occur in Plates 20, 32, 37 and 39.)

The plosives. In most cases a plosive sound is represented by a sequence of acoustic segments. A common feature of all Polish plosives in all positions is a pulse-like segment. On spectrograms, this appears in the form of a single vertical stroke. An ideal pulse would give a stroke whose breadth would only depend on the time constants of the analysing and registering circuits, and which would stretch along the entire frequency range under analysis. Since in the actual speech wave the segments here considered are only approximations to pulses, the duration is of the order of 15 ms, the stroke is rarely seen along the whole frequency range, and it is usually broken, thus showing some energy concentrations. The pulse-like segment may be seen on spectrograms of both the voiceless and the voiced plosives.

If it is absent from a spectrogram of a plosive, this only means that the sound is too weak relative to others in the word or syllable. With sufficient gain on reproduction (often with overload on vowels) the pulse-like segment can always be detected. It is seen in Plates 29, 30, 31 and 37. The spectrogram of a voiceless plosive in a non-initial position shows a gap lasting between 120 and 180 ms. In voiced plosives the pulse is preceded by a near-periodic segment with only a few low harmonics. The pulse is followed, almost always in voiceless plosives, but rarely in voiced plosives except [ʝ], by an aperiodic segment. In the bilabial, dental and velar plosives this segment shows energy concentrations in rather narrow frequency bands. In the dental and velar plosives there is one 'burst' between 1 kHz and 2·5 kHz and another between 4 and 5 kHz. The latter is stronger in the dentals than in the velars. The labials also have a burst in the region between 1 kHz and 2·5 kHz but the one above 4 kHz is very weak or not detectable. The bilabials have another burst between 3 and 4 kHz and sometimes a weak one below 1 kHz. The exact position of the burst between 1 kHz and 2·5 kHz depends on the context, and in the labials there are often two peaks rather than one in this region. In the palatals the main energy concentration has a broader frequency band between 2·5 and 4 kHz and is longer in duration, often exceeding 100 ms in [c] as compared with about 50 ms in [p, t, k]. The Russian plosives are phonetically equivalent to the Polish plosives and our data on the frequency of the bursts are in good agreement with those published by Fant (1960), Fischer-Jørgensen (1959), and later Halle, Hughes and Radley (1957) who showed that the problem of vowel transitions preceding or following a stop consonant is much more complex than would have appeared from earlier publications. The most recent and the most extensive study of vowel transitions as revealed by spectrograms is that by Lehiste and Peterson, (1961). Our investigations of the transitions have not been as detailed, but the results seem to support Lehiste and Peterson's findings. We shall here have to limit ourselves to the general statement that the transitions depend both on the type of plosive and the type of vowel as well as on the position of the consonant relative to the vowel.

The fricatives. Every fricative sound is represented by a segment which is either aperiodic (voiceless consonant) or periodic-aperiodic (a super-position–voiced consonant). There are four pairs of fricative phonemes in Polish, each with a voiced and a voiceless member and another phoneme which has no distinctive feature of voicing, its allophones being either voiceless (in most positions) or voiced (in specific positions). The four pairs are: labiodental, postdental, palato-alveolar and alveolo-palatal. The voiceless fricatives are monosegmental, and so are the voiced fricatives except in utterance-initial position. In this position the periodic-aperiodic segment is preceded by a periodic one with just a few low harmonics and some traces of energy at higher frequencies. The duration of this segment is of the order of 50 ms and it is not easily perceived as a separate auditory unit unless attention is drawn to it. The energy concentration in the low frequencies is greater in the first element of the bisegmental fricative than in the second. An example of a bisegmental voiced fricative is seen in Plate 38. The differences among the four pairs are in the frequency range of the noise and the position of energy maxima in the spectrum. The noise spectra of these fricatives are as follows: the frequency range extends from approximately 4 or 5 kHz well beyond 8 and even 10 kHz (as was shown by additional analysis) in the postdentals and from approximately 2·5 to 8 kHz in the palato-alveolars. The lower limit lies at about 2·8 in the alveolo-palatals, but the upper limit varies largely between 6 and 8 kHz. In the labiodentals the range is 1·5 to 10 kHz. In the last-named fricatives the energy is distributed fairly evenly, though slight maxima may be observed between 1 and 3 kHz and above 8 kHz. In the other fricatives the maxima are very distinct. In the dentals their frequencies vary largely, but there are usually two of them at least between 5 and 8 kHz. Another regular energy concentration in the [s–z] pair lies at 1·5 kHz. It is therefore a separate narrow band of noise. Its level is between 25 and 35 dB below the peak at the higher frequencies so that it is rarely detectable in ordinary Sonagrams. Our data for the labiodentals and postdentals are quite similar to those obtained for the corresponding English sounds by Hughes and Halle (1956). An analogous, stronger band of noise is also found in the palato-alveolars, but its frequency largely depends on the F_2 of adjoining vowels. Figure 6 represents the word /'tɕiʃa/, and this noise band is seen to link the second formant of [i] with the second formant of [a]. Further maxima in [ʃ] and [ʒ] are found just below 3 kHz, between 3 and 4 kHz, and there are one or two more at less fixed frequencies, between 4 and 7 kHz. The alveolo-palatals differ from the palato-alveolars in having a considerably weaker low-frequency noise, rarely present on Sonagrams. It lies about 0·5 kHz higher than in [ʃ, ʒ]. The other maxima, too, are approximately 0·5 kHz higher in the alveolo-palatals than in the palato-alveolars. Further examples of the fricatives just discussed appear in Plates 20 and 38 (the labials), 22, 26, 33 and 34 (the dentals), 35 (the voiceless palato-alveolar) and 32, 37 and 39 (the alveolo-palatals). The voiceless velar fricative is represented by two narrow bands of noise. The higher-frequency noise has a narrow band with a centre at about 4 kHz. The central frequency of the lower band depends on the neighbouring sounds. If these are vowels, this noise band has a frequency which is near that of F_2. Plates 19 and 34 show this very clearly because here the [x] is in an intervocalic position, so that the centre of the noise band moves up or down making a link between the differing second formants of the vowels. There is usually also a third, very narrow band of noise with a centre at the frequency of F_1 of a neighbouring vowel. With no vowel preceding or following the two lower bands of noise are at 0·4 and about 1·3 kHz. The rare voiced variant of /x/ i.e. [ɣ] is shown in Plate 27. A detailed study of fricatives was recently published by Strevens (1960) and our findings are in good general agreement with his data. Strevens also investigated differences in overall level and experiments with speech synthesis show that these differences are important in the process of auditory recognition.

The affricates. Polish has three pairs of affricates, corresponding to the postdental, palato-alveolar and alveolo-palatal fricatives. They are essentially combinations of varieties of [t] or [d] with the appropriate fricative. Usually, the pulse-like segment typical for the plosives is here immediately followed by an aperiodic segment whose spectral pattern is the same as that of the corresponding fricative. The duration of the fricative portion of an affricate is less than that of a fricative consonant in comparable circumstances. If an affricate is preceded by a homorganic fricative there may be, instead of a gap and a pulse, a gradual decrease of the noise energy followed by a gradual increase. This is shown in Plate 36. Other examples of affricates are found in Plates 15, 16, 17 and 27.

The figures which we have given are typical values for male voices. In female voices the values are 10–20 per cent higher.

The above description has of course been very fragmentary and sketchy, but it should be noted that our knowledge of the acoustics of speech is in any case very far from complete, one important reason for this being that the number of languages which have been analysed by the methods of acoustic phonetics is still severely limited. It is quite essential for the further development of the various branches of general phonetics that the number of institutions in several countries applying electro-acoustic analysis techniques should quickly increase.

References

FANT, C. G. M. (1960), *Acoustic Theory of Speech Production*, Mouton, The Hague.

FISCHER-JØRGENSEN, E. (1959), 'Acoustic analysis of stop consonants', *Miscellanea Phonetica II*, pp. 42–59.

HALLE, M., HUGHES, G. W., and RADLEY, J. P. (1957), 'Acoustic properties of stop consonants', *J. acoust. Soc. Amer.*, vol. 29, pp. 107–16. Excerpt reprinted here, pp. 162–76.

HUGHES, G. W., and HALLE, M. (1956), 'Spectral properties of fricative consonants' *J. acoust. Soc. Amer.*, vol. 28, pp. 303–10. Excerpt reprinted here, pp. 151–61.

LEHISTE, I., and PETERSON, G. E. (1961), 'Transitions, glides and diphthongs', *J. acoust. Soc. Amer.*, vol. 33, pp. 268–77.

LISKER, L. (1957a), 'Minimal cues for separating /w, r, l, y/ in intervocalic position', *Word*, vol. 13, pp. 257–67.

LISKER, L. (1957b), 'Linguistic segments and synthetic speech', *Language*, vol. 33, pp. 370–74.

O'CONNOR, J. D., GERSTMAN, L. J., LIBERMAN, A. M., DELATTRE, P. C., and COOPER, F. S. (1957), 'Acoustic cues for the perception of initial /w, j, r, l/ in English', *Word*, vol. 13, pp. 25–43. Reprinted here, pp. 298–314.

PETERSON, G. E., and LEHISTE, I. (1960), 'Duration of the syllable nuclei in English', *J. acoust. Soc. Amer.*, vol. 32, pp. 693–703.

STREVENS, P. (1960), 'Spectra of fricative noise in human speech', *Language and Speech*, vol. 3, pp. 32–49. Reprinted here, pp. 132–50.

8 Peter Strevens

Spectra of Fricative Noise in Human Speech[1]

Peter Strevens, 'Spectra of fricative noise in human speech', *Language and Speech*, vol. 3 (1960), pp. 32–49.

The phonetic category of voiceless fricatives comprises speech sounds consisting solely of turbulant noise, or *hiss*. Nine different voiceless fricatives were selected for analysis in the present study. They are only some of the total members of the class, and were selected to provide a wide coverage of different places of articulation and shapes of orifice. The sounds are those commonly referred to by the following symbols and articulatory labels:

Φ (bi-labial); f (labio-dental); θ (dental); s (alveolar); ʃ (palato-alveolar); ç (palatal); x (velar); χ (uvular); h (glottal).

It should be made clear that the term *voiceless* is used throughout this paper in its normal, general phonetic sense. Voiceless fricatives are sounds produced with no vibration of the vocal cords. Their spectrum is basically that of aperiodic random noise.

The author has been concerned in the operation for research purposes of P A T, the parametric artificial talking device designed by W. Lawrence (Lawrence, 1953; Strevens, 1958a, 1958b; Strevens and Anthony, 1958). It was clear from an early stage that the work must include the adequate simulation of at least the voiceless fricatives of English. In practice it was found that the available data were not sufficient to programme P A T to do this. The investigation now described was undertaken with a view to providing the basic data for the purpose.

Voiceless fricatives are all produced by turbulent air-flow caused by a constriction in the vocal tract at some point in or above the larynx. The constriction may vary as to position in the tract, degree of constriction, area of constriction and shape of orifice. Further, although it is customary to think of the vocal tract as if it were a tube having a cylindrical cross-section, it must not be forgotten that the tract is in places highly mobile, and that it may alter its shape to a considerable extent independently of

1. This work was undertaken under a contract between the Ministry of Supply and the University of Edinburgh for research into the specification of speech by means of acoustic parameters.

constrictions such as those under discussion. Finally, the air-stream may vary as to pressure or rate of flow. A variation of any combination of these factors can be expected to cause a variation in the physical nature of the resulting sound in any of three ways: by altering the spectrum of the original source of sound; by altering the filter function of the tract as a whole; by altering the intensity of the acoustic energy produced.

The spectrum of the sound-source will depend on the degree and the area of constriction, on the shape of the orifice or orifices, and to a minor extent on the rate of air-flow. The chief effect of increased air-flow is to increase the overall acoustic energy. The filter function will depend largely (though not wholly) on the position of the constriction within the vocal tract, since this position will decide what portions of the vocal tract are contributing to the shaping of the source spectrum.

Because of the interdependence of the physiological and the physical events it is necessary to consider them both; the following order will be employed: first, the modifications of the vocal tract which impede the air-stream and give rise to turbulent flow; second, variations in air-pressure and their relation to acoustic intensity; third, the spectrographic analysis of voiceless fricatives; fourth, an extension of the results thus obtained to consideration of other sounds containing a component of noise.

Modifications of the vocal tract

The position of the constriction within the vocal tract is possibly the chief cause of identifiable differences of sound quality in voiceless fricatives. (This is indeed true of all consonants; a traditional method of defining consonants is in terms of 'place of articulation'.) The organs of articulation concerned in the production of the nine selected voiceless fricatives /Φ f θ s ʃ ç x χ h/ and the typical positions within the vocal tract at which the constriction (and hence the turbulent air-flow) occurs, are as follows:

1 /Φ/ is produced with the constriction at the lips. Its occurrence in British forms of English is limited to certain Scottish and Irish dialects and to the exclamation 'Phew!'

2 /f/ is produced with the upper teeth close to the inner surface of the lower lip. The air-stream passes between the teeth and the lower lip, and also through some of the interstices between the upper teeth.

3 /θ/ is produced with the tip of the tongue close to, or touching, the inner edge of the upper incisors. However, there is a good deal of personal variation in the place of articulation of this sound: it has been described as occurring with the tip of the tongue protruding between the upper and lower teeth; but a tip-teeth articulation is believed to be the commonest one.

4 /s/ is produced with either the tip or the blade of the tongue raised to approach the alveolar ridge.

5 /ʃ/ is produced with the blade of the tongue, or the tip and blade, approaching the palate approximately at the part where the alveolar ridge merges into the main body of the hard palate.

6 /ç/ is produced with the front of the tongue, i.e. roughly that part of its surface which opposes the dome of the palate when the tongue is at rest, approaching the hard palate somewhat forward of its highest point.

7 /x/ is produced with the back of the tongue approaching the middle of the soft palate.

8 /χ/ is produced with the back of the tongue approaching the back of the soft palate and the back wall of the pharynx.

9 /h/ is the subject of some controversy. It is thought by many that the turbulent air-flow is produced somewhere in the larynx; others believe 'cavity-friction' to be generated throughout the vocal tract. The exact mechanism is not clearly understood.

Each of the articulations thus briefly described occurs at a different point in the vocal tract and can therefore be expected to lead to a different shaping of the source spectrum. The source spectrum itself will differ to some extent according to the nature of the orifice formed at the place of constriction. A short description of typical orifices for each of the nine sounds will demonstrate the occurrence of a wide variety of orifice shapes.

1 /Φ/ is produced with a long narrow slit between the lips.

2 /f/ is produced with a narrow opening between the upper teeth and the lower lip. There may also be a contribution through slits between the teeth.

3 /θ/ is produced with a narrow slit between the bottom of the upper teeth and the surface of the tongue; the configuration of the teeth affects the quality of the sound produced.

4 /s/ is produced with a narrow slit which may sometimes be accompanied by a deep groove and pit in the tongue.

5 /ʃ/ is produced with a wider slit or groove than for /s/ (with a greater area of turbulence). Further, the main body of the tongue assumes a different posture for /ʃ/ than for /s/.

6 In the production of /ç x χ/ the constriction is far back in the mouth. The chief difference between them is the place at which the constriction occurs.

7 /h/ is produced with increased air-flow through the larynx; the area of turbulence is probably very extensive.

The above set of statements is to be taken as an approximation and a normalization, and is not presented as an absolute or final description. Palatographic studies, especially those using the direct photography method (Anthony, 1954; Abercrombie, 1956; Ladefoged, 1957; Way, 1957), show that there are often large variations of the shape of the orifice and even of the place of constriction, within the speech of a single individual as well as between different speakers. Further, the description of these items by no means exhausts even commonly observed methods of production of hiss. The air-flow in most cases passes over the median line of the tongue, but it may for some voiceless fricatives pass over one or both sides of the tongue; the tongue may be grooved or flat, or 'pitted'; there may be more than one constriction at one time; the nasal cavity may be coupled-in with an air-flow sufficient to cause nasal turbulence, and so on.

It is clear that there are available to the speaker compensatory processes which enable him to produce an acceptable quality of voiceless fricative using quite a variety of different articulatory postures. (These processes are familiar to all those who have lost or acquired teeth.) The foregoing descriptions, then, are a catalogue of some configurations that *do* occur, not of those that *must* be used.

Variations of air-flow

A factor which must now be studied is the acoustic *intensity* of these sounds. Two assumptions underlie this section of the paper: first, that variations in the air-flow of speech have a major effect upon the *intensity* but only a negligible effect upon the *spectrum* of the sound produced; secondly, that the amount of acoustic energy produced during a voiceless fricative is closely related to the rate of air-flow involved.

It is a common observation that, to put it roughly, all the voiceless fricatives occur sometimes loud and sometimes soft, but some are loud most of the time while others are soft most of the time. It is of importance to discover whether this is because of inherent differences of acoustic energy or because of other factors such as those arising in the initiation and modification of the pulmonic air-streams.

In English (and presumably in all languages using only an egressive pulmonic air-stream) the pressure of the expiratory air is operated upon by two variables: (1) the *affective variations* of pressure; (2) variations of *phonetic impedance*. These labels need brief explanation:

1 During most speech, the mean pulmonic air-pressure remains relatively constant. Figure 1 shows the relation between the sub-glottal pressure and the volume of air in the lungs during a normal conversational utterance. As speech begins the air-pressure rises to an appropriate level (about 3 cm aq.

for normal speech). The pressure-level appropriate to shouting is higher than that for quiet speech. Pressure levels above the minimum for speech are decided by the general degree of loudness at which the speech is to be produced. The monitoring of this factor is entirely subjective and automatic; the term *affective variations* is proposed, to describe the gross changes in air-pressure level which produce the required loudness.

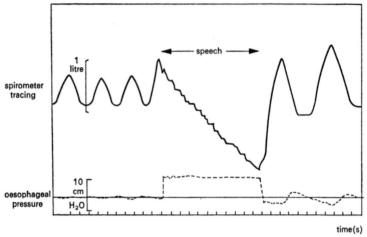

Figure 1 Two parameters of the air stream used in respiration and speech (by courtesy of P. Ladefoged)

2 The load on the air-stream varies in complex ways. The air-stream itself above the larynx has two modes of flow; breath and voice, the former being normally at a higher total rate of flow than the latter. In either mode the flow may be either free or impeded to some extent. Both the extent and the duration of the obstruction will vary from one sound to another. Stops have a momentary but complete obstruction – an infinite phonetic impedance – while fricatives have a lower phonetic impedance of a longer duration. These changes in impedance are added to the changes in pressure brought about by muscular activity in the form of 'chest pulses' (Draper, Ladefoged and Whitteridge, 1957, 1959; Ladefoged, Draper and Whitteridge, 1958). Between them they produce rapidly fluctuating peaks of pressure superimposed upon the speech level.

It is now appropriate to describe some preliminary attempts to relate acoustic energy to tracheal air-pressure.

A microphone, set at a distance of 1 ft from the speaker's mouth, was connected through a pre-amplifier to a valve millivoltmeter. Variations in the acoustic intensity of the nine voiceless fricatives could thus be read as variations in voltage. A nasal catheter tube terminating in a small, lightly inflated rubber bulb, was passed into the oesophagus of the two subjects, Peter Ladefoged and the author.

Experiments have shown (Draper, Ladefoged and Whitteridge, 1959) that since the oesophagus is separated from the trachea by only a thin membrane, the variations of pressure on the air-filled bulb could be treated as variations in the pressure of the pulmonic air-stream. Further, the oesophagus is on the lungward side of all the places of constriction of the nine sounds under investigation. The catheter tube was connected to a transducer incorporating a movable anode whose output was taken to a second voltmeter. The apparatus as a whole can be calibrated by a manometric device.

The subjects spoke a large number of examples of each of the nine voiceless fricatives, using degrees of muscular effort ranging from shouting to little more than a whisper. The two voltages corresponding to acoustic intensity and air-pressure were read simultaneously for each test item. It was found that peristalsis of the alimentary tract interfered increasingly with experimental readings as the next meal-time approached. Nevertheless sufficient readings were taken for the following points to become clear: (a) similar articulations could be made to produce acoustically different sounds; (b) after some little practice, a subject could learn to vary the intensity and pressure readings to some degree independently of each other; (c) a given sound may be produced habitually by a given speaker at a much higher or lower level of intensity than is used by another speaker.

The intensity reading of each item was divided by the pressure reading of each item. In this way it was possible to arrive at a single index for each sound, and a mean for all examples of a given sound by a given subject. There were strong correspondences between the indices of the two subjects; the indications are that the nine sounds as produced by these two subjects in these tests may be arranged as in Table 1:

Table 1 Rank order of intensity
per unit air-pressure

1 (lowest) Φ
2 θ
3 f
4 χ
5 s
6 x
7 ʃ
8 h
9 (highest) ç

The results of this preliminary experiment should be regarded with reserve, until there has been an opportunity to verify them using a more rigid experimental procedure and a larger number of subjects. When this has been done, it will be possible to establish an order (which may be similar to that given above) representing the relative intensities of the different fricatives when they occur in a sample of speech with a given mean pulmonic air-pressure level, e.g., as shown in Figure 1.

The programme of spectrographic analysis

Spectrographic analysis had not been attempted in the few papers previously published on these sounds (Halle, Hughes and Radley, 1957; Hughes and Halle, 1956; Meyer-Eppler, 1956). A small pilot investigation was undertaken with a view to discovering what the drawbacks would be in using spectrographic analysis, whether adequate data could be obtained, and what procedures should be used.

It was found at once that voiceless fricatives occurring in connected speech rarely gave usable spectral information for two reasons: first, the overall acoustic energy of the voiceless fricatives is generally much lower than for the stressed vowels by whose peaks the signal level is usually adjusted, consequently the full spectral pattern of the fricatives is too weak to appear; secondly, the duration of these items is often quite short, so that the quantity of pattern available for study is inadequate. The apparatus available for this study included a Kay Sonagraph; the first practical task was to find a technique of using the instrument which would overcome these difficulties. A sample of speech was recorded with the aim of studying the voiceless fricatives which occurred in that utterance; the expedient was tried of setting the recording level by these fricative items, and not by the peaks of energy occurring during vowels. This meant that the stressed vowels and many other voiced sounds were badly overloaded, but it was immediately apparent that greater detail was visible during the voiceless fricatives, and that the patterns for a given fricative were consistent between one utterance and another.

To overcome the problem of the short duration of naturally occurring fricatives the possibility was considered of using the sounds in isolation and of deliberately lengthening them. Given good listening conditions, e.g., the close proximity of speakers and the low background noise usual for quiet conversation, listeners experienced no difficulty in identifying voiceless fricatives spoken in isolation even when no visual clues were present. Lengthening the sounds in isolation only made their identification more immediate and certain. A scheme of investigation was therefore prepared on the assumption that the spectra of isolated, lengthened utterances of the voiceless fricatives would contain all the clues necessary for their auditory identification, and would not contain any undue quantity of spurious components. (The voiceless fricatives occur more frequently with a short duration, but the additional length used in this investigation is not necessarily an unreal factor. The following occurrences of lengthened voiceless fricatives are relatively common: /ΦΦΦ/ when expressing relief after a narrow escape; /sss/ expressing disapproval at the theatre; /fff/ when talking to children ('Pufff, puffff. . .', etc.); /ʃʃʃ/ asking for silence, etc.

The list of items was selected, as already mentioned, so as to cover a reasonable range of possible places of production within the vocal tract. Thirteen past and present staff and post-graduate students of the Phonetics Department of Edinburgh University acted as subjects. Each subject spoke each of the items in isolation, lengthened to approximately one second. Using as subjects people with a professional training in phonetics enabled satisfactory recordings to be obtained very quickly with the minimum of instructions and rehearsal. The utterances were checked both at the time they were made and from the recordings to ensure that the instructions had been carried out. The recordings were made on a Ferrograph tape recorder, with a flat frequency response from 50 to 10 000 Hz $\pm$ 2 dB, running at 15 inches per second. The recording technique was critical: the subject had to be close enough to the microphone to provide an adequate signal, yet his breath-stream had to be directed in such a direction as not to impinge on the microphone.

Once the recordings were complete the spectrographic analysis was begun. Various displays were tried. The best results compatible with the time and labour involved were obtained from two spectrograms per utterance; (i) a broad-band spectrogram of the normal scale of 0–8000 Hz; (ii) two amplitude sections of each utterance, chosen one from the first half and the other from the second half.[2]

Each recording was followed by a calibration tone consisting of a short 'pip' of square waves from a signal generator set at a frequency of 500 Hz. The display given by this 'pip' was arranged to provide a calibration scale at each edge of the spectrogram.

Spectrograms of each of these three types were made for each of the nine utterances of each of the thirteen speakers. The spectrograms were then inspected visually. Two things were immediately apparent: first, there were systematic variations of pattern between one item and another in the analysis of a given speaker; secondly, there were similarities of pattern within a given item in the analyses of all speakers.

Many alternative methods were tried in a search for a simple presentation of the patterns which occur in these spectrograms. The least unsatisfactory

2. In the original publication two spectrograms were shown. Owing to the difficulty of reproducing them, they have been omitted here.

is to produce an 'average line spectrum' for each utterance. These line spectra indicate the range of frequencies within which energy is shown to be present on the spectrograms. The variation of upper and lower limits of frequency within any one spectrogram is surprisingly small, and once it was decided that extremes of variation were to be ignored and only typical frequency limits shown, the preparation of line spectra was easy.

On these lines cross-bars are marked at frequencies when peaks of energy occur. No distinction is made between peaks of different height, or of different breadth; the cross-bars mark simply frequencies at which peaks of some kind occur. The reason for not indicating the magnitude of the peaks is a purely practical one: there is no simple way of describing them. It is arbitrary enough to decide by visual inspection that a peak is or is not present, but distinctions between different sizes or shapes of peak are not feasible, as anyone will confirm who has studied fricative spectra.

Here it may be mentioned that the amplitude cross-sections were considerably less helpful than might have been imagined. One single cross-section per fricative yields apparently helpful information about peaks of energy. A second cross-section from the same utterances, however, almost invariably gives information that conflicts in its details with the previous analysis. The operative point is that the conflict concerns the *details*: the rough outline is generally similar. Presumably the reason for the discrepancies is that we are dealing with the acoustic shaping of aperiodic noise. The general aspect of the cross-section is determined by the shaping which in turn is conferred by the configuration of the vocal tract; but the random nature of the sound is illustrated by variations of detail from one instant to another. To sum up, one cross-section per utterance gave a spurious appearance of firm detail, while two per utterance gave conflicting evidence. The line spectra and the cross-bars indicating frequency were therefore compiled chiefly from the broad-band spectrograms. These line spectra are shown as Figure 2, diagrams (a) to (i). Diagram (j) is composed of one typical spectrum of each item for comparison.

No account can be taken of the upper limits of frequency above 8 kHz since the frequency response of the spectrograph dropped away sharply above that point. From rough tests made with recordings played at half speed and then given the same analysis it appears that in the spectra shown as reaching 8 kHz, some energy is in fact present in most cases up to 10 kHz, and in a few cases up to at least 12 kHz. But the evidence is not sufficient to be presented here and no systematic study of the upper limits of frequency has been attempted, where these lie above 8 kHz.

The averaged line spectra shown in the diagrams must be accompanied by a verbal description of the average spectra of each of the nine voiceless fricatives; this will include a statement of intensity. By this is meant the

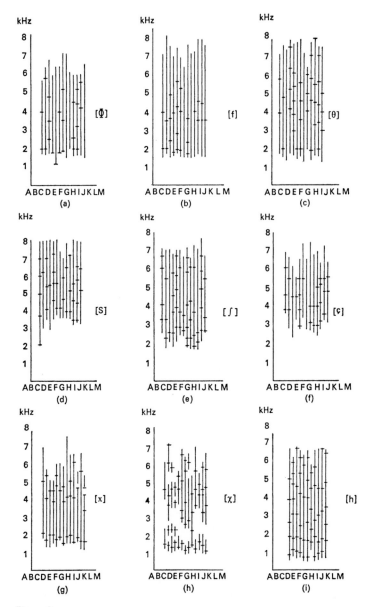

Figure 2

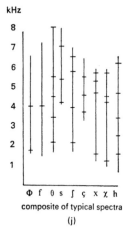

kHz

Φ f θ s ʃ ç x χ h

composite of typical spectra

(j)

Figure 2 *cont.*

order of ranking from the investigation of intensity per unit pressure described above. It must be repeated that no general validity is claimed for this figure.

1 /Φ/ (Figure 2a) Lowest frequency at which energy is visible on the spectrogram is between 1600 and 1650 Hz. Low peaks of energy tend to occur around 1800–2000 Hz, 4000–4500 Hz, and 5500 Hz. Energy rarely above 6500 Hz. Intensity ranking: lowest of 9.

2 /f/ (Figure 2b) Lowest frequency is around 1500–1700 Hz. Low peaks of energy tend to occur around 1900 Hz, 4000 Hz, and occasionally 5000Hz. Upper limit of frequency is rarely below 7000 Hz, usually around 7500 Hz. In general, a higher upper limit than 1. Intensity ranking: 3rd in ascending order.

3 /θ/ (Figure 2c) Lowest frequency varies, but lies between 1400 and 2000 Hz. Low peaks of energy tend to occur, the lowest being close to 2000 Hz, the upper peaks varying somewhat, but tending to lie about 1000 Hz apart. Upper limit of frequency rarely below 7200 Hz; some speakers reach 8000 Hz. In general, a somewhat higher upper limit than 2. Intensity ranking: 2nd in ascending order.

4 /s/ (Figure 2d) Lowest frequency almost always above 3500 Hz. Peaks of energy tend to occur with no apparent pattern, except that they do not lie closer to one another than 1000 Hz. Upper limit of frequency exceeds 8000 Hz in most cases. Intensity ranking: 5th in ascending order.

5 /ʃ/ (Figure 2e) Lowest frequency varies between 1600 and 2500 Hz. Peaks of energy tend to occur not less than 1000 Hz apart and the aspect of amplitude cross-sections shows a weighting towards the bottom of the pattern. Upper limit of frequency shows a sharp cut-off around 7000 Hz. Intensity ranking: 7th in ascending order.

6 /ç/ (Figure 2f) Lower limit of frequency varies generally between 2800 and 3600 Hz. Peaks of energy tend to appear at roughly 1000 Hz intervals; these peaks are sharper than those in 5. Upper frequency limit very variable, but usually between 6000 and 7200 Hz, i.e. lower than for either 4 or 5. The general shape of the spectrum is like that of 4, /s/, but with all values transposed 1000 Hz down. Intensity ranking: greatest of all 9 items.

7 /x/ (Figure 2g) Lower limit of frequency usually between 1200 and 1500 Hz. There is always a strong peak of energy below 2000 Hz, with others above about 3500 Hz. The aspect of amplitude cross-sections gives a hint of formant-like structure; the low peak is steeper than the upper peaks, which are often double peaks, some 500–600 Hz apart. Upper frequency limit is very variable, usually between 5000 Hz and 7500 Hz. A considerable variety of different sound qualities was obtained from the subjects, as was to be expected. Versions judged in phonetic terms to have a more back place of articulation tended to approach more closely to a formant-like structure. Intensity rating: 6th in ascending order.

8 /χ/ (Figure 2h) Lower limit of frequency varies between 700 Hz and 1200 Hz. All spectra bear a marked resemblance to vowels, with a 'formant' of one or two high peaks between 1000 and 2400 Hz. Sometimes there are three or even four 'formants' altogether, with one or two of them having rather high peaks of intensity, in the region from 3000 to 6000 Hz. At first glance the spectrographic pattern is that of a vowel rather than a voiceless fricative. Upper limit of frequency variable between 6000 and 7000 Hz. Intensity rating: 4th in ascending order.

9 /h/ (Figure 2i) Lower limit of frequency usually varies between 400 and 700 Hz. The peaks of intensity which occur are so marked as to suggest a multi-formant vowel. One major peak occurs around 1000 Hz, one around 1700 Hz. At least five major peaks occur in each pattern; spectra for women subjects exhibit more of these peaks than for men. Upper limit of frequency is usually around 6500 Hz. Intensity ranking: 8th in ascending order, but for technical reasons the data (and thus the ranking) for this item are suspect.

A consideration of the data provides a basis for distinguishing three groups of voiceless fricatives, the members of each group sharing certain features. It happens (not surprisingly) that the groupings reflect major differences in place of articulation. The groups may therefore be labelled as follows: *Front* (containing the labial and dental sounds /Φ f θ/), *Mid* (containing the alveolar and palatal sounds /s ʃ ç/) and *Back* (containing the velar, uvular and pharyngal sounds /x χ h/). The groups are distinguished in terms of spectral pattern in the following way:

Front Group /Φ f θ/ Long spectrum, covering a range of some 5000 to 6000 Hz; a peak of energy frequently occurs below 2000 Hz, but in general the peaks are un-patterned and 'spiky'; the relative intensity is the lowest of the three groups.

Mid Group /s ʃ ç/ Short spectrum, covering a range of some 3000 to 4000 Hz; one or more major 'humps' around the middle of the pattern; the relative intensity is the highest of the three groups.

Back Group /x χ h/ Medium spectrum covering a range of some 4000 to 5500 Hz; a marked 'formant-like' structure with invariably a major peak or 'formant' around 1500 Hz; the relative intensity is the middle of the three groups.

The above characteristics identify the groups and can be stated with some confidence. The factors which distinguish members within a group are not so clear-cut, and are put forward with some reserve. It is suggested that it is within these groups, rather than between them, that confusions and mis-identifications most frequently occur under conditions of restricted efficiency of communication, e.g., on poor telephone circuits. The distinctions between different members of a group may reside in the following criteria:

Front Group 'Centre of gravity'. It seems from a study of the amplitude cross-sections that the sequence /Φ f θ/ (that is, going progressively further back in place of articulation) displays an increasing weighting of the upper end of the spectrum, accompanied to some extent by a higher upper limit of frequency.

Mid Group A combination of upper and lower frequency limits. The sequence /s ʃ ç/ (that is, going progressively further back in place of articulation) is accompanied by a change of upper limit from highest to lowest; the lower limit changes in the same sequence from highest to lowest to intermediate.

Back Group Doubtful: possibly the frequency of lower limit of frequency, which becomes progressively lower in the sequence /x χ h/ (that is, progressively further back in place of articulation). The foregoing features are summarized in Table 2.

The sounds with which this investigation has been concerned are well known as being aperiodic in nature. Unfortunately it has often been

Table 2 The special characteristics of nine voiceless fricatives

Sounds	Articulation group	Relative intensity	Spectrum length	Distinction between members of the group
Φ f θ	front (labial and dental)	low	long (5000–6000 Hz)	Φ lowest 'centre of gravity' f intermediate 'centre of gravity' θ highest 'centre of gravity'
s ʃ ç	mid (pre-velar)	high	short (3000–4000 Hz)	s highest bottom limit, highest top limit of frequency ʃ lowest bottom limit, intermediate top limit of frequency ç intermediate bottom limit, lowest top limit of frequency
x χ h	back	medium	medium (4000–5500 Hz) with 'formant-like' structure	x highest bottom limit of frequency χ intermediate bottom limit of frequency h lowest bottom limit of frequency

assumed that they should be equated with the classical case of random, aperiodic vibration, known as 'white noise'. It is now quite clear that the randomness of the sound source is greatly modified by the acoustic shaping characteristics of the vocal tract, and that this shaping varies in several ways. To extend the 'white noise' metaphor it might be said that voiceless fricative speech sounds consist of 'grey noise, streaked with white and black'.

Extrapolations

Once the analysis and classification of voiceless fricatives has been performed on lengthened, isolated segments, it becomes possible to recognize many or all the features already described from their occurrence in spectrograms of normal connected speech. More important, the same sets of features begin to be seen, at least partially, in spectrograms of voiced fricatives, voiceless and voiced stops, and voiceless and voiced affricates.

No detailed analysis of any of these sounds has been attempted by the author but a combination of general phonetic considerations with extrapolations from the data on voiceless fricatives would lead one to expect with considerable confidence the existence of certain predictable features. The following paragraphs summarize these expectations.

We have seen that when turbulent air-flow occurs its spectrum will be related to the place where it occurs, the shape of the orifice concerned and the flow of air through the constriction. If other sounds containing a component of fricative noise are now considered in the light of the data described above, strong indications may be seen as to the probable nature of the hiss. It is convenient to discuss these sounds in categories according to their method of production.

Voiced fricatives (e.g.: /β v ð z ʒ j ʁ ɦ/)

These sounds are made up of two components: a component of hiss and a component of 'vocal tone' or *voice*. It can reasonably be assumed that the acoustic characteristics of the hiss will correspond in most respects to those of the voiceless fricatives. The major difference in articulation is that in voiced fricatives for a given air-pressure the *air-flow* is less than for the voiceless items, since the breath stream is being interrupted and reduced in flow by the action of the vocal cords. For a given air-pressure the acoustic intensity of the hiss component of voiced fricatives is inherently less than that of the corresponding voiceless items.

Evidence tending to confirm this may be found in spectrograms of ordinary speech. It is instructive to compare two amplitude displays (not cross-sections) of the same utterance, using a flat amplifier response for one and high frequency emphasis for the other. The amplitude of the trace during voiceless fricatives is greatly increased by the high frequency emphasis; the voiced fricatives, on the other hand, are only slightly higher than in the flat-response condition. The energy present at the higher frequencies is clearly less in the voiced fricatives than in the voiceless ones.

Nevertheless hiss remains comparatively easy to identify, even at low intensities and when accompanied by vocal cord vibration. In teaching general phonetics, there is little difficulty in teaching students to identify the presence of hiss, and the hiss seems not to be masked by voice.

Stops

Voiceless. Many languages contain voiceless stops, in the production of which the air-stream is momentarily obstructed, then released with a 'burst' of fricative noise, more or less short in duration. The spectrum of the hiss on any given occasion will inevitably be like the spectrum of a closely homorganic fricative. Thus in English when the voiceless stops /p t k/ are released with a burst of hiss, the spectrum of this affrication must be virtually identical with /Φ s x/ respectively, since /Φ/ and /p/ are homorganic, as are /s/ and /t/ and also /x/ and /k/. This is what one tends to find on close examination of suitable spectrograms. (See also Fischer-Jørgensen, 1954.)

Voiced. Perceptible affrication after voiced stops is much less common, at least in English. The reduced rate of air-flow resulting from vibration of the vocal cords causes a smaller build-up of pressure behind the occlusion, duration for duration, than in the case of voiceless stops. This means that when the stop is released the air-flow may be insufficient to cause audible friction. Even when hiss does occur, it is both short in duration and extremely low in level compared with the voiced components. The spectrum is identical with that of the voiceless counterpart.

Affricates

Voiceless. Affricates combine in sequence some of the articulatory features of the stops (e.g., complete but momentary obstruction of the air-stream) with other features characteristic of the fricatives (e.g., partial obstruction of the air-stream). An important additional point is that the place of articulation of the stop release is frequently not the same as the place of the fricative articulation within the same sound. The relative levels of the stop release and fricative portions may also be different. Consequently the hiss portion of an affricate may consist of two segments having different spectra. Thus /tʃ/ in *church* begins with a short 'stop-release' burst having a spectrum closely similar to /s/ and is followed without a break by a longer 'fricative' segment having the spectrum of /ʃ/.

Voiced. In voiced affricates (as in *judge*) the considerations for voiced stops and voiced fricatives apply. The stop-release portion will be at a much lower level of intensity, both absolutely and relatively, than in a voiceless plosive. The 'fricative' portion will have audible friction with a spectrum appropriate to its place of articulation at a relatively lower level of intensity.

Fricative sounds in speech synthesis

Although the foregoing remarks on hiss in sounds other than voiceless fricatives have been presented as a sequel to the discussion of fricatives they also received some practical attention. In the preparation of synthetic speech utterances for Lawrence's PAT, the following observations have been made:

1 Variations of hiss spectrum, in the general direction of simulating the spectra described above, lead to improved acceptability and intelligibility of synthetic speech;

2 even if the transitions have been faithfully simulated, voiced fricatives provided with some hiss of the appropriate spectrum are much more

acceptable than the same sounds without hiss or with hiss of some different spectrum;

3 in synthesizing affricates a great improvement is obtained by working to a pattern of the appropriate 'stop-release' spectrum portion, plus the appropriate fricative spectrum. These *ad hoc* observations are no substitute for a careful series of experiments in the synthesis of hiss sounds, but they provide much empirical confirmation and no refutation of the general validity of the foregoing remarks.

Furthermore, the quality of synthetic speech which PAT can produce is already very greatly improved as a result of this analysis of the acoustic spectra of voiceless fricatives; it is now at last possible to write some physical specification of the sounds that the machine is to be instructed to simulate.

Experiments on the identification of stops and of fricatives have been described previously by several writers, notably by workers at the Haskins Laboratories (Liberman, Delattre and Cooper, 1952; Cooper, Delattre, Liberman and Gerstman, 1952; Liberman, Delattre, Cooper and Gerstman, 1957). The fricative noise used in the experiments described consists of white noise of 600 Hz spectrum width; the only systematic variations reported are variations of the centre frequency of the band of short-spectrum hiss. The exception is Dr Harris (1956, 1958) who used wide-band white noise in some experiments and recordings of human fricatives in others, and experimented with variations in the relative intensity of vowel and fricative.

The question arises whether substantially different results might be expected from these synthetic speech experiments if they were to be repeated using hiss spectra more closely resembling those found in human speech. The conclusions of Schatz (1954) support the contention that the fricative portions of voiceless stops are in many circumstances sufficient clues for identification, without reference to vowel transitions. It seems probable, therefore, that listeners' judgements on any occasion will be influenced in the direction of the naturally occurring hiss spectrum most closely resembling the synthetic hiss.

Acknowledgements

The foregoing spectrographic investigations and the descriptions of articulatory and physiological facts owe a great deal to the cooperation of the author's colleagues at Edinburgh University. The original recordings and 400 spectrograms were produced by Miss Shiona Harkness, M.A., now of the College of Arts, Science and Technology, Zaria, Northern Nigeria. Many facts about articulations, almost the whole of the information about air-pressures, the instrumentation for the preliminary work on intensities and much fruitful discussion were generously given by Dr Peter Ladefoged; Dr Frances Ingemann read the manuscript and made several helpful suggestions; Mr David Abercrombie, Head of the Phonetics Department, encouraged the work throughout and contributed much information about articulations. Mr J. Anthony supervised the technical standards. To all these and to many others who have helped as subjects or with illustrations or secretarial assistance, grateful acknowledgement is made.

References

ABERCROMBIE, D. (1956), 'Direct palatography', *Z. Phonet. USW*, vol. 10, p. 21.

ANTHONY, J. (1954), 'New method for investigating tongue positions of consonants' *Science Technologists Assn Bull.*, vol. 4, p. 2.

COOPER, F., DELATTRE, P. C., LIBERMAN, A., and GERSTMAN, L. (1952), 'Some experiments on the perception of synthetic speech sounds', *J. acoust. Soc. Amer.*, vol. 24, p. 597. Reprinted here, 258–72.

DRAPER, M., LADEFOGED, P., and WHITTERIDGE, D. (1957), 'Expiratory muscles involved in speech', *J. Physiol.*, vol. 138, p. 17.

DRAPER, M., LADEFOGED, P., and WHITTERIDGE, D. (1959), 'Respiratory muscles in speech', *J. Speech Hearing Res.*, vol. 12, p. 1.

FISCHER-JØRGENSEN, E. (1954), 'Acoustic analysis of stop consonants', *Miscellanea Phonetica II*, p. 42.

HALLE, M., HUGHES, G., and RADLEY, J. (1957), 'Acoustic properties of stop consonants', *J. acoust. Soc. Amer.*, vol. 29, p. 107. Excerpt reprinted here, pp. 162–76.

HARRIS, K. (1956), 'Some acoustic cues for the fricative consonants', *Quarterly Progress Report*, Haskins Laboratories, New York.

HARRIS, K. (1958), 'Cues for the discrimination of American English fricatives in spoken syllables', *Language and Speech*, vol. 1, p. 1. Reprinted here, pp. 284–97.

HUGHES, G., and HALLE, M. (1956), 'Spectral properties of fricative consonants', *J. acoust. Soc. Amer.*, vol. 28, p. 303. Excerpt reprinted here, pp. 151–61.

LADEFOGED, P. (1957), 'Use of palatography', *JSHD*, vol. 22, p. 764.

LADEFOGED, P., DRAPER, M., and WHITTERIDGE, D. (1958), 'Syllables and stress', *Miscellanea Phonetica III*, p. 1.

LAWRENCE, W. (1953), 'The synthesis of signals having a low information rate', W. Jackson (ed.), *Communication Theory*, Butterworth, p. 460. Reprinted here, pp. 208–18.

LIBERMAN, A., DELATTRE, P. C., and COOPER, F. (1952), 'The role of selected stimulus variables in the perception of the unvoiced stop consonants', *Amer. J. Psychol.*, vol. 65, pp. 497–516.

LIBERMAN, A., DELATTRE, P. C., COOPER, F., and GERSTMAN, L. J. (1954), 'The role of consonant–vowel transitions in the perception of the stop and nasal consonants', *Psychol. Mongr.*, vol. 68, no. 8. Reprinted here, pp. 315–31.

MEYER-EPPLER, W. (1953), 'Untersuchungen zur Schallstruktur der stimmhaften und stimmlosen Geräuschlaute', *Z. Phonet. USW*, vol. 7, p. 89.

SCHATZ, C. (1954), 'The role of context in the perception of stops', *Language*, vol. 30, p. 47.

STREVENS, P. (1958a), 'The performance of "PAT", the six-parameter speech synthesiser designed by W. Lawrence', *Revista do Laboratório de Fonética Experimental, Coimbra*, vol. 4, p. 5.

STREVENS, P. (1958b), 'Edinburgh's artificial talking machine', *University of Edinburgh Gazette*, vol. 20, p. 4.

STREVENS, P., and ANTHONY, J. (1958), 'The performance of a six-parameter speech synthesizer', *Proceedings of the 8th International Congress of Linguists* (Oslo), p. 214.

WAY, R. (1957), *The Articulation of Certain 'Alveolar' Plosives*, Dissertation for University of Edinburgh Diploma in Phonetics, 1957 (unpublished).

9 George W. Hughes and Morris Halle

Spectral Properties of Fricative Consonants[1]

Excerpt from George W. Hughes and Morris Halle, 'Spectral properties of fricative consonants', *Journal of the Acoustical Society of America*, vol. 28 (1956), pp. 303–10.

Standard English has the following fricative consonants: /f/ as in 'leaf', /s/ as in 'lease', /ʃ/ as in 'leash', /v/ as in 'leave', /z/ as in 'Lee's', /ʒ/ as in 'rouge', /θ/ as in 'teeth', and /ð/ as in 'seethe'. These consonants can normally be distinguished by English speakers in identical phonetic contexts, regardless of whether these contexts are meaningful utterances of English or are nonsense syllables. It follows, therefore, that the cues on which this differentiation is based can only reside in the acoustical stimulus. The purpose of our investigation was to establish what cues are contained in the spectra of the fricative portions taken in isolation.[2] We have investigated in detail all but /θ/ and /ð/, since we believe that a solution of this problem will come only after the mechanism involved in their production is more fully understood. A few sample spectra of these two fricatives are given in Figure 1.

Procedure

A master tape was prepared by recording a number of English speakers, both male and female, reading a list of isolated words. The list was so designed as to place all fricatives in contexts before and after the major classes of vowels. Tape loops containing one word each were recorded from the master tape. Care was taken to ensure a high signal-to-noise ratio and a wide frequency response.

The fricative portion of a syllable or word can be easily located and isolated by observing the oscilloscope trace, examples of which are shown in Plate 40. For our purposes we had to be able to select a segment of any length at any specified time in the sample. In order to do this we recorded

1. This work was supported in part by the Army (Signal Corps), the Air Force (Office of Scientific Research, Air Research and Development Command), and the Navy (Office of Naval Research).
2. Available evidence indicates that the primary cues are contained in the fricative portion; see Harris (1954), where it is shown that except for the differentiation between [f] and [θ] the transitions of the formants in the adjacent vowels contribute little towards the identification of the fricatives. For a summary of the literature on fricatives see Tarnoczy (1954).

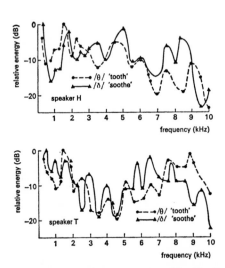

Figure 1 Energy density spectra of the fricatives /θ/ and /ð/

on the loops just before the sample a 10 kHz, tone, which was used to trigger an electronically controlled gate whose position and duration could be separately and accurately adjusted. The gate control circuits were such that the gate position settings could be noted down and the same segment reproduced to within ±2 to 3 ms for any number of measurements. This method was adequate, for when measurements of some sounds were repeated several months after the initial study, the two sets of data showed no significant discrepancies. The bottom part of Plate 40 shows how the gate was adjusted in a typical case. All spectral data on fricatives were taken with a gate length of 50 ms.

Energy density spectra of the gated fricative segments were measured by means of a fixed band-width filter whose center frequency was continuously variable over the range from 300 to 10 000 Hz. A Hewlett Packard wave analyser modified to have a band width of approximately 150 Hz was used.

The output of the wave analyser was amplified, squared or full-wave rectified, integrated, and the resulting d.c. voltage fed to a holding circuit and meter. The meter readings were made to be the same for all settings of the filter frequency by adjusting a precision calibrated attenuator in the amplifier. The relative energy values in dB were taken from the readings of this attenuator. A block diagram of the measurement system is shown in Figure 2. Under this system which ensured a relatively constant input voltage into the squarer or rectifier, fricative segments gave almost identical

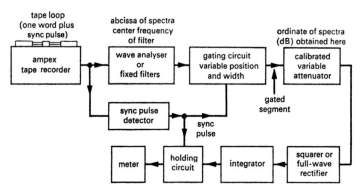

Figure 2

results using either an accurate squaring circuit or a full-wave rectifier. The results reported here were obtained employing the rectifier.

To evaluate the transfer characteristics of the system, the following three checks were made. The Hewlett Packard analyser was set to 2000 Hz, and 50 ms of a recorded 2000 Hz sine wave was gated into it. Plate 41 shows an oscilloscope trace of the input and output wave forms. The rise time of the filter is approximately 5 ms.

Energy density spectra of a 20 ms and a 50 ms portion of a 2000 Hz sine wave were measured using the same procedure as that in the case of the speech sounds. The resultant spectra, which indicate the effects of gating in only a burst of sound as well as the general dynamic range of the measurements, are shown in Figure 3.

Finally, to evaluate the overall input to output frequency characteristics, the output of a white noise generator was recorded on a loop and spectra

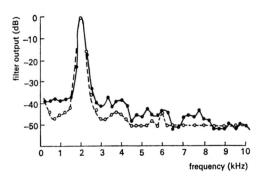

Figure 3

George W. Hughes and Morris Halle 153

obtained using a 50 ms gate width and several gate positions. Each spectrum was flat to within ±2 dB from 300 to 10 000 Hz and the ensemble showed no systematic spectral 'peaks' or 'valleys'.

Results

The spectra presented in Figures 4 to 6 were prepared in the above manner. Although the sounds were recorded as spoken and differed in intensity, each plot of the spectrum was normalized so that its highest peak is represented as 0 dB. The spectra are arranged in the following manner: each of the figures is devoted to spectra obtained from a single speaker. (Speakers H and E are male; speaker T is female.) The top two rows in each figure contain spectra of voiceless fricatives, the bottom two rows, spectra of voiced fricatives. Odd numbered rows contain spectra of fricatives in initial position; even numbered rows, spectra of fricatives in non-initial position. In the left-hand column the fricative is adjacent to a front vowel; in the middle column, to a central vowel; in the right-hand column, to a back vowel.

The discrepancies among the spectra of a given fricative as spoken by different speakers in different contexts are so great as to make the procedure of plotting these spectra on one set of axes a not very illuminating one. On the other hand, the differences among the three classes of fricatives (labial, dental, and palatal) are quite consistent, particularly for sounds spoken by a single speaker. To exhibit this consistency in our spectra we adopted the above method of presentation.

In spectra of the fricatives /v/, /z/, and /ʒ/ a very strong component in the region below 700 Hz is often found. In spectra of /f/, /s/, and /ʃ/ this region is never prominent. This strong component is due to the vibration of the vocal cords that often, though not always, occurs during the production of the former sounds, which are commonly known as 'voiced' (cf. spectra of speaker H, Figure 5, who is particularly consistent in producing the voicing component, with the spectra of 'zoom' (speaker E, Figure 4) and 'has' (speaker T, Figure 6), which do not possess this component). It appears, therefore, that the distinction between 'voiced' and 'unvoiced' fricatives is not necessarily made on the basis of a low-frequency component in the spectrum.[3] In the region above 1000 Hz the spectra of 'voiced' fricatives do not differ appreciably from those of the 'unvoiced'.

We now turn our attention to the frequency position of the most prominent energy density maximum (peak) in each spectrum. As a first approximation it may be illuminating to view the peaks as resonances of the effective portion of the vocal tract, i.e. of the portion between the point of

3. See pertinent remarks on this point in Jakobson *et al.* (1952, pp. 26 and 38); and Denes (1955).

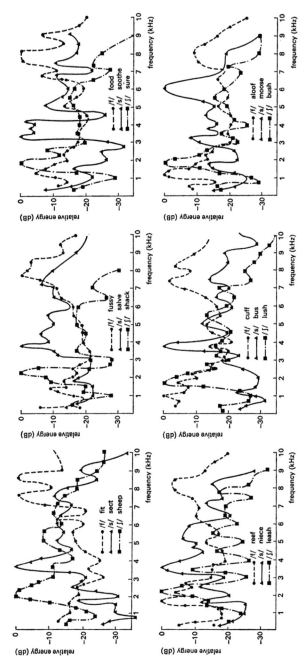

Figure 4 Energy density spectra of fricative consonants spoken by E (male)

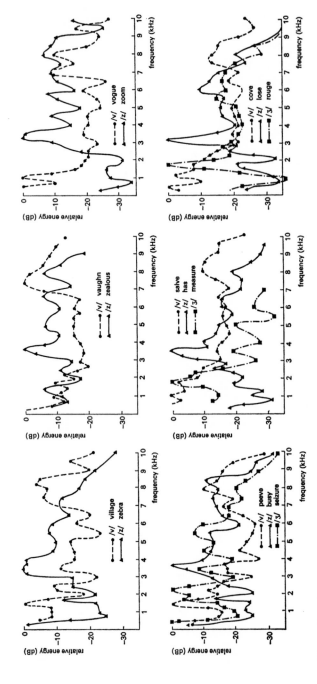

Figure 4 cont.

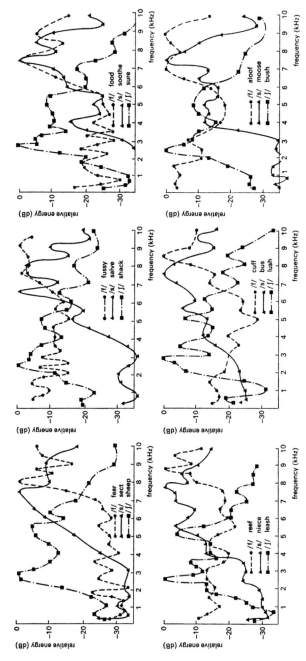

Figure 5 Energy density spectra of fricative consonants spoken by H (male)

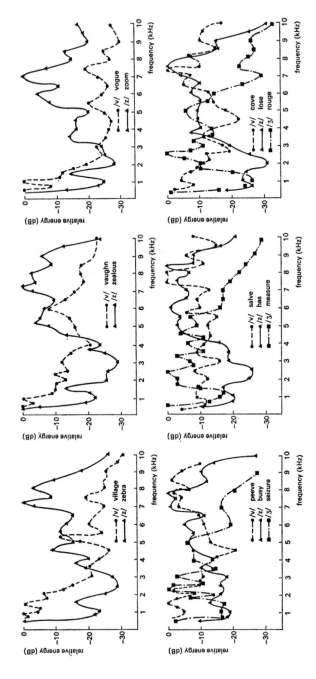

Figure 5 cont.

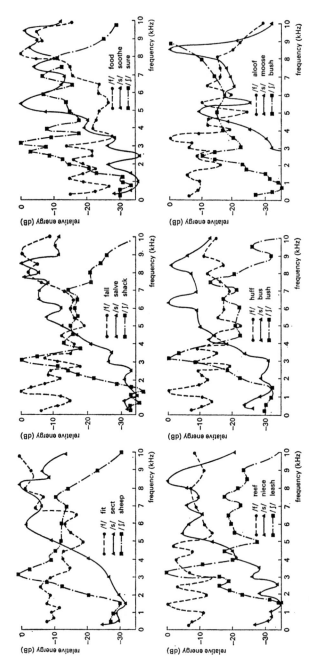

Figure 6 Energy density spectra of fricative consonants spoken by T (female)

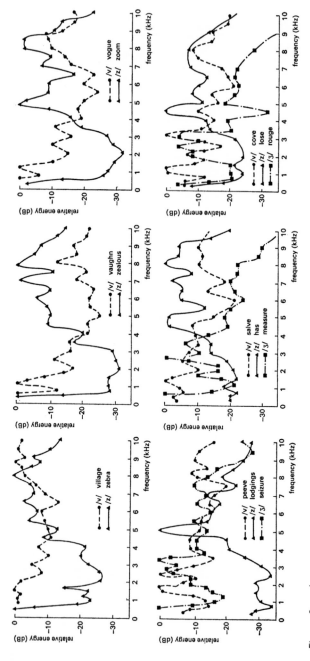

Figure 6 cont.

maximum constriction (point of articulation) and the lips. In such a case we expect an inverse relationship to hold between the length of the effective portion of the vocal tract and the frequency of the peak. Indeed for any single speaker the spectra of /s/ and /z/ have peaks at consistently higher frequency than those of /ʃ/ and /ʒ/. The situation is somewhat more complicated with respect to /f/ and /v/ where the point of articulation lies at the teeth, so that the effective length of the vocal tract is very small. Consequently in some spectra of /f/ and /v/ no high-frequency peak can be observed below 10 kHz. (Cf. the spectrum of 'fussy', in Figure 4 where a very prominent peak is to be seen at about 8000 Hz with that of 'huff' in Figure 6 where no peak is to be seen in the high frequencies.) The low-frequency peaks in spectra of /f/ and /v/ are due to factors which have been neglected in this approximation.

Individual differences in effective cavity length supply also a partial explanation for the overlaps between the peak frequencies of /s/ and /z/ of speaker E and those of /ʃ/ and /ʒ/ of the other speakers; see Figure 4 'zoom', 'lose', 'soothe', 'zebra', with Figure 6 'bush', 'leash', 'seizure'. For any one speaker, however, the order among the peak frequencies of different classes of fricatives is consistently maintained.

References

DENES, P. (1955), 'Effects of duration on the perception of voicing', *J. acoust. Soc. Amer.*, vol. 27, pp. 761–4.

HARRIS, K. S. (1954), 'Cues for the identification of the fricatives of American English', *J. acoust. Soc. Amer.*, vol. 26, p. 952.

JAKOBSON, R., FANT, C. G. M., and HALLE, M. (1952), *Preliminaries to Speech Analysis*, Technical Report no. 13, Acoustics Laboratory, MIT.

TARNOCZY, T. (1954), 'Die akustische struktur der stimmlosen Engelaute', *Acta Linguistica*, vol. 4, pp. 313–49, Budapest.

10 M. Halle, G. W. Hughes and J.-P. A. Radley

Acoustic Properties of Stop Consonants[1]

Excerpt from M. Halle, G. W. Hughes and J.-P. A. Radley, 'Acoustic properties of stop consonants', *Journal of the Acoustical Society of America*, vol. 29 (1957), pp. 107–16.

The stop sounds, /p/, /t/, /k/, /b/, /d/, /g/ are produced by a complex of movements in the vocal tract. With the nasal cavity closed, a rapid closure and/or opening is effected at some point in the oral cavity. Behind the point of closure a pressure is built up which is suddenly released when the closure is released.

During the period of closure the vocal cords may or may not vibrate; if they do, we have a voiced stop; if they do not, we have a voiceless stop. Although in many instances the presence or absence of voicing serves to distinguish /b/, /d/, /g/ from /p/, /t/, /k/, in English, voicing is not crucial to this distinction. The essential difference between these two classes of stops lies in the fact that in the production of the latter more pressure is built up behind the closure than in the production of the former. This difference in pressure results in higher intensity bursts and accounts for the well-known fact that /p/, /t/, /k/ bursts are often followed by an aspiration, which is not present in the case of /b/, /d/, /g/. Differences in the spectra of the bursts of these two classes of stops and in the duration of the preceding vowel can also be observed (see below). Since the role of the vocal-cord vibrations is thus relatively less important, the traditional terms 'voiced' and 'voiceless' seem somewhat inappropriate and will not be used here. Instead we shall refer to /p/, /t/, /k/ as 'tense' and to /b/, /d/, /g/ as 'lax' stops (Jakobson, Fant and Halle, 1952).

The acoustic correlates of the complex of movements involved in the production of stops are rapid changes in the short-time energy spectrum preceded or followed by a fairly long period (of the order of at least several centiseconds) during which there is no energy in all bands above the voicing component (above 300 Hz). This 'silence' is a necessary cue for the perception of a stop sound: if the 'silence' is filled by any other type of sound except voicing, a stop is not perceived.

1. This work was supported in part by the US Army (Signal Corps), the US Air Force (Office of Scientific Research, Air Research and Development Command), the US Navy (Office of Naval Research) and the National Science Foundation.

When the stop is adjacent to a vowel, the movement in the oral cavity to and/or from the closure results in rapid changes in the formant frequencies. These rapid changes in the vowel formants adjacent to a silence are known as *transitions* and they are important cues for the perception of the different classes of stops.[2] The rapid opening of the oral cavity is commonly accompanied by a short burst of noise. The spectral properties of the burst constitute another set of cues for the perception of the different classes of stops.

When a stop sound is adjacent to a vowel, we usually have all three cues: silence, burst and transition, or transition, silence and burst, as in 'tack' in Plate 42. Of these three, however, only the silence is a necessary cue – the silence with either transition or burst is a sufficient cue for identifying a stop. Thus, for example, in words like 'task' (see Plate 42) the identification of the final stop must evidently be attributed to the spectral properties of the stop burst; since the stop is not adjacent to any vowel, there can be no transition cue. On the other hand, in the ordinary pronunciation of words like 'tact' (see Plate 42), there is only a single silence followed by a single burst, although two stops, /k/ and /t/, are perceived. The cue for the stop /k/ must, therefore, be contained in the transitions of the vowel formants preceding the silence.

The objective of the research reported below was to study the burst and transition separately in order to establish ways in which they could be used in a mechanical identification procedure.

Spectral properties of stop bursts

For this phase of the study our corpus consisted of monosyllabic words spoken in isolation by two males and one female. The list of words contained the six stops of English in position before and after the vowels /i/ /ɪ/ /ʌ/ /ɑ/ /u/. In addition, the list contained the voiceless stops

2. Ever since it became clear that vowels are products of the resonances of different configurations of the vocal tract, it has also been obvious that these resonances had to change as the geometrical configuration of the vocal tract changed. Not until the development of the Sonagraph was it possible to follow these changes easily, although single investigators with unusually acute ears, like the Russian phonetician, A. Thomson, drew attention to these changes more than half a century ago. Thomson wrote: 'Depending on the pitch of the proper tone of the mouth cavity [pitch refers to the second formant] in its articulation of the preceding consonant, the vowel often begins considerably higher or lower, and then continuously and rapidly moves to its characteristic pitch on which it is held for a relatively long time. Towards the end, as it approaches the following consonant, the vowel again rapidly rises or drops, depending on the shape of the resonator characteristic of that consonant ... even in the central part of the vowel there is no complete constancy in pitch. The same movement from the characteristic pitch of the preceding consonant to that of the following consonant continues here too' (1905).

in non-vocalic contexts, e.g., in the word 'whisk', as well as words ending in the vowels /i/ /u/ /ɑ/.

Since we propose to study the bursts in isolation, the question might well be raised: Is a listener able to identify stop bursts isolated from their context as /p/, /t/ or /k/? We tried to answer this question by performing the following experiment. Words ending in stops produced with a burst and without vocal-cord vibration ('leap', for example) were selected from the corpus. The first 20 ms of each stop burst was gated out and rerecorded. Care was taken not to introduce any perceptible gating transients. The gated stop bursts were presented to listeners with instructions to judge them as /p/, /t/ or /k/. In the initial experiment, we experienced great difficulty in obtaining a reasonable response from our subjects, but with a certain amount of training it was possible to elicit fairly consistent responses. Our five best subjects gave the following percentages of correct responses: 65, 70, 75, 80 and 96. The last three subjects had had a considerable amount of experience with bursts in isolation; the first two subjects had received only a few minutes of instruction before the test. Since the percentages of correct responses of these five subjects were at least twice the percentages that might be obtained by guessing, we concluded that the bursts in isolation are identifiable as particular stops by listeners.

We hypothesized that the clues that make possible the identification of the bursts as different stops, reside in the spectrum. Consequently, we prepared detailed spectra of the stop bursts of all the words in our corpus. The first 20 ms of each stop burst, or the interval from the onset of the burst to the onset of the vowel – whichever was shorter – was fed into a filter of fixed band width whose center frequency was continuously variable over the range from 250 Hz to 10 000 Hz. For our filter we used a Hewlett Packard 300 A wave analyser modified so that its band width was approximately 150 Hz. The output of the wave analyser was amplified, full-wave rectified and integrated, and the resultant d.c. voltage was fed to a holding circuit and meter.[3] Samples of spectra are shown in Figures 1, 2 and 3.

In examining the spectra, we note that the three classes of stops associated with different points of articulation differ from each other as follows:

/p/ and /b/, the labial stops, have a primary concentration of energy in the low frequencies (500–1500 Hz).

/t/ and /d/, the postdental stops, have either a flat spectrum or one in which the higher frequencies (above 4000 Hz) predominate, aside from an energy concentration in the region of 500 Hz.

/k/ and /g/, the palatal and velar stops, show strong concentrations of energy in intermediate frequency regions (1500–4000 Hz).

3. Hughes and Halle (1956) give a detailed description of measuring procedure and equipment characteristics.

The differences among the various speakers were not very regular or marked. Much greater were the differences in the spectra of tense and lax stops. Since most of our lax stops were pronounced with vocal-cord vibration their spectra contained a strong low-frequency component. This component does not appear in the examples in Figures 1, 2 and 3, because we passed all lax stops through a 300 Hz high-pass filter before measuring them. The lax stops also show a significant drop in level in the high frequencies. This high-frequency loss is a consequence of the lower pressure associated with the production of lax stops and is therefore a crucial cue for this class of stops.

The most striking differences, however, were found in spectra of /k/ and /g/ in position before different vowels. Before front vowels, i.e., vowels having a second formant above 1200–1500 Hz, the spectral peak of the bursts was in the region between 2000 and 4000 Hz; before back vowels (second formant below 1200 Hz) the spectral peaks were at much lower frequencies. These differences are not surprising, since it is well known that in English the phonemes /k/ and /g/ have two distinct contextual variants; one, before front vowels, produced with a closure nearer the front of the vocal cavity, and the other, before back vowels, produced with a closure more to the rear of the oral cavity. In position after vowels these contextual differences were much less marked, which is to be expected since the 'silence' between the end of the vowel and the burst was of the order of 100 ms.

A number of spectra deviated from the norms described above. Two particularly striking examples are given in Figure 4; others can be found in Figures 1, 2 and 3.

In spite of these divergences, the spectra possessed enough uniformity to make possible a statement of criteria that separate the spectra into three classes which are associated with the different points of articulation: First, the intensity in the 700–10 000 Hz and 2700–10 000 Hz bands was measured for all bursts. When the burst possessed significant energy in the upper frequencies, these two values differed little (5 dB for tense stops, 8 dB for lax stops). When there was no significant energy in the higher frequencies, the two measurements differed greatly. As we have remarked, significant energy in the high frequencies is a characteristic of /t/ and /d/ and of the front variants of /k/ and /g/, while /p/ and /b/ and the back variants of /k/ and /g/ are characteristically weak in the high frequencies. We subjected our entire catalog of sounds to these two measurements and obtained correct classifications in 95 per cent of the cases.

This step classified all the sounds into two classes; one, which we shall call the *acute* class, contained /t/, /d/ and the front variants of /k/ and /g/; the other, which we shall call the *grave* class, contained /p/ and /b/ and the

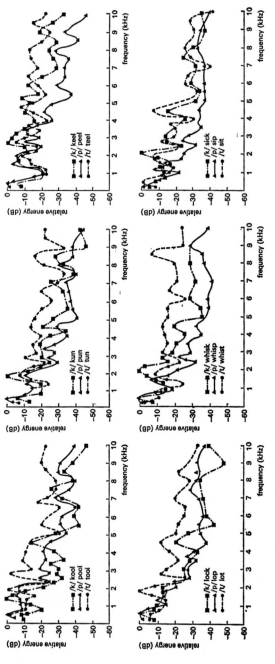

Figure 1 Energy density spectra of stop bursts as spoken by G (male)

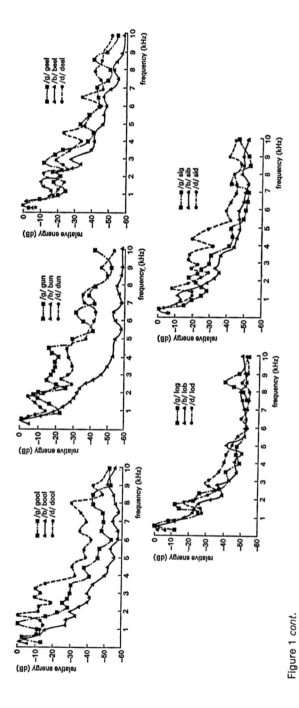

Figure 1 cont.

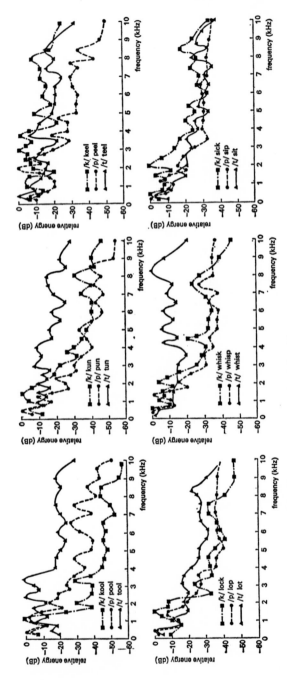

Figure 2 Energy density spectra of stop bursts as spoken by A (male)

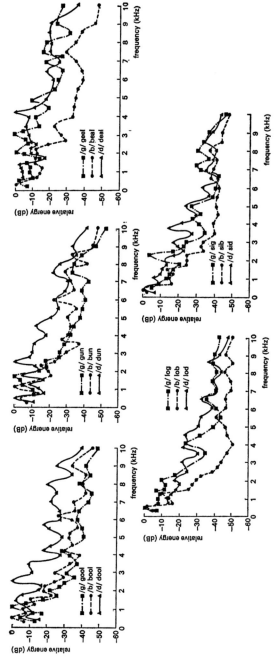

Figure 2 cont.

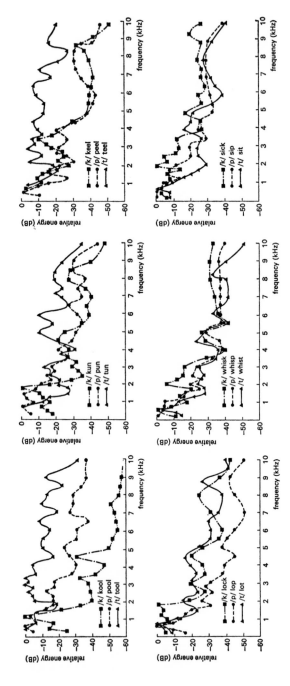

Figure 3 Energy density spectra of stop bursts as spoken by R (female)

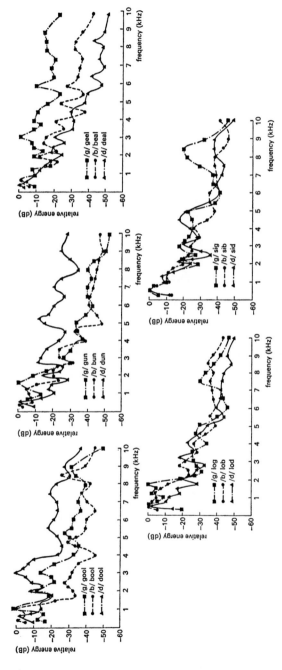

Figure 3 cont.

back variant of /k/ and /g/.[4] Acute /k/ and /g/ variants were rare in final position due to the 'silence' that separates the burst from the preceding vowel. The next task involves subdividing these two classes again into two;

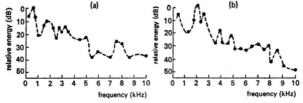

Figure 4 Deviant spectra of stop bursts; (a) for /k/ in 'leak' (G, male) and (b) for /p/ in 'peal' (A, male)

thus obtaining the correct identification of the stops. In order to do this we found it necessary to apply a different procedure for the grave consonants than for the acute.

For the grave consonants, we noted the difference in levels between the two most intense spectral maxima and plotted it as a function of the frequency position of the maximum of highest frequency. Such a plot is shown in Figure 5. By the simple expedient of drawing straight lines across these graphs (the higher line for tense than for lax stops can easily be justified on the grounds of correcting the effects of the high-frequency drop that is characteristic of lax stops), we obtained correct separation of 85 per cent of the tense bursts and approximately 78 per cent of the lax bursts. The only

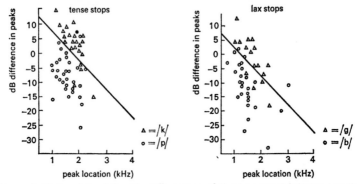

Figure 5 Plots of the intensity differences of the two most intense spectra maxima as a function of the frequency position of the maximum of highest frequency. The straight lines in each plot divide /k/ and /g/ bursts from /p/ and /b/ bursts

4. See Jakobson et al. (1952, pp. 26–36) for an explanation of the terms 'grave' and 'acute'.

really bad cases are the four low /g/s/ in final position. No special significance is to be attached to the shape or the position of the line other than that it separates what we know to be different.

We separated the acute stops into /t/, /d/ and /k/, /g/ by measuring graphically the average level of the spectrum between 300 and 10 000 Hz and comparing it with the average level of the spectrum between 2 kHz and 4 kHz. Since /k/ and /g/ had an energy concentration in the central frequencies, the spectrum level in these frequencies considerably exceeded (5 dB for tense stops, 8 dB for lax stops) the average level of the entire spectrum. These values yielded the correct classification in approximately 85 per cent of the cases. This procedure was very efficient in the case of the tense stops; for the lax stops it was not quite as reliable.[5]

Transitions

The other major class of cue that is important in the identification of the stop consonants is the transitions in the formants of the adjacent vowel. In recent years, a great deal of valuable information concerning this class of cue has been gathered by the researchers at the Haskins Laboratories in their work on the perception of synthetic speech stimuli in which certain features were systematically varied (Liberman, Delattre, Cooper and Gerstman, 1954). The problem, as we saw it, was to determine to what extent the uniformities observed with synthetic stimuli were applicable to natural speech.

We approached this problem from two directions: by studying a large number of spectrograms and attempting to correlate the observed formant transitions with the stop that was uttered by the speaker; and by conducting perceptual tests that were similar to those carried out by the Haskins group except that natural speech was used in place of synthetic stimuli.

Spectrographic studies[6]

For examining the transitions, the principal tool was a Kay Electric Sonagraph. The Sonagraph has certain limitations for a study of this kind, the most serious of which are the restricted range of automatic gain control and the fixed band widths of its analysing filter which make it impossible to obtain clearly defined formants for certain speakers. Nevertheless, in the majority of our samples the presentation was quite satisfactory.

The corpus in this study consisted of words, primarily monosyllables, in which the English vowels /i/ /ɪ/ /e/ /ɛ/ /æ/ /ɑ/ /ʌ/ /ɔ/ /o/ /u/ and /ʊ/ were

5. Attention is drawn to a similar scheme proposed for the identification of Russian stop sounds in Halle (1959).
6. For the material (including more than 500 Sonagrams) on which the following discussion is based, see Radley (1955).

combined with the six stops in initial and final position. The list was read twice by three males and one female whose dialects varied somewhat.

Our first problem, how to define a transition, illustrates well the difficulties that are encountered in the study of natural speech, but can easily be avoided when one has control over the stimulus (Delattre, Liberman and Cooper, 1955). In the Sonagrams, shown in Plate 43, there are a number of stop transitions that differ greatly in duration, rate of change and their terminal (beginning and end) points. In Plate 43a ('take', male speaker R), the final transition is considerably longer than 50 ms. The stop transition cannot be distinguished here from the change in the position of the vowel formants arising from the diphthongal pronunciation of the vowel. In Plate 43b ('tip', male speaker B), the vowel lasts only 100 ms and it is difficult to find any steady-state portion or to decide where the transition begins. In Plate 43c ('keep', male speaker H), the final transitions of the different formants start at different times. Note that here the final $F2$ transition lasts only 20 ms. The initial $F2$ and $F3$ transition can only be discerned with the greatest difficulty even if the aspiration is included with the vowel transition.

All of these difficulties show that it is not easy to decide what segment on a given Sonagram constitutes a transition. Specifically, it is often impossible to identify a transition by examining on a single Sonagram a fixed time interval before or after a silence or by looking for certain rates of change in the formant center frequency or the formant bandwidth.

We find, however, that by looking at sets of Sonagrams of minimally different words, e.g., 'seep', 'seat', 'seek', differences in the formant transitions, if they exist, can be easily pointed out. The transition, like so many other linguistic concepts, must be defined with respect to a set of entities that are otherwise identical.

The regularities that we observed were considerably more complex than the elegant 'locus' rules that summarize the results of the Haskins experiments. We found dependencies not only on the steady-state position of the adjacent vowel, but also on the position of the stop with respect to the vowel (preceding or following), and of the feature tense-lax in both the consonant and the vowel.[7]

The least satisfactory group was that of the tense stops in initial position. For these stops, generalizations are only possible about transitions in the lax vowels /ɪ/, /ʌ/ and /ʊ/ and in the tense vowel /u/. Before /ʌ/, $F2$ and $F3$ have neutral or negative transitions for /p/; $F2$ has a positive transition and

---

7. See Stevens and House (1956). Following common usage, we call a transition 'negative' if its terminal (beginning or end) point is of lower frequency than the steady-state or average position of the formant in the vowel; 'positive' if it is of higher frequency and 'neutral' if it is of the same frequency.

$F3$ has a negative or neutral transition for /t/; and $F2$ and $F3$ converge for /k/. Before /ɪ/, negative transitions in both $F2$ and $F3$ are associated with /p/, neutral or moderately positive transitions in both $F2$ and $F3$ are correlated with /t/, while /k/ is associated with a positive $F2$ and a neutral $F3$ transition, which can be thought of as a case of convergence. Before /ʊ/ and /u/, the $F3$ transition could not be seen in quite a few instances; in those cases in which it was visible it seemed to us to be neutral. $F2$ had positive transitions for /t/ and neutral or slightly negative transitions for both /p/ and /k/, which, however, could not be separated on the basis of their transitions.

In the case of tense stops in final position, the transitions are considerably more uniform. A partial explanation for this may be that imploded stops are quite common in final position. In these cases, the transition cue is not supplemented by a burst cue, as it is in initial position. The transitional cues fall into two classes: after /i/ /ɪ/ /ɛ/ /e/ /æ/ /ɑ/ /ɔ/ /ʌ/ and after the rounded back vowels /u/ /ʊ/ /o/. In the former class /p/ induces a markedly negative transition in $F2$, which is absent for /t/ and /k/. The latter two can be distinguished by noting that /k/ has a convergence of $F2$ and $F3$. In the case of /u/, /ʊ/, /o/ the cue for /t/ is a markedly positive $F2$ transition, which sometimes meets a descending $F3$, while the absence of such an $F2$ transition is the cue for /p/ and /k/, which do not differ significantly from each other.

For lax stops in initial position, /b/ has a more negative or less positive $F2$ and $F3$ transition than /d/ for every vowel except /i/, where the transitions may be similar. As we move along the vowel triangle from /i/ to /u/, /d/ gives progressively more positive $F2$ transitions, in conformity with the results obtained in the Haskins perceptual tests; but it was not possible to specify a 'locus' frequency. Before the front vowels, /i/ /ɪ/ /e/ /ɛ/ /æ/, /g/ has a more positive $F2$ transition than the other two stops, while before the back vowels, /g/ has a less positive transition than /d/. Convergence of $F2$ and $F3$ is common, though not universal, for /g/ transitions, particularly before back vowels.

In the case of the lax stops in final position, the rules are fairly similar to those stated for tense stops in final position. As with /p/, there is the very marked negative transition before /b/ in all vowels except those with the lowest $F2$: /u/ /o/. Again we find something like a 'locus' phenomenon in the behavior of /d/ transitions, which are slightly negative or neutral with vowels having a high second formant and become progressively more positive as $F2$ of the vowels is lower. After front vowels, /g/ has a more positive transition than /d/, and is further distinguished from /d/ by a negative $F3$, thus giving convergence. For the back vowels, however, the $F2$ transition is considerably more positive for /d/ than for /g/. In these instances, /g/ transitions cannot be differentiated consistently from /b/ transitions.

References

DELATTRE, P. C., LIBERMAN, A. M., and COOPER, F. S. (1955), 'Acoustic loci and transitional cues for consonants', *J. acoust. Soc. Amer.*, vol. 27, pp. 769–73. Reprinted here, pp. 273–83.

HALLE, M. (1959), *The Sound Pattern of Russian*, Mouton, The Hague.

HUGHES, G. W., and HALLE, M. (1956), 'Spectral properties of fricative consonants, *J. acoust. Soc. Amer.*, vol. 28, pp. 303–10. Excerpt reprinted here, pp. 151–61.

JAKOBSON, R., FANT, C. G. M., and HALLE, M. (1952), *Preliminaries to Speech Analysis*, Technical Report 13, pp. 36–9, Acoustics Laboratory, MIT.

LIBERMAN, A. M., DELATTRE, P. C., COOPER, F. S., and GERSTMAN, L. J. (1954), 'The role of consonant–vowel transitions in the perception of stop and nasal consonants', *Psychol. Mongr.*, vol. 68, no. 8, pp. 1–13. Reprinted here, pp. 315–31.

RADLEY, J.-P. A. (1955), *The Role of Transitions in the Identification of English Stops*, S. M. Thesis, Department of Electrical Engineering, MIT.

STEVENS, K. N., and HOUSE, A. S. (1956), 'Studies of formant transitions using a vocal tract analog', *J. acoust. Soc. Amer.*, vol. 28, pp. 578–85.

THOMSON. A. I. (1905), 'Fonetiteskie èt judy', *Russ. Filol. Vestnik*, vol. 54, pp. 199–244.

Part Three
Acoustic Cues in Speech

The most important development in acoustic phonetics in recent years has been a dramatic increase in our understanding of the functioning of acoustic cues in speech. Taking in speech requires the recognition of speech sounds which reach our ears and this process of recognition is not essentially different from recognition in other modes, for example the visual mode. When we recognize an object or an acquaintance we believe that we do so because we are 'seeing the same thing again'; in fact it is physically impossible that our eyes should receive exactly the same input on two occasions because there are always differences in the light and in the thing we are looking at. Recognition takes place despite differences in the physical input to our senses and depends upon the capacity of the brain to take note of diagnostic items of information, that is cues. When we recognize an acquaintance we make use of visual cues relating to his height, his build, his gait, his clothes and so on, and in this way we recognize him in a great variety of circumstances. It would not be possible to do this if the brain took equal account of every bit of information which came in through the senses. In speech the physical differences between the various occurrences of the 'same' sound are very much greater than in the case of an acquaintance seen in different lights and different circumstances; they are due to the great number of factors which affect the production of the sound by a single speaker and to the variations introduced by the speech habits of the many speakers who utter the sound. Recognition of speech sounds is possible only because the brain learns to pay attention to a restricted number of acoustic cues and to disregard the very great variability which is inherent in the production of a given sound by different speakers.

The wave-form of a stretch of speech embodies all the acoustic information supplied to the ear and even after acoustic analysis, for example by the sound spectrograph, the bulk of this information remains displayed. Acoustic analysis of itself cannot therefore tell us what cues the brain is making use of when it recognizes a given sound simply because it records too much of the variability of speech; it provides in fact too much information. However, the principal feature of the sound spectrograph is that it has been designed to reduce the variability and to throw into relief as far as possible acoustic similarities between sounds. Its great advantage is that it enables us to examine a mass of acoustic data and to discover, simply by inspection, pattern features which tend to recur with repeated occurrences of the 'same' sound. Almost all of our present knowledge about acoustic cues in speech has its foundation in this type of study.

The first step, therefore, is acoustic analysis, but we should not be justified in concluding that any acoustic feature that tended to recur was employed as a cue for recognition. It is necessary to demonstrate that a particular feature can be and is used by listeners in recognizing a given sound or sound-class. One way of doing this, as was said in the Introduction, is to take natural speech and to subtract from it acoustic information with respect to some dimension of the stimulus, and then to measure the effect of this subtraction on listeners' ability to recognize certain sounds. If this ability is substantially reduced, one can conclude that a cue or cues for the particular recognition are to be found in the information which has been taken away.

The two papers in this section provide examples of two methods by which this subtraction of information is often accomplished. The first is by filtering, that is by reducing or suppressing altogether sound energy in a particular frequency band. The section from Fletcher's book is an account of measurements made in the 1920s to determine the effect of filtering at different points in the frequency range upon the recognition of practically the whole ensemble of English speech sounds. The work was prompted by the need for information about the effect of telephone transmission on the reception of speech. The term *acoustic cue* was not then in use but it is clear that the experiments dealt with cues for speech sounds.

The paper by Miller and Nicely is an account of a very well-known series of experiments in which information is subtracted from speech signals by the introduction of masking noise as well as by the use of filters. The authors take a distinctive feature approach to consonant classification and seek to answer the question whether certain features are vulnerable to particular forms of distortion and noise, so that their experiments also concern acoustic cues for recognition although the term is not used. The paper is one of the first to present confusion matrices in this type of work, that is to say the data record not only the fact that a given sound is not recognized but also the sound for which it is mistaken in particular conditions.

11 Harvey Fletcher

Effects of Filtering and Masking

Excerpt from Harvey Fletcher, *Speech and Hearing in Communication*, Van Nostrand, 1953, pp. 418–423.

The articulation data were analysed to find the effect of filter distortion on each of the speech sounds. The results of this analysis are shown in Figures 1 to 6. These curves indicate that some of the sounds are fairly well localized in a limited frequency range while others seem to have characteristics extending throughout the entire range. For example, the sound /e/ could be recognized correctly 98 per cent of the time when either the range of frequencies above 1700 Hz or the range of those below 1700 Hz was

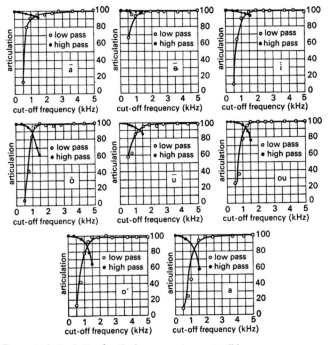

Figure 1 Articulation for the long vowels *v.* cut-off frequency

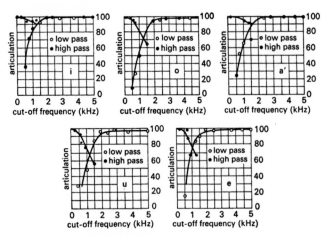

Figure 2 Articulation for the short vowels *v*. cut-off frequency

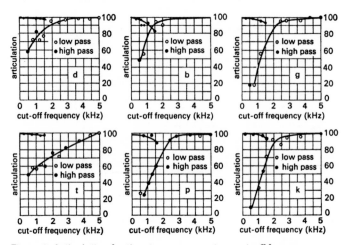

Figure 3 Articulation for the stop consonants *v*. cut-off frequency

used. On the other hand, the sound /s/ was only slightly affected by eliminating frequencies below 1500 Hz, but its characteristics were practically
destroyed by eliminating frequencies above 4000 Hz. The short vowels
/u, o, á, e/ are seen to have important characteristics carried by frequencies
below 1000. More than a 20 per cent error is made in recognizing these
sounds when the frequency components below 1000 are eliminated. On
the other hand, the elimination of frequencies above 2000 Hz for these

sounds produces only slight effects. The long vowels and the diphthong sounds seem to have sufficient distinguishing characteristics in either half of the frequency range to be identified. The intersection point of the curve for these sounds is always above 90 per cent, showing that by using a frequency range on either side of the intersection point, the sounds can be

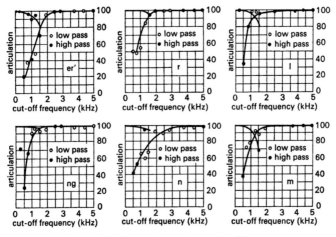

Figure 4 Articulation for the semi-vowels v. cut-off frequency

readily identified. The fricative sounds are seriously affected by the elimination of the high frequencies. The elimination of frequencies above 3000 reduces the articulation of the sound /s/ to 40 per cent, the sound /th/ to 66 per cent, the sound /z/ to 80 per cent, the sound /t/ to 81 per cent, and the sound /f/ to 85 per cent. All other sounds are reduced less than 10 per cent

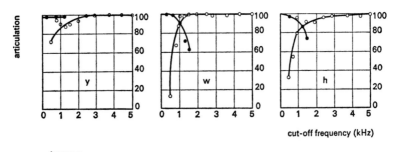

o low pass
• high pass

Figure 5 Articulation for the transitionals v. cut-off frequency

by the elimination of this frequency range. The pure vowels, the diphthongs, and the semi-vowels are affected only a negligible amount by the
elimination of this region. The curves indicate that for the unvoiced stop
consonants the frequencies in the region of 1000 and 3000 Hz are the important ones for carrying the recognition properties. The sound /t/ has a

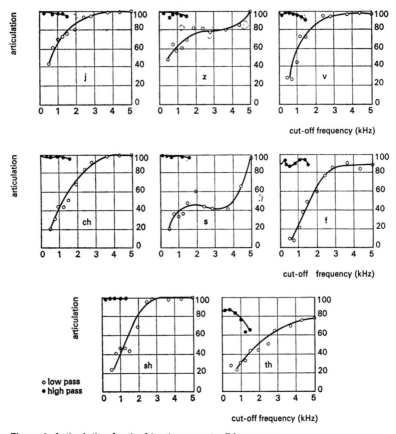

Figure 6 Articulation for the fricatives *v.* cut-off frequency

noticeable characteristic, namely, that the elimination of all sounds below
1500 Hz produces no noticeable effect upon its recognition. It is also the
first one of this group to be affected by the elimination of the high frequencies. The transitional sound /w/ has important characteristics in the
frequency region between 700 and 1500 Hz. The sound /y/ has characteris-

tics similar to the sounds /ĭ/ and /ē/. When all frequencies below 1500 Hz are eliminated, it still has an articulation of 99 per cent.

It must be remembered that in spite of the fact that high articulation values are obtained for these sounds under the distorting conditions

Table 1 Articulation error or the percentage of times the sound is misinterpreted

Speech sound	Key word	Average	Speech sound	Key word	Average
l	look	0·2	g	gold	1·0
ĭ	time	0·2	a	top	1·1
ou	town	0·3	b	ball	1·1
ng	sing	0·3	n	no	1·1
r	red	0·3	ē	team	1·2
z	zest	0·3	h	hat	1·2
ér	term	0·4	sh	ship	1·5
y	you	0·4	á	tap	1·5
ō	tone	0·5	ch	cheap	1·8
d	day	0·5	s	say	1·8
i	tip	0·6	k	keep	1·8
t	ten	0·6	ū	tool	2·2
m	man	0·7	u	took	2·5
j	jump	0·8	p	pay	2·5
o	ton	0·8	e	ten	2·8
ó	talk	0·8	v	view	3·9
w	we	0·9	f	fall	12·7
ā	take	1·0	th	then	17·3

mentioned, the quality of the sound is materially altered, that is, the naturalness is considerably reduced. However, there are some characteristics of the sound which seem to be sufficient to identify it in spite of its greatly altered quality. For example, /ē/ sounds very much like /ū/ when frequencies above 1000 Hz are eliminated, but from the fact that the per cent articulation at this point is over 90 per cent it is evident that some features are still preserved in the low-frequency region for the sound /ē/ that distinguish it from the sound /ū/.

12 George A. Miller and Patricia E. Nicely

An Analysis of Perceptual Confusions Among Some English Consonants

Excerpt from George A. Miller and Patricia E. Nicely, 'An analysis of perceptual confusions among some English consonants', *Journal of the Acoustical Society of America*, vol. 27 (1955), pp. 338–46.

The overall effects of noise and of frequency distortion upon the average intelligibility of human speech are by now rather well understood. One limitation of the existing studies, however, is that results are given almost exclusively in terms of the articulation score, the percentage of the spoken words that the listener hears correctly. By implication, therefore, all of the listener's errors are treated as equivalent and no knowledge of the perceptual confusions is available. The fact is, however, that mistakes are often far from random. A closer look at the problem suggests that we might learn something about speech perception and might even improve communication if we knew what kinds of errors occur and how to avoid the most frequent ones. Such was the reasoning that led to the present study.

Perhaps the major reason that confusion data are not already available is the cost of collecting them. Every phoneme must have a chance to be confused with every other phoneme and that large number of potential confusions must be tested repeatedly until statistically reliable estimates of all the probabilities are obtained. Such data are obtained from testing programs far more extensive than would be required to evaluate some specific system.

In order to reduce the magnitude of the problem to more manageable size, we decided to study a smaller set of phonemes and to explore the potential value of such data within that smaller universe. Since the consonants are notoriously confusable and are quite important for intelligibility, we decided to begin with a comparison of sixteen consonants: /p/, /t/, /k/, /f/, /θ/, /s/, /ʃ/, /b/, /d/, /g/, /v/, /ð/, /z/, /ʒ/, /m/ and /n/. These sixteen make up almost three quarters of the consonants we utter in normal speech and about 40 per cent of all phonemes, vowels included. It was our suspicion that when errors begin to occur in articulation tests, the culprits would usually be found among this set of sixteen phonemes. A further reason for being interested in consonants is that the information-bearing aspects of these sounds are less well understood than is the case for vowels; we hoped to pick up some clues as to what the important features of these phonemes might be.

The major portion of the work to be reported here was done with the aforementioned sixteen consonants. However, a number of other, even smaller, experiments were conducted with subsets of those sixteen. In general, the results of the smaller studies agree with and support the conclusions of the larger study. These results will be introduced into the discussion where appropriate, but the major emphasis will be placed on the sixteen-consonant data.

Experimental procedures

Five female subjects served as talkers and listening crew; when one talked, the other four listened. Since the tests lasted several months, some of the original crew members departed and were replaced; care was taken to train new members adequately before their data were used. The subjects were, with one Canadian exception, citizens of the United States. None had defects of speech or hearing and all were able to pronounce the sixteen nonsense syllables without any noticeable dialect. Since rhythm, intonation and vowel differences were not involved, we have assumed that regional differences in speech habits were not a significant source of variability in the data.

The sixteen consonants were spoken initially before the vowel /a/ (father). The list of 200 nonsense syllables spoken by the talker was prepared in advance so that the probability of each syllable was one in sixteen and so that their order was quite random within the list and from one list to the next. The syllables were spoken at an average rate of one every 2·1 seconds and the listeners were forced to respond – to guess, if necessary – for every syllable. When the speech was near the threshold of hearing, the listeners were kept in synchrony with the talker by a tone that was turned on at fixed intervals. Otherwise, a 2·1 second pause was inserted after every block of five syllables. With four listeners, there were 800 syllable-response events per talker for which confusions could be studied. Pooling the five talkers gives us 4000 observations at each condition tested.

At the completion of each test of 200 syllables, the talker went from the control room back to the rest room and the crew proceeded to tabulate their responses. Each listener had a table showing what syllable was spoken and what syllable she had written in response; each cell of the table represented one of the 256 (16×16) possible syllable-response pairs, and the number entered in that cell was the frequency with which that syllable-response pair occurred. We shall refer to such tables as 'confusion matrices'.

A headrest on the talker's chair ensured that the distance to the WE 633A microphone was constant at 15 inches. The speech 15 inches from the talker's lips was about 60 dB re 0·0002 dyne/cm². The speech voltage was amplified, then filtered (if frequency distortion was to be used), then mixed with noise, then amplified again and presented to the listeners by PDR 8 earphones. In all tests the noise voltage was fixed at −32 dB below one volt across the earphones and the signal-to-noise ratio was varied by changing the gain in the speech channel. A separate amplifier was used to drive a monitoring VU meter with the output of the microphone. The gain to the VU meter was fixed so that the talker could maintain her speech level at a constant value. The talkers did succeed rather well in keeping a constant level; several hundred sample readings of peak deflections gave an average of +0·18 VU with a standard deviation of 1·04. However, it should be noted that with this system, the signal-to-noise ratios are set by the peak deflection of the VU needle and that peak occurs during the vowel. The consonants, which are consistently weaker than the vowel, were actually presented at much less favorable signal-to-noise ratios than such a vowel-to-noise ratio would seem to indicate. It was, therefore, especially important to keep the same speech level for all tests since otherwise the vowel-to-consonant ratio might have changed significantly and the data would not be comparable.

The frequency response of the system was essentially that of the earphones which are reasonably uniform between 200 and 6500 Hz. A low-pass filter at 7000 Hz in the random noise generator ensured that noise voltages could be converted directly to sound pressure levels according to the earphone calibration. A Krohn-Hite 310 A variable band-pass filter was used to introduce frequency distortion into the speech channel; the skirts dropped off at a rate of 24 dB per octave and the cut-off frequency was taken as the frequency 3 dB below the peak in the pass band.

Results

The results of these tests are confusion matrices. Since these matrices represent a considerable investment and since other workers may wish to apply summary statistics differing from those which we have chosen, the complete confusion matrices are presented in Tables 1–17. Data for all listeners and all talkers have been pooled so that 4000 observations are summarized in each matrix; on the average, each syllable was judged 250 times under every test condition.

Tables 1–6 summarize the data obtained when the speech-to-noise ratio was −18, −12, −6, 0, +6 and +12 dB and the band width was 200–6500 Hz. Tables 7–12 summarize the data when the high-pass cut-off was fixed at 200 Hz and the low-pass cut-off was 300, 400, 600, 1200, 2500 and 5000 Hz with a speech-to-noise ratio corresponding to +12 dB for unfiltered speech. Tables 12–17 summarize the data when the low-pass cut-off was fixed at 5000 Hz and the high-pass cut-off was 200, 1000, 2000, 2500, 3000 and 4500 Hz with a speech-to-noise ratio that would have been +12 dB if the speech had not been filtered.

Table 1 Confusion matrix for $S/N = -18$ dB and frequency response of 200–6500 Hz

	p	t	k	f	θ	s	ʃ	b	d	g	v	ð	z	ʒ	m	n
p	14	27	22	23	25	22	14	15	16	7	17	11	12	11	16	12
t	16	26	21	15	15	18	14	7	10	6	17	9	13	11	9	13
k	20	22	24	15	14	29	12	4	11	9	12	10	16	11	17	14
f	27	22	27	23	13	12	10	19	20	14	16	16	15	3	13	18
θ	17	18	18	13	15	21	12	14	20	14	23	6	14	9	12	14
s	18	17	23	11	18	21	17	11	24	15	15	16	11	13	17	5
ʃ	16	20	27	17	13	37	14	10	21	7	20	18	9	8	16	15
b	12	11	24	15	19	15	12	24	20	19	24	12	15	11	18	17
d	16	24	18	13	15	15	14	22	25	21	25	17	18	13	15	25
g	11	20	29	9	18	18	15	26	30	14	18	14	16	20	24	22
v	9	17	18	11	7	12	9	25	14	13	15	15	19	11	12	17
ð	16	11	10	7	6	14	10	20	17	18	15	7	17	12	18	18
z	18	18	15	9	13	19	7	22	14	9	21	12	23	10	22	12
ʒ	8	16	17	14	12	15	7	22	18	8	15	11	15	11	18	13
m	19	24	15	14	14	14	8	14	15	12	13	8	11	6	25	28
n	11	18	20	6	9	18	9	14	14	13	9	8	10	12	33	32

In these tables the syllables that were spoken are indicated by the consonants listed vertically in the first column on the left. The syllables that were written by the listener are indicated horizontally across the top of the table. The number in each cell is the frequency that each stimulus-response pair was observed. The number of correct responses can be obtained by totalling the frequencies along the main diagonal. Row sums would give the frequencies that each syllable was spoken and column sums would give the frequencies that each syllable was written by the listeners.

A generalization of the articulation score

The standard articulation score is obtained from Tables 1–17 by summing the frequencies along the main diagonal and dividing the total by n, the number of observations. Although this score is useful, it tells us nothing about the distribution of errors among the off-diagonal cells. If we wanted to reconstruct an adequate picture of the confusion matrix, we would need other scores to supplement the usual articulation score.

In order to generalize the articulation score, we can combine stimuli (and their corresponding responses) into groups in such a way that confusions within groups are more likely than confusions between groups. Combining stimuli creates a smaller confusion matrix that shows the confusions between groups, and the sum along the diagonal gives a new articulation score for this new, smaller matrix. The new score will be greater than the original score, since all the responses that were originally correct remain so and in addition all the confusions within each group are now considered to be 'correct' in the new score. If the original score, A, is supplemented with such an additional score, A', we would reconstruct the data matrix by spreading the fraction A along the main diagonal. Then $A'-A$ would go off the diagonal but within groups, and $1-A'$ would be distributed off the diagonal between groups. This general strategy can be repeated quite simply if the several groupings used form a monotonic increasing sequence of sets: $A \leqslant A' \leqslant A''$, etc.

A simple example will illustrate this technique. A test was conducted at $S/N = -12$ dB over a 200–6500 Hz channel using six stop consonants in

Table 2 Confusion matrix for $S/N = -12$ dB and frequency response of 200–6500 Hz

	p	t	k	f	θ	s	ʃ	b	d	g	v	ð	z	ʒ	m	n
p	51	53	65	22	19	6	11	2		2	3	3	1	5	8	5
t	64	57	74	20	24	22	14	2	3	1	1	2	1	1	5	1
k	50	42	62	22	18	16	11	4	1	1	1	2			4	2
f	31	22	28	85	34	15	11	3	5		8	8	3		3	
θ	26	22	25	63	45	27	12	6	9	3	11	9	3	2	7	2
s	16	15	16	33	24	53	48	3	5	6	3	1	6	2		1
ʃ	23	32	20	14	27	25	115	1	4	5	3		6	3	4	2
b	4	2	2	18	7	7	1	60	18	18	44	25	14	6	20	10
d	3		1	4	7	4	11	18	48	35	16	24	26	14	9	12
g	3	1	1	1	4	5	7	20	38	29	16	29	29	38	10	9
v		1	1	12	5	4	5	37	20	23	71	16	14	4	14	9
ð		1	4	17	2	3	2	53	31	25	50	33	23	5	13	6
z	6	1	2	2	6	14	8	23	29	27	24	19	40	26	3	6
ʒ	3	2	2	1		6	7	7	30	23	9	7	39	77	5	14
m		1			1	1		11	3	6	8	11		1	109	60
n	1			1		1		2	2	6	7	1	1	9	84	145

Table 3 Confusion matrix for $S/N = -6$ dB and frequency response of 200–6500 Hz

	p	t	k	f	θ	s	ʃ	b	d	g	v	ð	z	ʒ	m	n
p	80	43	64	17	14	6	2	1	1		1	1			2	
t	71	84	55	5	9	3	8	1				1	2		2	3
k	66	76	107	12	8	9	4					1			1	
f	18	12	9	175	48	11	1	7	2	1	2	2				
θ	19	17	16	104	64	32	7	5	4	5	6	4	5			
s	8	5	4	23	39	107	45	4	2	3	1	1	3	2		1
ʃ	1	6	3	4	6	29	195		3							1
b	1			5	4	4		136	10	9	47	16	6	1	5	4
d							8	5	80	45	11	20	20	26	1	
g					2			3	63	66	3	19	37	56		3
v				2		2		48	5	5	145	45	12		4	
ð					6			31	6	17	86	58	21	5	6	4
z					1	1	1	7	20	27	16	28	94	44		1
ʒ								1	26	18	3	8	45	129		2
m	1							4			4	1	3		177	46
n					4			1	5	2		7	1	6	47	163

Table 4 Confusion matrix for $S/N = 0$ dB and frequency response of 200–6500 Hz

	p	t	k	f	θ	s	ʃ	b	d	g	v	ð	z	ʒ	m	n
p	150	38	88	7	13											
t	30	193	28	1												
k	86	45	138	4	1		1									1
f	4	3	5	199	46	4		1				1			1	
θ	11	6	4	85	114	10					2					
s		2	1	5	38	170	10			2						
ʃ		3	3			3	267									
b				7	4			235	4		34	27	1			
d									189	48		4	8	11		
g									74	161		4	8	25		
v				3	1			19		2	177	29	4	1		
ð								7		10	64	105	18			
z									17	23	4	22	132	26		
ʒ									2	3	1	1	9	191		1
m								1							201	6
n												3		1	8	240

Table 5 Confusion matrix for $S/N = +6$ dB and frequency response of 200–6500 Hz

	p	t	k	f	θ	s	ʃ	b	d	g	v	ð	z	ʒ	m	n
p	162	10	55	5	3							1				
t	8	270	14													
k	38	6	171	1												
f	5	1	2	207	57			3				1				
θ	5	1	2	71	142	3						2	2			
s		1		1	7	232	2			1						
ʃ						1	239									
b				1	2			214				31	12			
d									206	14		9	1	2		
g								11	64	194		4	2	1		
v				1	1			14		2	205	39	5			1
ð								2		4	55	179	22	2		
z									3	10	2	20	198	3		
ʒ									3	4			2	215		
m															217	3
n									1						2	285

Table 6 Confusion matrix for $S/N = +12$ dB and frequency response of 200–6500 Hz

	p	t	k	f	θ	s	ʃ	b	d	g	v	ð	z	ʒ	m	n
p	240		41	2	1											
t	1	252	1	1						1						
k	18	3	219													
f				225	24			5			2					
θ	9		1	69	185			3				1				
s						232										
ʃ							236									
b					1			242				24	12	1		
d									213	22				1		
g					1				33	203			3			
v								6			171	30			1	
ð					1			1		3	22	208	4			1
z									2	4	1	7	238			
ʒ														244		
m												1			274	1
n																252

Table 7 Confusion matrix for $S/N = +12$ dB and frequency response of 200–300 Hz

	p	t	k	f	θ	s	ʃ	b	d	g	v	ð	z	ʒ	m	n
p	47	61	68	15	11	17	9	3	3	1		1	2	2	3	1
t	59	63	64	19	15	14	13	3	4	1		5	2	2	2	2
k	37	47	56	10	13	15	10	1	2	1		2		1		1
f	21	29	21	38	37	47	19	2	2	1		2	2	3	3	1
θ	13	23	25	23	39	54	39	2	2	1		5	1		4	5
s	16	25	10	29	52	65	34	1	4	2	4	5	1	1	1	2
ʃ	15	33	23	18	28	70	41	1	1			7	3	1	1	2
b		1	1	8	8	5	3	98	28	17	38	19	9	2	8	7
d	1		1	11	7	12	5	70	84	33	12	10	24	9	1	
g	4	1	2	7	5	13	8	56	74	33	13	15	21	13	6	1
v		2	1	1	2	1	1	44	34	18	77	34	36	14	2	1
ð	1				3		1	22	16	19	45	46	45	23	11	8
z	2	3	2	2	4	3	2	15	15	20	46	35	64	21	2	
ʒ	1	1		1	2		1	11	15	24	54	42	70	39	2	5
m			1	1	2	2		1	3	3	4	5	1	4	161	60
n	1	3	2	1	1	1	2	1	3	2	2	4	2	2	133	108

Table 8 Confusion matrix for $S/N = +12$ dB and frequency response of 200–400 Hz

	p	t	k	f	θ	s	ʃ	b	d	g	v	ð	z	ʒ	m	n
p	72	68	90	20	15	4	1	2	4	1		1				2
t	73	72	74	20	8	6	3	1	2	2		2	1			
k	63	74	127	9	7	5	2			1		1	1	1		1
f	7	7	10	63	69	41	8	3	1	1	1	3		1	1	
θ	5	8	11	60	85	45	14	2	4	2	6	5	1			
s	1	6	5	19	49	125	60	5	2	1	2	9	4			
ʃ	2	6	8	8	22	69	89	2	4	1		3	5	1		
b		1	1	19	14	5		134	20	13	14	11	4	1	2	1
d			2		1	6	4	19	120	23	2	3	11	3		2
g			2	1		5	1	11	116	59	8	7	11	4	1	2
v		1		1	1	2		25	4	8	111	55	18	2	2	2
ð		1	1	6	5	1		43	16	15	75	66	23	11	1	4
z	2		2	1	5	5	2	21	20	17	18	33	91	25	1	1
ʒ						4	2	1	27	29	11	16	83	78	1	
m								12	3		1				219	57
n						1	1	12	3	1	1	2			99	120

Table 9 Confusion matrix for $S/N = +12$ dB and frequency response of 200–600 Hz.

	p	t	k	f	θ	s	ʃ	b	d	g	v	ð	z	ʒ	m	n
p	115	43	70	10	3	2							1			
t	69	63	71	4	4								1			
k	59	49	134	4	1						1					
f	2	3	2	126	89	11	1	2			1	8	1		1	1
θ	2	1	1	103	97	35	7	2	1		5	1				1
s	3	3		34	88	93	26	4	1			7		1		
ʃ	3	6	12	7	31	98	87	1	2	1	2	1	1			
b			1	10	5	1		201	13		13	4				
d		1		1	1	6	1	29	169	39	3	3	6	5		
g				1		7		12	99	97		4	8	11		1
v				5	2			14	1	2	141	57	9	4	1	
ð								10	6	10	109	90	31	7	1	
z						1	2	3	15	30	17	42	116	22		
ʒ			1				1		10	21	8	17	110	116		
m					1								1		215	39
n				1											119	120

Table 10 Confusion matrix for $S/N = +12$ dB and frequency response of 200–1200 Hz

	p	t	k	f	θ	s	ʃ	b	d	g	v	ð	z	ʒ	m	n
p	165	46	31	3	1								1			
t	91	83	68	4	1	2		1				2				
k	48	55	147	2	3							1				
f	16	4	3	146	60	3	2	11			1	2				
θ	4	3		109	76	17	2	12	1			2	1	1		
s	2	1	1	43	83	83	11	3		1	1	7				
ʃ	1	6	2	12	41	86	90		6	4		4				
b				14	5			223	4		5	1				
d	1			1		3	4	4	173	37		2	1	2		
g	1				1				102	107	1	2	7	7		
v	2	2		2	1			23	1	2	163	62	14	3	1	
ð				1		3	2	27	6	32	87	107	36	7		
z	1							4	12	48	10	15	114	39		1
ʒ							1	3		35	1	16	60	134	2	
m	1											1			229	9
n															5	247

Table 11 Confusion matrix for $S/N = +12$ dB and frequency response of 200–2500 Hz

	p	t	k	f	θ	s	ʃ	b	d	g	v	ð	z	ʒ	m	n
p	215	29	26	5	1											
t	74	91	47													
k	15	16	201													
f	6		1	186	31	2		3					7			
θ	1	5	1	93	81	25	1	1			2	2	4			
s	1	3	1	31	78	142	9	1		1			5			
ʃ		1	1			23	210			1						
b				11	6	1		206	4		11	1				
d							1	1	217	30			1			6
g				2		1	1	1	54	169			1			3
v				1	2	1		36		1	178	39	9		1	
ð				3	6	2		14		17	58	146	45	1		
z						2		17		40	7	24	122	20		
ʒ				1				5		9			11	265		
m															242	18
n															2	242

Table 12 Confusion matrix for $S/N = +12$ dB and frequency response of 200–5000 Hz

	p	t	k	f	θ	s	ʃ	b	d	g	v	ð	z	ʒ	m	n
p	228	7	7	1		1										
t		236	8													
k	26	5	213													
f	6	1	1	194	35			3			1	3				
θ		2	2	96	146	2		2	1		1	8				
s		2		1	31	204	1	1	9	4		7				
ʃ						1	243									
b				13	12			207	2	3	19	8			3	
d									240	9						3
g								1	41	199					2	1
v				3	3			20		2	182	47	2		1	
ð					7			10	3	22	49	170	19			
z					1			3	8	24	2	22	145	3		
ʒ							1			2			13	264		
m															213	11
n																248

Table 13 Confusion matrix for $S/N = +12$ dB and frequency response of 1000–5000 Hz

	p	t	k	f	θ	s	ʃ	b	d	g	v	ð	z	ʒ	m	n
p	179	9	44	6	3					2	1					
t		272	3					1								
k	15	1	227					1	1		2					1
f	12	1		162	28	3	1	34			6		1		4	
θ	8	2	7	39	125	13	2	6	2	1	4	19	3		1	
s				3	28	200		2	1	1	4	6	9	1		1
ʃ						1	221							2		
b	2			9	10	1		130		6	74	24			16	
d		2					1		195	35	6	2	2	8		5
g				2					48	151		3	4	5		11
v	1			28	8			48	1	3	145	33	3		17	1
ð	1			1	14			8	11	12	31	116	26	5	21	6
z		1			2	24	2	1	19	7	3	31	163	4	2	1
ʒ				1			20				2	2		207		
m	3		2	5	4	1		10			6				224	1
n			1	1	1			1	8	4	2	1	1	1		207

Table 14 Confusion matrix for $S/N = +12$ dB and frequency response of 2000–5000 Hz

	p	t	k	f	θ	s	ʃ	b	d	g	v	ð	z	ʒ	m	n
p	94	32	26	15	6	3	1	10	4	4	13	12	1	5	3	3
t	7	223	3	3	1		3	7	1	1	1	1		5	1	
k	24	25	126	4	7	4	2	3	6	15	1	3	1	2	7	2
f	38	7	19	72	24	5	2	24	3	12	28	11	4	3	12	4
θ	22	7	11	20	63	27		19	8	13	22	26	16		12	10
s	2	9	1	5	23	148		1	4	3	3	4	44	6		8
ʃ	1	1				208		1					1	28		
b	15	5	5	37	12	2		72	7	8	40	30	4		40	7
d	2	6	7		2			4	192	19	4	6	3	2	2	23
g	2	1	3	1	8	4	1	8	44	122	10	6	6	1	3	20
v	17	1	12	13	7		1	39	5	14	42	23	2	4	32	12
ð	5		6	9	20	5		17	16	19	17	64	20	1	36	25
z	3	2	2	5	8	44		5	22	7	1	13	99	5	7	9
ʒ							37			4				199	4	
m	10	4	3	8	7		1	9	5	10	10	16	2		113	26
n	2		2		3	2		1	20	11	3	7	6	3	4	192

Table 15 Confusion matrix for $S/N = +12$ dB and frequency response of 2500–5000 Hz

	p	t	k	f	θ	s	ʃ	b	d	g	v	ð	z	ʒ	m	n
p	69	30	37	26	16	4	4	21	9	18	13	12	9	3	7	10
t	4	164	9	2	2	2		1	4	4	1	2	2		3	
k	20	35	76	9	11	5	6	3	5	25	5	3	15	11	7	4
f	27	8	7	24	28	7	8	15	8	14	34	14	6	2	11	11
θ	15	19	7	20	49	10	8	12	16	16	13	20	10	5	16	16
s	6	8	2	1	19	160	4		16	10	8	11	27	2	7	11
ʃ	1	1	2	1	5	1	204	1				1	2	44		1
b	23	4	10	13	17		2	48	17	17	34	28	10	1	28	12
d	1	7	6	5	4	2	1	1	128	16	8	6	5	13	5	16
g	6	3	16	5	6	5	2	17	39	85	11	13	6	7	6	13
v	22	6	6	26	18	3	3	33	12	9	32	28	7	2	18	7
ð	21	11	9	16	28	4	2	35	14	22	20	44	10	2	24	22
z	4	5	1	2	9	60	5	1	27	21		12	86	6	2	3
ʒ	2	4	2			3	49	1	7	1	2	1	5	167		
m	18	3	7	11	16	8	2	13	16	12	16	21	3	1	68	37
n	8	4	12	7	9	2		10	22	17	13	8	5	4	16	119

Table 16 Confusion matrix for $S/N = +12$ dB and frequency response of 3000–5000 Hz

	p	t	k	f	θ	s	ʃ	b	d	g	v	ð	z	ʒ	m	n
p	31	15	15	15	14	11	6	19	11	8	15	15	5	9	12	19
t	11	184	16	6	5	5		8	9	3	4	2	5	3	6	4
k	15	35	50	7	16	7	2	14	14	24	7	9	8	9	8	7
f	19	12	12	15	19	8	2	25	16	25	15	12	6	2	17	11
θ	15	14	13	13	30	15	3	15	24	12	14	17	10	3	14	20
s	4	4	8	11	8	140	4	7	8	6	6	11	35	7	2	7
ʃ		6	2	3	1	4	177	1	2	2	1	6	1	23	7	
b	17	13	11	25	23	8	1	27	13	19	25	13	5	6	17	13
d	14	23	15	11	11	4	3	15	63	25	14	10	13	6	19	14
g	14	15	17	17	12	8	1	23	39	45	14	10	13	7	17	16
v	19	19	22	18	20	8	10	35	18	16	19	21	7		28	16
ð	19	13	12	12	24	8	6	22	24	15	24	21	10	5	33	16
z	9	21	1	7	17	59	6	6	11	13	10	15	41	4	10	14
ʒ	4	6	1	5	1	11	51	3	3	7	1	10	9	128	7	5
m	16	7	14	11	19	5	4	31	16	17	17	10	10	6	58	19
n	16	7	12	6	16	7	6	14	29	16	13	22	7	4	19	58

Table 17 Confusion matrix for $S/N = +12$ dB and frequency response of 4500–5000 Hz

	p	t	k	f	θ	s	ʃ	b	d	g	v	ð	z	ʒ	m	n
p	26	21	23	16	24	20	4	15	16	14	20	9	10	9	16	9
t	10	141	12	3	4	4	3	5	11	5	7	11	4	5	8	3
k	16	34	25	14	11	13	8	20	20	8	18	13	20	10	12	22
f	9	9	22	18	18	6	6	18	17	9	17	19	9	3	27	13
θ	16	21	25	5	20	10	2	29	23	24	27	28	11	5	16	10
s	8	5	15	7	11	138	7	6	4	11	13	7	34	5	6	7
ʃ	3	3	7	1	1	12	190	1	4	2	2	4	6	26	6	4
b	12	8	23	11	18	13	9	26	14	18	21	14	11	6	16	16
d	24	26	28	16	19	8	4	19	18	19	13	11	6	3	16	14
g	12	16	17	14	21	11	10	12	17	21	18	19	7	10	22	13
v	21	11	17	15	24	12	8	19	15	14	33	23	6	3	23	16
ð	18	19	15	16	20	7	5	24	16	16	22	28	9	11	24	10
z	8	12	8	8	7	64	5	12	10	9	12	17	51	11	6	8
ʒ	5	18	10	8	9	11	57	5	4	5	9	11	15	85	9	7
m	8	13	20	13	15	14	7	18	8	16	16	17	12	2	15	18
n	20	15	15	18	15	7	6	19	20	12	17	15	12	4	21	16

front of the vowel /a/. The confusion matrix for 2000 observations is given in Table 18. There are 882 entries on the main diagonal, so $A = 0.441$. If we group the consonants /pk/, /t/, /b/, and /dg/, there are 1366 correct responses, so $A' = 0.683$. If we again group /ptk/ and /bdg/, there are 1873

Table 18 Confusion matrix at $S/N = -12$ dB with a 200–6500 Hz channel

	p	t	k	b	d	g	Sum
p	117	58	115	14	10	2	316
t	74	101	103	8	4	6	296
k	105	109	153	5	8	4	384
b	13	9	10	217	45	26	320
d	3	4	5	47	200	117	376
g	3	11	8	45	147	94	308
							2000

correct responses, so $A'' = 0.9365$. Now if we wish to reconstruct the matrix from these three articulation scores, we would first divide the 882 correct responses equally among the six diagonal cells, which gives 147 observations per cell. When we add the four cells for /pk/ and /dg/ to the diagonal cells, the count increases from 882 to 1366, so the additional 484 observations must be divided equally among the four additional cells, which gives 121 per cell for /pk/ and /dg/ confusions. When we add the eight remaining cells for the /ptk/ and /bdg/ groups, the count increases from 1366 to 1873, so the additional 507 observations must be divided evenly among those eight cells, which gives 63·4 per cell. The remaining 127 observations are then divided equally among the 18 cells remaining in the lower left and upper right quadrants, which gives 7·1 per cell. In this way the generalized, three-valued articulation score gives a reasonably clear picture of the distribution of errors.

The procedure just described can lead to serious errors if the stimulus frequencies are quite disparate. For example, if one stimulus is presented much more often than any other, it will contribute more to the total number of correct responses and then the equipartition of correct responses among the diagonal cells will be in error. In such cases the original data matrix should first be corrected to the frequencies that would presumably have been obtained if the stimuli had been equally frequent. This correction is made by multiplying the entries in each row by n/kn_i, where n_i is the frequency of occurrence of the ith stimulus ($i = 1, 2, \ldots, k$) in a sample of n observations. Then the 'articulation scores corrected for stimulus frequencies' are calculated for the revised matrix. To reconstruct the data matrix, the corrected frequencies should be partitioned as before and then each row multiplied by kn_i/n in order to remove the correction and regain the original stimulus frequencies. Whenever an experimenter employs some unusual (non-uniform) distribution of stimulus frequencies, this fact should be stated explicitly in order to avoid misinterpretations of the articulation scores so obtained.

Some such generalization of the articulation score seems essential in order to preserve the data on clustering of errors. In our own analysis of the data, however, we have preferred a somewhat more elaborate statistical analysis. We have presented this simpler technique for the reader who feels that the information measures we have employed are too abstract or do not permit a simple reconstruction of the original matrix. Having pointed out this simpler technique, however, we shall make little use of it in the following discussion.

Linguistic features

For many years linguists and phoneticians have classified phonemes according to features of the articulation process used to generate the sounds. These features of speech production are reflected in certain acoustic characteristics which are presumably discriminated by the listener. When we begin to look for reasonable ways to group the stimuli in order to summarize the pattern of confusions, it is natural to turn first to these articulatory features for guidance. In order to describe the sixteen consonants used in this study we adopted the following set of features as a basis for classification.

Voicing. In articulatory terms, the vocal cords do not vibrate when the consonants /ptkfθs/ are produced, and they do vibrate for /bdgvŏzʒmn/. Acoustically, this means that the voiceless consonants are aperiodic or noisy in character, whereas a periodic or line-spectrum component is super-imposed on the noise for voiced consonants. In addition, in English the voiceless consonants seem to be more intense and the voiceless stops have considerable aspiration, a sort of breathy noise between the release of pressure and the beginning of the following vowels, and may be somewhat briefer than the voiced stops. Thus the articulatory difference is reflected in a variety of acoustic differences.

Nasality. To articulate /m/ and /n/ the lips are closed and the pressure is released through the nose by lowering the soft palate at the back of the mouth. The nasal resonance introduced in this way provides an acoustic difference. In addition, /mn/ seem slightly longer in duration than their stop or fricative counterparts and somewhat more intense. Also, the two nasals are the only consonants in this study lacking the aperiodic component of noisiness.

Affrication. If the articulators close completely, the consonant may be a stop or a nasal but if they are brought close together and air is forced between them, the result is a kind of turbulence or friction noise that distinguishes /fθsʃvŏzʒ/ from /ptkbdgmn/. The acoustic turbulence is in contrast to the silence followed by a pop that characterizes the stops and to the periodic, almost vowel-like resonance of the nasals.

Duration. This is the name we have arbitrarily adopted to designate the difference between /sʃzʒ/ and the other twelve consonants. These four consonants are long, intense, high-frequency noises, but in our opinion it is their extra duration that is most effective in setting them apart.

Place of articulation. This feature has to do with where in the mouth the major constriction of the vocal passage occurs. Usually three positions, front, middle, and back, are distinguished, so that we have grouped /pbfvm/ as front, /tdθsŏzn/ as middle, and /kgʃʒ/ as back consonants. Although these three positions are easy to recognize in the production of these sounds, the acoustic consequences of differences in place are most complex. Of the various accounts of the positional feature that have been given, the work done by the Haskins Laboratory seems to provide the best basis for an interpretation of our data (see Liberman, Delattre and Cooper, 1952; Liberman, Delattre, Cooper and Gerstman, 1954). For the voiced stops /bdg/ the most important acoustic clue to position seems to be in the initial portion of the second formant of the vowel /a/ that follows; if this formant frequency rises initially, it is a /b/, but if it falls it is /d/ or /g/. Since the vowel formant is relatively audible, the front /b/ is easily distinguished from the middle /d/ and the back /g/. The latter two positions are much harder to distinguish and probably cannot be differentiated until their aperiodic, noisy components become sufficiently audible so that high-frequency noise can be assigned to middle /d/ and low-frequency noise to

Table 19 Classification of consonants used to analyse confusions

Consonant	Voicing	Nasality	Affrication	Duration	Place
p	0	0	0	0	0
t	0	0	0	0	1
k	0	0	0	0	2
f	0	0	1	0	0
θ	0	0	1	0	1
s	0	0	1	1	1
ʃ	0	0	1	1	2
b	1	0	0	0	0
d	1	0	0	0	1
g	1	0	0	0	2
v	1	0	1	0	0
ð	1	0	1	0	1
z	1	0	1	1	1
ʒ	1	0	1	1	2
m	1	1	0	0	0
n	1	1	0	0	1

back /g/. For the voiceless stops /ptk/, however, the story is different because the transitional portion of the second formant occurs during the period of aspiration, before vocalization has begun, and is correspondingly much harder to hear. The plosive part of the voiceless stops is relatively intense, however, so that the high-frequency noise of middle /t/ distinguishes it from the low-frequency noise of front /p/ and back /k/. The distinction between /p/ and /k/ is slightly harder to hear because it seems to depend upon hearing the aspirated transition into the second vowel resonance. What acoustic representation there is for place of articulation of the fricative sounds is even more obscure. Probably the middle /sz/ are distinguished from the back /ʒ/ on the basis of the high-frequency energy in /sz/. The distinction between front /fv/ and middle /θð/,

George A. Miller and Patricia E. Nicely 199

however, is uncertainly attributable to slight differences in the transition to the following vowel. The distinctions between /f/ and /θ/ and between /v/ and /ð/ are among the most difficult for listeners to hear and it seems likely that in most natural situations the differentiation depends more on verbal context and on visual observation of the talker's lips than it does on

Table 20 Frequencies of correct responses in Tables 1–17

Condition	S/N	Band	All	Voice	Nasal	Frict'n	Durat'n	Place
1	−18	200–6500	313	2286	3200	2032	2600	1439
2	−12	200–6500	1080	3586	3742	2610	3095	1842
3	−6	200–6500	1860	3877	3921	3202	3429	2386
4	0	200–6500	2862	3977	3992	3706	3780	3099
5	6	200–6500	3336	3985	3998	3861	3910	3472
6	12	200–6500	3634	3985	3997	3916	3980	3691
7	12	200–300	1059	3725	3864	2922	2905	1717
8	12	200–400	1631	3801	3939	3402	3388	2088
9	12	200–600	1980	3903	3991	3696	3475	2341
10	12	200–1200	2287	3891	3994	3641	3526	2616
11	12	200–2500	2913	3927	3999	3778	3673	3224
12	12	200–5000	3332	3920	3999	3811	3853	3522
13	12	1000–5000	2924	3735	3861	3566	3801	3476
14	12	2000–5000	2029	3208	3573	3087	3689	2992
15	12	2500–5000	1523	2857	3472	2871	3552	2587
16	12	3000–5000	1087	2527	3283	2601	3390	2227
17	12	4500–5000	851	2283	3276	2463	3260	1927
Random guessing			250	2031	3125	2000	2500	1406

the acoustic difference. In any event, when we summarily assign these consonants into three classes on the basis of 'articulatory position', we are thereby concealing a host of difficult problems. The positional feature is by all odds the most superficial and unsatisfactory of the five features we have employed.

In Table 19 a digital notation is used to summarize the classification of these sixteen consonants on the basis of these five features. From Table 19 it is easy to see in what ways any two of the consonants differ.

Now if we apply the groupings given in Table 19 to the data matrices in Tables 1–17, we can obtain a set of articulation scores, one score for each feature. For example, we can group the voiceless consonants together *versus* the voiced consonants and so estimate the probability that the voicing feature will be perceived correctly – the articulation score for voicing.

The necessary summations for each feature for every table have been made and are given in Table 20.

References

LIBERMAN, A. M., DELATTRE, P. C., and COOPER, F. S. (1952). 'The role of selected stimulus variables in the perception of the unvoiced stop consonants', *Amer. J. Psychol.*, vol. 65, pp. 497–516.

LIBERMAN, A. M., DELATTRE, P. C., COOPER, F. S., and GERSTMAN, L. J. (1954). 'The role of consonant–vowel transitions in the perception of the stop and nasal consonants', *Psychol. Mongr.*, vol. 68, no. 8. Reprinted here, pp 315–31.

Speech Synthesis

As a result of the type of work described in the preceding section we have learned a great deal about the sort of acoustic information that the brain is likely to find important for the recognition of speech sounds. A further step is necessary, however, before we can be precise about any specific cue and its functions since by the use of the subtraction method we do not know how many cues may be contained in what has been taken away from the speech signal nor indeed how many there may be in what is left. To resolve doubts of this kind we need to be able to present to listeners signals which we can be fairly sure carry only one cue and then see what sounds this enables them to recognize reliably. Obviously such sounds for presentation to listeners would represent a drastically simplified version of natural speech and there would be the likelihood that the listeners were unable to consider them as speech at all. In practice what is done is to manufacture speech-like sounds, to select a particular cue dimension as the variable and then to set up a series of stimuli in which variations along this dimension are introduced while all other features of the sound are kept constant. Listeners' responses to the series of stimuli then provide a measure of the efficacy of the cue in recognition.

The production of artificial speech-like sounds is effected by the use of speech synthesizers. These consist basically of electronic circuits capable of generating the appropriate sound outputs and a means of controlling the action of these circuits. Classical work on acoustic cues in speech recognition was done by the research group at Haskins Laboratories and the first of the two synthesizers described here is the machine on which that work was carried out. The principle on which it operates is that of reversing the action of the sound spectrograph; the spectrograph accepts a sound input, analyses it into its components and presents the result as a visible pattern. The Haskins Pattern Playback starts with a visible pattern, which resembles a speech spectrogram in greater or less detail, and converts this into a sound output. Since the pattern which controls the sound output can be made as simple as is required, it is possible to generate speech-like sounds which contain acoustic information which is relevant to only one cue and thus to produce stimuli of the kind mentioned earlier.

The second synthesizer devised and described by Lawrence has also been used for much fundamental work in this field. Whereas the Haskins synthesizer produces sounds by generating and controlling individual harmonics, the Lawrence synthesizer imitates more closely the working of the speech mechanism in providing a source function, a train of pulses analogous to those set up by the vocal folds, and shaping these pulses after the manner of the vocal tract. The control system, like that of the Haskins synthesizer, makes use of a visible pattern.

Most speech synthesis now being done makes use of digital computers. Their use makes the control of synthesized sounds very much more flexible and reliable but does not of course change the essential nature of the work being done since the computer is generally involved only in the control of the synthesis and not in the generation of the sound.

13 Franklin S. Cooper, Alvin M. Liberman and John M. Borst

The Interconversion of Audible and Visible Patterns as a Basis for Research in the Perception of Speech[1]

Excerpt from Franklin S. Cooper, Alvin M. Liberman and John M. Borst, 'The interconversion of audible and visible patterns as a basis for research in the perception of speech', *Proceedings of the National Academy of Sciences*, vol. 37 (1951), pp. 318–22.

In investigating the acoustic aspects of speech it has long been the practice to convert these extremely complex sounds into a visible display, and so to enlist vision as an aid in dealing with a problem which lies largely in the area of auditory perception. Of the various displays which have been used, perhaps the most effective is provided by the sound spectrograph, which has come to be recognized as a valuable research tool for the study of the acoustic correlates of perceived speech (see Potter and Steinberg, 1950; Joos, 1948; Potter, Kopp and Green, 1947). By examining numerous spectrograms of the same sounds, spoken by many persons and in a variety of contexts, an investigator can arrive at a description of the acoustic features common to all of the samples, and in this way make progress toward defining the so-called invariants of speech, that is, the essential information-bearing sound elements on which the listener's identifications critically depend. The investigator can also take account of the variations among spectrograms, and by correlating these with the observed variations in pronunciation, he can begin to sort out the several acoustic features in relation to the several aspects of the perception.

There are, however, many questions about the relation between acoustic stimulus and auditory perception which cannot be answered merely by an inspection of spectrograms, no matter how numerous and varied these may be. For any given unit characteristic of the auditory perception, such as the simple identification of a phoneme, the spectrogram will very often exhibit several features which are distinctive to the eye and the information which can be obtained from the spectrogram is, accordingly, ambiguous. Even when only one feature or pattern is strikingly evident, one cannot be certain about its auditory significance, unless he assumes that those aspects of the spectrogram which appear most prominently on visual examination are, in fact, of greatest importance to the ear. That assump-

1. The research reported here was made possible by funds granted by the Carnegie Corporation of New York. The paper, as read before the Academy of 10 October 1950, employed recordings to illustrate various points in the discussion. Some revision of the text has therefore been necessary.

tion, as we shall try to point out later in this paper, is itself extremely interesting, but it has not been directly tested, nor, indeed, has it always been made fully explicit.

To validate conclusions drawn from visual examination of spectrograms, or, more generally, to determine the stimulus correlates of perceived speech, it will often be necessary to make controlled modifications in the spectrogram, and then to evaluate the effects of those modifications on the sound as heard. For these purposes, we have constructed an instrument, called a pattern playback, which reconverts spectrograms into sound, either in their original form or after modification.

The basic operating principle[2] is quite simple, as shown in Figure 1 (see Cooper, Liberman and Borst, 1949; Vilbig, 1950). The playback scans a spectrogram from left to right along the time axis, using a line of light modulated by a tone wheel at some fifty harmonically related frequencies

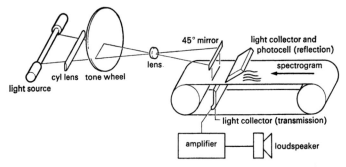

Figure 1 Operating principle of the pattern playback

which match approximately the frequency scale of the spectrogram. Those portions of the modulated light which are selected by the spectrogram – by transmission through a film transparency or by diffuse reflection from a painted design – are collected by an optical system and led to a phototube. Thus the photocurrent, amplified and fed into a loudspeaker, produces sounds which have, at every instant, approximately the frequency components shown on the spectrogram.

For convenience in research the playback is designed to operate from either of two kinds of spectrograms (see Plate 44). In the one case, the spectrogram is a film transparency, and the sound is produced by the light which is transmitted through the relatively transparent portions of the film. These transmission spectrograms, so called, are photographic copies (on film) of an original produced from recorded sound by a spectrograph

2. Potter, R. K., U S Patent no. 2 432 123 (1947).

designed specially for this purpose. The transmission spectrograms are most useful if one wishes to recreate the original sound as accurately as possible, or to make minor changes (especially deletions) in some detail of the spectrogram. In the other case, the playback operates from spectrograms which are drawn with white paint on a transparent plastic base, and the playback uses only the light which is reflected from the painted portions. The drawing is done by brush or pen, and the spectrograms can be prepared or modified in a variety of ways. These spectrograms are most appropriate then, if one wishes to make drastic changes in the sound, or, in the extreme case, to employ entirely synthetic patterns.

In general, the playback appears to be a most useful tool in research involving the experimental manipulation of speech sounds. By comparison with more conventional instruments for modifying the speech stream, the playback method is extremely flexible and convenient, and has the particular advantage that it allows considerable freedom in dealing with the dynamic or constantly varying aspects of speech. This was, indeed, the specific function for which it was designed. It is of course obvious that such a playback will be useful as a research tool only to the extent that it is able to produce intelligible speech which may then be degraded or dissected in various ways.

We have measured the intelligibility of the playback speech produced from transmission spectrograms, using for this purpose twenty standard test sentences, and have found it to be approximately 95 per cent. The intelligibility of reflection spectrograms will obviously depend on how they are drawn. In drawing these spectrograms we have attempted, in a preliminary way, to determine the extent to which they could be simplified without serious loss of intelligibility. The procedure was, first, to copy from an actual spectrogram the features which were most prominent visually, and then, largely on a trial-and-error basis, to make such further changes as were required for reasonable intelligibility. For the degree of schematization shown in Plate 44b, the median intelligibility is about 85 per cent, as determined with twenty test sentences. The experimental procedures and the nature of the simplifications will be reported in detail elsewhere (Cooper, Liberman and Borst, 1950). For present purposes it is important merely to note that the simplified spectrograms are, in general, a reduction of the originals to their most obvious visual patterns. Although the first rough paintings were modified in many details in order to produce these highly simplified spectrograms, the modifications have not destroyed the overall visual resemblance to the originals. To the extent that these similarities remain, and also to the extent that the simplified spectograms are intelligible, these results provide a partial validation of the assumption, referred to earlier, that the spectrogram displays most prominently to the eye those acoustic features which are of greatest importance in auditory perception. If this were not the case, the spectrograph would not be so useful a tool in describing the sounds of speech, and, more significantly for our purposes, the playback would have no special advantage as a means of manipulating speech.

That the playback does have special advantages is indicated by our experience with it, and that fact seems, moreover, to have theoretical implications which deserve examination. It does not appear that the advantage is solely one of stopping time, that is, of converting a transitory sound into a stationary visible display which can be modified and then reconverted into sound for aural evaluation. This is an obvious advantage and an important one in experimenting with speech, but it is neither unique nor quite sufficient. For example, sounds can be represented to the eye by means of an oscillograph, and the oscillogram can be reconverted into sound by a device somewhat like a phonograph, yet the oscillographic representation is virtually useless as a basis for experimenting with the sounds of speech. The critical requirement, and the one which is not adequately met by the oscillogram, is that the display must provide for the eye information which is organized into patterns corresponding to the acoustic patterns on which auditory identifications depend; that is, the conversion must be from patterned acoustic information to patterned visual information. When this is so, the significant aspects of the acoustic pattern become comprehensible to the eye, and the display will have conceptual and also experimental utility in manipulating the sounds of speech. We believe that a reasonable approximation to the required conversion is represented by the spectrograph-playback combination, which interconverts the x and y coordinates of visual space with time and frequency in the acoustic domain (preserving intensity as a parameter in both cases), and that this accounts for the special utility of these instruments as practical research tools.

References

COOPER, F. S., LIBERMAN, A. M., and BORST, J. M. (1949), 'Analysis and synthesis of speech-like sounds', *J. acoust. Soc. Amer.*, vol. 21, p. 461 (abstract).

COOPER, F. S., LIBERMAN, A. M., and BORST, J. M. (1950), 'Preliminary studies of speech produced by a pattern playback', *J. acoust. Soc. Amer.*, vol. 22, p. 678 (abstract).

JOOS, M. (1948), *Acoustic phonetics*, Language Monograph, no. 23, Baltimore.

POTTER, R. K., KOPP, G. A., and GREEN, H. C. (1947), *Visible Speech*, Van Nostrand.

POTTER, R. K., and STEINBERG, J. C. (1950), 'Toward the specification of speech', *J. acoust. Soc. Amer.*, vol. 22, pp. 803–23.

VILBIG, F. (1950), 'An apparatus for speech compression and expansion and for replaying visible speech records', *J. acoust. Soc. Amer.*, vol. 22, pp. 754–61.

14 W. Lawrence

The Synthesis of Speech from Signals Which Have a Low Information Rate

W. Lawrence, 'The synthesis of speech from signals which have a low information rate', in W. Jackson (ed.), *Communication Theory*, Butterworth, 1953, pp. 460–69.

Experimental apparatus has been constructed which enables speech to be synthesized from slowly varying parameters. The parameters specify the resonant frequencies of the vowel cavity system, and the excitation applied to it. The synthetic speech has good intelligibility and the information content of the controlling signals is estimated to be less than one fiftieth of that of normal telephonic speech signals.

The general problem of speech compression

The paper deals with one aspect of the problem of reducing the channel capacity required for the transmission of telephonic speech. It is shown that speech having good intelligibility can be synthesized from signals having an information rate estimated to be no more than a fiftieth of that of a normal telephonic signal.

The paper does not deal with the complementary problem of obtaining these signals from live speech. It is believed, however, that the signals used are all analytically derivable, at any instant, from the past history of the speech waveform, and that this method of signalling linguistic information may ultimately form part of a two-way telephonic system.

Speech generation described in acoustic terms

Speech is caused by the excitation of the vocal cavities with acoustic stimuli. The vocal cavities form a linear system having a number of damped resonances. The excitation is provided by the larynx in the form of a recurrent series of impulsive shocks, and also by turbulent air flow through restricted passages.

Sound is radiated when orifices connect this resonant system to the surrounding air. The radiation draws energy from the system and therefore acts as a load on it.

An analogous electrical generating system

Figure 1 shows an electrical generating system analogous to the acoustic generating system considered above. The excitation is represented by a voltage source. The vocal cavity system is represented by a four-terminal network. The load resistance represents the effect of the radiation of sound, and the current flowing in the load has the waveform of the radiated sound wave.

The source is described by means of a function of time called the driving function. The network is described by means of a system function, which is a mathematical device for expressing the form of the differential equation relating the input voltage to the output current. The sounds that we interpret as intelligible speech can be described in terms of the properties of

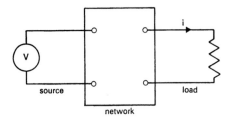

Figure 1 Electrical analogy

these two functions. By considering the properties of each function separately, a greater insight is obtained into the nature of speech. The system function relates to the instantaneous position of the vocal cavities. The driving function describes the means by which they are excited – the 'grunts' and 'puffs' that are the active causes of speech sounds. The two functions are varied by different sets of muscles, responding to different nerve messages from the brain.

If all the ways in which these two functions vary from moment to moment could be signalled, it would be possible to reproduce the speech wave exactly at a distant point. All the possible variations of the functions are not equally significant. A variation is only significant if it produces a difference in the sound wave that the ear can detect. In this paper we shall go farther, and consider as significant only those variations which help the listener to differentiate between sounds that have different linguistic or semantic significance.

The distinction between significant and non-significant variation is the heart of the problem of speech compression. In the next section we shall consider what kinds of variation are possible and which of these are likely to be significant. After this we shall describe the experiments designed to test these conclusions, and give some of the results so far obtained.

The driving function

Only two types of driving function are used in speech making, correspond-ing to the phonetic classification of 'larynx excitation' and 'fricative ex-citation'.

The larynx excitation can be represented by a driving function consisting of a recurrent series of short impulses. It is adequately specified by two parameters, of which one defines its amplitude and the other its recurrence frequency. Other variations, such as the exact shape of the impulse, are believed to be non-significant. We can distinguish two types of amplitude variation; one is a comparatively rapid 'on-off' variation, and the other a slow variation of the maximum. It is the 'on-off' variation that is primarily significant.

The fricative excitation can be represented by a driving function of the type sometimes called 'white noise'. This is defined as a random time function whose instantaneous value has a specified probability distribution, and whose power spectrum is uniform over the band of frequencies con-sidered, in this case the audio frequency range. The only significant variation is its intensity. Other possible variations are the form of its probability distribution, and its spectral weighting. The former is almost certainly non-significant, and the variations of the latter can be considered as variations of the system function.

The system function

The system function defines the response of the vocal cavity system to shock and noise excitation. An acoustic system consisting of a number of coupled cavities can be represented by an analogous electrical network having lumped constants.

The properties of such a system can conveniently be defined in terms of its response to a single unit impulse. If this is known we can also deduce its response to a recurrent series of impulses and to 'white noise'.

The response of linear systems to shock excitation has been extensively studied from the mathematical point of view. Only two types of response are possible, namely, resonant and non-resonant, and only the resonant type will be considered here. The most general type of resonant response may be expressed as the sum of a number of terms having the form

$$Ae^{-at} \cos (\omega t + g) \quad \text{for} \quad t > 0,$$

where $t = 0$ defines the instant of excitation

A = amplitude of the response to unit excitation

a = damping factor

ω = resonant angular frequency

g = phase constant.

The complete description of the system function may involve four or five such terms. Since each of the four parameters of each term may vary during speech, it would seem at first sight that it might be necessary to provide twenty signals to convey the required information.

It does not follow, however, that all these parameters vary significantly. The variations in the phase constant are almost certainly non-significant, as we know that the ear cannot distinguish phase changes of sustained sinusoidal components. The variations in the relative amplitudes of the various resonances are, perhaps, not entirely without significance, but are unlikely to be important, since variations in relative frequency response of an audio system have little effect upon intelligibility. Variations in damping are also unlikely to be significant. The speaker does not consciously control the damping, and it does not in fact vary markedly during speech. Experimental evidence supporting these conclusions will be given below.

This leaves us with the frequency parameters, which are the main information-bearing variables. It is found, moreover, that intelligible speech can be synthesized if only the three most prominent resonances are considered.

The minimum number of significant parameters

From the foregoing argument, it would seem possible that intelligible speech could be synthesized from a knowledge of the time variations of a few simple parameters, specifying properties of the system function and the driving function that vary significantly. The following is a list of the properties whose variation is considered most significant.

System function

1 ⎫
2 ⎬ The frequencies of the three most prominent resonances
3 ⎭

Driving function
4 The amplitude of the larynx excitation
5 The intensity of fricative excitation
6 The frequency of the larynx excitation

Since all these variations occur in speech as a result of actual muscular movements, it seems likely that the signals used in conveying the information will only vary slowly and can be passed over channels having very narrow bandwidth.

The parameters considered as properties of the speech waveform

The parameters have been defined above in relation to the means whereby the speech sounds are produced. It will now be shown that their values can be inferred from a study of the sounds themselves. The instantaneous values of the frequencies of the resonances can be obtained from the representation of speech known as the 'Speech Spectrogram'.[1] The Spectrogram is a two-dimensional plot in which time is measured horizontally and frequency vertically. The density of the marking of any point on the plot is proportional to that part of the sound energy whose frequency lies near the value given by the ordinate of the point, at a time given by the abscissa of the point. The spectrogram reveals that the energy tends to be concentrated at or near a few discrete frequencies, known as formant frequencies, which appear as dark 'bars'.

From the observed frequencies of the bars we can infer the resonant frequencies of the cavity system. It is worth noting, however, that the conceptions are essentially different. The resonance frequency parameters relate to static physical properties of the cavity system, and have definite values whether it is excited or not. The frequencies of the bars, on the other hand, relate to the spectral maxima of actual sound waves.

The instantaneous values of the parameters describing the driving function can be inferred by considering only the 'envelope' or 'instantaneous power' of the speech wave. If this shows a recurrent sharp rise, followed by an exponential fall, then larynx excitation is present, and the time interval between successive rises gives the recurrence frequency. If the envelope has an irregular outline, fricative excitation is present. The amplitude of larynx excitation and the intensity of fricative excitation are given by the mean height of the envelope.

The apprehension of speech by the listener

The distinction between the properties of the driving function and those of the system function is also apparent when we consider the apprehension of speech by the listener. The interpretation of speech proceeds by inference. We hear a certain sound which we identify as speech and assume that it is made by a vocal mechanism similar to that which we use ourselves. We can then infer which of a small number of possible causes were operative to produce the sound heard at a given moment.

The properties of the driving function alone give the timing of word and syllable. They also enable us to distinguish vowels from consonants, and to classify the consonants into broad categories. For example, plosives can be distinguished from fricatives and voiced consonants from unvoiced. Finer shades of difference are established by the properties of the system function which enables us to tell one vowel from another, one voiced fricative from another, and to make other similar distinctions within the main groupings.

1. For a description of the Speech Spectrograph, with numerous examples of Spectrograms, see Potter, Kopp and Green (1947).

The system function gives information relating to the mouth positions, and it is reasonable to suppose that the listener makes these distinctions by inferring, unconsciously, the mouth positions that could have produced the sounds he hears. Mouth positions, and sequences of mouth positions, are indeed closely associated in our minds with linguistic sounds and words. So much is this so, that a reader will sometimes mouth words silently as he reads. Even if he does not, he will find that he can do so if he wishes, with little or no extra mental effort.

The next section of the paper describes apparatus designed to check these arguments experimentally, and also to establish an estimate of the channel capacity required for transmitting the signals.

The experimental approach

To test the validity of the above hypotheses, two instruments have been constructed, called the Speech Generator and the Controller. The Speech Generator produces waveforms similar to those that would be produced by specified driving functions when applied to specified system functions. The parameters specifying the driving function and the system function can be varied by means of signals supplied by the Controller.

The Controller

The signals from the Controller correspond to the nervous messages from the brain of a speaker. Time graphs of the required signal voltages are painted on a glass slide as shown in Figure 2. The length of the time scale is about 1 second.

When the 'operate' button is pressed, signal voltages, varying in the prescribed manner, appear in separate output circuits. This is achieved by placing the slide between a cathode ray oscilloscope and a photo-electric cell, and causing the spot of the oscilloscope to scan the slide.

In the interests of simplicity the Controller has been constructed to give only four simultaneous signals. The first three signals, S_1, S_2 and S_3, are used to specify the three resonant frequencies of the system function. The signal S_4, by means of the scheme shown in Table 1, specifies the properties of the driving function.

Only two values of larynx excitation amplitude (corresponding to ON and OFF) can be signalled and only two values of fricative excitation intensity. Simultaneous larynx and fricative excitation cannot be signalled. These are undesirable limitations imposed in the interests of simplicity.

The Speech Generator

The action of the Speech Generator will be more easily understood if larynx and fricative excitation are considered separately.

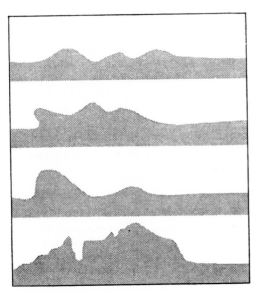

Figure 2 'How d'you do?'

Table 1

Value of S_4 (arbitrary scale 0–10)	Type of driving function
0–3	Off
3–5	Fricative excitation
5–10	Larynx excitation, recurrence frequency proportional to S_4 $S_4 = 5$; recurrence frequency 100 Hz $S_4 = 10$; recurrence frequency 200 Hz

When the signal S_4 exceeds the value 5 a relaxation oscillator is started, having a frequency controlled by the value of S_4. Figure 3a gives the output waveform, and from it the envelope waveform of Figure 3b is generated. A 10 kHz oscillator is modulated by this, producing the waveform Figure 3c, which is passed through a filter to eliminate products of modulation near the harmonics of 10 kHz.

The modulated 10 kHz wave is then heterodyned with a fixed-amplitude variable-frequency oscillator, having a frequency of $(10 + f_1)$ kHz. This produces a difference frequency component as shown at Figure 3d which

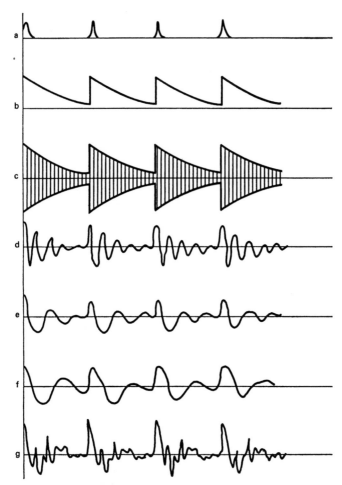

Figure 3 Speech Generator waveforms

has the frequency f_1 and the envelope of Figure 3b. The value of the frequency f_1 is controlled by the signal S_1.

The same modulated 10 kHz wave is heterodyned with two other variable frequency oscillators controlled by S_2 and S_3 to produce two other outputs shown at Figures 3e and 3f. The three outputs are then added together to produce the combined output shown at Figure 3g.

Simple relaxation oscillators of the multi-vibrator type are used for the fixed and variable oscillators. These are easily controlled in frequency from a variable voltage signal. In order that the phase of the output wave may have a fixed relationship to the excitation impulse shown in Figure 3a, all oscillators are stopped for a short interval and re-started in phase at the beginning of each recurrence cycle of the envelope function.

The output corresponding to fricative excitation is synthesized in a somewhat similar manner. It is necessary to produce random signals with energy concentrated near the formant frequencies. This is achieved as follows. A noise source is provided and the noise passed through a weighting network that attenuates frequencies above about 100 Hz progressively. When S_4 lies between 3 and 5, this is applied to a balanced modulator, modulating the 10 kHz fixed frequency oscillator. The output consists of two side bands of noise in the neighbourhood of 10 kHz. When these side bands are heterodyned with the variable frequency fixed amplitude oscillators, difference frequency noise signals are obtained, with energy concentrated in the regions of the spectrum specified by the signals S_1, S_2 and S_3.

Results of tests

Only preliminary results are yet available for report. A small number of short phrases have been synthesized. The intelligibility is fairly good, probably quite adequate for commercial telephony.

It has been found that variations of the relative amplitude of the different resonances do not affect intelligibility even if made during speech. It is found that variations of damping are unimportant. It is also found that the variations in the third resonance frequency do not contribute much to intelligibility, indicating that the use of a fourth resonance parameter is unnecessary.

The information content of the signals

The Speech Generator and the Controller can be used to supply experimental evidence for estimating the channel capacity required for transmitting the signals.

This can be done by supposing that each of the four signals is transmitted by a system of pulse code modulation, with a sampling rate and number of digits just adequate for that signal. The channel capacity for each signal is then given by the product of the number of samples per second and the number of binary digits ('bits') per sample. The total channel capacity in bits per second is the sum of channel capacities required for individual signals.

It is not necessary to make an actual pulse code modulator for this purpose. A quantized version of the slide shown in Figure 2 can be made, as shown in Figure 4. By experimenting with different sizes of rectangles it

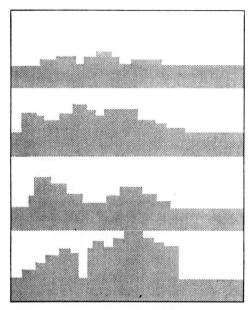

Figure 4 'How d'you do?' (quantized version)

should be possible to arrive at a figure for the permissible loss of detail due to quantizing.

A programme of work along these lines is now in hand. The estimate given in Table 2 is based on preliminary results.

Table 2

S_1	top formant	25 samples/s	2^3 levels $=$	75 bits/s
S_2	middle formant	50 samples/s	2^4 levels $=$	200 bits/s
S_3	bottom formant	25 samples/s	2^3 levels $=$	75 bits/s
S_4	driving function	50 samples/s	2^4 levels $=$	200 bits/s

Total 550 bits/s

This may be compared with straight PCM which requires, say, 8000 samples/s, 2^5 levels, or 40 000 bits/s showing an improvement ratio of over 70:1.

The improvement ratio estimated above can only be translated into a reduction in band-width if we can exchange signal-to-noise ratio for bandwidth on ideal terms. A more realistic basis for comparison, where bandwidth is the criterion, can be made by considering only the number of samples per second required, and assuming that the signal-to-noise ratio is adequate for the required number of levels to be distinguished. On this basis the improvement ratio is about 50: 1, as 150 samples/s are required for synthetic speech in place of 8000 for normal telephony.

Future developments

The experimental work described in this paper is intended to establish that sounds recognizable as speech, and having good intelligibility, can be synthesized from a very small amount of information. Before this knowledge can be made the basis of a telephone communication system a complementary problem must be solved. It will be necessary to invent means for obtaining the information in this form, continuously, from live telephonic speech waveforms. This analysis problem may very well prove much more difficult than the problem of synthesis. The experimental synthesis, however, helps to define the exact type of analysis required, and in this way may be regarded as a logical first step.

In addition to the analysis and synthesis, there is also the problem of combining the signals efficiently into a single signal of the type best suited to the link over which the speech is to be sent.

Acknowledgement is made to the Chief Scientist, Ministry of Supply and to the Controller of H M S O for permission to publish this paper.

References

POTTER, R. K., KOPP, G. A., and GREEN, H. C. (1947), *Visible Speech*, Van Nostrand.

Perceptual Experiments

The papers which make up the next two sections represent the core of the experimental work which has done so much to increase our understanding of the process of speech recognition and of the use of acoustic cues in speech. All that is necessary by way of introduction is to outline once more the steps by which the results are obtained. First a considerable amount of acoustic analysis is necessary in order to discover what acoustic features tend to recur with given sounds or classes of sound and are thus available to the listener as cues for recognition. These observations must of course be quantitative with respect to the relevant dimensions since they are to be the basis for synthesis. Measurements refer to frequency, intensity or time or to some combination of these. The second step is to select a specific cue dimension and the set of sounds to which it may refer. In the papers reprinted here the cue dimensions include formant frequency, formant transitions, frequency of noise and, in the succeeding section, the onset of voicing. Next, stimuli are synthesized which embody a range of variation with respect to the selected cue dimension, the range of values being largely determined by the range of the analytical measurements. Finally the stimuli are presented in random order and repeatedly to subjects who are asked to respond to every stimulus by signalling their recognition of one out of a restricted set of sounds, usually in a forced choice situation.

All of the experiments reported here make use of this basic technique and have yielded significant results. They have shown that the identification of a given sound does not depend on the operation of a single specific cue but rather on the working of a system of cues which parallels in some sense the phonological system. In English the whole set of the plosives plus the affricates is marked off from the rest of the system by the interruption in sound occasioned by the stop. The affricates are distinguished from the plosives by the length of the noise which succeeds the interruption. The voiced plosives are differentiated from the voiceless by the early onset of voicing and by the weak burst of noise which accompanies the release of the stop compared with the strong noise burst in the voiceless sounds. The bi-labial, the alveolar and the velar stops are distinguished from each other by the frequency of the noise burst and by the direction of the second formant transition, though not in a simple manner since the vowel with which the stop is combined may affect both of these cues. The recognition of any one out of the set of plosive consonants may therefore involve the use of some or all of these cues or a particular combination of them depending on the circumstances of speech reception.

There can be no doubt of the very complex nature of the process of speech sound recognition and one direction in which this work is likely to move in the future is towards a closer examination of the interactions which take place between acoustic cues, since it is already clear that they do not for the most part act independently.

15 Pierre C. Delattre, Alvin M. Liberman, Franklin S. Cooper and Louis J. Gerstman

An Experimental Study of the Acoustic Determinants of Vowel Color; Observations on One- and Two-Formant Vowels Synthesized from Spectrographic Patterns

Pierre C. Delattre, Alvin M. Liberman, Franklin S. Cooper and Louis J. Gerstman, 'An experimental study of the acoustic determinants of vowel color; observations on one- and two-formant vowels synthesized from spectrographic patterns', *Word*, vol. 8 (1952), pp. 195–210.

Introduction[1]

This paper will report the results of an attempt to synthesize the sixteen cardinal vowels of the International Phonetic Association[2] by converting hand-painted spectrographic patterns into sound. The conversion from spectrogram to sound is accomplished with a special-purpose instrument (called a pattern playback) which, by making it possible to listen to spectrograms, provides a basis for evaluating the effects of a wide variety of experimental modifications in the acoustic pattern, and thus affords a convenient method for determining the role of various acoustic features in the perception of speech.[3] This method is most appropriate, perhaps, for investigating the dynamic, or constantly varying, aspects of speech sounds; it is not primarily designed, nor is it necessarily ideally suited, for work with steady-state vowels, though it can be used, as it has been in this study, for that purpose. Our interest in producing these steady-state vowels with the pattern playback stemmed from our need for highly simplified, but still identifiable, synthetic vowels which could be used in combination with some of the consonants we were interested in studying.

1. Some of the data of this study have been published in an earlier paper, Delattre, Liberman and Cooper (1951). In that article we were concerned primarily to display the results of our syntheses graphically and to compare that graph with the IPA articulatory charts.
2. The vowels which served as our models were produced by one of the authors, a phonetician whose native language is French. Naturally his conception of the color of the cardinal vowels might differ slightly from that of Daniel Jones whose pronunciation of these vowels on a well-known recording has long served as the standard. However, we should guess that the differences, if any, are very small, since for eleven of the sixteen vowels the IPA offers French vowels as guides to pronunciation. (See *The Principles of the International Phonetic Association*, University College, London. 1949.)
3. Descriptions of the technique and of some of the results obtained with it are to be found in Cooper (1950); Cooper, Liberman and Borst (1951); Liberman, Delattre and Cooper (1952); Cooper, Delattre, Liberman, Borst and Gerstman (1952).

Previous investigations,[4] using various techniques of analysis and synthesis, have suggested that three, two, and, in some cases, one formant might be sufficient to produce all the vowel colors, and have defined, at least within broad limits, the frequency positions which those formants should occupy. In a recent monograph, for example, Joos (1948) reports that he was able to produce reasonable approximations to normal vowel color with no more than two formants, though he hesitates to draw a final conclusion because his work with these synthetic vowels was essentially exploratory. Our own preliminary investigations convinced us that two formants were, indeed, sufficient to produce identifiable vowels. It was clear, however, that much would be gained by trying to find those formant positions which would give the closest approximations to various vowel colors. The attempt to find those positions becomes, then, the primary purpose of this investigation. Taking the sixteen cardinal vowels of the IPA as our standard, we have separately and systematically varied the frequency positions of each formant in synthetic two-formant patterns and then selected from among these many sounds those which formed the best vowels. We have tested the identifiability of the vowels which were finally selected, and we have investigated in a preliminary fashion the effects of variations in the relative intensities of the two formants. On the basis of the results of varying the relative intensities of the two formants, we were led, finally, to experiment with single-formant vowels.

Apparatus and technique for producing the synthetic vowels

The playback with which the vowels of this study were synthesized produces 50 modulated bands of light corresponding in frequency to a fundamental of 120 Hz with its harmonics up to and including the 50th at 6000 Hz. These modulated beams of light are made to scan a spectrogram from left to right along the time dimension, the light being spread across the spectrogram to match the frequency scale of the spectrogram. Painted portions of the spectrogram then act to select the light which is modulated at frequencies corresponding to the position of the painted areas and to reflect this light into a phototube whose current is fed, after amplification, into a loudspeaker. The intensity of the sound can be controlled by altering the width of the painted lines, by using paints of different reflectance, or by placing filters in the path of the light beams.

The playback 'equalizes' the intensities of the sounds it produces by reducing intensity 9 dB per octave in the frequency range above 1500 Hz.

4. Summaries of and references to many of these studies are to be found in Chiba and Kajiyama (1941). More recent studies are described or referred to in Dunn (1950); Peterson and Barney (1952).

This rate of attenuation corresponds roughly to the distribution of energy in normal human speech.

The vowel sounds of this study were synthesized by drawing a spectrographic representation of the desired vowel and then converting the spectrogram into sound. An inspection of spectrograms of spoken vowels reveals, generally, from three to five frequency regions (called *formants*) in which there is a relatively high concentration of acoustic energy. For a male voice pitched at about 120 Hz, the spectrogram typically shows from two to four harmonics within each formant. One also sees that the harmonic nearest the center of the formant is usually more intense than the harmonics on either side. For the synthetic vowels, we have used not more than two formants; in regard to width of formant and to the distribution of energy within the formant, we have tried to make the synthetic vowels correspond rather closely to actual speech. (The width of the formants and the distribution of energy within them, as well as their frequency positions, are shown in Figure 3.)

Although the playback tones are spaced 120 Hz apart, it is possible to achieve the effect of finer gradations of formant frequency, i.e. 10 to 30 Hz, by altering the relative widths of the three contiguous harmonics which comprise the formant, thereby shifting its center of intensity. Wherever we have resorted to this procedure, we have estimated the equivalent frequency of the 'unbalanced' formant on the basis of the relative widths of the lines; otherwise we have given the frequency value corresponding to the middle harmonic.

Procedure for selecting the formant frequencies and the results obtained

We first did a considerable amount of exploratory research to satisfy ourselves that reasonable approximations to the cardinal vowels could, in fact, be synthesized from two-formant hand-painted spectrograms, and to determine how best to set up a series of vowel-like sounds from which the most nearly adequate vowels might be selected. Using the results of this exploratory work as a basis, we then drew two series of two-formant patterns (a total of 235 vowel patterns) which represented a fairly systematic and comprehensive variation in frequency position for each of the formants. In the one set of vowel patterns the frequency of the *lower formant* was fixed in turn at each of four values, while for each of these settings the higher formant was varied in steps of 120 Hz over a rather considerable range; in the other set, the frequency of the *higher formant* was fixed while the frequency of the lower formant was varied in steps of approximately 30 Hz. (As is well known, relatively smaller steps at the low frequencies produce as much difference for the ear as relatively larger steps at the higher frequencies.)

The first set of vowels can be divided into four groups according to the frequency position of the fixed lower formant (formant 1). For the four positions of this formant, we used frequency values corresponding to the four frequency regions into which formant 1 normally falls in French sustained vowels (1: /i y u/, 2: /e ø o/, 3: /ɛ œ ɔ/, 4: /a ɑ/), choosing French vowels for this purpose because of their known similarity to cardinal vowels. Thus, the first part of the first set combined a fixed formant frequency of 250 Hz (which is the position of formant 1 in a French pronunciation of /i/) with a formant 2 which varied from 280 to 3000 Hz in 20 steps of 120 Hz each. We listened to these vowels many times and finally

Table 1 Results of the attempt to find the closest two-formant (synthetic) approximations to the sixteen cardinal vowels of IPA obtained with the first formant fixed at each of four positions (corresponding to /i e ɛ a/ of French) while the second formant varied over the range indicated below[a]

Frequency at which 1st formant was fixed (Hz)	Frequency range within which 2nd formant was varied (Hz)	Vowel approximated	Frequency of second formant which gave best approximation (Hz)
250	480–3000	i	2900
		y	1900
		ɯ	1050
		u	700
360	500–2520	e	2400
		ø	1650
		ɤ	1100
		o	800
510	840–2040	ɛ	2000
		œ	1450
		ʌ	1150
		ɔ	950
720	960–1800	æ	1650
		a	1300
		ɒ	1200
		ɑ	1100

[a]It should be remembered that in order to obtain any frequency which was not an integral multiple of 120 Hz we had to resort to the unbalancing procedure described earlier. The frequency values given here are estimates based on the relative intensities of the harmonics composing the formant.

selected those sounds which, in our judgment, most closely approximated the four cardinal vowels /i y ɯ u/. Because it appeared that the steps of 120 Hz did not permit us to get the very best approximation to the desired vowel, we proceeded, by the method described in the preceding section, to try to improve each vowel by making finer adjustments in the frequency positions of formant 2. Table 1 summarizes the procedures and results obtained with the first set of vowels.

In the second set of experimental vowels we fixed formant 2 at the values given in Table 1 and went on then to vary the frequency of formant 1 (in steps of 30 Hz) over frequency ranges which extended a considerable distance on either side of the fixed frequency we had used in the first set. After much listening to this second set of vowels we concluded that the formant 1 frequencies which gave the best vowels were identical with those

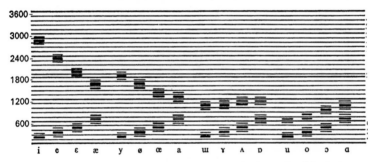

Figure 1 The synthetic approximations to the cardinal vowels of the IPA, showing the precise composition and frequency position of each formant

we had used in the first set of experimental vowels, except for the formant 1 of /æ a ɒ ɑ/. In the first set we had fixed the first formant of these vowels at 720 Hz; after listening to the second set, we decided that better approximations to the vowels /æ a ɒ ɑ/ were obtained when formant 1 was moved up to 750 Hz.

In Figure 1 are shown the synthetic spectrograms which, when converted into sound, most closely match the sixteen cardinal vowels. Figure 2 shows the position of each of these synthetic vowels in a two-dimensional space in which the Y-axis gives the frequency of the first formant and the X-axis the frequency of the second formant.[5] To make this acoustic plot

5. A disk recording of the synthetic vowels described here is available. This recording includes the synthetic vowels that were selected finally as the closest approximations to the sixteen cardinal vowels and separately the series of 235 experimental vowels from which the selection was made. The disk can be obtained, at cost, by writing to The Haskins Laboratories, 270 Crown Street, New Haven, Conn. 06510.

Pierre C. Delattre, *et al.* 225

resemble more closely the familiar vowel quadrilateral (whose coordinates have an articulatory reference), we have reversed the usual order of the frequency scales on both the vertical and horizontal axes and have made the frequency scales logarithmic. (For a detailed comparison of articulatory and acoustic vowel charts, see Joos, 1948, pp. 49–59.) It should be noted

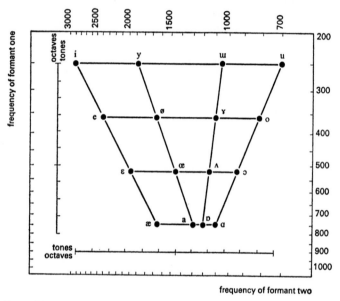

Figure 2

that these results were obtained with sounds having a fundamental frequency of 120 Hz; no attempt has been made in this study to determine what adjustments in formant-frequency positions might be needed for other values of the fundamental.

To test the identifiability of our synthetic vowels we arranged the final group of sixteen sounds in three test formats and presented them to students in phonetics for judgment. Test A included the entire group of sixteen cardinal vowels /i e ɛ æ y ø œ a ɯ ʏ ʌ ɒ u o ɔ ɑ/; Test B consisted of the ten vowels (out of the group of sixteen) which are to be found in French /i e ɛ y ø œ u o ɔ a/; and Test C contained the seven 'outside' vowels /i e ɛ a ɔ o u/, a group of sounds which should be reasonably familiar to speakers of English. For each test the vowels were first presented in quick succession, and identified, in order to familiarize the subject with the total range of vowel-like sounds which were to be included in the test. The synthetic patterns were then presented in random order (at the rate of one every four seconds) for identification by the subjects. The tests were presented to eleven subjects in the order A, B, C, and then, a second time, in reverse order. Five additional subjects took Tests B and C. Most of the subjects had English as a native language, but were studying phonetics and French.

In Figures 3, 4 and 5, we see the formant positions of the synthetic vowels, plotted as in Figure 2, and in the circles corresponding to the location of the vowels are values which summarize the results of the tests.

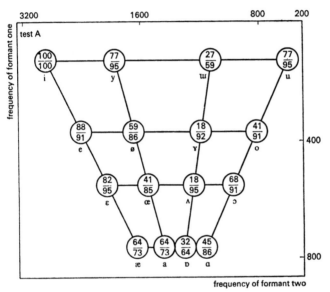

Figure 3 The accuracy of listeners' identifications of the sixteen synthetic vowels

The upper number in each circle is simply the percentage of times the synthetic vowel was judged correctly. The lower number is a composite score, made up of the percentage of correct identifications plus the percentages of identifications which were incorrect by not more than one 'step' on the vowel chart, e.g. an /æ/ identified as /ɛ œ a/ is counted as a one-step error.

It is apparent that in Test C the accuracy of judgment was quite high, and, except for 6 per cent of the judgments of /u/, such errors as did occur were never more than confusions with the nearest neighboring vowel. The percentage of correct identifications is somewhat lower in Test B and lower

Pierre C. Delattre, et al. 227

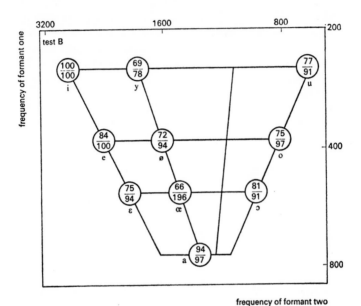

Figure 4 The accuracy of listeners' identifications of the ten synthetic vowels that have analogues in French

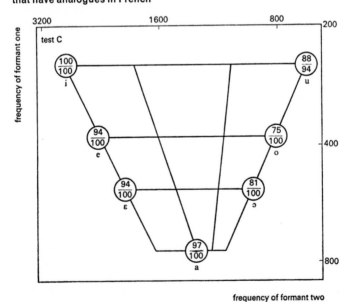

Figure 5 The accuracy of listeners' identifications of seven of the 'outside' synthetic vowels

still in Test A, a result which may quite safely be attributed to the differences among the tests in the number of stimuli to be identified, and to the fact that Tests A and B – particularly Test A – contain vowel sounds /ø œ ɯ ɣ/ with which our subjects are not very familiar.[6]

It is also to be seen in Figures 3, 4 and 5, that the vowels differed greatly among themselves in identifiability. In Test A, for example, /i/ was judged correctly 100 per cent of the time while /ɣ/ and /ʌ/ were called correctly in only 18 per cent of the judgments. These differences are explicable, perhaps, in terms of the differential familiarity of the vowels and, also, by the positions of the vowels in the vowel chart. In general, those vowels which occur in English were identified with fewer errors than those which do not, e.g. /ɯ/ and /ɣ/, which occur in none of the Latin or Germanic languages and which were unknown to our subjects until the time of the test, were identified most poorly of all. We note, also, some evidence that a familiar vowel at the outside edges of the chart will be identified more easily than an equally familiar vowel which has its locus in the inside quadrilateral, e.g. /ʌ/ was identified less accurately than /ɔ/. If we assume that distances on our vowel charts (Figures 2, 3, 4 and 5) correspond, however roughly, to perceived similarities, we may suppose that the 'outside' vowels, having fewer neighboring vowels with which to be confused, are at an advantage by comparison with the 'inside' vowels.

Effects of intensity variations

Starting with the 'equalized'[7] formant intensities of our synthetic vowels, we proceeded to reduce by small steps the intensity of each formant separately (until the formant was effectively extinguished), and to observe the effects on the vowel sound as heard. The reduction in intensity was accomplished by interposing filters of appropriate density in the path of the modulated light beams, thus reducing the intensity of the light before it reached the painted formant.

6. For comparison with the identifications of our synthetic sounds, we presented to the same subjects, in such a way as to duplicate the test conditions of Tests B and C, a group of vowels spoken by one of the authors. (We did not include the vowels of Test A because we doubted our ability to speak several of the vowels correctly.) In all of the identifications of these spoken vowels there was only one error.

7. For the purposes of this part of the investigation, all the vowel formants, including those of /o/ and /u/, were made equally wide; when converted into sound, however, they were not of the same intensity, inasmuch as the playback is so constructed as to produce a reduction in intensity along the frequency scale amounting to 9 dB per octave in the frequency range above 1500 Hz. As we pointed out earlier, this attenuation corresponds roughly to the distribution of energy in normal human speech; it should be noted, however, that this rate of reduction in intensity is correct only on the average and hence is not necessarily perfectly appropriate for any particular speech sound.

The effects of reducing the intensity of the lower formant

For those vowels in which the two formants are relatively far apart /i e ɛ y ø œ/, progressive reductions in the intensity of the first formant resulted finally, for each of these vowels, in a destruction of vowel color. Beyond a certain amount of attenuation, somewhat different for each of the vowels listed above, the vowel color was replaced by a non-vowel sound which corresponded to the pitch of the higher formant. In no case did a reduction in the intensity of the lower formant cause a clear *shift* in vowel color.

In the case of those vowels whose two formants are relatively close together /u o ɔ ɑ/ a very different result was found. Here reductions in the intensity of the lower formant caused, not a loss of color, but rather a change in color toward an adjacent vowel; /u/ went to close /ɔ/, /o/ to open /ɔ/, /ɔ/ to /ɑ/, and /ɑ/ to /æ/. This finding can, perhaps, be accounted for if we assume that the ear effectively averages two vowel formants which are close together, receiving from these two formants an impression which is highly similar to that which would be heard from one formant placed at a position somewhere intermediate between them. We should suppose, then, that reducing the intensity of the lower formant, for example, would have the effect of increasing the higher formant's relative contribution to the 'mean' and would thus effectively raise the mean formant. On this basis reducing the intensity of the lower formant of /u/ could raise the mean impression to a level equivalent to the mean impression received from the normal formant intensities of a close /ɔ/. All of this suggests, of course, that those back vowels in which the formants are close enough to permit averaging are, in effect, one-formant vowels.[8]

With the vowels /ɯ ɤ ʌ/, reductions in the intensity of the first formant caused /ɯ/ to become vague /ɑ/, /ɤ/ to become vague /a/, and /ʌ/ to become vague /æ/. It should be noted that these color changes are superficially quite different from those which occurred when the first formant of the back vowels was reduced in intensity. In the case of the back vowels the shift in color was to a vowel quite near to the original, e.g. /ɔ/ went to /ɑ/, whereas the vowels /ɯ ɤ ʌ/ move over a rather considerable distance, e.g. /ɯ/ shifts to /ɑ/. (The term *distance* may be taken in its literal sense to refer to the two-dimensional space in which the synthetic vowels are arrayed in Figure 2.) As has been pointed out, the shifts which occur with the back

8. Fletcher pointed out in 1929 that early investigators had failed to detect the relatively weak second formant of the back vowels and had concluded, therefore, that these vowels were 'singly resonant' (Fletcher, 1929). Our results suggest that these back vowels may, indeed, be single-formant vowels, but only in the very special sense that, because of 'averaging', formants 1 and 2 of the spoken vowel can be replaced, in any synthetic production, by a single formant which is located at an intermediate position.

vowels suggest that the ear averages the two not widely separated formants of the back vowels, which is to say that the two formants should be replaceable by one formant which is properly intermediate. In the case of /ɯ ɤ ʌ/ we may suppose, to take one group of examples, that the second formant frequency of /ɤ/ (1100 Hz) is equal to the mean impression of the two formants (750 and 1300 Hz) of /a/. Reducing the intensity of the lower formant of /ɤ/ leaves us then with a single formant whose frequency happens to correspond to the 'mean' impression created by the lower and higher formants of a vowel /a/, although the latter is quite far removed from /ɤ/ on the vowel chart.

It was also noted that /a ʌ ɔ ɑ/ became slightly nasalized when the intensity of the first formant was reduced by as much as 7 dB.

The effects of reducing the intensity of the higher formant

For /i e ɛ y ø œ/, and also /ɯ ɤ ʌ/, small attenuations of the higher formant caused the vowel to acquire a quality that can best be described as 'dull'. With further reductions in the intensity of the higher formant each of these vowels changed to a close form of that particular back vowel whose first formant it shares. Thus /i y ɯ/ went to close and rather vague /u/; /e ø ɤ/ became a close and vague /o/; /ɛ œ ʌ/ became a close and vague /ɔ/. Reducing the intensity of the second formants of the back vowels /u o ɔ/ has, of course, the same final result since /u/ has the same first formant as /i y ɯ/, /o/ has the same first formant as /e ø ɤ/, and /ɔ/ has the same first formant as /ɛ œ ʌ/: /u/ became a close /u/, /o/ became a close /o/, and /ɔ/ became a close /ɔ/. When the second formant of /æ a ɒ ɑ/ is reduced there is a shift in vowel color to open /ɔ/.

In all these cases reduction in the intensity of the higher formant leaves us finally with a single formant of relatively low frequency, and we should suppose, on the basis of our assumptions about 'averaging', that the vowel color of that one formant would correspond to an 'average' impression produced by the two formants of some back vowel. For /æ a ɒ ɑ/ we see clearly that this happens: the lower formant of these vowels (750 Hz) is intermediate between the first (510 Hz) and second (950 Hz) formants of /ɔ/, and we find, as reported in the preceding paragraph, that the first formant of these vowels, by itself, does indeed sound like a vowel in the /ɔ/ category. We might have expected, similarly, that the first formants of /ɛ œ ʌ ɔ/ (510 Hz) would sound like /o/ (first formant, 360 Hz, second formant 800 Hz), and that the first formant of /e ø ɤ o/ would sound like /u/ (first formant, 250 Hz, second formant, 700 Hz). In fact, /ɛ œ ʌ ɔ/ move only to close /ɔ/, when the higher formant is omitted, and /e ø ɤ o/ go only as far as close /o/. We should suppose, then, that in the case of the vowels /o/ and /u/ the correct average is at a value very close to the first formant.

One-formant equivalents of the synthetic two-formant vowels

The results described in the preceding section imply that the two formants of some of the back vowels are replaceable by a single formant. We have attempted by several techniques to secure evidence which might bear rather more directly on this question. In one exploratory investigation we tried simply to find those single formants which will most closely approximate the ten synthetic cardinal vowels /i e ɛ æ a ɒ ɑ ɔ o u/ which lie on the perimeter of the vowel chart. For each two-formant vowel we listened to a series of single formants which sampled the frequency range between the first and second formants of the two-formant vowel. (These single formants were 2½ harmonics wide, and successive single formants were 120 Hz apart.) The sounds were arranged by pairs: the first member of the pair was the two-formant vowel, and the second member of the pair was one of the above series of one-formant vowels. The judgments were made by a guest phonetician and the authors of this paper. In general, the results were reasonably consistent with the conclusions obtained by varying the relative intensities of the two formants. For the vowels /u o ɔ ɒ ɑ a/, where the two formants are relatively close together, the judges were able to find reasonably good one-formant equivalents. The best one-formant approximations were very near in frequency to the *first* formants (of the two-formant synthetic vowels) for the two extreme back vowels /u/ and /o/, and were, in general, at positions progressively nearer the middle of the frequency interval separating the two formants of the synthetic vowels in the series /ɔ ɒ ɑ a/. It was difficult to find one-formant equivalents for /æ ɛ e/, in which the two formants are rather far apart, but for /i/, which has the greatest separation of first and second formants, a single formant near the normal position of the *second* formant seemed to produce the /i/ color rather well.[9]

It is perhaps worth noting that the results were quite different when we attempted to match single intermediate formants to arbitrarily chosen two-formant patterns which did not sound like vowels. In these cases we found it generally impossible to locate a single formant which sounded like the two-formant pattern. It was our impression that the two formants of the non-vowel patterns, however close together they might be, did not fuse into a single sound, but tended rather to be heard as two-component chords. (We have noticed the same kind of thing in listening to those synthetic cardinal vowels which are outside the range of our linguistic experience.) Inasmuch as the two formants of the non-vowels do not blend

9. It is relevant here that /i/ is an extreme vowel (none has a higher second formant), and the kind of judgment-anchoring which so often occurs at the extremes of a stimulus series might account for the fact that a high-frequency formant was so often identified as /i/.

into a single sound, one ought not, perhaps, to expect to find an equivalent 'average'.

As a further test of the apparent averaging of the two-formant vowels, we constructed a series of 24 one-formant representations which sampled the range 240 to 3000 Hz at intervals of 120 Hz. (Again, each formant was 2½ harmonics wide.) These sounds were arranged in a random order and presented to five listeners (one phonetician and the authors) with instructions to try to identify each sound as a vowel and to indicate on a three-point scale how 'good' a vowel it was. There was considerable agreement among the judges in identifying the vowels /u/ through /ɔ/ – /u/ at 240 Hz, /o/ at 360 and 480 Hz, and /ɔ/ at 600 and 720 Hz – and these one-formant sounds were felt by all the judges to be rather highly identifiable. The judges did not agree so well in identifying the other stimuli, and were generally less confident about their judgments, except in the case of formants above 2760 Hz which were unanimously called /i/. For /e ɛ a/, the closest approximations appeared to be 2520 Hz, 2160 Hz, and 1200 Hz, respectively.[10]

Using the results of these two exploratory studies as a basis, we selected the best one-formant approximations to seven of the 'outside' cardinal vowels /i e ɛ a ɔ o u/ and arranged them for Test D in a format identical with that used to determine the identifiability of the two-formant vowels in Test C. The center frequencies of the single-formant vowels in Test D were: /u/—240 Hz; /o/ — 480 Hz; /ɔ/—720 Hz; /a/—1200 Hz; /ɛ/—2160 Hz; /e/—2520 Hz; /i/—3000 Hz. These sounds were presented to fourteen of the sixteen listeners who had judged the two-formant vowels of Test B and C. The results of the test are presented in Figure 6. By comparing the percentages of correct identification in Test D with the analogous values in Test C (Figure 5) we see that the identifications were, in general, less accurate for the one-formant than for the two-formant vowels. Of greater interest, however, is the fact that, with the exception of /i/, the one-formant front vowels lost relatively more in identifiability than the one-formant back vowels. (The percentages of correct identification go from 100 for /i/, 94 for /e/, and 94 for /ɛ/, in the two-formant version, to 89 for /i/, 64 for /e/, and 61 for /ɛ/ in the one-formant version; the values for the back vowels, on the other hand, go from 88 for /u/, 75 for /o/, and 81 for /ɔ/ in the two-formant version, to 86 for /u/, 82 for /o/, and 75 for /ɔ/ in the one-formant case.) This result would appear in general to confirm the conclusion already presented that the back vowels (whose formants are

10. Köhler matched single pure tones to the pitch of sung vowels and arrived at equivalent frequencies of 3480 for /i/, 2265 for /e/, 1140 for /a/, 470 for /o/, and 225 for /u/. These values are very close to those which we arrived at by the very different technique described above. Köhler's results are reported in Boring (1942, pp. 373–4).

close together) can be rather closely approximated by a single formant, whereas the front vowels, with the possible exception of /i/, cannot.

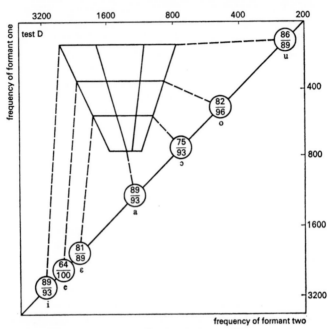

Figure 6 The accuracy of listeners' identifications of the seven one-formant vowels. Each one-formant vowel has a locus on the straight line where formant one equals formant two. The broken lines direct the eye to the original two formant positions on the vowel chain

Comparison of spoken and synthetic vowels

Figure 7 provides a basis for comparing the formant frequencies of our two-formant synthetic vowels with the frequencies of spoken French vowels.[11] Of the sixteen synthetic vowels, ten have their analogues in spoken French.

We see that the frequencies of the lower formants are about the same for synthetic and spoken vowels in the case of the close, mid-close, and mid-open vowels. For the open vowels the formant 1 frequencies of the synthetic vowels are slightly higher than those of the spoken vowels.

The frequencies of the higher formant show much larger differences between synthetic and spoken vowels. The largest difference, as can be seen in

11. For a specification of the frequency positions of the first two (lower) formants of French spoken vowels, see Delattre (1948).

the figures, is for /i/. A most extreme French /i/ has its second formant at 2500 Hz, while our synthetic /i/ has the second formant at 2900 Hz, a difference of 1·3 tones. For /e/ there is a difference which is somewhat smaller (¾ of a tone) but in the same direction; also, for /ɛ y ø œ/, the second formant of the synthetic vowel is higher than that of the spoken vowel,

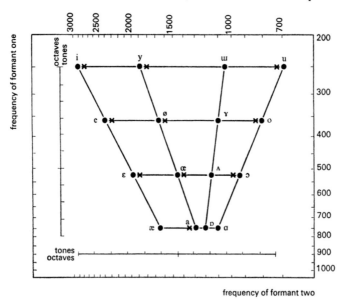

Figure 7 Acoustic locations of spoken French vowels for comparison with the synthetic vowels of Figure 2. The French vowels, indicated by crosses, are plotted according to the frequencies of their first and second formants

although the difference is less than in /i/ or /e/, amounting only to about ¼ of a tone. These differences between synthetic and spoken vowels can, perhaps, be accounted for on the basis of two assumptions: (a) that the third formant (of spoken vowels) makes a significant contribution to vowel color in the case of these (front) vowels, and (b) that the ear effectively averages two formants – the second and third, in this case – which are relatively close together. (The latter assumption has been made and supported in the preceding sections of this paper.) What we have done, then, in our synthetic vowels is to arrive at a 'compromise' second formant which has its position somewhere between the second and third formants of spoken vowels, this compromise formant being closer to the third formant (as in /i/) or closer to the second (as in /ɛ/) depending on the relative importance of the second and third formants in determining vowel color.

Pierre C. Delattre, *et al.* 235

If one attempts to define the essential acoustic features of vowels by examining spectrograms of actual speech, it is tempting to conclude that the third formant is of negligible importance for the perception of the vowel, since its frequency position changes very little from vowel to vowel. This is, of course, an altogether reasonable inference from the spectrographic data, but if our interpretation of our own results is correct, we must assume that the third formant, however stationary, can be quite important for its contribution to the 'mean' impression of formants two and three when these are close together.

For the back vowels /u o ɔ/ we see that the synthetic versions have second formants somewhat higher than the spoken vowels. This difference amounts to $\frac{2}{3}$ to $\frac{1}{2}$ a tone; we have found, however, that the higher formant of these back vowels can be lowered in frequency to the extent of two tones or more without destroying the cardinal vowel color.

Summary

A series of 235 two-formant patterns, representing systematic variations in formant-frequency position, were prepared and converted into sound by an instrument called a 'pattern playback'. From this experimental series, the authors selected those sounds which, in their collective judgment, most closely approximated the sixteen cardinal vowels of the International Phonetic Association. These sixteen synthetic sounds were presented to a group of students in phonetics for identification as vowels; the results indicated that the synthetic vowels were rather highly identifiable.

Variations in the relative intensities of the formants in the two-formant synthetic vowels caused some of the sounds simply to lose vowel color and to become vague, while others seemed to change color and to become different vowels. The changes in color which did occur are all consistent with the assumption that the ear effectively 'averages' two formants which are relatively close together (as is the case for the back vowels), and receives from them an overall quality roughly equivalent to that which would be produced by a single intermediate formant.

To test this assumption more directly, an attempt was made to locate those single formants which, as heard, most closely resemble the synthetic two-formant vowels. In general, it was relatively easier to find satisfactory one-formant equivalents for the back vowels (whose first and second formants are rather close in frequency) than for the front vowels (where the frequency separation of the formants is relatively great). An exception to this generalization is the vowel /i/, which can be very closely approximated by a single high-frequency formant. The best one-formant approximations to seven of the cardinal vowels /i e ɛ a ɔ o u/ were selected, and their identifiability was tested with the same listeners and by the same technique used to measure the identifiability of the two-formant synthetic vowels. As might be expected on the assumption of 'averaging' and from the observations about the relative ease or difficulty of finding one-formant equivalents, the identifiability of the back vowels was not appreciably less in the one-formant than in the two-formant form, while, with the exception of /i/, the difficulty of identifying the one-formant front vowels was rather considerably increased.

A comparison of the frequency positions of the two-formant synthetic vowels with the first- and second-formant positions of the corresponding French vowels *as spoken* shows certain differences, especially in the second formants of the front vowels. These differences appear to be explicable on the assumption that the third formant of the spoken front vowels makes an important contribution to their color and, further, that the second formant of the synthetic vowels, which is generally higher than the second formant of the spoken vowels, represents again an 'average' of formants which lie close together in the spoken vowel.

In conclusion we should like to acknowledge that this research was made possible in part by funds granted by the Carnegie Corporation of New York and in part through the support of the Department of Defense in connection with Contract DA49–170-sc-274.

References

BORING, E. G. (1942), *Sensation and Perception in the History of Experimental Psychology*, Appleton-Century-Crofts.

CHIBA, T., and KAJIYAMA, M. (1941), *The Vowel: Its Nature and Structure*, Tokyo-Kaseikan, Tokyo.

COOPER, F. S. (1950), 'Spectrum analysis', *J. acoust. Soc. Amer.*, vol. 22, pp. 761–2.

COOPER, F. S., LIBERMAN, A. M., and BORST, J. M. (1951), 'The interconversion of audible and visible patterns as a basis for research in the perception of speech', *Proc. nat. Acad. Sci.* vol. 37, pp. 318–25. Excerpt reprinted here, pp. 204–7.

COOPER, F. S., DELATTRE, P. C., LIBERMAN, A. M., BORST, J. M., and GERSTMAN, L. J. (1952), 'Some experiments on the perception of synthetic speech sounds', *J. acoust. Soc. Amer.*, vol. 24, pp. 597–606. Reprinted here, pp. 258–72.

DELATTRE, P. C. (1948), 'Un triangle acoustique des voyelles orales du français' *French Review*, vol. 21, no. 6.

DELATTRE, P. C., LIBERMAN, A. M., and COOPER, F. S. (1951), 'Voyelles synthétiques à deux formants et voyelles cardinales', *Le Maître phonétique*, vol. 96, pp. 30–37.

DUNN, H. K. (1950), 'The calculation of vowel resonances, and an electrical vocal tract', *J. acoust. Soc. Amer.*, vol. 22, pp. 740–53.

FLETCHER, H. (1929), *Speech and Hearing*, Van Nostrand.

JOOS, M. (1948), *Acoustic Phonetics*, Language Monographs, no. 23, Baltimore.

LIBERMAN, A. M., DELATTRE, P. C., and COOPER, F. S. (1952), 'The role of selected stimulus variables in the perception of the unvoiced stop consonants', *Amer. J. Psychol.*, vol. 65. pp. 497–516.

PETERSON, G. E., and BARNEY, H. L. (1952), 'Control methods used in a study of the vowels', *J. acoust. Soc. Amer.*, vol. 24, pp. 175–84. Reprinted here, pp. 104–22.

16 Dennis B. Fry, Arthur S. Abramson, Peter D. Eimas and Alvin M. Liberman

The Identification and Discrimination of Synthetic Vowels[1]

D. B. Fry, Arthur S. Abramson, Peter D. Eimas and Alvin M. Liberman, 'The identification and discrimination of synthetic vowels', *Language and Speech*, vol. 5 (1962), pp. 171–89.

In previous studies of the acoustic cues that may be used in the identification of English consonants, it has been found that, at least for certain classes of consonant, there is a strong tendency for listeners to hear speech sounds in a categorical fashion. The evidence for this has been gained by presenting to listeners a series of synthetic speech sounds, differing from each other by some very small step on a single acoustic dimension, asking them to label each sound in the series with an appropriate phonemic label and also measuring their sensitivity to change in this acoustic dimension. For the consonant group /b, d, g/, for example, a set of stimuli was used in which the transition of the second formant ($F2$) was systematically varied (Liberman, Harris, Hoffman and Griffith, 1957; Griffith, 1957). The subjects' labelling of these stimuli placed the sounds in three well-defined classes, corresponding to the three phonemic units, with a sharply marked boundary between each class and the neighbouring one. The measures of discrimination showed that subjects were in fact more sensitive to change in the region of the phoneme boundary than at other points in the continuum of change. The labelling and the discrimination data taken together suggested very strongly that subjects were in fact hearing this series of sounds categorically and the discrimination data were therefore re-examined on the assumption that listeners were able to discriminate only to the extent that they were able to identify the sounds as belonging to different phonemes. It was found that the major variations in the ability to discriminate which would be predicted on the basis of this extreme assumption were actually present in the data but that the general level of discrimination was somewhat higher than purely categorical hearing of the sounds would require.

Later experiments dealing with a variety of acoustic dimensions, but most of them concerning at least in part the broad class of stop consonants, have reinforced this view of consonant perception and lent support to the theory that a listener's own articulatory habits may be an important factor in determining the way in which he perceives speech sounds. In the case of

1. This work was supported in part by the Carnegie Corporation of New York.

/b, d, g/ there is clearly a discontinuity at the articulatory level between /b/ and /d/ and between /d/ and /g/; it is not in fact possible for a human speaker to produce a series of sounds that changes smoothly from /b/to/d/. The tendency to hear such sounds categorically may well be connected, therefore, with the existence of such articulatory discontinuities. If this were so, then we should expect that there will be marked differences between various classes of speech sound as to the way in which they are perceived, since there are certainly differences in the degree of articulatory discontinuity.

We are, of course, concerned here only with groups of sounds in which change with respect to a single acoustic dimension is a sufficient cue for phonemic differences. Within this limitation, there are cases such as change in the mid-point of a noise band as a cue to the difference between /s/ and /ʃ/, and change in third formant transition as a cue to /l/ and /r/, where the articulatory discontinuity is very much less obvious than in the change from /b/ to /d/. We might therefore expect to find that in these instances perception might also be less categorical in character. There is, however, a class of sounds, the vowels, in which continuous articulatory change from one member of the class to another is possible (at least insofar as English vowels are concerned) and vowels therefore provide an excellent testing-ground for the hypothesis that categorical hearing of speech sounds and articulatory discontinuity are related to each other.

It is well established that the frequencies of the first and second formants ($F1$ and $F2$) taken together are a sufficient cue for vowel differences and that these frequencies are very largely dependent on tongue articulation. Analytical acoustic studies of vowels have shown that $F1$ and $F2$ vary over a wide range in the case of a single vowel uttered by many different speakers and that there is considerable overlap in the plots of $F1$ and $F2$ when data for all the vowels in the English system are taken together (Peterson and Barney, 1952). Since the correlation between $F1$ and $F2$ and tongue articulation is close, this overlapping in the acoustic data indicates that vowel articulation not only can be changed continuously but that it in fact is so varied if we take into account utterances from different speakers in different contexts. The experiments reported in this paper represent a preliminary attempt to explore the perception of synthetic stimuli in which $F1$ and $F2$ are varied systematically in such a way as to cover the range corresponding to several vowel phonemes. The stimuli were used as the basis for labelling and discrimination experiments similar to those carried out for /b, d, g/ and the results constitute in the first place a contribution to the study of the relation between articulation and perception.

There are, however, a number of other reasons for attempting this kind of perceptual experiment with vowels. The consonant–vowel dichotomy has appeared in discussions of language from the most ancient times and has persisted down to the present despite some questioning in recent years of the validity and the necessity of the distinction. If the two classes of sound fulfil different functions in speech we may expect to find differences correlated with their occurrence at a number of different levels, among them the perceptual level. Experimental results showing that listeners perceive vowels and consonants in different ways would form at least contributory evidence to suggest that the two classes are functionally distinct.

One important respect in which vowels and consonants differ seems to be in their informational loading. This is indicated in a qualitative way by the observation that English speech in which all vowel distinctions have been artificially eliminated is many times more intelligible than English in which all consonant differences have been removed. The same principle is recognized in the alphabetic spelling of such languages as Hebrew where all the essential information is conveyed by the consonant letters. Reliable quantitative studies of this difference would need to be based on computations of the number of possible choices available at succeeding points in actual phonemic sequences and a comparison of the numbers for vowel and consonant phonemes, having regard to the total information content of the sequence. Data concerning this aspect of English will shortly be available as a result of computer work on phonemic transcriptions of English speech (Denes, 1963). Meanwhile one could argue theoretically that if the loading of consonants were high, then the most important part of consonant reception by the listener would consist in placing the sound in its appropriate phonemic category; it would be essential that this operation should be done accurately and also quickly, requirements which would be efficiently met by the kind of categorical hearing for which there is already a good deal of evidence in the case of consonants. It is quite clear that vowels, whatever their loading from the phonemic point of view, carry other kinds of information. They are the principal vehicle for rhythm and intonation, they carry the voice quality of the speaker, convey his emotional state and, in English especially, provide most of the information about dialect. All these kinds of information are borne by relatively long time segments and hence are delivered at rates very much slower than the phonemic rate. Rhythm and intonation patterns occupy a span usually equivalent to that of a number of phones; the listener's appreciation of a speaker's dialect is the cumulative effect of hearing a number of vowels over and over again, a process which may take a matter of minutes. For these purposes, rapid and accurate phonemic categorization of the vowels is not important and if it should turn out that the loading of the vowels with respect to phonemic information is relatively low, then there would be good grounds for expecting that vowels should be perceived rather differently from consonants.

The differences in vowel quality that must be perceived in comparing the vowels of one dialect with those of another are very much smaller than the differences between the constituent vowels of one speaker's vowel system so that in making judgments of dialect a listener is discriminating subphonemic vowel differences which would be imperceptible to him if vowels were perceived in the categorical way that has been found to hold for stop consonants. Something much more in the nature of continuous hearing seems to be called for in the case of the vowels where in general it is possible to trade speed for fineness of discrimination. In comparing the perception of stop consonants and vowels we may, therefore, be dealing with opposite ends of a scale ranging from rapid, categorical and hence relatively coarse hearing at one extreme to relatively slow, continuous but highly discriminating hearing at the other.

One further difference is implied in the contrast between categorical and continuous hearing. In order to provide a basis for quick and accurate decoding, the former must deal in categories which are relatively fixed and independent of context. If context exerts a great influence on the perception of sounds, this must lead either to a great number of errors in decoding or to the need for more time in which to take in and allow for the nature of the neighbouring sounds. The results of some experiments with stop consonants (Eimas, 1962), which we shall have occasion to discuss later in this paper, indicate very little influence of context. In labelling stimuli as /b, d, g/, for example, listeners' judgments of a given stimulus were not much affected by the preceding stimulus; the categories they were using seem to be rather sharply defined and most stimuli fell clearly into one or another of them. In any case where the listener is not functioning in this way, where he is discriminating comparatively fine differences and dealing with a continuum rather than discrete classes, that is to say in what we have referred to as continuous hearing, we should expect that context might play an important part. There will be a tendency for the subject's judgment to be determined largely by the fact that x is 'light' compared with y, or that z is 'dark' compared with x rather than by a longer-term conviction that x and y are in the class 'light' and z in the class 'dark'.

There is already some evidence that the perception of vowels is greatly dependent on context. Experiments by Ladefoged and Broadbent (1957) have shown that subjects' identification of the vowel in an English monosyllable can be influenced by the formant patterns used in a preceding carrier sentence. These results not only demonstrate an effect of context on vowel perception but also support the view which has been generally held for a very long time that in dealing with vowels uttered by a particular speaker, listeners rapidly form an appropriate reference frame against which they judge the quality of and identify the sounds which occur. The reference frame is readily changed when utterances from another speaker are received and it is clearly dependent on judgments of the relations between vowel qualities. Essentially this is a matter in which context is bound to exert considerable influence and the categories that the listener is using will be shifting classes determined by the interrelations within a system rather than well-defined absolute categories. This is not to say, of course, that listeners experience serious difficulty in placing vowel sounds into phonemic categories. In the experiments by Broadbent and Ladefoged, for example, the subjects showed no hesitation in selecting the syllable that they heard, and in general listeners are able to assign vowel sounds to phonemes. The important point is that the particular phonemic category selected is dependent on context, that is more specifically on the vowel reference frame which is operative for the listener at the time of reception.

In these circumstances, then, we expect the identification of vowels in a labelling test to be rather dependent on context and if this effect is strong enough there will be trends in the experimental data to indicate that the sequence in which the stimuli are presented to the subjects is a factor of some weight. A later section of this paper gives an account of a method of treating the data so as to find out whether this factor is important.

Procedure

The purposes of this experiment required, first, that we have as stimuli a series of synthetic vowels that vary along an articulatory and acoustic continuum from one phoneme to another. The relevant data are obtained then, by presenting these vowels to listeners (a) for identification as phonemes and (b) for discrimination on any basis whatsoever. In this way we determine whether or not there are peaks in discrimination at the phoneme boundaries and, also, to what extent the listener can or cannot hear intraphonemic differences. In general we were at pains to make the procedures of this experiment correspond as closely as possible to those of earlier studies on consonant perception; this was done in order that the results of the several studies might be more easily compared.

Stimuli

We chose to synthesize /ɪ/, /ɛ/ and /æ/, and to divide the space between them so as to have a total of thirteen stimuli. Our aim is best described by asking the reader to imagine a two-dimensional acoustic space whose coordinates represent the frequencies of the first and second formants, scaled logarithmically, and then to consider that our stimuli would, ideally, lie at equal distances along a straight line drawn through the points at which /ɪ/, /ɛ/ and /æ/ are located.

The vowels were synthesized on a machine called 'Alexander', a formant-type terminal analogue synthesizer designed and built at the Haskins Laboratories.[2] It can be controlled manually for steady-state sounds or by means of a pattern on an optically scanned acetate loop for the synthesis of running speech. It has four formant generators connected in parallel. Only two of them, excited by buzz pulses of variable repetition rate, were used for the present study. Smooth onsets and offsets of vowel amplitude and fundamental frequency envelopes were obtained by circuitry that gave an exponential rise and decay.

Appropriate formant frequencies for the three vowels were obtained by reference to data available in the literature (see Peterson and Barney, 1952), supplemented by the results of our own exploratory work. There is, of course, some error and uncertainty in the control of the synthesizer, just as there is in the measurement of the sounds the synthesizer has produced. After synthesizing the thirteen vowels that were to constitute the stimuli of the experiment, we measured the formant frequencies by inspection of wide- and narrow-band spectrograms as well as narrow-band sections made on the Kay Sonagraph. A 1200 Hz/inch scale was used for better visual resolution than the standard 2000 Hz can give. The harmonics of a complex wave of 400 Hz were used for frequency calibration. After arriving at formant frequencies this way, we then repeated the procedure with another

Table 1 Formant frequencies of the synthetic vowel stimuli

Stimulus number	First formant (Hz)	Second formant (Hz)
1	330	1980
2	380	1970
3	410	1960
4	460	1930
5	490	1910
6	500	1890
7	550	1880
8	580	1860
9	650	1860
10	700	1820
11	780	1820
12	830	1780
13	890	1760

2. No technical description has been published as yet, but the general design is similar in many respects to other formant-type synthesizers in use elsewhere. For a discussion of them, see Fant (1958).

set of spectrograms and sections for each of the variants. Table 1 gives the averages of the two sets of measurements of the formants of the synthetic vowels. These numbers have been rounded to the nearest 10 Hz as a realistic estimate of the attainable precision. We estimate the formant bandwidths to be about 100 Hz throughout. The average difference in intensity between *F1* and *F2* in the same stimulus is 8 dB. The difference in overall intensity between stimuli occurring in one triad does not exceed 1 dB.

The spectrographic examination of the stimuli revealed that we did not always succeed in coming as close to the intended frequencies as we might have wished. In particular, the differences between numbers 5 and 6 is considerably smaller than it was supposed to be.

Measurement of discrimination

A forced-choice A B X method was used to determine how well the listeners could discriminate the synthetic vowels. In this method the stimuli are arranged in triads, the first, A, and second, B, being always different, and the third, X, being always identical with the one or the other. The listener's task is to determine whether X is identical with A or with B and to guess if necessary.

We undertook to measure discrimination between each stimulus and those that were one, two and three steps away from it on the stimulus scale. This made a total of 33 A-B pairs. Each A B X triad was arranged in all possible permutations (A B A, A B B, B A A and B A B) to counterbalance series or order effects. Given thirty-three A-B pairs and four A B X permutations of each one, there was, then, a total of 132 A B X triads. These triads were presented to the subjects in random order, the number of presentations being such as to provide twenty judgments per stimulus comparison (A-B pair) for each subject. Three of the subjects worked longer and made a total of forty judgments of each stimulus pair.

Phoneme identification

To determine how the various stimuli were assigned to the three phoneme classes (/ɪ/, /ɛ/ and /æ/), we presented to the subjects the same A B X arrangements of stimuli that had been used in the discrimination tests, but instead of asking whether X was identical with A or with B, as we had in measuring discrimination, we instructed the subjects to label each stimulus as /ɪ/, /ɛ/ or /æ/. No other responses were accepted, and the subjects were asked to guess if necessary. The triads were presented in random order. Obviously the stimuli near the middle of the continuum will appear more often than those near the ends; the number of judgments per stimulus varied accordingly from 84 to 184.

Subjects

Eight paid volunteers attending the University of Connecticut summer school served as subjects. They had been selected from a group of seventeen on the basis of a special pre-test in which they had been found to be most consistent in applying phoneme labels to the synthetic vowels.

Results

In presenting the results of the vowel experiments it is necessary to stress once more that these are preliminary attempts at studying the discrimination and labelling of vowel sounds and the results too must be considered as being preliminary. We shall have occasion to compare the vowel data with those for stop consonants, particularly /b, d, g/, and it will be immediately apparent that the former are very much less tidy than the consonant data. There are several reasons for the greater amount of noise in the vowel data. The first is to be found in the experimental stimuli themselves since past experience has shown that a great deal of experimentation is necessary before one can produce the best synthesized sounds for a given set of discriminations. The vowel-like sounds used in the present series of experiments were adequate but no more, and it should be possible in future work to effect some improvement in the stimuli. More exact specification and closer control of formant frequencies, intensities and band-widths is needed, the signal to noise ratio in the test tapes should be improved and it is advisable to examine the desirability or otherwise of introducing constant third or higher formants and to determine the most suitable time course for overall intensity and fundamental frequency variation.

A second reason for the scatter of the results is also connected with the stimuli but is one which is inherent in the nature of the experiment. A prerequisite for this type of measurement is that we should find a single dimension such that variation with respect to it is a sufficient cue for phonemic differences. In the case of the vowels the $F1/F2$ plot may justifiably be considered as forming a single dimension and thus satisfies the conditions, but the situation is nonetheless different from that encountered in the consonant experiments. The variation of $F2$ transition in the /b, d, g/ case gave rise to a set of stimuli which cued the recognition of these three consonants but which nowhere in the progression suggested to the listener some other English consonant; it was, as it were, a linear sequence. An $F1/F2$ plot, on the other hand, is a point on a plane on which it is possible to define an area bounded by extreme values of $F1/F2$ either for all vowels occurring in a given language or, more generally, for all vowels that can be produced. Such an area represents a physical projection of a space containing a great range of vowel qualities perceived by listeners. The correlation between the physical and the perceptual is, of course, not simple and when we set out to find a series of *F1/F2* plots forming a progression from /ɪ/ through /ɛ/ to /æ/ we cannot take it as axiomatic that these values will lie on a straight line in the physical space, nor even that they will necessarily lie on a smooth curve. We know already from analytical data that the sounds corresponding to a given phoneme will cover a considerable area in the *F1/F2* space so that there will clearly be a number of paths which will form a progression from one vowel to another and to determine the best path for the purposes of labelling and discrimination experiments is an empirical matter. Further, even assuming that we have found the optimum progression, there is the added difficulty that any deviations from this through small errors in setting up the stimuli may produce sounds which suggest to the listeners some vowel other than the three which are the basis for the labelling.

Such difficulties as these were in fact encountered in the preparation of the test stimuli in the experiments reported here. They represent in themselves a particular facet of the fundamental reason for the scatter of the data which is simply that subjects do find it difficult to label vowel sounds consistently. The variability of the vowel sounds produced by speakers, reflected in the large area of the *F1/F2* space occupied by the sounds belonging to a single vowel phoneme, is matched by a corresponding inconsistency on the part of listeners when they are asked to label vowel sounds. As we shall see from the results and in the subsequent discussion, vowel categories are not as sharply defined nor as absolute as some consonant categories and vowel judgments are very highly susceptible to the effects of context. In these circumstances, improvements in the stimuli in future work may be expected to get rid of some of the variability in the data but there will remain that part of it which is, it seems, inherent in the judgments we have been trying to investigate.

Vowel identification results

Figure 1 shows the pooled responses of eight subjects to the vowel identification test. The stimuli evoked a considerable number of identifications in each of the phonemic categories, though there were in all rather fewer judgments in the /æ/ category than in either of the other two. Stimuli 1 and 13 set an artificial boundary to the /ɪ/ and /æ/ categories and we cannot, of course, make a valid comparison of the extent of all three categories unless the range of stimuli is enough to take listeners into a fourth and fifth category at either end. The range used appears to be quite satisfactory for the purpose of these experiments, that is, to show boundaries between the /ɪ/ and /ɛ/ and the /ɛ/ and /æ/ phonemes, and the judgments are not unduly weighted in favour of any one phoneme.

It is, perhaps, worth noting that the labelling functions of Figure 1 are less sharp than those that have been obtained when comparable procedures are carried out with synthetic stops (Eimas, 1962). Such a comparison reveals another difference in that in the case of the consonants the degree of agreement or consistency reaches a high level in all three categories whilst in the vowels the middle category does not produce as high a level as the

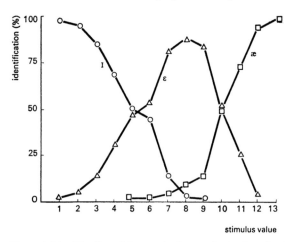

Figure 1 Identification of the synthetic vowel stimuli as English /ɪ/, /ɛ/ or /æ/ as a function of first- and second-formant frequency combinations as shown in Table 1

other two. These are indications of the effect of context on vowel judgments, which will be discussed in a later section. It will be enough to point out here that the context effect in vowels works by *contrast* which means, if we express it in terms of phonetic classification, that a given vowel sound will appear more open when preceded by a sound closer than itself and more close after a sound more open than itself. In the case of the stimuli used in these tests, every sound in the series strikes the listener as being more open than stimulus number 1 so that the effect of context here is to increase the number of judgments that number 1 is /ɪ/; similarly, all sounds appear closer than stimulus number 13 and this increases the judgments that 13 is /æ/. For all the stimuli labelled as /ɛ/, however, there are included in the test some sounds that make them appear closer and others that make them appear more open. Hence these stimuli are labelled less consistently and this fact is reflected in the labelling function for /ɛ/. More generally, of course, all the vowel stimuli other than those at the extreme of the continuum will tend to be labelled according to the context in which they are presented; this will reduce the consistency with which the labels are applied and thus produce the sloping functions of Figure 1 rather than the more nearly quantal functions found with the stops.

Vowel discrimination results

The curves of Figure 2 show the percentage of correct responses in discriminating between stimuli which differ by one, two and three steps. The series of stimuli are set off on the horizontal axis in arbitrarily equal steps and in the same order as in the case of the labelling data. The continuous curve in each part of the figure indicates the pooled results for all subjects.

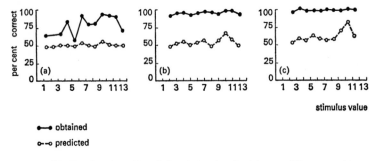

•—• obtained

o--o predicted

Figure 2 Obtained and predicted discrimination for (a) one-, (b) two- and (c) three-step differences among the synthetic vowel stimuli

It has been noted above that the step between stimuli 5 and 6 was considerably smaller than other steps and this accounts for the fact that at this point in the graph the level of discrimination falls to nearly 50 per cent. The mean level of discrimination for the one-step differences is, however, very close to 75 per cent which would normally be taken as a threshold criterion. When the difference between test items is as large as two steps on the stimulus scale, the percentage of correct responses is very near to 100 per cent, and there is very little room for improvement on this in the case of the three-step differences.

In the course of previous work on the discrimination of consonants a model has been developed which enables us to consider to what extent discrimination is influenced by categorical perception and to predict from labelling data the level of discrimination to be expected if subjects were able to discriminate only to the extent that they could place the same stimuli consistently in phonemic categories. In the case of a variety of consonantal discriminations it has been found that the discrimination functions obtained experimentally lie quite close to the functions predicted on the basis of labelling data. Usually the subjects' level of discrimination is slightly better than the predicted level but the major inflections in the predicted functions, which appear at the region of the phoneme boundaries, are found also in the experimental data. The broken lines in Figure 2 represent the discrimination function for the vowels predicted in the same way, that is to say on the assumption that subjects can discriminate only as well as they can label. In the case of the one-step discriminations, the predicted scores do not differ materially from the chance score of 50 per cent. For the two-step differences, the level of the predicted scores rises a little and there is a pronounced maximum for the discrimination of stimulus 9 from stimulus 11, the sounds which lie closest to the phoneme boundary indicated in the labelling data. This maximum is, of course, still more marked in the predicted scores for the three-step differences but for other parts of the range the predicted scores remain quite low. In the obtained scores for the one-step discriminations, the low level of discrimination at stimulus 5 rather confuses the picture, but there is no doubt that the obtained level is far above the predicted level. At two and three steps the difference between the obtained and the predicted scores is even more striking and the discrimination is so good throughout the range of stimuli that there is no room for improvement in the region of the phoneme boundaries. On the basis of these data we have to say that the perception of the vowels is continuous rather than categorical. There is no evidence of discontinuities in the discrimination functions at phoneme boundaries. More generally, it is clear that discrimination is much better than that which is predicted on the extreme assumption that the listeners can only hear phonemically, i.e. categorically.

There is a marked difference between this result and the discrimination data for /b, d, g/ obtained by Eimas (1962) and shown in Figure 3.[3] We should remark here that the comparison between the vowel data and the results of Eimas' study is a reasonable one. In both cases there were three phoneme classes; these three classes were divided into fourteen stimulus steps in the case of the stops and thirteen in the case of the vowels. It is clear from Figure 3 that the perception of the stops tends to be categorical. There are obvious peaks in discrimination in the regions of the phoneme boundaries, and in general discrimination is very little better than is predicted on the basis of the extreme assumption that the listeners can only

3. This part of Eimas' study, which was intended to provide a basis for certain other comparisons between continuously and categorically perceived stimuli, was much like the earlier experiments of Liberman, Harris, Hoffman and Griffith (1957) and Griffith (1957). Eimas' procedures were more like those of the present study, however, in that the stimuli were presented for labelling in A B X triads and the results for all subjects were pooled.

discriminate as well as they can apply the three phoneme labels. Thus, in the case of the stops the subjects take very little notice of anything but phonemic distinctions, while in the vowels, on the other hand, they discriminate quite well between sounds within the same phonemic category. It was suggested earlier that in order to recognize dialectal differences a listener

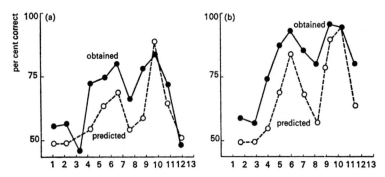

Figure 3 Group obtained and predicted discrimination functions for the /b, d, g / stimuli at (a) two and (b) three steps. Reproduced from Eimas (1962), Figure 4

would in fact need to take account of differences in vowels which are considerably smaller than the phonemic differences within the system of a single speaker. The experimental results provide strong evidence that listeners are well able to do this.

The effect of context on identification

In discussing the identification data we have already mentioned that the sequence in which sounds were presented for labelling was a factor which influenced the results. The same test tapes were used in both the labelling and discrimination experiments so that many of the stimuli for identification were heard in quick succession (at intervals of one second) and in groupings (ABA and ABB) which would tend to maximize the effect of context. The rather gradual slope of the identification functions, the high level of consistency in labelling the end-points of the range of stimuli, the relatively inconsistent labelling of the middle phoneme category, it has been suggested, may all be signs that context is playing an important part in identification. In the present section we shall consider further treatment of these data intended to give us some idea of the magnitude of the effect.

Let us consider first the case in which a listener hears a sound, x, paired with another sound, y, that is, either followed or preceded by y. If context or sequence has some effect on what he perceives, it must operate in one of two directions: either y will seem more unlike x because of its proximity in time, or it will seem more like *x*. In the first case we should say that context was working in the direction of *contrast* and in the second, of *assimilation*. Previous work on the perception of vowels suggests that the effect is more likely to be one of contrast. In the experiments reported by Ladefoged and Broadbent, for example, the lowering of *F1* in the carrier sentence made the test item sound more open in quality, that is as though it had a higher *F1*.

The stimuli for the vowel experiments, which are numbered from 1 to 13 in Table 1, are ranged in order from the most /ɪ/-like to the most /æ/-like vowel, that is from the closest sounding to the most open sounding. If the effect of context was in the direction of contrast, then any stimulus which in the test sequence was paired with a stimulus of lower number than itself would tend to sound more open; when paired with a stimulus of higher number it would sound closer because of this proximity. We can obtain a very simple and crude measure of the context effect therefore if we examine

Table 2 Hypothetical examples of maximum context effect

	Example 1 (%)		Example 2 (%)		Example 3 (%)		Example 4 (%)	
	/ɪ/	/ɛ/	/ɪ/	/ɛ/	/ɪ/	/ɛ/	/ɪ/	/ɛ/
total response distribution	50	50	50	50	60	40	60	40
response distribution when paired with higher numbered stimuli	100	0	0	100	100	0	20	20
response distribution when paired with lower numbered stimuli	0	100	100	0	20	80	100	0
maximum context effect	100		−100		80		−80	

the labelling responses for each stimulus in the range and break the judgments down into two groups, those made when the stimulus was paired with another of higher number and those made when paired with one of lower number. The greatest effect that context could possibly have would be exemplified when for a given stimulus, *x*, all the labelling judgments were swung in a particular direction when *x* was paired with higher numbered stimuli and in the opposite direction when paired with lower numbered stimuli. The way in which this simple measure was applied can best be seen from hypothetical examples such as those shown in Table 2.

In the first example we suppose that of all responses to stimulus *x*, 50 per cent labelled it as /ɪ/ and 50 per cent as /ɛ/. We now divide the responses into those made when x was paired with a stimulus having a higher number and those when it was paired with one with a lower number. Assume now that every time that x was paired (in the ABX triads) with a stimulus having a higher number, the label applied to x was /ɪ/ and that every time x was paired with the stimulus having a lower number, the label was /ɛ/. This would represent the maximum contrast effect, expressed in our example by subtracting the percentage of /ɪ/ judgments when x was paired with higher valued stimuli from that when x was paired with lower valued stimuli, giving the value 100 (the positive sign has been chosen arbitrarily to denote contrast). In the second example we have the same total distribution of responses, but the effect of context is now reversed since x is labelled /ɛ/ whenever paired with stimuli above it and /ɪ/ when paired with stimuli below it. By the same procedure as before this gives the value of −100 for the context effect, which represents maximal assimilation.

It will more frequently happen that /ɪ/ and /ɛ/ are not equally divided in the total distribution of responses and examples 3 and 4 show maximum context effects computed for the case of some other division of the total. Stimulus x is paired equally with higher and lower numbered stimuli. If now 60 per cent of the total responses are /ɪ/, the maximum contrast effect would mean that x was labelled /ɪ/ in all instances when paired with higher numbered stimuli and also in 20 per cent of the pairings with lower valued stimuli. We arrive at the value for maximum context effects in the same way as before, obtaining the value of 80 (contrast). In example 4, the effect is again reversed and maximum context effect is −80 (assimilation).

In dealing with the data, we have used this method to compare both the maximum possible and the actual effect of context for the various synthetic vowels.[4] The actual effect can vary between zero and the maximum possible; the extent to which the actual effect approximates the maximum possible is a rough measure of the influence of context on perception.

In Figure 4 the broken lines show the maximum, and the continuous curves the actual context effects for one-, two- and three-step differences. Clearly there was an effect of context, and, just as clearly, the effect was consistently in the direction of contrast. By comparing the actual effect with the maximum one sees, further, especially in the two- and three-step cases, that the context effect was very large in relation to what it might have been. This is to say that wherever there was variation in the response to a vowel, that variation was not primarily random, but was rather determined almost entirely by the context in which the vowel was judged.

To determine how great these relative magnitudes of context effect are it

4. Context effects of the kind described here could not be calculated for the stimuli at either end of the continuum, since these could be paired only with stimuli lying to one side or the other.

is instructive to compare the results of this experiment on the vowels with results of similar studies of some consonants and certain simple non-speech stimuli. Eimas (1962) has made just such comparisons, using the voiced stops /b, d, g/, a set of cards of varying reflectance, and various durations of

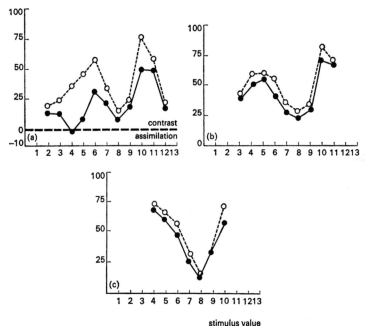

stimulus value

Figure 4 Actual and maximum context for (a) one-, (b) two- and (c) three-step differences, averaged over all eight subjects

white noise. He found the effect of context in the perception of the stops to be much smaller than that which we have observed here with the vowels. In the case of the non-speech stimuli the context effect was rather variable, but in general it was less than the vowels and greater than the stops.

Discussion

On the evidence of the results presented in this paper there are clearly grounds for believing that listeners perceive vowels in a way somewhat different from that in which they perceive the stop consonants. The chief basis for this conclusion is to be found in the fact that the ability to discriminate vowels is far superior to what would be required merely in order to assign them to categories and that there appears to be no particular sharpening of sensitivity in the region of phoneme boundaries, whereas discrimination of /b, d, g/ was very little if at all superior to labelling and showed the predicted increase in sensitivity near the phoneme boundaries.[5] It seems that we may here be dealing with two extremes in speech perception, in the case of the stops with perception that is maximally categorical and in the vowels with the extreme of continuous perception. In experiments involving plosive consonants it has often been commented upon by both experimenters and subjects that when one listens to the stimuli there indeed seems to be a rather sharp switching over between categories. This was particularly noticeable in the /b, d, g/ experiment (Liberman *et al.*, 1957), the /d, t/ experiments (Liberman *et al.*, 1961a), and the /sl, spl/ experiments (Bastian, Eimas and Liberman, 1961). If the vowels and the stops do represent extremes in this matter, then one would expect that some other classes of sound may be perceived in a manner which falls somewhere between the categorical and the continuous, and it would obviously be profitable to explore other cases of labelling and discrimination from this point of view. It might be particularly interesting in this connection to study the fricatives, nasals and liquids.

In the introduction to this paper it was suggested that some association was to be expected between categorical perception and the effect of context on perception. Sharply defined and strongly marked categories would be rather in the nature of absolute categories and in assigning sounds to them a listener would be rather little influenced by temporal sequence. In this respect, too, the vowels present an extreme case, for the influence of context on the vowel judgments is almost as great as it can possibly be in the conditions of the experiments. Indeed, as we pointed out earlier, the effect of context is greater on the vowels than on simple non-speech stimuli. Thus it appears that listeners have a strong tendency to judge a vowel by comparing it with one they have just heard. This fact lends support to the idea which has often been expressed in the past (see, for example, Joos, 1948; Broadbent and Ladefoged, 1960) that in dealing with vowels a listener establishes for himself a frame of reference appropriate to a given listening situation. In particular he is likely to set up a reference system of vowel qualities for an individual speaker and to judge all vowel sounds occurring in this individual's speech by comparing them with the reference values. A listener who is decoding the speech of a total stranger usually manages in quite a short time to erect the reference frame by making use of the redundancy of the language, which in most cases will determine with a very high probability what vowel 'must' have occurred, and then judging a particular vowel quality by comparison with those that have preceded it.

5. Related studies on phonemic tones (Abramson, 1961) and phonemic vowel duration (Bastian and Abramson, 1962) in Thai yielded results similar to those of the present vowel study.

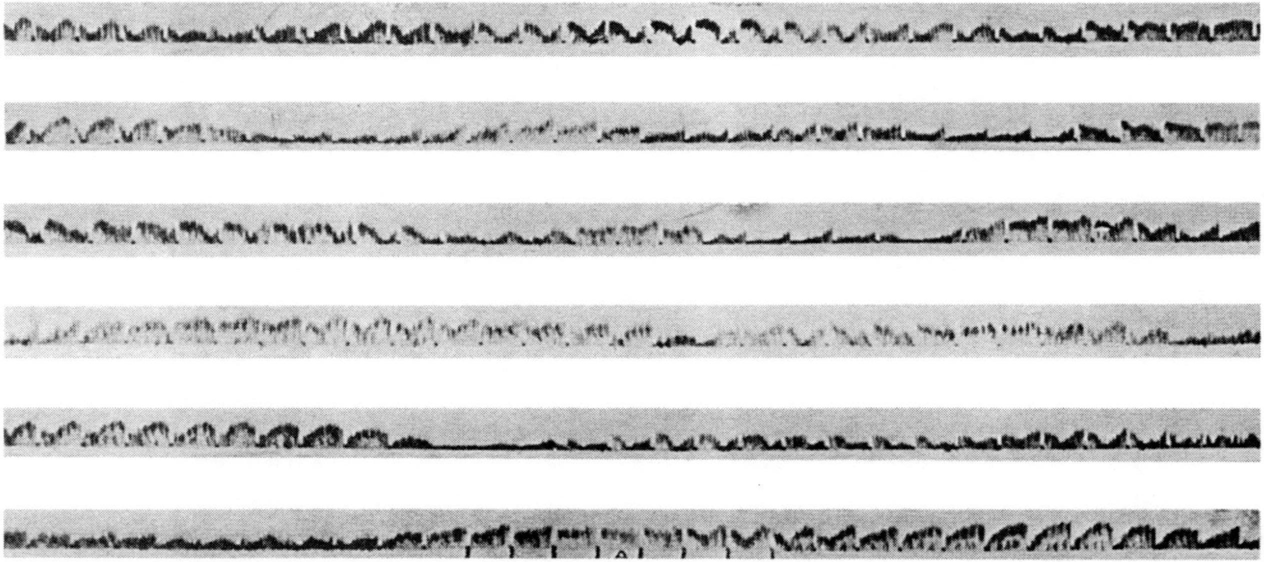

Plate 1.

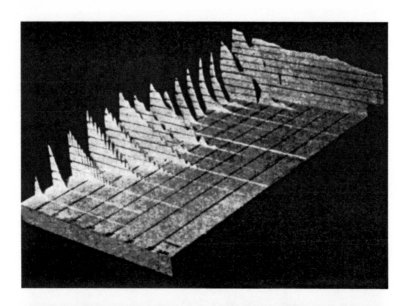

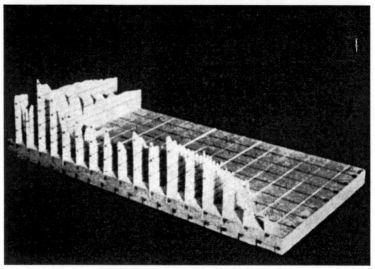

Plate 2.

Plate 3. The words are 'visual telephony for the deaf'

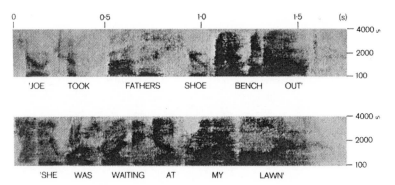

Plate 4. Spectrograms made with the first laboratory model assembled from available equipment

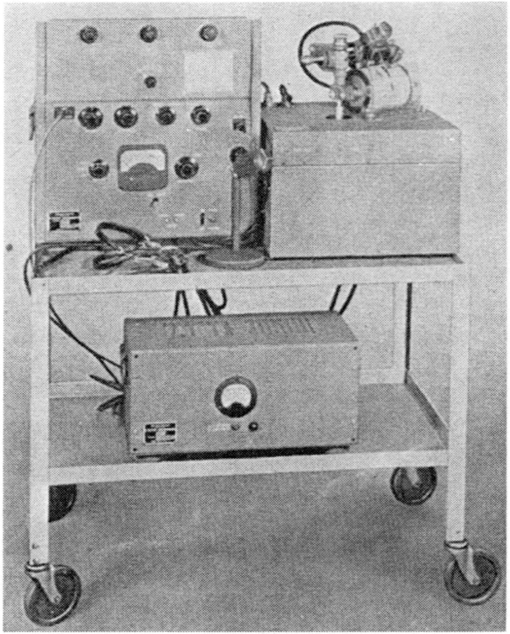

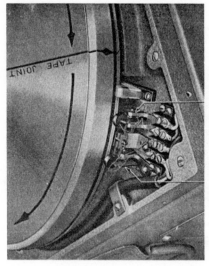

TAPE JOINT
recording-reproducing pole piece, 40 ml face
erasing pole piece 50 ml face

Plate 6 (above). View with cover removed, showing the magnetic tape and the pole pieces. The butt-joint in the tape is exaggerated in this picture

Plate 5 (left). The present model of the sound spectrograph, built in three parts for portability

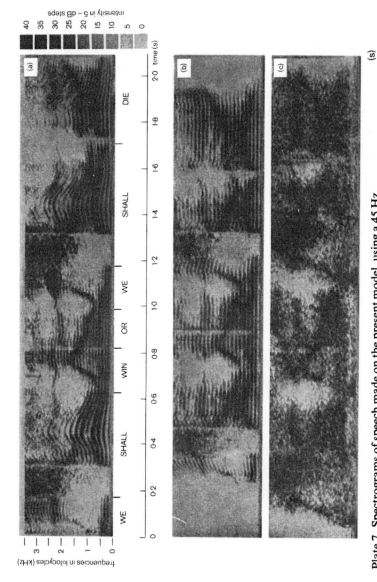

Plate 7. Spectrograms of speech made on the present model, using a 45 Hz analysing filter. Section (A) normal speech (B) monotone (C) whisper

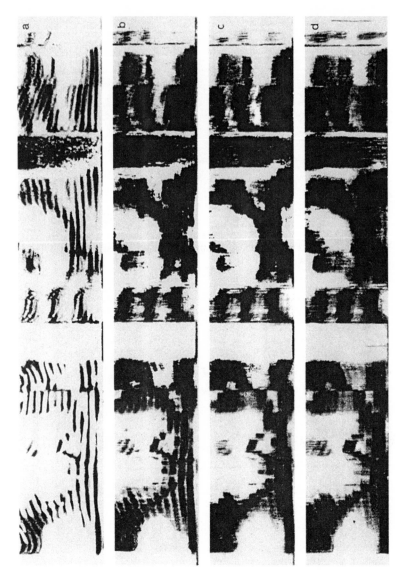

Plate 8.

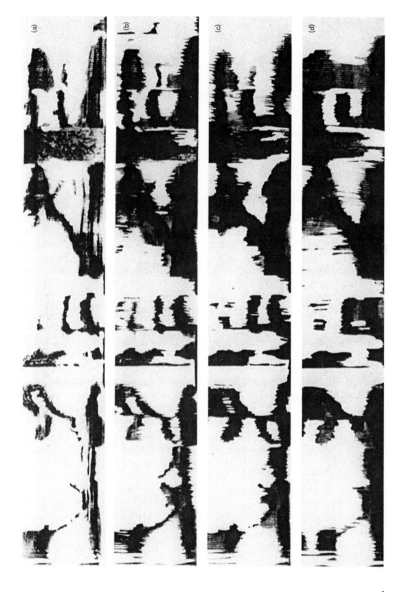

Plate 9.

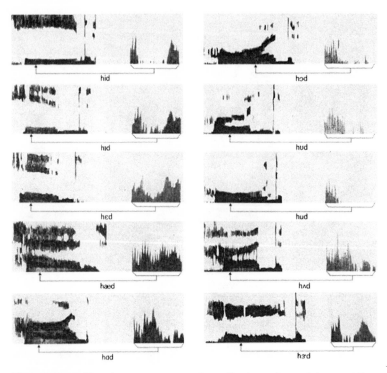

Plate 10. Broad band spectrograms and amplitude sections of the word list by a female speaker

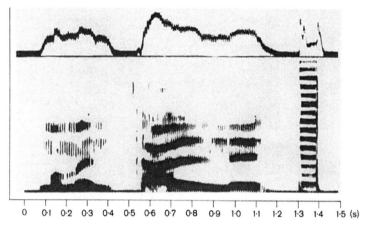

0   0·1   0·2   0·3   0·4   0·5   0·6   0·7   0·8   0·9   1·0   1·1   1·2   1·3   1·4   1·5 (s)

Plate 11. /momenˈtalnɨ/*momentalny*

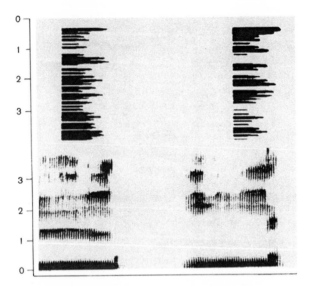

Plate 12a. Spectrograms and sections of /m, n/

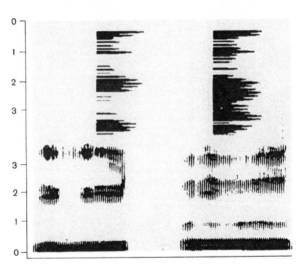

Plate 12b. Spectrograms and sections of /ɲ, ŋ/

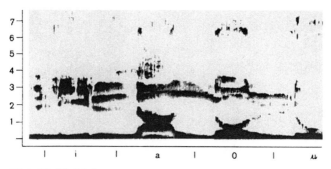

Plate 13. [lilalolu]

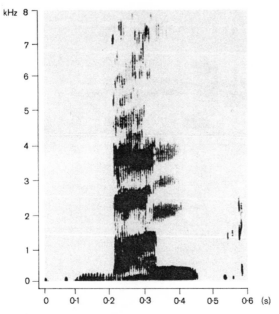

Plate 14. /baŋk/*bank*

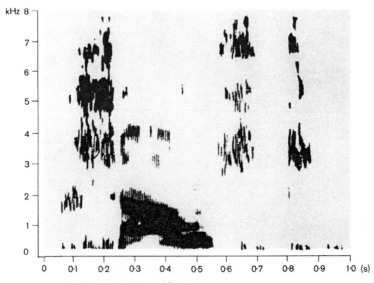

Plate 15. /xʃoɲʃtʃ/*chrząszcz* (*fem.*)

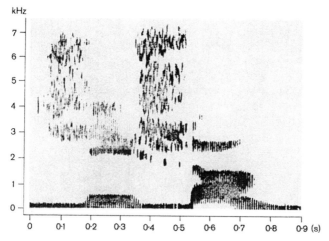

Plate 16. /tɕiʃa/*cisza*

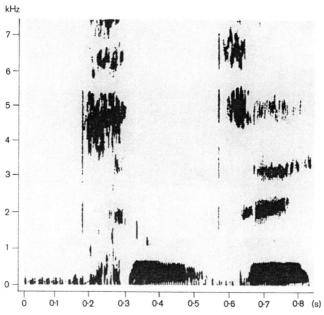

Plate 17. /ˈtsudzi/*cudzy* (*fem.*)

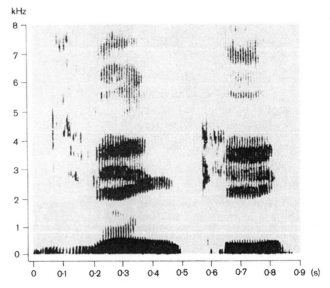

Plate 18. /dzvjeŋci/*dźwieki*

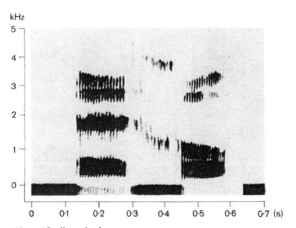

Plate 19. /ˈexo/*echo*

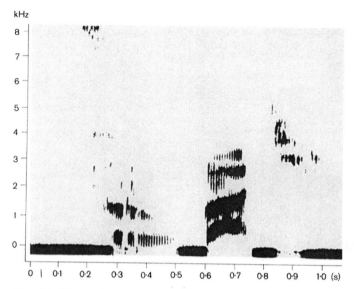

Plate 20. /ˈfruvatɕ/*fruwać*

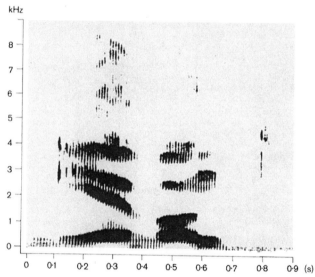

Plate 21. /ˈjevont/*Giewont*

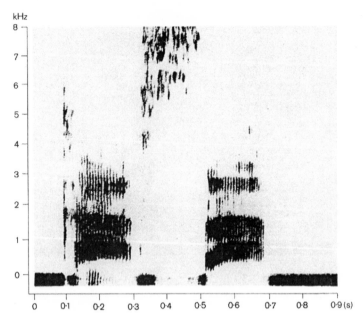

Plate 22. /ˈkasa/*kasa*

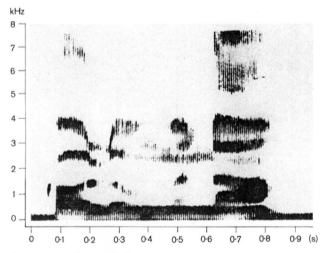

Plate 23. /koˈlumna/*kolumna*

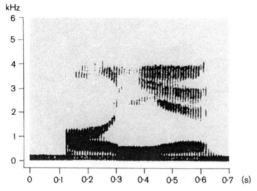

Plate 24. /ˈkoɲe/*konie*

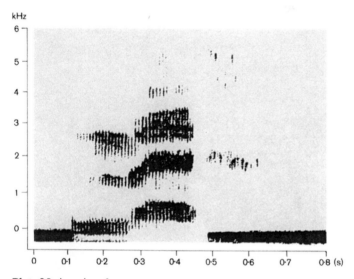

Plate 25. /mex/*mech*

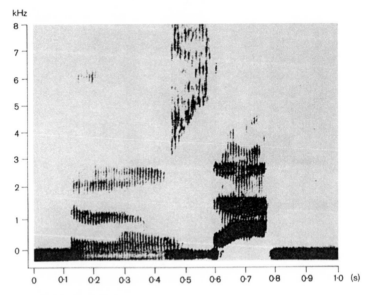

Plate 26. /ˈmuza/*muza*

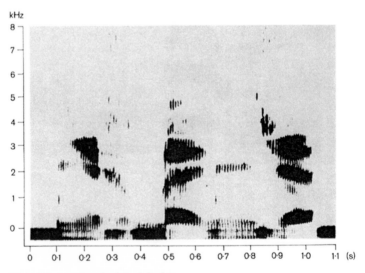

Plate 27. /ɲexˈbɛndze/*niech będzie*

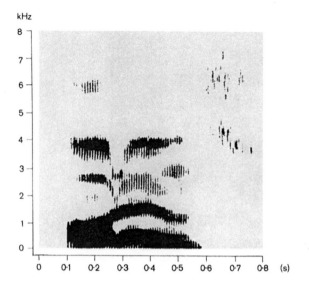

Plate 28. /oreɲʃ/*oręz*

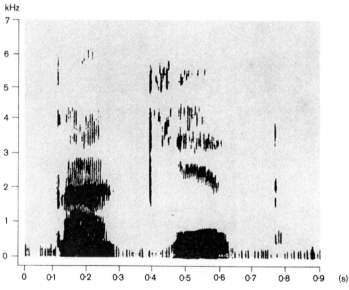

Plate 29. /ˈpacet/*pakiet* (*fem.*)

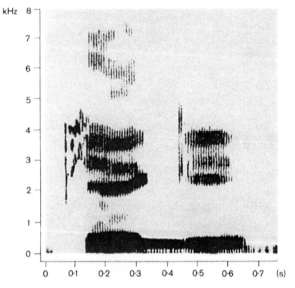

Plate 30. /ˈpjeɟi/*picgi*

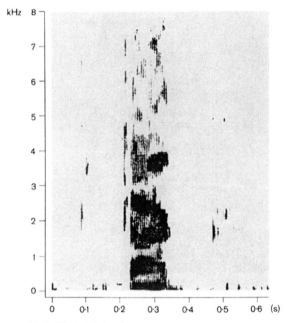

Plate 31. /ptak/*ptak*

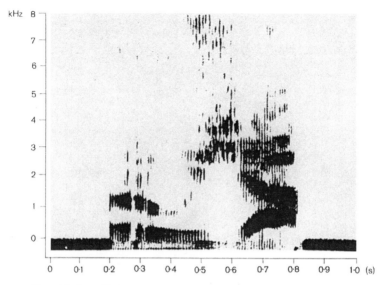

Plate 32. /ruza/*Rózia*

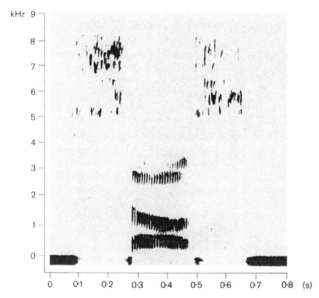

Plate 33. /sos/*sos*

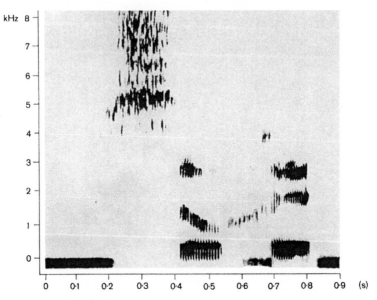

Plate 34. /ˈsuki/*suchy*

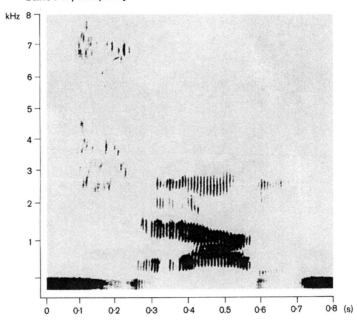

Plate 35. /ʃron/*szron*

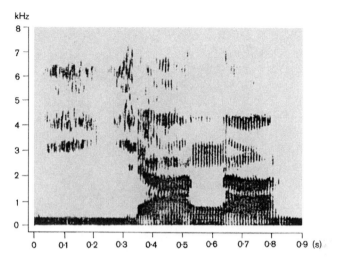

Plate 36. /ɕtɕana/*ściana*

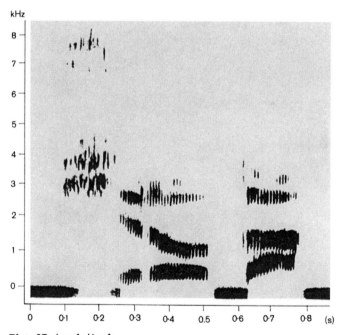

Plate 37. /ɕroda/*środa*

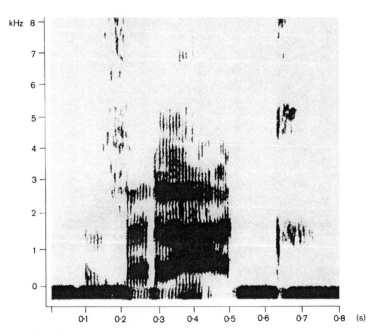

Plate 38. /vrak/*wrak*

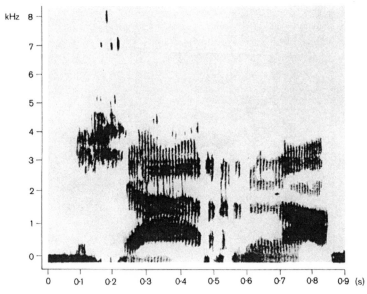

Plate 39. /zarno/*ziarno*

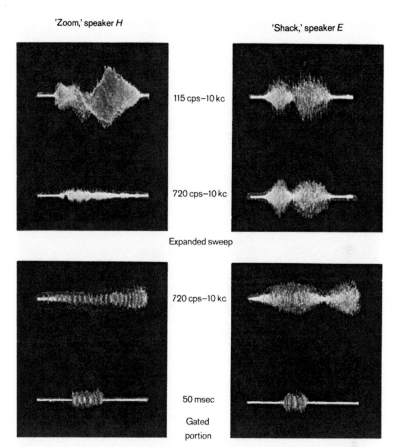

'Zoom,' speaker *H*

'Shack,' speaker *E*

115 cps–10 kc

720 cps–10 kc

Expanded sweep

720 cps–10 kc

50 msec

Gated

portion

Plate 40. Oscillograms of two words showing a typical placement of the gate. Note that the unvoiced /ʃ/ in 'shack' is almost entirely unaffected by the elimination of frequencies below 720 Hz

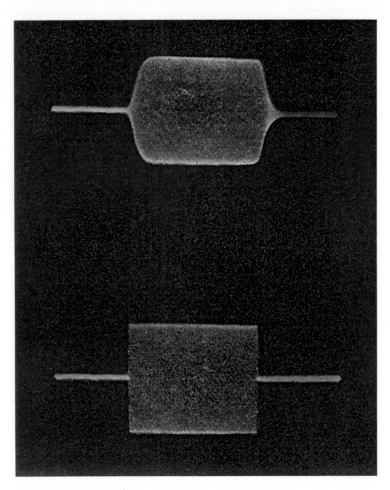

Plate 41.

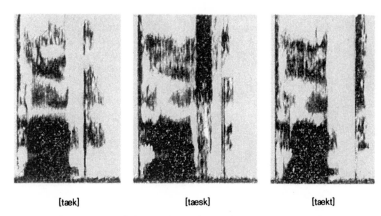

[tæk]   [tæsk]   [tækt]

Plate 42. Sonograms of the words 'tack', 'task' and 'tact' (G, male). In the /k/ of 'tack' both transition and burst are present; in that of 'task' only the burst is present, while in that of 'tact' the transition alone is present

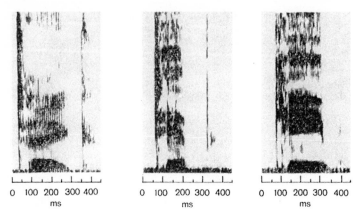

Plate 43.

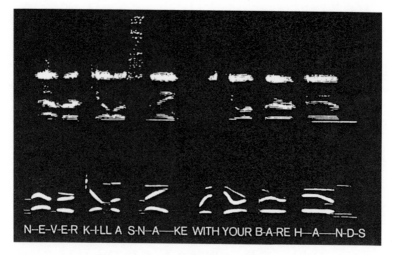

Plate 44. (a) Transmission spectrogram copied photographically from an original spectrogram without modification. (b) Reflection spectrogram drawn by hand as a simplified version of the original spectrogram. (c) Text of the sentence

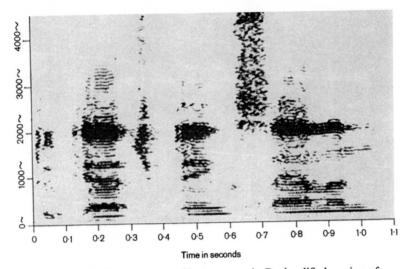

Plate 45. A : sound spectrogram of human speech. B : simplified version of the same phrase painted by hand

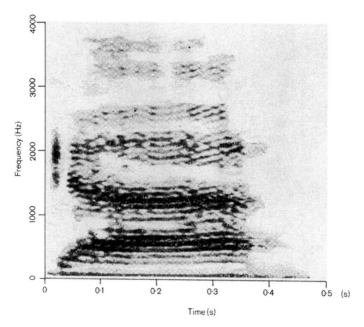

Plate 46. Spectrogram of the syllable /ga/ showing a burst and a transition

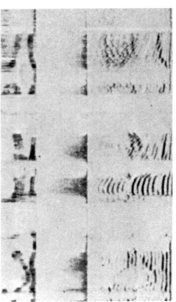

Plate 47. (a) pəvə́t (b) pə́vət (c) iŋklái̯n (d) íŋklai̯n

Nevertheless, when faced with speech showing very marked features of a dialectal pronunciation far removed from his own, a listener may require to hear some considerable stretch of speech before he is able with certainty to assign a vowel to the correct category in sequences where redundancy does not resolve all ambiguities. It is only by paying a good deal of attention to the sequence of vowel qualities and by remembering them that he builds the frame of reference.

The situation with regard to the stop consonants is plainly different. Even when the /b, d, g/ stimuli were presented in triads, as in the experiment by Eimas (1962) referred to earlier, the effect of context on the judgments was very small and certainly nowhere near to the maximum possible effect. The categories here appear to be rather more absolute and classification is more or less independent of sequential effects. There can be no doubt that the series /b, d, g/ includes marked discontinuities on the articulatory plane and, as we have already said, the association of categorical perception and articulatory discontinuity in this class of consonants formed the starting point for the theory that perceptual and articulatory continuity or discontinuity might be linked. Vowels present clearly a case of articulatory continuity and the present results, as far as they go, indicate continuous perception[6] but this evidence is not of course critical for the theory. It would be quite possible for articulatory continuity to be associated with well-defined categories established on some other, perhaps purely perceptual, basis. On the other hand, if it could be shown that continuous perception in speech was possible for a series of sounds which included marked articulatory discontinuities, this would certainly be a contra-indication to the theory. Material for such critical experiments might be found in the fricative series in English since it contains varying degrees of articulatory continuity. The change from /ʃ/ to /s/ involves very little break, there is a rather more decided one between /s/ and /θ/ and an even greater one between /θ/ and /f/. The difficulty here is that no single cue has equal weight in all these discriminations, as has been shown in experiments with naturally produced speech (Harris, 1958). It would therefore be difficult to generate a completely satisfactory series of stimuli to cover the whole group of fricatives, but it might be possible in separate experiments to discover how closely articulatory discontinuity is linked with sharpness of the phoneme boundary.

It has been suggested in previous papers that many of the data hitherto obtained concerning the perception of speech sounds show that this is a rather special kind of perception. In all cases where there was evidence of well-marked categories, the discrimination function showed peaks in the

6. As do the studies on phonemic tones and phonemic vowel duration (fn. 4). These phonemic distinctions also lie along articulatory continua.

region of the phoneme boundaries and the general level of discrimination was such as to suggest that listeners could discriminate between sounds only very little better than they could place these sounds in appropriate phoneme categories; they could in fact distinguish only about as many different sounds as they could identify. This result is very different from those obtained in psychophysical experiments with non-speech stimuli. It has generally been found that in judging stimuli varied with respect to a single dimension, subjects are able to discriminate many more stimuli than they can identify with certainty; they can distinguish more different pitches or brightnesses than they can label correctly. The comparison between speech and non-speech stimuli has been directly made in experiments already reported (Liberman *et al.*, 1961a, 1961b) in which the discrimination of speech stimuli was compared with that of non-speech stimuli which were as physically similar to the speech stimuli as it was possible to make them. The results showed two important differences between the two types of perception: first, for the non-speech sounds there was not the degree of fluctuation in discriminability that was found with the speech sounds and, second, discrimination was generally worse for non-speech stimuli than for comparable speech stimuli. This led to the conclusion that the sharpening of sensitivity to change at the region of phoneme boundaries must be the result of linguistic training in the listener.

Experiments with non-speech controls have so far been limited to the class of stop consonants (discrimination of /d, t/, /sl, spl/, /p, b/) but it is significant that in each case discrimination of speech sounds has proved to be superior to that for the non-speech controls. It is clear that listeners have learned to make the speech discrimination as a result of linguistic training. In the case of vowels, there are certain difficulties inherent in obtaining suitable controls in order to find out how far the discrimination of vowels may be the result of training, particularly where the physical variable is to be formant frequency. A transposition of the formant frequencies on the frequency scale is likely to result in sounds which are either still too speech-like or too musical. Discrimination of the latter might not be influenced by linguistic training but would be dependent on musical training and this factor might mask the effect that was being studied. It is quite possible that suitable control stimuli for vowel experiments may be found empirically but meanwhile little comment can be made about the effect of linguistic training on vowel discrimination except in one respect, that is, with regard to the evidence provided by the measures of context effect.

It was pointed out in the section on results that the influence of context on the perception of stop consonants was very weak and certainly less than in the case of the non-speech stimuli that were examined. For the synthetic vowels, on the other hand, the effect of context was, if anything, greater than for the non-speech stimuli. This suggests the very interesting conclusion, if this observation proves, in the light of further experimental evidence, to be well founded, that linguistic training in the case of vowel perception may include learning to make the maximum use of context. It is possible that English speakers, at least, learn both to make the necessary vowel phonemic distinctions and to appreciate the sub-phonemic differences involved in the recognition of different dialects, basing both operations on the maximum use of short-term memory for vowel quality. In other words, they learn to shift the frame of reference for vowels very frequently and very rapidly under the influence of sounds heard in the immediate past. If this were indeed so, vowel perception would not only present a very special case of perception but would also appear to be quite justifiably considered as being different from consonant perception.

References

ABRAMSON, A. S. (1961), 'Identification and discrimination of phonemic tones', *J. acoust. Soc. Amer.*, vol. 33, p. 842 (abstract).

BASTIAN, J., EIMAS, P. D., and LIBERMAN, A. M. (1961), 'Identification and discrimination of a phonemic contrast induced by silent interval', *J. acoust. Soc. Amer.*, vol. 33, p. 842 (abstract).

BASTIAN, J., and ABRAMSON, A. S. (1962), 'Identification and discrimination of phonemic vowel duration', *J. acoust. Soc. Amer.*, vol. 34, p. 743 (abstract).

BROADBENT, D. E., and LADEFOGED, P. (1960), 'Vowel judgments and adaptation level', *Proc. Roy. Soc. B.*, vol. 151, p. 384.

DENES, P. B. (1963), 'On the statistics of spoken English' *J. acoust. Soc. Amer.*, vol. 35, pp. 892–904.

EIMAS, P. D. (1962), 'A study of the relation between absolute identification and discrimination along selected sensory continua', Ph.D. dissertation (Connecticut).

FANT, C. G. M. (1958). 'Modern instruments and methods for acoustic studies of speech', *Proceedings of the 8th International Congress of Linguists* (Oslo), p. 282.

GRIFFITH, B. C. (1957) 'A study of the relation between phoneme labelling and discriminability in the percep on of synthetic stop consonants', Ph D. dissertation (Connecticut).

HARRIS, K. S. (1958), 'Cues for the discrimination of American English fricatives in spoken syllables', *Language and Speech*, vol. 1, pp. 1–7. Reprinted here, pp. 284–97.

JOOS, M. (1948), *Acoustic Phonetics*, Language Monograph, no. 23, Baltimore.

LADEFOGED, P., and BROADBENT D. E. (1957), 'Information conveyed by vowels', *J. acoust. Soc. Amer.*. vol. 29, p. 98.

LIBERMAN A. M., HARRIS, K. S., HOFFMAN, H. S., and GRIFFITH, B. C. (1957), 'The discrimination of speech sounds within and across phoneme boundaries', *J. exp. Psychol.*, vol. 54. p. 358. Reprinted here, pp. 333–47.

LIBERMAN, A. M., HARRIS, K. S., KINNEY, J. A., and LANE, H. (1961a), 'The discrimination of relative onset-time of the components of certain speech and nonspeech patterns', *J. exp. Psychol.*, vol. 61, p. 379.

LIBERMAN, A. M., HARRIS, K. S., EIMAS, P. D., LISKER, L., and BASTIAN, J. (1961b), 'An effect of learning on speech perception: the discrimination of durations of silence with and without phonemic significance', *Language and Speech*, vol. 4, p. 175.

PETERSON, G. E., and BARNEY, H. L. (1952) 'Control methods used in a study of the vowels', *J. acoust. Soc. Amer.*, vol. 24, pp. 175–84. Reprinted here, pp. 104–22.

17 Franklin S. Cooper, Pierre C. Delattre, Alvin M. Liberman, John M. Borst and Louis J. Gerstman

Some Experiments on the Perception of Synthetic Speech Sounds[1]

Franklin S. Cooper, Pierre C. Delattre, Alvin M. Liberman, John M. Borst and Louis J. Gerstman, 'Some experiments on the perception of synthetic speech sounds', *Journal of the Acoustical Society of America*, vol. 24 (1952), pp. 597–606.

The program of research on which we are engaged was described in general terms at the preceding Speech Communication Conference (Cooper, 1950). As we pointed out there, and in more detail in another paper (Cooper, Liberman and Borst, 1951), our work on the perception of speech was based on the assumption that we would have a flexible and convenient experimental method if we could use a spectrographic display to control or manipulate speech sounds. Workers at the Bell Telephone Laboratories had developed the sound spectrograph, which made it instrumentally feasible to obtain spectrograms of relatively long samples of connected speech, and it had become evident that the spectrographic transform has important advantages over the oscillogram as a way of displaying speech sounds to the eye. We were interested in using the spectrogram, not merely as a representation of speech sounds, but also as a basis for modifying and, in the extreme case, creating them. For that purpose we built a machine called a pattern playback which converts spectrographic pictures into sound, using either photographic copies of actual spectrograms or, alternatively, 'synthetic' patterns which are painted by hand on a cellulose acetate base. Having determined first that the playback would speak quite intelligibly from photographic copies of actual spectrograms, we proceeded to prepare hand-painted patterns of test sentences[2] which were, by comparison with the original spectrograms, very highly simplified (see Plate 45). In drawing the hand-painted spectrograms we tried, as the first step, to reproduce as well as we could those aspects of the original pattern which were most apparent to the eye, and then, by working back and forth between hand-painted spectrogram and sound, we modified the patterns, usually by trial and error, until the simplified spectrograms were rather highly intelligible.

1. This research was made possible in part by funds granted by the Carnegie Corporation of New York and in part through the support of the Department of Defense in connection with Contract DA49-170-sc-274.
2. We employed sentence lists prepared by Egan and co-workers. See Egan (1948).

The work with simplified spectrograms did not provide unequivocal answers to questions about the minimal and invariant patterns for the various sounds of speech, but it did enable us to develop our techniques, and, further, it suggested certain specific problems which appeared to warrant more systematic investigation. In our research on these problems we have departed from the procedure of progressively simplifying the spectrograms of actual speech and have undertaken instead to study the effects on perception of variations in isolated acoustic elements or patterns. Thus, we can hope to determine the separate contributions to the perception of speech of several acoustic variables and, ultimately, to learn how they can be combined to best effect.

Stop consonants: bursts of noise

A careful inspection of actual spectrograms suggests, and our experience with simplified spectrograms seems to confirm, that one of the variables that may enable a listener to differentiate /p/, /t/ and /k/ is the position along the frequency scale of the brief burst of noise which constitutes the acoustic

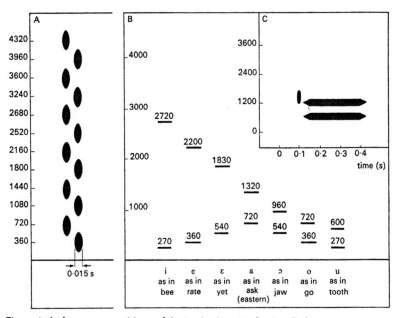

Figure 1 A: frequency positions of the twelve bursts of noise. B: frequency positions of the formants of the two-formant vowels with which the bursts were paired. C: one of the 84 'syllables' formed by pairing a burst of noise and a two-formant vowel. (Source: *American Journal of Psychology*)

counterpart of the articulatory explosion. In an attempt to isolate this variable and determine its role in perception, we prepared a series of schematized burst-plus-vowel patterns in which bursts at each of twelve frequency positions were paired with each of seven cardinal vowels. As can be seen in Figure 1, the bursts were constant as to size and shape, and the vowels, which maintained a steady state throughout, were composed of two formants only.[3] All of the combinations of burst and vowel – a total of 84 syllable patterns – were converted into sound and presented in random order to thirty college students with instructions to identify the initial component of the syllable as /p/, /t/ or /k/.

Figure 2 shows, for each of the vowels, how the subjects' identifications varied according to the frequency position of the burst. In general, it appears that this one variable – the frequency position of the burst – provides the listener with a basis for distinguishing among /p/, /t/ and /k/.

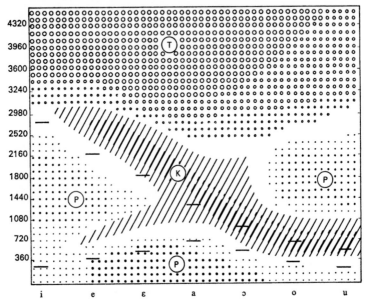

Figure 2 The twelve center frequencies of the bursts of noise are shown along the *y* axis: the seven vowels are arranged in the order front-to-back along the *x* axis with formant positions given. The zones show the burst-vowel combinations for which one of the three responses was dominant and indicate roughly the extent of dominance. (Source: *American Journal of Psychology*)

3. For a complete account of the experimental work leading to the choice of the formant frequencies of these vowels, see Delattre, Liberman and Cooper (1951)

We see that high frequency bursts were heard as /t/ for all vowels. Bursts at lower frequencies were heard as /k/ when they were on a level with, or slightly above, the second formant of the vowel; otherwise they were heard as /p/. It is clear that for /p/ and /k/ the identification of the consonant depended, not solely on the frequency position of the burst of noise, but rather on this position in relation to the vowel. In other words, the perception of these stimuli, and also, perhaps, the perception of their spoken counterparts, requires the consonant–vowel combination as a minimal acoustic unit.[4]

Stop consonants: transitions

We turned next in our study of the stop consonants to another aspect of the acoustic pattern which is often evident in spectrograms, namely, the consonant–vowel transitions. These transitions are seen as rapid shifts in the frequency positions of the vowel formants where vowel and consonant join and are typically most marked for the second formant, although they are usually present in some degree for the other formants as well.

The interpretation of these transitions is a major problem. In articulatory terms it is clear that the positions of the speech organs for consonant and vowel are, in general, different and that the rapid movement from one position to the other will usually produce an equally rapid shift in the acoustic output. The parallel interpretation in perceptual terms is that these rapid changes in the sound stream are no more than the necessary transitions (hence, the name) between the sounds that serve to identify successive phonemes; by implication, the transitions are merely nulls which dilute, or even confuse, the acoustic message.

An alternative interpretation is that these rapid changes are heard as important distinguishing characteristics of the sound stream and may indeed serve as a principal acoustic cue for the perception of the consonant–vowel combination – the syllable or 'half-syllable', as the case may be (Joos, 1948, p. 122). Since a vowel is usually loud and long (hence, identifiable by itself) whereas a consonant is often weak or of very short duration, the practical effect is that the transitional portion of the vowel is transferred to the acoustic counterpart of the consonant. But whether one considers the syllable as separable in this restricted sense or as an indissoluble unit, the second interpretation of transitions gives far more weight to their role in speech perception than the term 'transition' would imply. The first step in exploring this question experimentally was to select one vowel and to draw synthetic spectrograms in which a variety of 'transitions' were added to the two-formant version of the vowel. Such a series is shown in Figure 3. In the

4. For a detailed account of the experiment and a further discussion of the results, see Liberman, Delattre and Cooper (1952).

upper line, the first formant has always the same rising transition, but there is a systematic variation in the transitions of the second formant: rising sharply at the left of the figure, straight in the center and falling steeply at the right. In the lower line, the same sequence of second-formant transitions is repeated, but the first formant has a very small rising transition. One observation that came from this sort of exploratory work was that the

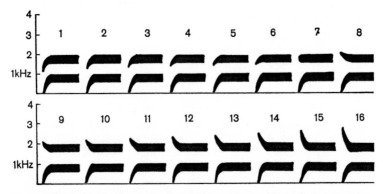

Figure 3 Variations in the onset of vowel formants used in exploring the role of transitions. When the patterns shown in the upper line are converted into sound by the playback, the syllables /ba/, /da/ and /ga/ are heard in succession as the second formant transitions vary from rising to falling. The upper and lower lines differ only in the extent of the first-formant transitions: this seems to contribute to the voiced (upper) or unvoiced (lower) characteristics of the consonants

transitions of the first formant appear to contribute to voicing of the stop consonants, while transitions of the second formant provide a basis for distinguishing among /b/, /d/ and /g/, or their cognates /p/, /t/ and /k/. (The sounds corresponding to these painted spectrograms were presented by means of magnetic tape recordings.[5] These sounds were generated by passing the patterns of Figure 3 through the pattern playback.)

Our first attempts to generalize from the second-formant transitions for /ba/, /da/ and /ga/ to the corresponding transitions for a different vowel showed quite clearly that matters would be more complicated – that we were again dealing with interactions or interrelations between the acoustic counterparts of consonant and vowel when they occur together as a syllable.

This exploratory work was followed by systematic tests of a range of

5. The authors will supply, at cost, copies of the sound demonstration on magnetic tape or disk.

second-formant transitions applied to each of the seven vowels that had previously been used in the /ptk/-burst experiment. The resulting test syllables are very much like those shown in Figure 3 except that the extent of second-formant transitions was increased by one degree at the left and two at the right, giving a total of eleven different degrees of transition. Thus, with seven vowels, there were seventy-seven consonant–vowel stimuli to be judged. The results are shown in the upper left-hand corner of Figure 4. There are, for each vowel, three bars showing the distribution of

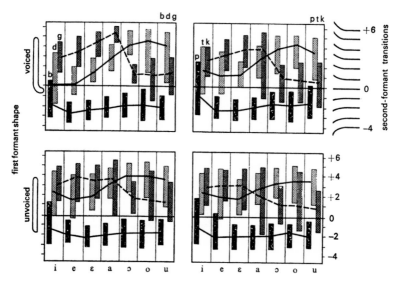

Figure 4 Results of four experiments on the contribution of second-formant transitions to the identification of the stop consonants

judgments among /b/, /d/ and /g/ as a function of the direction and extent of the second-formant transition. All first formants had rising transitions similar to those in the upper half of Figure 3. The length of the bar gives a rough indication of the range of different transitions included within the group judgment for each sound and, hence, some indication of the degree of overlap or confusion among the sounds. Specifically, the connecting lines pass through the median judgments, and the bars end at the quartile points. Thus, the array shows that most of the subjects heard a rising second-formant transition as /b/ and that falling transitions might be heard either as /g/ or /d/, depending on the vowel.

In the lower left-hand quadrant of Figure 4 are the results of a comparable test in which all of the first formants were straight, or 'unvoiced'.

Also, the two right-hand arrays of Figure 4 give comparable data for the two sets of test stimuli mentioned above when, however, the subjects were instructed to choose among /p/, /t/ and /k/. In a general way, the four arrays are similar. The results agree in the predominance of /b/ (or /p/) judgments for rising second-formant transitions and in the existence of a crossover between /d/ (or /t/) and /g/ (or /k/) judgments for falling transitions. It does appear that the cognate relationships between /ptk/ and /bdg/ are effectively cued by the second-formant transitions. A problem remains, however, of finding adequate cues for the distinction between voiced and unvoiced stops.

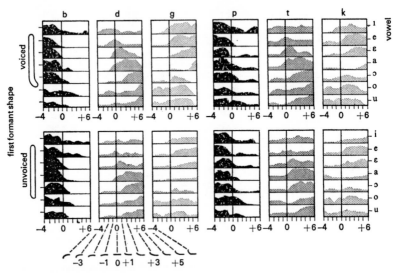

Figure 5 Distributions of judgments of the stop consonants obtained with variations in second-formant transitions

Transitions of the first formant make some difference, and, of course, the presence or absence of a 'voice bar' at the fundamental frequency plays a role.

The same data are presented somewhat more directly in Figure 5. Vowel color is now displayed along the y axis, and the extent of second-formant transition is the x dimension, as shown pictorially at the lower left; the heights of the 'mountains' show the percentage distributions of the responses indicated by the column headings (/b/, /d/, /g/ or /p/, /t/, /k/) for the various stimulus combinations of transition plus vowel. One is somewhat reassured, in dealing with experiments of this kind, to find that some of the stimuli do yield unanimous agreement and that the variations, both with degree of transition and with vowel color, seem to be smooth and continuous. At the same time, it is evident that these transitions do not suffice in all cases; there are a few consonant-vowel combinations for which none of the transitions gives an unambiguous cue. However, a comparison of the data on transitions with the previous results for bursts shows that most of the ambiguous cases would possibly be resolved if *both* of these cues were being used.

Nasal resonants: m and l

A class of sounds which are cognate to /b/, /d/, /g/ and /p/, /t/, /k/ consists of the nasal resonants /m/, /n/ and /ŋ/. Another series of exploratory experiments indicated that each of these consonants involves a vowel transition and also a steady-state resonant sound whose intensity and frequency characteristics are different from those of the vowel. We were interested, in the first instance, in segregating the effects of the transitions, and this seemed to require that we find a neutral position for the resonant portion which would convey the impression of resonant nasal consonants as a class without providing important cues to the identity of the particular consonant. This is probably an oversimplification, but it does permit us to collect data for a comparison of the resonants with the voiced and voiceless stops. We have run a first set of tests in which the previous seven vowels and eleven degrees of transition were paired in all possible combinations in syllables which also contained a neutral nasal resonance portion. The consonant was placed in terminal position since initial /ŋ/ does not occur in English. This work is still in process; hence, no figure will be presented. In a general way, we find about the same distributions that appeared in the /bdg/-transition test. Thus, the second-formant transitions which were regularly heard as /b/ (or /p/) in the preceding test now give the cognate /m/, and there is a comparable crossover in which /n/ parallels /d/ (or /t/) and /ŋ/ parallels /g/ (or /k/). There are some indications in the data that we are not dealing with a monovalent stimulus in this case; probably we shall have to explore variations in the supposedly neutral resonance.

The exploratory work that precedes systematic tests of the kind that we have been discussing tends to become divergent almost without limit, but also it turns up interesting leads, such as the example shown in Figure 6. We find that a transition from higher to lower frequency which is followed by a steady-state resonant sound is often heard as /m/ but may at times sound like /l/ instead. Our best guess at the moment and on the basis of cut-and-try experiments with only two vowels is that the distinctions between /l/ and /m/ are multiple, involving (a) the rate of transition of the second formant – a gradual transition favors /l/, a rapid transition favors /m/, (b) the frequency position of the low formant of the resonant portion – /l/ is favored by a higher frequency: and (c) the behavior of the second formant in passing from vowel to resonance – if the second formant of the resonant portion forms a plausible continuation of the second formant of the vowel, one tends to hear /l/, whereas a sudden discontinuity contributes to an /m/ impression. The first three lines of Figure 6 illustrate these three pattern

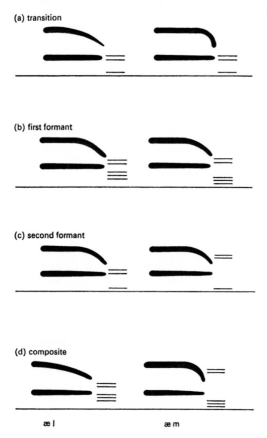

(a) transition

(b) first formant

(c) second formant

(d) composite

æ l   æ m

Figure 6 Spectrographic patterns showing three acoustic cues which contribute to the perceptual differentiation of /l/ and /m/ following the vowel /æ/

differences; the fourth line shows a composite pattern which incorporates all three differences. These are tentative results, but they indicate the kind of thing that one finds in the exploratory phase. (The sounds which correspond to these syllables were demonstrated, line by line, and in both forward and reverse directions.)

Vowels

In this review we shall pass over a sizable block of work on two-formant and one-formant synthetic vowels, except to say that some of the results are most readily explained on the basis that the ear can, and sometimes does perform an averaging operation on two formants which lie close together; thus, the first and second formants of the back vowels may at times be replaceable by a single formant, or the second and third formants of /i/ by a single high formant. We have not so far found it necessary to use three formants to obtain reasonably good vowel color for the cardinal vowels, but an exploratory investigation has indicated that *transitions* of the third formant may contribute to consonant identification. Of course, the behavior of the third formant in spectrograms of the Midwestern /r/ and of nasal vowels is well known (see Joos, 1948, p. 93; Potter, Kopp and Green, 1947).

Some future directions

The general directions in which the present work should be extended are fairly obvious. We have studied various acoustic cues in isolation. We can reasonably expect that the synthetic sounds will be identified with greater accuracy if two or three cues are provided *simultaneously*. We can even hope that *not more* than two or three acoustic cues will be required to give high intelligibility, even though the resulting sounds may still not be entirely lifelike. In addition, it is quite possible that such speech will be more resistant to noise than normal speech. As to the effectiveness of multiple cues, we know already that a transition added to a burst of noise improves the stop consonants, but we have yet to investigate what adjustments in burst position and in extent of transition may be required for the best combination of these two cues and just how much improvement will result. Also, while it is clear that bursts and transitions complement each other in the sense that when one cue is weak, the other is usually strong, nevertheless, there may remain some syllables for which both cues together may not suffice, and one must then search for other cues. One such possibility is a transition in the third formant of the vowel, and we do have some exploratory evidence of contributions from this quarter, However, the problem is not merely to find additional acoustic cues which make a contribution, but rather to sift out the two or three most efficient cues: that is, we should like eventually to rank-order the cues in terms of their *relative* contributions to intelligibility. Also, we need to run tests in which a greater variety of stimuli are presented and wider ranges of judgments are allowed, until finally all of the phonemes of American English have been studied in their usual combinations.

The step from phoneme combinations to connected speech will involve a variety of additional problems, but we ought, eventually, to be able to synthesize connected speech on the sole basis of rules, or principles, of the same general kind that we are beginning to derive for the stops and the resonants. This is not our primary objective, but it does provide an overall check on the validity of the acoustic descriptions.

Some speculations

In addition to the pragmatic objectives of synthesizing speech and giving simplified acoustic descriptions of the speech sounds, we may hope that eventually an acoustic counterpart of the linguistic structure of the language might emerge – and indeed, that the regularities of the one structure might complement those of the other. Figure 7, for example, shows one attempt

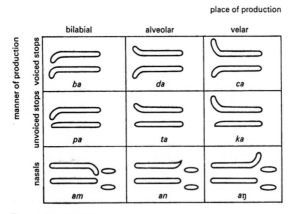

Figure 7

to correlate some of our acoustic data with the articulatory and linguistic patterns of English. There the schematic patterns for the voiced and voiceless stops and the nasal resonants (paired with the vowel /a/) are arranged in a 3-by-3 array based on articulatory features. It does seem that the acoustic data fit naturally into the array, with the distinctions among columns being given by the transitions of the second formant, and, among rows, by three 'markers', namely, rising transitions of the first formant for the voiced stops, no transitions of the first formant (also bursts of noise not shown in the figure) for the unvoiced stops, and a steady resonant portion for the nasal resonants. (The playback sounds corresponding to the patterns of Figure 7 were played, row by row and column by column.) We should probably not try to generalize from these limited data; we have not yet made the corresponding comparisons for a range of vowels, and some changes in interpretation may be necessary when we do.

As a second point, it may be of interest to examine the data from the point of view that perception involves a set of binary choices. You will recall that bursts of noise preceding a vowel were always heard as /t/ when the center frequency of the burst was high, but that low bursts were heard as /p/ or /k/, depending on the vowel that followed:

$$\text{bursts:} \quad \frac{\text{high } (+) = \quad /t/}{\text{low } \ (-) = /p/ \text{ or } /k/}.$$

You will also recall that transitions of the second formant, if rising, were always heard as /p/, and if falling as /t/ or /k/, depending on the vowel that followed:

$$\text{transitions:} \quad \frac{\text{falling } (+) = /t/ \text{ or } /k/}{\text{rising } \ (-) = \quad /p/}.$$

We have then a basis for deciding among /p/, /t/ and /k/, when both cues are given: /p/ $= - -$ (low burst, rising transition), /t/ $= + +$ (high burst, falling transition), /k/ $= - +$ (low burst, falling transition). It would appear, then, that perceptual distinctions among /p/, /t/ and /k/ might conceivably be made on the basis of only two separate binary decisions.[6] If this is correct, we should be able to synthesize satisfactory stop consonants without regard to the exact placement of bursts or to the precise degree of transition, but merely on the basis of 'high' or 'low' bursts and transitions. We are by no means confident that this can be done.

For a third point, let us return to the general subject of transitions. It seems fairly clear that transitions are important in speech perception, and one could wish for a name that would carry *this* implication rather than its opposite. You have seen how the identification of a particular transition (or burst) seems to depend also on the vowel, so that, apparently, one is perceiving an acoustic unit having the approximate dimensions of a syllable or half-syllable. Now this is not really very surprising if spectrograms are taken at face-value, but we – and perhaps some other workers as well – had undertaken to find the 'invariants' of speech, a term which implies, at least in its simplest interpretation, a one-to-one correspondence between something half-hidden in the spectrogram and the successive phonemes of the message. It is precisely this kind of relationship that we do *not* find, at least for these stripped-down stops and nasal resonants. It may be useful to phrase this departure from a one-to-one correspondence between phoneme

6. We should, perhaps, point out that the kind of binary scheme being considered here differs in several respects from the system put forward by Jakobson, Fant and Halle (1952).

and sound in the technical jargon of cryptography, thereby borrowing a well-established distinction, and say that we seem to be dealing, at the acoustic level, with an *encoded* message rather than an *enciphered* one – or, more probably, with a mixture of code and cipher. But the important point, however phrased, is a caution that one may not always be able to find the phoneme in the speech wave, because it may not exist there in free form; in other words, one should not expect always to be able to find acoustic invariants for the *individual* phonemes.

The problem of speech perception is then to describe the decoding process either in terms of the decoding mechanism or – as we are trying to do – by compiling the code book, one in which there is one column for acoustic entries and another column for message units, whether these be phonemes, syllables, words, or whatever.

One more bit of speculation, if we may. The results of the /ptk/-burst experiment – and also the results with transitions – provide some extreme cases which suggest that the perceived similarities and differences between speech sounds may correspond more closely to the similarities and differences in the *articulatory* domain than to those in the *acoustic* domain; that is to say, the relation between perception and articulation may be simpler than the relation between perception and the acoustic stimulus. In Figure 2, the set of bursts which were called /k/ differ markedly in acoustic terms, despite the fact that they are heard as the same speech sound and are spoken in about – although not quite – the same way. On the other hand, the bursts at 1440 Hz are identical sounds in acoustic terms, but they are heard as different speech sounds when paired with different vowels, e.g. /pi/, /ka/ and /pu/. Here, the perceived *differences* in the consonant are in contrast to the acoustic '*similarities*', but they might very well parallel articulatory differences if it is reasonable to assume that a person, in attempting to duplicate the sound of these bursts, would find it easiest to use his lips when his mouth is set to say /i/ or /u/ (close vowels) but would find it easiest to use the arch of the tongue with his mouth in position to say /a/ (open vowel).

These are examples of what we mean in saying that perception may at times be more closely and simply related to the articulatory movements than to the acoustic stimuli. This is not a new concept – the central idea has been stated in various ways by various workers (see Stetson, 1951; Joos, 1948, p. 98) – but we do believe that these considerations must be taken into account in any theory of speech perception; obviously, they are most directly related to the functioning of the decoding mechanism.

Synthesis of connected speech

In discussing future directions for the general program of work that has been described here, we mentioned the synthesis of connected speech as a long-range objective. It is possible, of course, to attempt synthesis using only the limited information we now have about only a few of the sounds of speech. We shall play for you some examples of words and sentences which were synthesized on the basis of rules derived from our experiments. It is fairly evident that the rules alone are inadequate at this stage and that

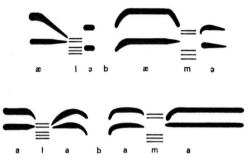

Figure 8 Simplified spectrograms of the word 'Alabama', drawn, as far as possible, according to the rules derived from our research on the component phones

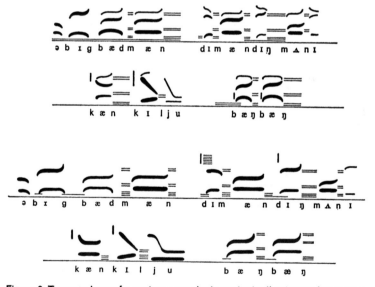

Figure 9 Two versions of a sentence employing principally stop and resonant consonants. Both were highly intelligible when converted into sound by the playback

these examples do benefit from extrapolations of the cardinal vowels to the vowels of American English and from some hunches about diphthongization, syllable length and stress. However, in all cases, the words were created *de novo* – without reference to actual spectrograms – and employed bursts and transitions for the production of the stop and resonant consonants. (This portion of the demonstration consisted of the following recordings from the playback: (a) 'Alabama', from the patterns of Figure 8. The upper version yielded a Southern dialect; the lower version gave the word as it might have been pronounced by a Frenchman. (b) Spondees taken from the lists prepared at the Psycho-Acoustic Laboratory: 'backbone, bonbon, outlaw, pancake, cookbook, cupcake, nutmeg'. (c) Sentences: 'Oh my aching back.' 'At MIT meet Lick and Locke.' 'A playback can talk back.' (d) The sentence of Figure 9, in two versions; the lower is the first draft, painted directly from the typewritten page; the upper version benefited from revisions by ear. Some transitions of the third formant were introduced, in addition to the use 'by rule' of second-formant transitions and bursts.)

Apparently most of you understood some, if not all, of the examples; even so, it is clear that much remains to be done to achieve a working mastery of the rules governing the acoustic stimuli by which we perceive speech.

References

COOPER, F. S. (1950), 'Spectrum analysis', *J. acoust. Soc. Amer.*, vol. 22, pp. 761–2.

COOPER, F. S., LIBERMAN, A. M., and BORST, J. M. (1951), 'The interconversion of audible and visible patterns as a basis for research in the perception of speech', *Proc. nat. Acad. Sci.*, vol. 37, pp. 318–25. Excerpt reprinted here, pp. 204–7.

DELATTRE, P. C., LIBERMAN, A. M., and COOPER, F. S. (1951), 'Voyelles synthétiques à deux formants et voyelles cardinales', *Le Maître phonétique*, no. 96, pp. 30–37.

EGAN, J. (1948), 'Articulation testing methods', *Laryngoscope*, no. 58, pp. 955–91.

JAKOBSON, R., FANT, C. G. M., and HALLE, M. (1952), 'Preliminaries to speech analysis', *Technical Report*, no. 13, Acoustics Laboratory, MIT.

JOOS, M. (1948), *Acoustic Phonetics*, Language Monograph, no. 23, Baltimore.

LIBERMAN, A. M., DELATTRE, P. C., and COOPER, F. S. (1952), 'The role of selected stimulus variables in the perception of the unvoiced stop consonants', *Amer. J. Psychol.*, vol. 65, pp. 497–516.

POTTER, R. A., KOPP G. A., and GREEN, H. C. (1947), *Visible Speech*, Van Nostrand.

STETSON, R. H. (1951), *Motor Phonetics*, Oberlin College.

18 Pierre C. Delattre, Alvin M. Liberman and Franklin S. Cooper

Acoustic Loci and Transitional Cues for Consonants[1]

Pierre C. Delattre, Alvin M. Liberman and Franklin S. Cooper, 'Acoustic loci and transitional cues for consonants', *Journal of the Acoustical Society of America*, vol. 27 (1955), pp. 769–73.

In an earlier experiment (see Cooper *et al.*, 1952) we undertook to find out whether the transitions (frequency shifts) of the second formant – often seen in spectrograms in the region where consonant and vowel join – can be cues for the identification of the voiced stop consonants. For that purpose we prepared a series of simplified, hand-painted spectrograms of transition-plus-vowel, then converted these patterns into sound and played the recording to naïve listeners for judgment as /b/, /d/ or /g/. The agreement among the listeners was, in general, sufficient to show that transitions of the second formant can serve as cues for the identification of the stops and, also, to enable us to select, for each vowel, the particular transitions that best produced each of the stop consonant phones. These transitions are shown in Figure 1.

We found in further experiments (Liberman *et al.*, 1954) that these same second-formant transitions can serve as cues for the unvoiced stops /ptk/ and the nasal consonants /mnŋ/, provided, of course, that the synthetic patterns are otherwise changed to contain appropriate acoustic cues for the voiceless and nasal manners of production. Moreover, and more important for the purposes of this paper, the results of these experiments plainly indicated a relationship between second-formant transition and articulatory place of production. Thus, the same second-formant transitions that had been found to produce /b/ proved to be appropriate also for the synthesis of /p/ and /m/, which, like /b/, are articulated at the lips; the second-formant transitions that produced /d/ produced the consonants /t/ and /n/, which have in common with /d/ an articulatory place of production at the alveoles; and, similarly, the second-formant transitions were found to be essentially the same for /g/, /k/ and /ŋ/, which are all produced at the velum.

It is an obvious assumption that the transitions seen in spectrograms reflect the changes in cavity size and shape caused by the movements of the

1. This work was supported, in part, by the Carnegie Corporation of New York and, in part, by Department of Defense Contract. Some of the results of this research were reported in a paper read before the Acoustical Society of America on 15 October 1953.

articulators, and if we further assume that the relation between articulation and sound is not too complex, we should suppose, on the basis of the evidence of the preceding paragraph, that the second-formant transitions rather directly represent the articulatory movements *from* the place of production of the consonant *to* the position for the following vowel. Since the articulatory place of production of each consonant is, for the most part, fixed, we

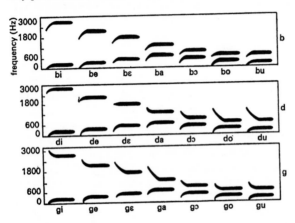

Figure 1

might expect to find that there is correspondingly a fixed frequency position – or 'locus' – for its second formant; we could then rather simply describe the various second-formant transitions as movements from this acoustic locus to the steady-state level of the vowel, wherever that might be.[2] As may be seen in Figure 1, the various transitions that produce the best /d/ with each of the seven vowels do, in fact, appear to be coming from the same general region, and on the assumption that the first part of the acoustic transition is somehow missing, one may suppose that the transitions originate from precisely the same point. Clearly, /d/ is the best case. For /b/ the transitions all appear to be coming from some point low on the frequency scale, but an exact position for the /b/ locus is not evident. In the case of /g/, there would appear to be a single high frequency locus for the front vowels /i/, /e/, /ε/, and the mid-vowel /a/; but for the back vowels /ɔ/, /o/,

2. We do not wish to restrict the concept of locus to the second formant, nor do we mean to relate it exclusively, on the articulatory side, to place of production. By 'locus' we mean simply a place on the frequency scale at which a transition begins or to which it may be assumed to 'point'. We have found this to be a useful concept, since, for first and second formants, there appear to be many fewer loci than there are transitions.

The locus is in certain respects similar to the concept of the 'hub' as developed by Potter, Kopp and Green (1947, pp. 39–51).

and /u/ the acoustic pattern breaks sharply, and it is obvious that the same /g/ locus cannot serve for all vowels. In this connection it is known that the articulatory place of production of /g/ is displaced somewhat according to the vowel that follows it, but there is no evidence that there is in this displacement the kind of discontinuity that occurs at the acoustic level in the sudden and large shift of the /g/ transition. It would appear, then, that in this particular instance the relationship between place of production and sound has become rather complex, and a simple correspondence between this articulatory variable and a second-formant acoustic locus is not found.

In the series of experiments to be reported here we have, first, undertaken to collect additional evidence concerning the existence and position of the second-formant loci for /b/, /d/ and /g/, and, in particular, to determine whether these loci are independent of vowel color as, indeed, they must be if the concept is to have any utility; second, we have tried to determine whether, in the case of the stops, the locus can be the actual starting point for the transition, or whether, alternatively, the locus is a place to which the transition may only point; and, third, we have collected evidence concerning a first-formant locus.

Apparatus and general procedure

All the acoustic stimuli used in this study were produced by converting hand-painted spectrograms into sound. The special-purpose playback that accomplishes this conversion has been described in earlier papers (Cooper, 1950; Cooper, Liberman and Borst, 1951). It produces 50 beams of light, separately modulated at each of the first 50 harmonics of a 120 Hz fundamental, and spreads them across the hand-painted spectrogram in such a manner that the frequency of the modulated light at any point corresponds approximately to the frequency level of the place at which it strikes the spectrogram. The painted portions of the spectrogram reflect the appropriately modulated beams of light to a phototube whose current is amplified and fed to a loudspeaker.

As shown in Figure 2, the hand-painted patterns consisted of two formants, each of which included three contiguous harmonics of the 120 Hz fundamental. A: rising transition in the first formant and a straight transition in the second; B: a straight transition in the first formant and a falling transition in the second. The intensity of the central harmonic of the formant was 6 dB more than the two outlying ones; the frequency of that harmonic is used in specifying the frequency position of the formant. All transitions of either formant were always painted and heard in initial position in the syllable. A transition is called 'rising' or 'falling' according to whether it originates at a frequency lower than (rising) or higher than (falling) the steady state of the corresponding formant of the vowel.

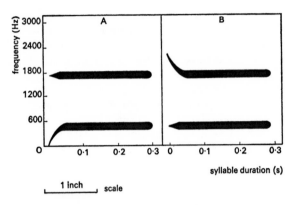

Figure 2 Scale drawings of sample two-formant patterns used in this study

Second-formant loci

The purposes of this part of the investigation were to find the positions of the second-formant loci of the stop consonants, and to test whether their existence and position are independent of vowel color and, also, of the extent of first-formant transition. Accordingly, we prepared the series of

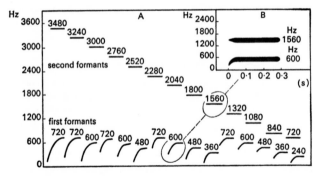

Figure 3 Schematic display of the stimuli used in finding the second-formant loci of /b/, /d/ and /g/

patterns shown schematically in Figure 3, and converted them to sound for evaluation by ear. A: frequency positions of the straight second formants and the various first formants with which each was paired. When first and second formants were less than 240 Hz apart, they were permitted to overlap. B: a typical test pattern, made up of the first and second formants circled in A.

As shown in the figure, each stimulus pattern had a straight transition of the second formant and some degree of rising transition of the first formant. This arrangement was dictated by two considerations: first, the possibility that the initial part of the transition is not sounded, in which case we should suppose that only a straight second formant can 'point' precisely to the frequency position of the locus;[3] and, second, the fact that with zero transition of the second formant, a consonant will be heard, if at all, only when the first formant is curved.

When the first and second formants of Figure 3 are paired in all combinations, 65 vowels are produced, comprising a wide variety of colors and including many that do not correspond to known speech sounds. The extent of first-formant transitions was varied as shown in the figure. Each of the two-formant patterns was converted into sound and listened to carefully by the authors of this paper, who identified and evaluated each sound as /b/, /d/ or /g/. When the judgments thus obtained are appropriately tabulated, the following conclusions emerge:

1 Rather clear stop consonants are heard at particular positions of the second formant. The best /g/ is produced by a second formant at 3000 Hz, the best /d/ at 1800 Hz, and the best /b/ at 720 Hz.[4] We shall suppose that these three frequencies represent the acoustic loci of /g/, /d/ and /b/, respectively. At other frequency levels of the straight second formant a stop-like sound is heard, the identity of which is more or less clear depending on its nearness to one of the three frequencies given above. At about 1320 Hz the sound is indifferently /b/, /d/ or /g/.

3. Potter, Kopp and Green (1947, pp. 81–103) located the 'hub' of each of the stop consonants by a technique which obviously takes account of the same consideration. They made spectrograms of each of the stops paired with a variety of vowels and then looked for those patterns in which the second formant was straight. The syllables /dæ/ (as in 'dad') and /bu/ (as in 'book') yielded straight second formants, and they concluded that the hub of /d/ is in the same position as the hub of /æ/ and that, in similar fashion, /b/ goes with /u/. The hub of /g/ was found to be variable.
4. One would infer from the graphs of Figure 1 that the locus of /b/ must be somewhere below the second formant of /w/ (720 Hz), since the best /bu/, as indicated by the amount of agreement among our naïve listeners in the earlier transition study, was formed when the second formant had a rising transition. We believe that the discrepancy between that result and the present one is to be attributed to differences of detail in the patterns used in the two studies.
As is indicated in Figure 3, the straight second formants were spaced at intervals of 240 Hz. After it had begun to appear that the stop consonant loci were in the vicinity of 3000, 1800 and 720 Hz, we experimented, on an exploratory basis, with straight second formants 120 Hz on either side of each of these three values, and found that none of the stops was significantly improved by these adjustments. Of the three stops that are produced when the straight second formants are at the loci, the /d/ (at 1800 Hz) is the most compelling, the /b/ (at 720 Hz) is slightly less so, and /g/ (at 3000 Hz) is, perhaps, the least satisfying.

Pierre C. Delattre, Alvin M. Liberman and Franklin S. Cooper 277

2 The steady-state level of the first formant has essentially no effect on either the strength or identity of the consonant impression, with the exception that when the straight second formant is about midway between the /g/ locus (at 3000 Hz) and the /d/ locus (at 1800 Hz), raising or lowering the level of the first formant tends to push the sound toward /d/ or /g/. Otherwise, it appears that the second-formant loci are independent of the changes in vowel color that are produced by varying the position of the first formant.

3 The extent of the first-formant transition has little or no effect on the identity of the stop consonant. Such variations do, however, affect the strength of the consonant impression. As was pointed out earlier, the first formant must have some degree of rising transition if a consonant is to be heard at all when the second formant is straight. Our observations in this experiment point additionally to the conclusion that in the case of the voiced stops the consonant impression is stronger as the first-formant transition is larger. The strongest stop is obtained when the first formant starts at the lowest frequency (120 Hz) and rises from that point to the steady-state level appropriate for the following vowel.

The locus and the start of the transition

This part of the investigation was designed to determine whether the transitions can start from the locus and move to the steady-state level of the vowel, or whether the transitions must only point to this locus, as they appeared to do in Figure 1. For that purpose we used the locus values that had been found in the first part of this investigation, and, making the assumption that the transition can actually originate at the locus, we prepared a series of patterns like those shown schematically in A of Figure 4. There we have, with a fixed lower formant, a choice of second formants which all originate at the /d/ locus, i.e. at 1800 Hz, and move from that point to their respective steady-state positions. When these patterns are sounded – the fixed first formant with each of the second formants in turn – we do not hear /d/ in every case. Rather, we hear /b/ when the steady state of the second formant is in the range 2520 Hz through 2040 Hz, then /d/ from 1920 Hz through 1560 Hz. With second-formant levels from 1440 Hz through 1200 Hz, /g/ is heard, and then /d/ again when the second-formant level goes below about 1200 Hz.

We find, however, that if we erase the first 50 ms of the transition, creating a silent interval between the locus and the start of the transition, as shown in B of Figure 4, then reasonably good /d/s are heard in all cases. A silent interval less than 50 ms does not produce /d/ at all steady-state levels of the second formant, and intervals greater than 50 ms also fail, at least at some second-formant levels, to give /d/. As we pointed out earlier in this paper, the second-formant locus of a consonant presumably reflects the articulatory place of production, and the transition can be assumed to show the movement from that place to the articulatory position appropriate for the following vowel. The fact that the transition serves best if it does not begin at the locus might be taken as an indication that no appreciable sound is produced until at least part of the articulatory movement has been completed. Note that there is no silent interval in the first formant,

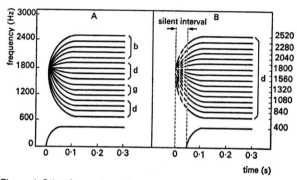

Figure 4 Stimulus patterns (shown schematically) and identifications with and without a silent interval between the second-formant locus and the onset of the transition

but that it has been displaced along the time scale so that its onset is, as in A, simultaneous with that of the second formant. Similar adjustments in the time of onset were made for all the silent intervals tested in this experiment. The introduction of a silent interval into the first formant weakened the consonant, but did not affect its identity.

In all the patterns of Figure 4, the time interval between the locus and the steady state of the second formant was 100 ms. We should suppose that this corresponds to some particular rate of articulation. To find out what might happen at other articulatory rates we have repeated the procedures described above with sets of patterns in which the total interval between locus and steady state of the vowel, was 40, 60, 80 and 120 ms; that is, for these additional total intervals we prepared and listened to patterns in which the transition went all the way to the locus, and also to patterns in which various amounts of the initial part of the transition had been erased. For total intervals of 80 and 120 ms the results are almost identical with those that were obtained with a total interval of 100 ms, except that the 'best' silent intervals (that is, the ones at which /d/ is most clearly heard at all steady-state levels of the second formant) are about 40 and 60 ms, respectively. From these values (together with that of 50 ms which was best for a

Pierre C. Delattre, Alvin M. Liberman and Franklin S. Cooper 279 total interval of 100 ms) it would appear that the best silent interval is approximately half the total interval. When the total interval is 60 ms or less, we do not get good /d/s at any silent intervals.

We have repeated these procedures with the /b/ locus (at 720 Hz) and with the /g/ locus (at 3000 Hz). It is reasonably clear in these cases, as it was with /d/, that the transition cannot start at the locus and go all the way to the steady state. The length of the silent interval that gives the best results seems to depend on the total duration of the interval (from locus to steady state), the best silent interval, as with /d/, is approximately half the total interval. With /b/ and /g/ the best results are obtained (with the appropriate silent intervals) when the total interval is 80 or 100 ms. Both these sounds are relatively poor (at all silent intervals) with a total duration of 120 ms; at total durations of 60 and 40 ms, /g/ suffers rather more loss in clarity than /b/.

The results obtained with /b/ and /g/ are in certain other respects different from those that were found with /d/, and they are also, perhaps, somewhat less definite. When the transition started at the /d/ locus, consonants having other than the /d/ (alveolar) place of production were clearly heard at some levels of the second-formant steady state. (Thus, as shown in A of Figure 4, /b/ was heard at relatively high levels of the second formant, and /g/ was heard when the steady-state level of the second formant was in the range 1440 Hz to 1200 Hz.) When the transition starts at the /b/ locus, however, we hear /bw/ (which has the same place of production as /b/) for steady-state levels from 2520 Hz through 1440 Hz, and then from 1200 through 960 Hz we hear something that sounds very vaguely like /gw/. The alveolar consonant, /d/, is not heard at all in the /b/ series, and the /g/ in the /gw/ cluster is very weak. Thus, the impossibility of starting the transition at the locus is less strikingly demonstrated for /b/ than it was for /d/, and the improvement in the /b/ which results from the introduction of a silent interval is, accordingly, less dramatic than the effects that are produced when a silent interval precedes the /d/ transitions.

The results obtained with the /g/ locus were different from those with /b/ and /d/ in that there is, apparently, no silent interval that will produce /g/ at all steady-state levels of the second formant. In the best case – that is, with the best silent interval – one hears /g/ from a steady state of 2520 to one of approximately 1200 Hz. Below the latter value we hear /d/. This result is not surprising, since it was quite clear from our earlier data on transitions as cues that the same /g/ locus could hardly apply to all vowels.

First-formant locus

In the first part of this investigation, which was concerned primarily with finding the second-formant loci, it appeared that the best stop consonants were produced when the curved first formant started at the lowest possible frequency. The purpose of the third part of the study was to explore further the problem of the first formant, using straight first formants and curved second formants. The straight first formant will presumably serve here, as the straight second formant did in the first part of the investigation, to avoid the problems introduced by the possibility that the transition does not reach all the way to the locus; the transition in the second formant will be necessary, as was the first-formant transition of the earlier experiment, to produce a consonant effect.

The experimental patterns are shown schematically in Figure 5. Four first formants were used having frequencies appropriate for the first formants of the cardinal vowels /i/, /e/, /ɛ/ and /a/. These were paired with various second formants as shown in the figure where A shows the frequency positions of the straight first formants and the various second formants

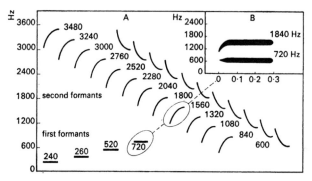

Figure 5 Schematic display of the stimuli used in finding the first-formant locus of /b/, /d/ and /g/

with which they were paired. All combinations of first and second formants were used, except for eight cases in which the two formants were so close together as to overlap. The formant shown at 520 Hz is composed, in slightly unequal parts of the fourth harmonic at 480 Hz and the fifth harmonic at 600 Hz; 520 Hz is an estimate of its equivalent frequency. The second formants always had transitions that rose or fell through four harmonics (of the 120 Hz fundamental). These patterns were converted into sound by the playback and judged by the authors of this paper.

As we should have expected from the results we had previously obtained in our work on second-formant transitions, the listeners heard /g/ or /d/ when the transition of the second formant was falling, and /b/ when it was rising. (With falling transitions of the second formant, /g/ was heard for steady-state levels from 3000 to 2280 Hz; between 2280 and 1320 Hz the sound could be identified either as /g/ or /d/; and below about 1320 Hz it was clearly /d/.) It will be remembered, however, that our primary interest was not in the second formant, but rather in the first, and, more particularly, in the effects of its frequency level. In this connection we found that the stop consonant – whether /b/, /d/ or /g/ – was best when the first formant was at the lowest position (240 Hz). When the first formant was raised from 240 Hz, there was, apart from the change in vowel color, a weakening of the stop consonant; however, the identification of the stop as /b/, /d/ or /g/ was not affected by the frequency level of the first formant. It would appear, then, that the locus of the first formant is at 240 Hz for all the voiced stops, but inasmuch as we did not, and, indeed, with our playback could not, center the first formant much lower than 240 Hz, we should rather conclude that the first-formant locus is somewhere between that value and zero.

Discussion

The experiments reported here were concerned only with the voiced stops, /b/, /d/ and /g/. We know, however, that the same second-formant transition that produces /b/, for example, will also produce other consonants, such as /p/ and /m/, which have the same articulatory place of production. From some experiments now in progress it appears, further, that with an appropriate lengthening of its duration, this same transition will produce the semivowel /w/. We should suppose, then, that /b/, /p/, /m/ and /w/ might have the same second-formant locus, which would correspond, as it were, to their common place of production, and that we might generalize the results of this study by assuming that the second-formant loci we found here are appropriate not only for /b/, /d/ and /g/, but, more broadly, for the three places of production (bilabial, alveolar and velar) that these stop consonants represent.

Although we expect that consonants with the same place of production will be found to have the same second-formant locus, we do not think that they will necessarily have the same best silent interval. In the case of the stops it is clear that approximately the first half of the total interval from locus to steady state must be silent. With a semivowel like /w/, on the other hand, it appears on the basis of exploratory work that the second-formant transition can be made to go all the way from the locus to the steady state of the vowel without adversely affecting the identifiability of the sound – indeed, it may well be that the best semivowel is made in this way.

The results of these experiments indicate that the locus of the first formant is not different for /b/, /d/ and /g/. We might guess, then, that the first-formant locus has little or nothing to do with *place* of production. Evidence from experiments now in progress suggests rather that it is closely related to the articulatory dimensions of *manner*.

We know from earlier experiments that third-formant transitions are cues for the identification of the stop consonants according to place of production, and we might expect, therefore, that there would be a third-formant locus for each of the stops. We have been trying to find these loci by procedures analogous to those used in the present study, that is, by varying the frequency position of a straight third formant. These procedures have yielded some evidence that the third-formant loci do exist. The results are less clear than for the second-formant loci, however, and it appears that additional and more sensitive techniques will be required.

References

COOPER, F. S. (1950), 'Spectrum analysis', *J. acoust. Soc. Amer.*, vol. 22, pp. 761–2.
COOPER, F. S., DELATTRE, P. C., LIBERMAN, A. M., BORST, J. M., and GERSTMAN, L. J. (1952), 'Some experiments on the perception of synthetic speech sounds', *J. acoust. Soc. Amer.*, vol. 24, pp. 597–606. Reprinted here, pp. 258–72.
COOPER, F. S., LIBERMAN, A. M., and BORST, J. M. (1951), 'The interconversion of audible and visible patterns as a basis for research in the perception of speech', *Proc. nat. Acad. Sci.*, vol. 37, pp. 318–25. Excerpt reprinted here, pp. 204–7.
LIBERMAN, A. M., DELATTRE, P. C., COOPER, F. S., and GERSTMAN, L. J. (1954), 'The role of consonant–vowel transitions in the perception of the stop and nasal consonants', *Psychol. Mongr.*, vol. 68, no. 8. pp. 1–13. Reprinted here, pp. 315–31.
POTTER, R. K., KOPP, G. A., and GREEN, H. C. (1947), *Visible Speech*, Van Nostrand.

19 Katherine S. Harris

Cues for the Discrimination of American English Fricatives in Spoken Syllables[1]

Katherine S. Harris, 'Cues for the discrimination of American English fricatives in spoken syllables', *Language and Speech*, vol. 1 (1958), pp. 1–7.

This paper will be concerned with the first steps in an investigation of the cues which listeners use in discriminating among the members of the class of unvoiced fricatives /f/, /θ/, /s/ and /ʃ/, and among their voiced counterparts, /v/, /ð/, /z/ and /ʒ/.

If one examines spectrograms of these sounds in consonant-vowel syllables, they are found to be made up of two successive segments – a period of noise, which we shall call the friction, succeeded by a segment with well-marked formant structure, which we shall call the vocalic portion.[2] Cues for identifying the phonemes might well be in either or both of the two portions. Indeed, one might infer from research with other groups of consonants that both parts are important. For example, the friction of the fricatives is much like the burst of the stop consonants; it has previously been found that the frequency position of this burst is significant in determining which stop will be perceived (Liberman *et al.*, 1952). Transitions of the second and third formant in the vocalic part of the syllable have been shown to be important for distinguishing among the liquids and semi-vowels (O'Connor *et al.*, 1957), among the nasals, and among the stops (Liberman *et al.*, 1954).

As a step towards isolating the acoustic cues for the fricatives, then, it has seemed reasonable in this experiment to assess the overall relative contribution of the friction and vocalic portions of fricative-vowel syllables. Detailed examination of particular cues within each of the two parts will be left for later study.

1. This work was supported in part by the Carnegie Corporation of New York and in part by the Department of Defense in connection with Contract DA 49-170-sc-2159. Some of the results were reported at a meeting of the Acoustical Society of America in New York in June 1954.
2. These characteristics of spectrograms of fricatives have been noted in two previous studies. Potter, Kopp and Green (1947) have called the two parts of fricatives described above the 'fill' and the 'consonant influence on the vowel', while Joos (1948) has called them the 'noise patch', and the 'glide' or 'transition'.

Procedure

A simple means of assessing the relative importance of cues in the friction and vocalic portions would be to split the friction segment away from the vocalic segment of the syllable, and then recombine friction and vocalic portions from different syllables. Presumably, the more important part of the sound would determine which phoneme a listener would hear.

A similar technique of recombination has been used by Schatz (1954) in a study of changes in stop consonants from one vowel to another. In her study, magnetic tape recordings of the stop consonants were made, and then the burst of noise at the beginning of the stop was split away from the vocalic portion, and interchanged with the burst from another stop consonant-vowel syllable. In the present experiment, we have used the same technique to interchange friction and vocalic parts of different fricative-vowel syllables.

The first step was to make tape recordings of a number of repetitions of each of the four syllables /fi/, /θi/, /si/ and /ʃi/, spoken by a single male speaker. Since we wanted to split the syllables between friction and vocalic portions, we needed to put a marker on the magnetic tape at the join of the two. To do this, the tape was run back and forth over the playback head of a tape recorder by hand, and the output monitored by listening and by watching the face of an oscilloscope; the join of the friction and vocalic parts of the syllable could be seen and heard by the change from low-intensity, high-frequency noise to high-intensity, low frequency periodic sound waves. Through the use of this method, all the tapes were marked and cut at the marked points. A friction portion from each of the four syllable types was combined with a vocalic portion from each, to make sixteen combination stimuli. The recombinations produced are schematized in Figure 1. The dotted line at the top of the figure indicates the point in the recorded sound at which the magnetic tapes were cut.

A similar set of four repetitions of each of the four fricatives before each of the vowels /e/, /o/ and /u/ was recorded, and each set was recombined to make sixteen stimuli for each vowel, analogous to the combinations for the vowel /i/ designated in the preceding paragraph. All sixty-four stimuli, sixteen for each of the four vowels, were then re-recorded.

The naturalness of the recombined syllables was dependent on the accuracy of the location of the original cut between the friction and the vocalic parts of the syllable. This location was checked after the rejoining operation and the re-recording by turning the original tape to the oxide side and running a magnetized knife blade along the splices between friction and vocalic parts of each syllable, so that there was a sharp click placed at the join of the two. When spectrograms were made, the click appeared as a black line at the point of join. One could then tell by visual examination whether or not the cut had been made at the point intended. (Of course, it was necessary to use the re-recording made before the insertion of the test clicks for the final test tape.)

After all the rejoined syllables had been checked in the manner described above, the re-recording was made into a test tape by rearranging all the

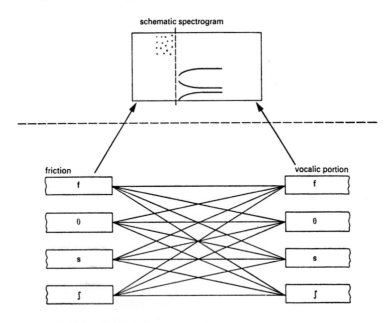

Figure 1 Test stimuli generated from the spoken syllables /fi/, /θi/, /si/ and /ʃi/

stimuli in random order, and spacing them in such a way that each syllable was repeated once after an interval of 0·9 s, and successive pairs of syllables appeared 6 s apart. This recording of the sixty-four stimuli will be referred to below as the unvoiced fricatives test.

A similar test was made for the four voiced fricatives. The male speaker who recorded the unvoiced fricatives recorded /v/, /ð/, /z/ and /ʒ/, before the same set of four vowels, /i/, /e/, /o/ and /u/. The syllables were recombined as before and checked for splice position. We should note, however, that the spectrographic checking technique used is somewhat less accurate in the case of a voiced fricative, since the boundary between friction and vocalic portions is harder to define from a spectrogram than the boundary for an unvoiced fricative. The sixty-four stimuli were made into a test in the manner described above; this recording will be referred to below as the voiced fricatives test.

The voiced and unvoiced fricatives tests were presented to twenty-two listeners, volunteers from undergraduate and graduate courses at the University of Connecticut. The subjects were present for two sessions, each of which contained one presentation of each test. Within the session, half the subjects heard the unvoiced fricatives test first, while half heard the voiced fricatives test first. All subjects were instructed to judge the stimuli as /f/, /θ/, /s/ or /ʃ/, for the former test, or as /v/, /ð/, /z/ or /ʒ/, for the latter.

We thought that the judgments made might be affected by the intensity level of the tests, since the friction portions of the different phonemes vary considerably in intensity; to control for this possibility we presented the stimuli at two different intensity levels in the two experimental periods. These intensity levels cannot be specified meaningfully in the usual units, because the listeners were seated in an experimental room listening to a loudspeaker, rather than listening on earphones. The two levels selected were, first, the lowest speaker output level at which the experimenter could hear the friction when seated in the subject's chair farthest from the loudspeaker, and, second, the highest level at which the sound could be presented without distortion. Analysis of the data has shown that this variable had no effect on the listeners' judgments over the range selected; therefore, results are not presented separately for the two intensities.

Results

The results for the unvoiced fricatives test are shown in Figure 2. The data were obtained from twenty-two subjects, each of whom heard each syllable twice. Each histogram represents the responses of the subjects to one of the sixty-four stimuli of the experiment. For example, the upper left-hand histogram in the upper left-hand quadrant indicates the responses of the subjects to a stimulus made up of /f/ friction and /f/ vocalic portion, with the vowel /i/. Approximately 95 per cent of the subjects identified the resulting syllable as /fi/, while 5 per cent heard the syllable as /θi/.

Before describing the results in detail, we should note that the results are the same for the four vowels. This can be seen by examining the corresponding histograms in each of the four quadrants, which represent the four vowels. We will therefore describe the data hereafter without reference to specific vowels.

As can be seen in Figure 2, the results of the test were quite different for /s/ and /ʃ/, on the one hand, and /f/ and /θ/, on the other. When /s/ friction was paired with any vocalic portion, the resulting stimulus was judged as /s/; similarly, when /ʃ/ friction was paired with any vocalic portion, the

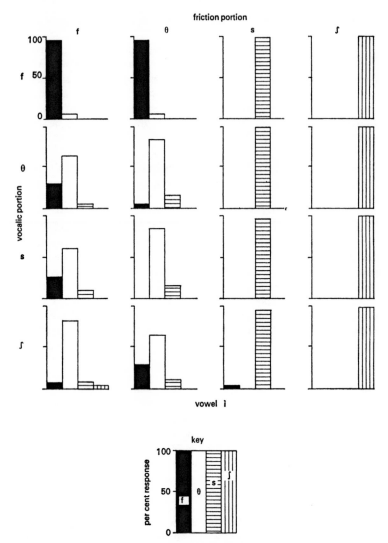

Figure 2 Responses to stimuli made up of friction from one unvoiced fricative-vowel syllable paired with the vocalic portion of another

friction portion

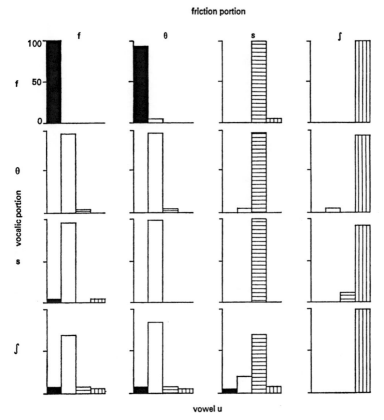

Figure 2 cont.

vowel u

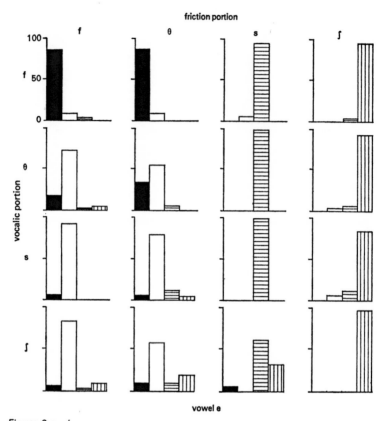

Figure 2 *cont.*

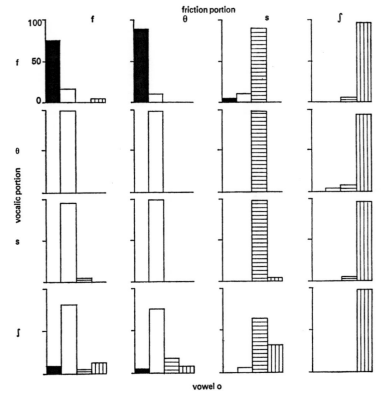

Figure 2 *cont.*

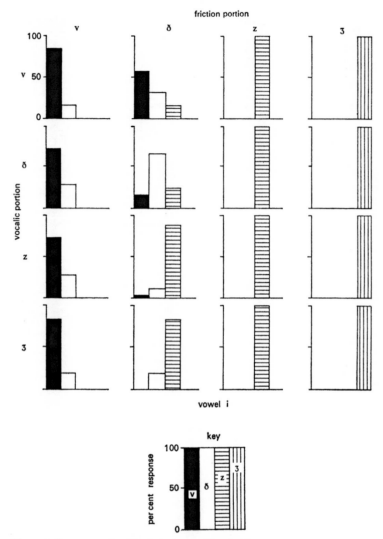

Figure 3 Responses to stimuli made up of friction from one voiced fricative-vowel syllable paired with the vocalic portion of another

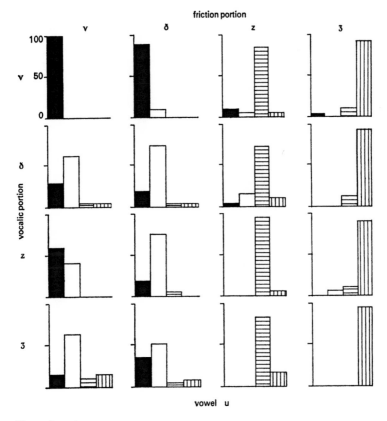

Figure 3 *cont.*

friction portion

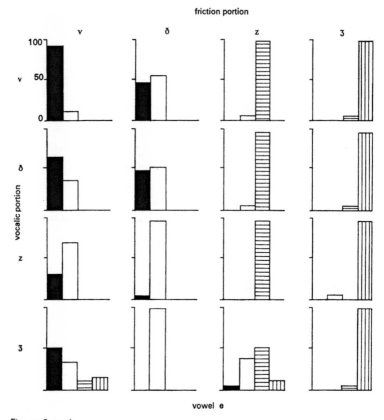

Figure 3 *cont.*

vowel e

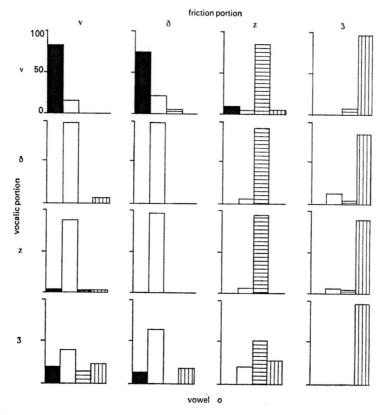

Figure 3 cont.

resulting stimulus was judged as /ʃ/. None of the other eight stimuli was judged as /s/ and /ʃ/ with any great frequency. Apparently, then, the friction of /s/ and /ʃ/ provide the necessary and sufficient cues for their identification, and override whatever cues may be provided by the vocalic portions.

The situation was somewhat more complicated for /f/ and /θ/ judgments. In general, only stimuli with /f/ or /θ/ friction were judged as either /f/ or /θ/, but which of the two judgments was made depended largely on the vocalic part of the syllable. Most of the listeners tended to judge a syllable with /f-θ/ friction as /f/ when it had /f/ vocalic portion, and as /θ/ when it had any other vocalic portion.[3]

The results of the voiced fricatives test, shown in Figure 3, were similar to those just described, though not as clear. The phonemes /z/ and /ʒ/ behaved like their unvoiced counterparts /s/ and /ʃ/ for all vowels, in that both /z/ and /ʒ/ were identified almost entirely by their friction portions. The results for /v/ and /ð/, on the other hand, were variable from vowel to vowel. When the vowel was /o/ or /u/, syllables with /v/ friction and /ð/ friction were identified as /v/ or /ð/ depending on the vocalic portion; in other words, with these vowels the sounds behaved in the same way as /f/ and /θ/. For /i/ and /e/, however, there appeared to be some contribution from both friction and vocalic portions. In this connection, it should be remembered that, as we noted above, the join of the friction and vocalic portions is less clear for the voiced fricatives; consequently, the original splicing may not have been made as well and we might expect somewhat more variability in the results.

By way of summary, then, we may say that the results suggest a general way of describing the perception of the four fricatives (with their voiced counterparts). The listener may be said to behave as if he first decided on the basis of friction, whether the syllable belonged to the /s-ʃ/ class or to the /f-θ/ class. If /s/ or /ʃ/, he uses the friction again to decide which of these alternatives it was. If, on the other hand, the first decision had been that the sound belonged in the /f-θ/ class, then the listener uses the vocalic portion to decide which of the two sounds, /f/ or /θ/, he had heard.

3. Hughes and Halle (1956) have recently reported some experimental results which are in general agreement with the results of the unvoiced fricatives test. In their study, several speakers produced syllables containing /f/, /s/ and /ʃ/ with various vowels. The isolated friction segments of the syllables were then presented to listeners who were asked which of the three phonemes had been spoken. All three were identified quite well. The result is not surprising for /s/ and /ʃ/, since we had concluded that friction provided the necessary and sufficient cues for their identification. Furthermore, we would expect that /f/ friction would be discriminable in the set of alternatives presented since in our experiment, /f/ friction was not confused with any friction except /θ/, and /θ/ was not a possible response in Hughes' and Halle's experiment.

References

HUGHES, G. W. and HALLE, M. (1956), 'Spectral properties of fricative consonants', *J. acoust. Soc. Amer.*, vol. 28, pp. 303–10. Excerpt reprinted here, pp. 151–61.

JOOS, M. (1948), *Acoustic Phonetics*, Language Monograph, no. 23, Baltimore.

LIBERMAN, A. M., DELATTRE, P. C., and COOPER, F. S. (1952), 'The role of selected stimulus-variables in the perception of the unvoiced stop consonants', *Amer. J. Psychol.*, vol. 65, pp. 497–516.

LIBERMAN, A. M., DELATTRE, P. C., COOPER, F. S., and GERSTMAN, L. J. (1954), 'The role of consonant–vowel transitions in the perception of the stop and nasal consonants', *Psychol. Mongr.*, vol. 68, no. 8, pp. 1–13. Reprinted here, pp. 315–31.

O'CONNOR, J. D., GERSTMAN, L. J., LIBERMAN, A. M., DELATTRE, P. C., and COOPER, F. S. (1957), 'Acoustic cues for the perception of initial /w, j, r, l/ in English', *Word*, vol. 13, pp. 24–43. Reprinted here, pp. 298–314.

POTTER, R. K., KOPP, G. A., and GREEN, H. C. (1947), *Visible Speech*, Van Nostrand.

SCHATZ, C. D. (1954), 'The role of context in the perception of stops', *Language*, vol. 30, pp. 47–56.

20 J. D. O'Connor, L. J. Gerstman, A. M. Liberman, P. C. Delattre and F. S. Cooper

Acoustic Cues for the Perception of Initial /w, j, r, l/ in English[1]

J. D. O'Connor, L. J. Gerstman, A. M. Liberman, P. C. Delattre and F. S. Cooper, 'Acoustic cues for the perception of initial /w, j, r, l/ in English', *Word*, vol. 13 (1957), pp. 24–43.

In investigating the acoustic cues for the perception of speech it is usually convenient and often necessary to study only a relatively small group of phonemes in any single experiment. Thus, our own earlier research and that of our colleagues at Haskins Laboratories has dealt separately with the stop, nasal and fricative consonants (Liberman, Delattre and Cooper, 1952; Liberman, Delattre, Cooper and Gerstman, 1954; Harris, 1954). In the experiments to be reported here we have chosen to study /w, j, r, l/ as a group and to try to find the physical stimuli essential to the recognition of these phonemes in (absolute) initial position before vowels.

The selection of /w, j, r, l/ is necessarily arbitrary, at least in some degree; it is not random, however, since these phonemes have certain articulatory and distributional properties which tend to set them off from the other English consonants. From an articulatory standpoint, they differ from the constrictive consonants (stops, fricatives) in the degree of oral stricture present,[2] and from the nasals by their oral articulation. On the basis of distributional characteristics too, /w, j, r, l/ can be distinguished as a group from other sub-classes of English consonants. Their most obvious distinguishing mark is that they, and they alone, can constitute the third member of an initial three-term consonant cluster – for example in words like *screw*, *splint*, *skew* and *square*. In other initial clusters these consonants must occupy the position immediately before the vowel and cannot have any other consonant intervening between them and the vowel.[3] Similarly, where they occur in final consonant clusters they must, again, occupy the

1. This research was supported in part by the Carnegie Corporation of New York and in part by the Department of Defense in connection with Contract DA49-170-sc-1642.
2. The majority of the allophones of /w, j, r, l/ are voiced oral resonants, and the occurrence of voiceless fricative allophones of all four phonemes in the same phonetic environment, i.e. after a voiceless stop or fricative in the same syllable, whilst no doubt connected with their phonemic distribution, is an added mark of their coherence as a class.
3. In many, perhaps most, dialects of English this would be an exclusive class-marker but, in the case of those dialects where 'new' = /nu/, the phoneme /n/ shares this distributional characteristic.

place nearest the vowel, as in words like *melts* and *birds*.[4] The one exception to this is in words such as *snarl* or *world*, where /r/ comes between the vowel and /l/. We can, therefore, generalize the distribution of these sounds by saying that they must occupy a position in the syllable in immediate contact with the vowel (or with the vowel plus /r/), and that they are the only sounds permitted as the third term of a three-term initial consonant cluster.[5]

The fact that /w, j, r, l/ can be grouped together on articulatory and distributional grounds permits us to hope that they will have certain significant acoustic features in common. We should expect, then, that some of the acoustic cues which enable the listener to distinguish within the class will be found to lie on the same acoustic dimension, and, further, that these common acoustic features will serve, at least in part, to distinguish this class of phonemes from other classes.

Method

The inspection of acoustic spectrograms is a rewarding study which has already made a notable contribution to linguistic work, and it was upon such study that we relied for our preliminary observations. If a spectrogram has a fault, however, it is in the abundance of its revelations, which lead an investigator to wonder what, in a given stretch of speech, is linguistically basic and what dispensable. Often, too, the acoustic features are only vaguely shown on a spectrogram, making it difficult to know the precise characteristics of those features which are revealed. These difficulties can to some extent be overcome by use of the pattern playback, a machine with which hand-painted patterns, resembling spectrograms more or less closely, may be converted to sound.[6] This provides a convenient method for making experimental modifications in various presumably important parts of the pattern and then evaluating the effects of these changes on the sound as heard. The present investigation was based primarily on this technique.

We were concerned in this experiment with the recognition of phoneme sequences as such. This is, of course, only one stage in the process by which speech is understood: the sounds perceived must be set against the pattern of both linguistic and extra-linguistic probabilities and a balance struck. In the experiments being reported here we have minimized the effect on

4. This sets them off from all English phonemes except /ŋ/ which must also occupy the immediately post-vocalic position, although it is quite unlike /w, j, r, l/ in its general distribution.
5. For a more detailed statement of the combinatory latitudes of /w, j, r, l/ see O'Connor and Trim (1953).
6. For a description of the pattern playback see Cooper (1950); Cooper Liberman and Borst (1951); Cooper (1953).

intelligibility of any but the immediate sound contexts by working exclusively with nonsense syllables of the pattern CV. The vowels used were seven in number, corresponding approximately to the cardinal vowels [i, e, ɛ, a, ɔ, o, u] (see Delattre, Liberman and Cooper, 1951).

The experiments fell into two parts. In Part 1 we explored a wide variety of acoustic variations and attempted to determine, always by our own listening, which of these variations were important for the perception of /w, j, r, l/ and which were not. It is difficult to know precisely how many patterns and pattern changes were made and listened to, but the number is in the thousands. This is an important consideration only because it means that we were unable to control perfectly the contexts in which, and occasions on which, we listened to and judged the various patterns. The possibility exists, therefore, that our judgments were made against a background or standard that varied somewhat from week to week and from one context to another. As a partial control against this possibility, and also in order to have judgments from a group of naïve listeners, we carried out the experiment reported in Part 2. For the purposes of the second part of the study we sampled from the various acoustic dimensions we had found to be important in Part 1, arranged these stimuli in a random order, and presented them to naïve college students for judgment as /w/, /j/, /r/ or /l/.

Part 1

Figure 1 shows patterns that contain the cues we believe to be most important for the perception of /w, j, r, l/. These patterns are, in general, like those we have found in previous studies to be appropriate for other CV syllables in that they consist primarily of formant transitions, or frequency shifts, followed by a steady state.[7] It had been found in the earlier studies that the transitions contain important, and in many cases sufficient, cues for the perception of the consonants (see Liberman, Delattre, Cooper and Gerstman, 1954), while, as is well known, vowel color depends largely on the frequency position of the steady-state formants.[8] As can be seen from these patterns, the distinctions among /w, j, r, l/ depend primarily on the transitions of the second and third formants. The second-formant transition is sufficient to distinguish /w/ from /r-l/ from /j/: for /w/ this transition

7. We have drawn all our transitions as straight lines even though the transitions of real speech are necessarily curvilinear. Using straight lines enables us to control the patterns more precisely, and it does not significantly alter the auditory impression.
8. This has been demonstrated by several methods: from a statistical analysis of the vowel productions of many speakers by Peterson and Barney (1952); from tests constructed at the pattern playback by Delattre, Liberman, Cooper, and Gerstman (1952); and from vowel synthesis employing electronic analogs of the vocal tract by several investigators. See Dunn (1950); Stevens, Kasowski and Fant (1953); Stevens and House (1955).

originates at a low frequency, for /r/ and /l/ it begins nearer the middle of our frequency range, while /j/ requires that the transition start high. The distinction between /l/ and /r/ seems to depend primarily on the third-formant transition: for /r/ the third formant begins at a point just slightly above the second formant and then rises to its steady-state level, while for /l/ the third formant starts at a level at least as high as the steady-state.

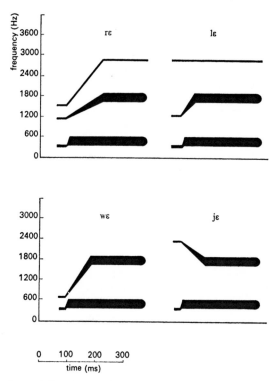

Figure 1 Hand-painted spectrograms that produce reasonable approximations to /rɛ/, lɛ/, /wɛ/ and /jɛ/ when converted into sound by the pattern playback

There is also at the beginning of each formant a relatively short steady state which, for convenience, we will refer to as a 'steady-state onset'. These steady-state onsets represent what we have previously referred to as the consonant loci,[9] and they are, quite obviously, the acoustic counterparts of the starting points of the consonant articulation. It is of considerable interest that the loci are explicit for /w, j, r, l/ because in this respect these four

9. For a discussion of the 'locus' concept, see Delattre, Liberman and Cooper (1955).

phonemes are different as a class from the stop and nasal consonants. In the case of the stops (and presumably for the nasal consonants, too) we had found for the second formant that the transition may not begin at the locus but must rather start at a point somewhat delayed in time. The steady-state onsets we see in Figure 1 indicate that for /w, j, r, l/ the formants not only begin at the loci but spend from 30 to 50 ms there before proceeding to the steady-state positions of the vowel.

Steady-state onsets similar to those of Figure 1 were found in an earlier study to be necessary for the synthesis of the nasal consonants in initial position, but in this respect /w, j, r, l/ are very different from the nasal consonants in that the steady-state onsets are always continuous with the transitions for the former, but typically differ in frequency from the starting points of the transitions for the latter. This is so, presumably, because in the case of the nasal consonants the steady-state onset is produced as a consequence of the addition of the nasal resonator and is little affected by the (buccal) articulatory position, which nevertheless determines the starting frequency of the formant transitions. With /w, j, r, l/ the steady-state onsets reflect the start of the buccal articulation.

Having made these rather general comments about the acoustic cues that distinguish among /w, j, r, l/, and about certain characteristics of these four phonemes as a class, we should like to proceed to a more detailed discussion of our results.

Number of formants needed

As shown in Figure 1, a distinction may be made at the outset between /w, j/ on the one hand, and /r, l/ on the other, in that the former can be synthesized satisfactorily with only two formants, while the latter require three. In the case of /w, j/ this is no more than might be expected, bearing in mind the well-known possibility of two-formant vowel synthesis, and the articulatory relationship between [i] and /j/ and between [u] and /w/. We find for /r/ and /l/, however, that a third formant is clearly necessary in order to synthesize these two consonants before the full range of vowels. As can be seen in Figure 1, and as we will have occasion to discuss in greater detail later, the second-formant starting points are not very different for /r/ and /l/ – they both begin in the middle of our frequency scale – so it is not surprising that we cannot distinguish these phonemes by means of two formants alone. This does not mean that the more-or-less common /r-l/ second formant will produce, with all vowels, a phoneme which is indifferently /r/ or /l/. In fact, we find with two-formant patterns that when the second-formant transition rises from the /r-l/ region to the frequency levels appropriate for front vowels we hear /r/, but when the transition falls to a back vowel we hear /l/.

Duration of steady-state onsets

Steady-state onsets were found to be useful, not for any distinctive function they might have within our group of consonants, but to avoid a potential confusion with clusters of stop + /w, j, r, l/. When the onset phase was omitted and the transition begun immediately, the resulting stimulus appeared to have an explosive beginning, a stop of some kind being clearly apprehended though not always identified with certainty. The duration of steady-state necessary to avoid this clustering effect differs as between /r, l/ and /w, j/. For /r/ and /l/ a steady-state onset period of about 50 or 60 ms was needed – below this the explosive beginning started to make itself heard – whilst at greater durations, from 70 ms upwards, the effect was of syllabicity, often leading to the identification of a schwa vowel before the consonant. For /j/ and /w/ the onset duration could apparently be smaller; 30 ms was sufficient to eliminate the explosive beginning, and 40 ms upwards gave the effect of a full vowel, /i/ or /u/, despite a reduction in intensity of the steady-state onsets *vis-à-vis* the following vowel formants.

Recent work suggests that the steady-state onsets can perhaps be dispensed with for /w/ and /j/ without causing an explosive beginning to the syllable, provided that the first-formant transition begins at a sufficiently high frequency (discussed in the next section). We have also found it possible to hear /r/ without initial steady states, provided that the intensity onset is gradual, but we have never been able to synthesize an acceptable /l/ using transitions alone. We note that none of the four phones is harmed by the presence of appropriate steady-state onsets, and indeed, that spectrograms typically show, if not a steady state preceding the transitions, at least a very much slower rate of frequency change than pertains to the transition phase.

Starting frequencies of the transitions (*steady-state onset frequencies*)

In the preceding section we observed that appropriate steady-state onsets serve mainly to distinguish the class /w, j, r, l/ from other groups of phonemes. Since these onsets have durations up to 60 ms, it is not inconceivable that they might also themselves be identifiable as /w/, /j/, /r/ or /l/, but our observations suggest that for the most part they are not; rather, it is the transitions, particularly those of the second and third formants, which play the main part in distinguishing among the four phonemes. Steady-state /w/ and /j/ are quite out of the question since the absence of transitions can result only in /u/ and /i/. The onset of /l/ contains some identifying information, but naïve listeners have considerable difficulty in perceiving the steady state as /l/. For /r/ there is more information in the steady-state onset, to the extent that the onset approximates an /r/-colored vowel.

Bearing in mind that the transition directions and extents are the most important cues for distinguishing among /w, j, r, l/, we will nevertheless specify these variables by reference to the frequency positions of the steady-state onsets, since they are always continuous in frequency with the start of the transition. These starting points provide a convenient way of describing the transitions because the onsets remain relatively fixed while transition directions and extents shift radically with changes in the formant positions of the following vowel (Delattre, Liberman and Cooper, 1955).

First-formant onset. It will be obvious from the patterns of Figure 1 that the onset of the first formant does not distinguish among /w, r, j, l/ since, for the same following vowel, its form is unchanged throughout. It does, however, serve the very important function of distinguishing /l/ from the nasal consonants. If the onset of the first-formant transition is located at 240 Hz, the resulting sound will be identified more often as a nasal than as /l/ even when the second and third formants are given their best /l/ values, whereas with the first-formant onset at 360 Hz, or above, the identification will be /l/. The best /l/ results were obtained with the steady-state onset located at or slightly below the frequency of the first formant of the following vowel, but no lower than 360 Hz. In subsequent work the first-formant onset was placed at 480 Hz for [a], and 360 Hz for the remaining vowels.

For both /w/ and /j/ one would expect the frequency of the first-formant onset to be in the neighborhood of 240 Hz (the first-formant frequency of both /i/ and /u/), and this proved to be well founded. In fact, there was not much freedom to deviate from that value lest either of two complications occur: when the steady-state onset was located at 120 Hz, the semivowels acquired stop-like beginnings, /bw/ or /gj/, an effect that we have discussed in other papers;[10] when the onset was placed much above 360 Hz, the impression of /w/ was destroyed, while a non-speechlike whistle was introduced into /j/.

The influence of the first-formant starting frequency on /r/ was small. If a pattern contained second- and third-formant transitions, satisfactory for /r/, the only difference made by a first-formant onset between 120 and 600 Hz was a difference of 'color', corresponding at the bottom of the range to extreme lip-rounding and at the top to lip-spreading.

We see, then, that /l/ imposes more stringent requirements upon the

10. Delattre, Liberman and Cooper (1955); Liberman, Delattre, Gerstman and Cooper (1956). The first formant locus for the stop consonants was found to be at the lowest frequency attainable with the pattern playback (120 Hz). Any higher frequency caused the stops to sound less like stops and more like semivowels. This effect was slight, however, as compared to the strong influence of transition duration: patterns were heard as semivowels or stops depending on whether the transitions were more or less than 50 ms.

first-formant onset frequency than the other three phonemes. However, when we use values appropriate for /l/ we also satisfy the restrictions imposed by /w, j, r/.

Second-formant onset. The onset frequency of the second-formant transition has a very considerable effect on the perception of /w, j, r/. Other things being equal, high frequencies (about 2760 Hz) give /j/, low frequencies (about 600 Hz) give /w/, and intermediate frequencies give either /l/ or /r/. The frequency ranges of /l/ and /r/ overlap.

For /w/ and /j/ the starting frequencies are, again as one would expect, in the neighborhood of the second formants of [u] and [i], respectively, but the opener and closer semi-vocalic allophones are clearly reflected in the differing ranges before different vowels. Before the vowel [i], the lower limit of the /j/ range has the same frequency as the second formant of the vowel (2760 Hz), the glide effect being obtained by the transition of the first formant and the gradual increase in the intensity of the transitions; more satisfactory results are obtained, however, with a higher second-formant onset frequency and consequent falling transition. Before [e] (second formant at 2160 Hz), the lower limit of the range is 2280 Hz. One cannot start /j/ below 2280 Hz for any following vowel without producing the effect of a glide from [ø] or [y]. There is virtually no upper limit for /j/, 3600 Hz still being entirely satisfactory.

The frequency range of the second-formant onset for /w/ before [u] (second formant at 720 Hz), is the very low and restricted one of 360–480 Hz; before [o] on the other hand the upper limit is 600 Hz, and for the remaining vowels, 840 Hz.

For /r/ the frequency range of the second-formant onset before [i, e, ɛ] is 840–1560 Hz, before [ɔ] 840–1200 Hz, and before [o, u] 600–1200 Hz. In the lower part of the range the acoustic counterpart of labio-velarization is heard, leading to confusion between /r/ and /w/ below the lower limit, whilst in the higher part of the range an effect of palatalization is heard.

For /l/ before [i, e, ɛ] the frequency range is 960–1800 Hz, before [a] 840–1800 Hz, and before [ɔ, o, u] it is 840–1680 Hz. In the lower part of these ranges the /l/ was of a dark or velarized variety, the lower the frequency the darker the /l/; at the higher frequencies the /l/ was clearer or more palatalized, until, above the upper limits here given, the effect of laterality was lost, and was replaced by a vowel glide from [e] or from [ɪ].

We can therefore distinguish /w/, /l, r/ and /j/ by reference to the second formant. Although the starting point of the second-formant transition should be somewhat higher for /l/ than for /r/, this does not provide a reliable differential between the two phones.

Third-formant onset. The third formant is the crucial factor, as we suggested earlier, in distinguishing /l/ from /r/, but contributes little to the perception of /w/ and /j/. The third-formant starting frequency for /l/ is close to that of the vowel third formant, whereas the third-formant onset of /r/ needs to be lower in frequency, fairly close to the second-formant onset. This being the case, it is possible to pass from /l/ to /r/ by no other change in the pattern than a gradual lowering of the starting frequency of the third formant. If /w/ and /j/ are to have a third formant, the transition can be similar to that required for /l/, although as we have pointed out, such a third formant contributes very little to the perception of the semivowels.

We have already mentioned that the need for third-formant transitions in distinguishing /l/ from /r/ varies as between front and back vowels, so it should not be surprising to find these differences reflected in the permissible ranges of third-formant starting frequencies. For the vowels [i, e, ɛ], where the second-formant transition is rising and only two formants are required to hear /r/, the third-formant onset for /r/ can vary from 840 Hz (the lower limit for the second-formant onset) to as high as 1920 Hz; this means in effect that the frequency ranges of the second- and third-formant onsets are virtually identical for /r/, whereas the third-formant onset for /l/ must be no lower than the third formant of the vowel. For the vowels [ɔ, o, u], where the second-formant transition is falling and a two-formant pattern is heard as /l/, the restrictions are now reversed: the third-formant onset for /l/ may be as low as 1920 Hz, but for /r/ it may be no higher than 1680 Hz. It is possible, of course, to find starting frequencies for the second and third formants which cancel out each other, so that neither /r/ nor /l/ is perceived with clarity; we may make /r/ and /l/ maximally discriminable, however, by placing the third-formant onset either as low as the second-formant onset permits, or as high as the third formant of the vowel.

Precise specification of formant starting frequencies. The reader will have noted that we summarized our observations about the starting frequencies of the second- and third-formant transitions in terms of ranges rather than as specific values. Thus, for example, we placed the second-formant onset frequency of /re/ between 840 and 1560 Hz, but did not say that any particular value between these extremes gave a 'better' /re/ than any other.

We believe that this is the most realistic way of stating our findings, since in different idiolects and dialects, there are many phonetically discriminable sounds which are nevertheless readily identifiable as /r/. Similarly, two different frequencies within our range will produce sounds which are distinguishable, but which are, in our estimation, both identifiable as /r/. We do not claim that every sound produced from different frequencies within a stated range makes an equally natural impression on us, or would do so on a wider selection of listeners – a very clear [l] initially may sound as odd to some listeners as a very dark [l] does to others – but we do believe that every such sound is recognizable phonemically.

The limits of the ranges are usually difficult to draw, since a given stimulus, evaluated phonetically, may contain auditory features reminiscent of both, say, /w/ and /r/, or /r/ and /l/; further, a stimulus identified by the phonetician as [ø] might well be categorized by the naïve listener as /j/, for lack of any other oppositional category in which to place it, even though [ø] is not normally found as an allophone of /j/. We have always tried to draw the line at a point where the identification seems to us to be still positive; the same identification might be made beyond the limits we have laid down, but we would expect more confusion in these areas and more uniform responses within our ranges.

Our observations indicate that the range of starting frequencies is shifted somewhat (on the frequency scale) according to the following vowel, and this is no doubt a function of conditioned allophonic variation: we should suppose that to produce a given allophone we must change the starting frequency as we change the vowel. However, our frequency ranges reflect a good deal more than the allophones of a single idiolect or even of a single dialect, within which we would not necessarily expect so wide a range of frequencies.

Since our own judgments, whilst basically phonemic, are necessarily also partly phonetic, it will be particularly interesting to see, in Part 2, whether the shifting of starting points in relation to the following vowel is confirmed by naïve listeners judging on what we assume to be a purely phonemic basis.

Transition duration

Transition duration is another factor in the perception of /w, j, r, l/. Its role seems to be similar to that of the steady-state onsets in that it does not serve to distinguish among the four phonemes (with the minor exception to be noted below), but does aid in differentiating /w, j, r, l/ as a class from other groups of consonants. If the transitions are of too brief duration, there is confusion with nasals and stops, while with transitions that occupy too much time in moving from the steady-state onsets to the steady-state vowel formants, there is the danger of losing the consonant impression entirely in favor of a vowel of changing color. Between these extremes there is a middle range of durations which serves reasonably well for all four consonants, although the particular values that give the most realistic sounds are somewhat different for each phoneme.

A duration of 100 ms is suitable for the second- and third-formant transitions of all four phonemes. Briefer values give slightly better /l/ identifications, while longer ones help /r/. When /l/ is made as brief as 30 ms, there is the possibility of confusion with the nasal consonants, but at 60–70 ms this ambiguity has disappeared, leaving /l/ at its most generally satisfactory value. When the transitions of an otherwise satisfactory /r/ pattern are reduced to 50 ms or less, one hears a retroflex flapped sound, but, on the other hand, durations of up to 300 ms do not destroy the /r/ effect.

Experiments with two-formant /w/ and /j/ showed that durations of 50 and 100 ms were satisfactory, though the latter gave a somewhat more realistic sound; below 50 ms the effect was of a vowel plus stop or flap.[11] At 150 ms /j/ was still good, but an otherwise satisfactory /w/ pattern, before the vowels [i, e, ɛ], was heard as /wr/; this effect is undoubtedly due to the large rising transition of the second formant coupled with a comparatively slow rate of frequency change. The rising second-formant transition is often sufficient to produce an /r/ without the parallel rising third-formant transition that we have found to be so potent a cue for /r/. We find that a relatively broad rising second formant produces nearly the same effect as second- and third-formant rising transitions running parallel and in near contiguity. As one would expect, the /wr/ effect disappears when the transition durations are made briefer (thus speeding up the rate of frequency change), or when a straight third formant is added.

The first-formant transition for /w, j, r/ may have a duration identical to those of the second and third formants. For /l/, however, there is something of a special problem, since even at the briefest durations used with second and third formants (50 ms), the first-formant transition seemed to be too gradual, giving the impression of a vocalic glide. It is apparently not without significance that spectrograms of spoken /l/ show a very abrupt frequency change between the first-formant onset and the following vowel. We sought to obtain this effect synthetically by reducing the transition duration to 10 ms, with the result that /l/ identifications were definitely improved. We found, further, that the patterns for /w, j, r/ were not adversely affected by this special first-formant transition, and have incorporated it into all the patterns used in Part 2.

Part 2

In this section we shall describe the results we obtained when we presented some of the stimuli of Part 1 to phonetically naïve listeners for judgment as /w, j, r, l/. We are concerned here only with the cues that distinguish among these four phonemes. Accordingly, we have varied only those aspects of the pattern that had been found in our earlier investigations (see Part 1) to be important for those distinctions, and we have asked our listeners to restrict their choices to /w/, /j/, /r/ or /l/. In regard to those acoustic variables which distinguish these phonemes from other classes, we

---

11. These effects correspond exactly to those obtained with naïve subjects who were able to hear the series /bɛ, wɛ, uɛ/ or /gɛ, jɛ, iɛ/ solely as a function of changes in transition duration. See Liberman, Delattre, Gerstman and Cooper (1956).

have selected values which favored /w, j, r, l/ and held them constant in all the stimulus patterns.

The patterns seen in Figure 2 illustrate, for the vowel [e], the stimulus variables we used in this experiment. As shown in the top row, there were six second-formant transitions, so chosen as to cover the range that had been found earlier to be important for /w, j, r, l/. We should note, however,

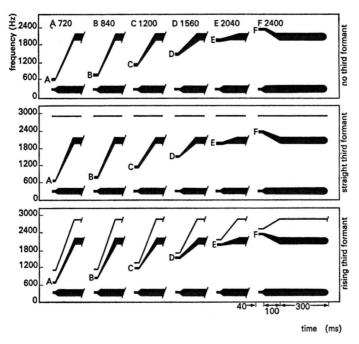

time (ms)

Figure 2 Schematic representation of the stimulus variables used in Part 2. At the extreme right of each row are complete, hand-painted spectrograms illustrating some actual patterns from which the test stimuli were produced

that the range is sampled in rather large steps. By converting these two-formant patterns into sound we produced six of our test stimuli. Another twelve stimuli were made by combining each of these various second-formant transitions with a straight third formant and with a rising third formant as shown in the middle and bottom rows of Figure 2. The straight third formant and the rising third formant had seemed on the basis of our earlier research to be reasonably appropriate for /l/ and /r/, respectively. There was, then, a total of eighteen stimulus patterns for the vowel [e]. In the bottom row of the figure we see that the rising third-formant transitions always started at a point just slightly above the starting point of the second-formant transitions.

There were, in addition, eighteen stimulus patterns each for the vowels [a] and [o], constructed in essentially the same fashion as the stimuli for [e] in Figure 2. Figure 3 summarizes the stimuli for [e, a, o] together. In

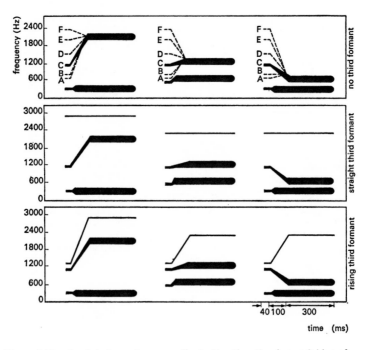

Figure 3 Hand-painted spectrograms illustrating the stimulus variables of Part 2 with all three vowels [e, a, o]

the top row we see that the starting points of the second-formant transitions were identical for all three vowels. The middle and bottom rows illustrate, respectively, straight and rising third formants for a single second-formant starting point.

These patterns were converted into sound and presented in random order to a group of forty-four phonetically naïve listeners, all of whom were undergraduate students at the University of Connecticut. Each listener was asked to identify every sound as /w/, /j/, /r/ or /l/, and to guess if necessary.

The results of this experiment are to be found in the judgments of our listeners, all of which are shown in Figure 4. There we have plotted the /w, j, r, l/ responses, expressed as per cents, against the second-formant onset frequencies, which are labelled on each abscissa by letter and identified by frequency in the key at the bottom of the figure. The three third-formant conditions (no third formant, straight third formant, and rising third formant) are the parameters, coded as shown in the upper right-hand corner. To avoid the difficulties in reading that would have been caused by many more or less overlapping curves, we have put the curves into separate plots according to responses (columns) and vowels (rows).

In general, the results obtained here are similar to those we described in Part 1. The starting point of the second-formant transition distinguishes /w/, /r-l/ and /j/. This formant starts at a low frequency for /w/, at a middle frequency for /r/ and /l/, and at a high frequency for /j/. The third formant tends to distinguish /r/ from /l/, /r/ being helped by the rising third formant and /l/ by the straight third formant. Straight and rising third formants have little effect on /w/ and /j/, except that the rising third formant, in favoring /r/, tends to reduce the number of /w/ responses.

As we pointed out earlier, the stimuli that were presented for judgment in this experiment represent a rather large-step sampling of the various ranges, and it is, therefore, idle to draw conclusions which depend upon exact comparisons of the various curves, particularly in regard to the positions and heights of their peaks. However, some of these more specific effects are sufficiently large, and sufficiently consistent within the experiment, that we can be reasonably confident that they would be reproduced, at least in their grosser aspects, if the experiment were repeated with a much finer sampling of the stimulus range.

Perhaps the most important of these more specific results is the tendency of the peaks of both the /l/ and /r/ curves to occur at different positions on the abscissa as we go from the vowel [e] through [a] to [o]. These shifts in the response peaks mean that to produce the best /r/s and /l/s we must adjust the starting frequency of the second-formant transition according to the frequency level of the second formant of the following vowel. The starting point of the second-formant transition should be somewhat higher when the second formant of the vowel is high (as in [e]), and it should be somewhat lower when the vowel formant is low (as in [o]). We see, however, that the variations in the starting points of the transitions are quite small in relation to the frequency range through which the vowel formant moves. All of this confirms what we had previously observed and reported in Part 1, and considerably increases our confidence in the result. The result itself is of some general importance, we believe, for when we take into account that /r/ and /l/ transitions begin at the actual loci (as many other consonant

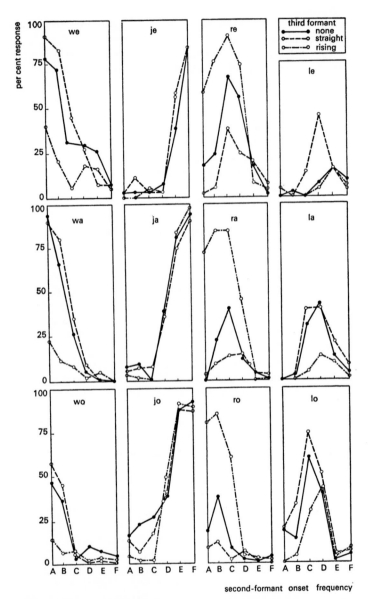

Figure 4 Responses of forty-four phonetically untrained listeners, plotted as a function of second-formant onset frequency for each of the three third-formant conditions, where A = 720 Hz, B = 840 Hz, C = 1200 Hz, D = 1560 Hz, E = 2040 Hz and F = 2400 Hz

transitions do not), we see that we have here a clear case in which the frequency position of a consonant locus varies with changes in the frequency level of the vowel formant. This variation in the position of the locus is relatively small, which is fortunate for the utility of the locus concept as a simplifying assumption, but it clearly occurs, and we have remarked on it at some length because it is the first direct evidence we have had that a consonant locus will behave in this manner.[1][2]

The judgments of our naïve listeners tend to agree with our own impressions (as reported in Part 1) in several other particulars. We see in Figure 4, for example, that the best starting point for the second-formant transition is at a somewhat higher frequency for /l/ than for /r/, though this difference would not appear from these data to provide a very good basis, in itself, for the perceived distinction between these two phonemes. It is also reasonably clear from the results with naive listeners that with two formants alone, /l/ is relatively good with the back vowels, while /r/ is relatively good with the front vowels.

It had been our feeling in working with these sounds that our /l/ was, at best, inferior to the other three phonemes, but we were somewhat surprised to discover how very poor our naïve listeners found it. We believe that certain rather detailed changes in the first-formant steady-state onset and transition will considerably improve the /l/ for our naive listeners.

We see in Figure 4 that /w/ before the vowel [o] was rather poor. This is not surprising when we consider that there were no patterns for [o] in which the starting point of the second-formant transition was below the steady state of the vowel (720 Hz). Starting the transition at a somewhat lower frequency will probably improve the /wo/ considerably.

References

COOPER, F. S. (1950), 'Spectrum analysis', *J. acoust. Soc. Amer.* vol. 22, pp. 761–2.
COOPER, F. S. (1953), 'Some instrumental aids to research on speech', *Report of the Fourth Annual Round Table Meeting on Linguistics and Language Teaching*, pp. 46–53, Institute of Languages and Linguistics, Georgetown University, Washington, DC.
COOPER, F. S., LIBERMAN, A. M., and BORST, J. M. (1951), 'The interconversion of audible and visible patterns as a basis for research in the perception of speech', *Proc. nat. Acad. Sci.*, vol. 37, pp. 318–25. Excerpt reprinted here, pp. 204–7.

12. Stevens and House (1956) have demonstrated that precisely this kind of locus movement can be expected, on the basis of their calculations, to occur for the second-formant loci of /b/ and of /g/. In our own earlier research on the second-formant loci of /b/, /d/ and /g/, we had to contend with the difficulties arising from the fact that the second-formant transitions do not (and indeed, cannot) begin at the locus, but must only point to it. As a result, we had to rely on a series of straight second formants (at various frequency levels) in order to find the /b/, /d/ and /g/ loci. By the very nature of that procedure, it was impossible to detect the kind of locus movement that we have here found with /r/ and /l/ and that Stevens and House would expect to find with /b/ and /g/.

DELATTRE, P. C., LIBERMAN, A. M., and COOPER, F. S. (1951), 'Voyelles synthétiques à deux formants et voyelles cardinales', *Le Maître phonétique*, vol. 96, pp. 30–37.

DELATTRE, P. C., LIBERMAN, A. M., COOPER, F. S., and GERSTMAN, L. J. (1952), 'An experimental study of the acoustic determinants of vowel color: observations on one- and two-formant vowels synthesized from spectrographic patterns', *Word*, vol. 8, pp. 195–210. Reprinted here, pp. 221–37.

DELATTRE, P. C., LIBERMAN, A. M., and COOPER, F. S. (1955), 'Acoustic loci and transitional cues for consonants', *J. acoust. Soc. Amer.*, vol. 27, pp. 769–73. Reprinted here, pp. 273–83.

DUNN, H. K. (1950), 'The calculation of vowel resonances and an electrical vocal tract', *J. acoust. Soc. Amer.*, vol. 22, pp. 740–53.

HARRIS, K. S. (1954), 'Cues for the identification of the fricatives of American English', *J. acoust. Soc. Amer.*, vol. 26, p. 952 (abstract).

LIBERMAN, A. M., DELATTRE, P. C., and COOPER, F. S. (1952), 'The role of selected stimulus variables in the perception of the unvoiced stop consonants', *Amer. J. Psychol.*, vol. 65, pp. 497–516.

LIBERMAN, A. M., DELATTRE, P. C., COOPER, F. S., and GERSTMAN, L. J. (1954), 'The role of consonant–vowel transitions in the perception of the stop and nasal consonants', *Psychol. Mongr.*, vol. 68, no. 8. Reprinted here, pp. 315–31.

LIBERMAN, A. M., DELATTRE, P. C., GERSTMAN, L. J., and COOPER, F. S. (1956), 'Tempo of frequency change as a cue for distinguishing classes of speech sounds', *J. exp. Psychol.*, vol. 52, pp. 127–37.

O'CONNOR, J. D., and TRIM, J. L. M. (1953), 'Vowel, consonant and syllable – a phonological definition', *Word*, vol. 9, pp. 103–22.

PETERSON, G. E., and BARNEY, H. L. (1952), 'Control methods used in a study of the vowels', *J. acoust. Soc. Amer.*, vol. 24, pp. 175–84. Reprinted here, pp. 104–22.

STEVENS, K. N., and HOUSE, A. S. (1955), 'Development of a quantitative description of vowel articulation', *J. acoust. Soc. Amer.*, vol. 27, pp. 484–93.

STEVENS, K. N., and HOUSE, A. S. (1956), 'Studies of formant transitions using a vocal tract analog', *J. acoust. Soc. Amer.*, vol. 28, pp. 578–85.

STEVENS, K. N., KASOWSKI, S., and FANT, C. G. M. (1953), 'An electrical analog of the vocal tract', *J. acoust. Soc. Amer.*, vol. 25, pp. 734–42.

21 Alvin M. Liberman, Pierre C. Delattre, Franklin S. Cooper and Louis J. Gerstman

The Role of Consonant–Vowel Transitions in the Perception of the Stop and Nasal Consonants[1]

Alvin M. Liberman, Pierre C. Delattre, Franklin S. Cooper and Louis J. Gerstman, 'The role of consonant–vowel transitions in the perception of the stop and nasal consonants', *Psychological Monographs*, vol. 68, no. 8 (1954).

In spectrograms of stop consonant-plus-vowel syllables one commonly see several acoustic variables that might conceivably be important in the auditory identification of the stop consonant phones. One such variable is a short burst of noise, found near the beginning of the syllable, as in Plate 46, and presumed to be the acoustic counterpart of the articulatory explosion. By preparing hand-drawn spectrographic patterns of burst-plus-vowel and then converting these patterns into sound, we found in an earlier experiment that the frequency position of the burst could serve as a cue, though not necessarily as a completely adequate one, for distinguishing among /p/, /t/ and /k/.

Bursts above 3000 Hz were, in general, judged to be /t/. Below that level, the perception of the burst was determined by its frequency position in relation to the vowel with which it was paired: the burst was heard as /k/ when it lay at or slightly above the second formant of the following vowel: otherwise, it was identified as /p/. The effect of the vowel on the perception of the burst was shown most strikingly in the case of one burst, centered, at 1440 Hz which was heard as /p/ before /i/ and /u/, but as /k/ before /a/ (Liberman, Delattre and Cooper, 1952).

A second possible cue to the perception of the stops lies in the transition between consonant and vowel, seen in Plate 46 as a curvature of the formants[2] during the vowel onset. Such shifts in the frequencies of the vowel

1. This research was supported in part by the Carnegie Corporation of New York and in part by the Department of Defense in connection with Contract DA49-170-sc-773. The first of the two experiments reported here was described at the 1952 meeting of the American Psychological Association: also, it was summarized in a discussion of related research at the 1952 Conference on Speech Analysis.
2. Formant: a relatively high concentration of acoustic energy within a restricted frequency region. In spectrograms the formants appear as dark bands whose general orientation is parallel to the horizontal (time) axis of the graph. Typically, three or more formants are seen, as, for example, in Plate 46; these several formants are conventionally referred to by number, formant one being the lowest in frequency and in position on the spectrogram, formant two the next higher, and so on.

formants presumably reflect the articulatory movements that are made in going from one position to another; one expects, then, to find these shifts in the region where two phones join.[3]

In their discussion of the cues that might be used in 'reading' speech spectrograms, Potter, Kopp and Green (1947, pp. 81–103) have noted the transitions between stop consonant and vowel, especially in the second formant, and have described in general terms the forms that these transitions seem characteristically to take. According to these authors, the movement of the second formant is typically upward when the vowel follows /p/ or /b/; after /t/ or /d/ the second formant of the vowel starts at a position 'near the middle of the pattern', with the result that this formant will then rise or fall depending on whether its normal, steady-state position in the vowel is higher or lower than the /t-d/ starting point; after /k/ or /g/ the second formant starts at a position slightly above its steady-state position in the vowel, wherever that may be, and the transition is always, therefore, a relatively small shift downward. Joos (1948, pp. 121–5), also, has noted that the transitions are characteristically different for the various syllabic combinations of stop and vowel, and, in addition, has made explicit the assumption that the transitions may well be important cues for the perception of the stops. Without this latter assumption, he points out, one may have difficulty in explaining how listeners distinguish among the stop sounds, since the explosive portions are sometimes of very low intensity.

Further analysis of spectrograms may result in a more nearly precise description of the typical patterns of transition for the various combinations of stop consonant and vowel. It will be no less necessary, however, to isolate the transitions experimentally if we are to determine whether they are perceptual cues or nulls, since the transitional movements do not occur independently of other possible cues in spectrograms of actual speech. To find whether or not the transitions can, in fact, enable a listener to distinguish among the stop consonants, we have, in the first experiment to be reported here, varied the direction and extent of second-formant transitions in highly simplified synthetic syllables and presented the resulting sounds to a group of listeners for identification as /b/, /d/ or /g/ and, separately, as /p/, /t/ or /k/.

Since the nasal consonants /m/, /n/ and /ŋ/ are closely related in articulatory terms to the voiced and unvoiced stops – /p-b-m/ are all articulated by the lips, /t-d-n/ by the tip of the tongue against the alveoles, and /k-g-ŋ/

3. We do not mean to imply that frequency shifts occur only between regions of steady-state resonance. It is, in fact, not unusual, especially in spectrograms of connected speech, to find that the formants are in almost constant movement. We shall deal here, however, with consonant–vowel syllables in which the vowel does assume a steady state following the transitional movement at the vowel onset.

by the hump of the tongue against the velum – we might guess that the transitional cues for /p-t-k/ or /b-d-g/ would also serve to distinguish among /m-n-ŋ/. A second experiment was carried out, then, to determine whether the variable second-formant transitions of the first experiment could function as cues for the perception of the nasal consonants. For that purpose we added to the patterns of vowel-plus-transition a certain neutral and constant resonance that had been found to impart to these patterns, as heard, the color or character of nasal consonants as a class. The sounds produced from these patterns were presented to subjects for judgment as /m/, /n/ or /ŋ/.

Experiment 1: stop consonants

Apparatus. All the stimuli of this experiment were produced by using a special purpose playback to convert hand-painted spectrograms into sound. This playback, which has been described in earlier papers (Cooper, 1950; Cooper *et al.*, 1951) produces 50 bands of light modulated at harmonically related frequencies that range from a fundamental of 120 Hz through the fiftieth harmonic at 6000 Hz. The modulated light beams are arranged to match the frequency scale of the spectrogram. Thus, when a spectrogram, painted in white on a transparent base, is passed under the lights, the painted portions reflect to a phototube those beams whose modulation frequencies correspond to the position of the paint on the vertical (frequency) axis of the spectrogram.

Stimuli. As shown in Figure 1, the second-formant transitions, which constituted the experimental variable of this study, differed in direction and extent. From the frequency at which the second formant begins to the frequency at which it levels off, the transitions vary in steps of one harmonic (120 Hz) from a point four harmonics (480 Hz) below the center of the steady-state portion of the second formant to a point six harmonics (720 Hz) above the second formant. This range of transitions was judged, on the basis of exploratory work, to be sufficient. For two of the synthetic vowels, /o/ and /u/, the close proximity of first (lower) and second (higher) formants made it impossible to extend the transition as much as 480 Hz below the second formant; in these cases the transitions that rise from points below the second formant were varied in four half-harmonic steps.

For convenience in reference, the direction and extent of second-formant transitions will be indicated as in section A of Figure 1. Transitions that go through a frequency range lying below the steady-state formant of the synthetic vowel will be called 'minus' (−); those that cover a range of frequencies above the steady-state formant will be called 'plus' (+). The extent of a transition will be given by the number of harmonics (of the 120 Hz fundamental) through which the formant moves before arriving at its steady-state position: A transition of −3, for example, is one that goes through the first three harmonics below the steady state of the vowel.

In determining the curvature of the transitions, we tried simply to approximate the transitions we have seen in spectrograms of actual speech. The duration of the transition, i.e. the time interval between the beginning and end of the frequency shift, varied linearly with the size of the transition,

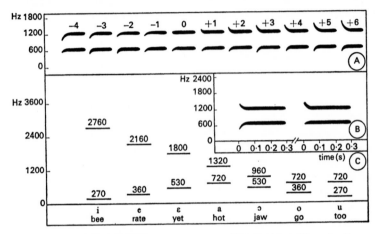

Figure 1 The stimuli of experiment 1. A: second formant transitions for the vowel /a/. B: large and small transitions of the first formant. C: two-formant synthetic vowels

from 0·04 s for a transition of +1 or −1, to 0·08 s for a transition of +6. This made it possible to keep the shape of the transition (as judged by eye) roughly constant. We have found in exploratory work that variations in the duration of the transition or in curvature do not cause the sound to change from one stop consonant to another.

The two-formant synthetic vowels used in this study, and arranged in section C of Figure 1 along an articulatory continuum of front-to-back tongue positions, represent a rather systematic sampling of the vowel triangle. They have been adapted from a set of synthetic vowels that had been found in an earlier study (Delattre *et al.* 1952) to approximate rather closely the color of the corresponding cardinal vowels as spoken; with the exception of /u/, the vowels of the present experiment are substantially identical with those used in an earlier experiment (Liberman *et al.*, 1952) on bursts as cues for the stop consonants. The frequency extent of each formant is three harmonics of the 120 Hz fundamental. The value that is to be found just above each formant in section C of Figure 1 gives the frequency that corresponds approximately to the center of the formant.[4] Each pattern of transition-plus-vowel has a total duration of 0·3 s.

In our essentially exploratory attempts to produce acceptable stop consonants with nothing more than a transition and a schematic vowel, we had adopted for the first formant the constant minus transition seen in section A of Figure 1.[5] This first-formant transition seemed to increase the realism and identifiability of the sounds, but it imparted to all of them a rather strong voiced quality; that is, it made them sound, much more like /b-d-g/ than /p-t-k/. Although we were not concerned in this study to isolate the cues that distinguish the voiced stops from their voiceless counterparts, we did wish to investigate the role of second-formant transitions in both classes of sounds, and, on the assumption that phonetically naïve listeners might have difficulty in trying to identify the voiced sounds as voiceless, we thought it wise to try to 'unvoice' the sounds before presenting them for judgment as /p-t-k/. The closest approximation we could achieve, without adding the burst of noise that appears to characterize /p-t-k/, was obtained by considerably reducing the transition of the first formant.[6] This reduces somewhat the impression of voicing; it makes the stops resemble the unaspirated voiceless stops used, for example, by a native speaker of French, but it does not succeed in producing the clearly unvoiced quality typical of aspirated /p-t-k/ in an American pronunciation. The 'unvoiced' and 'voiced' types of first-formant transition are illustrated in section B of Figure 1.

4. Although the tones produced by the playback are spaced 120 Hz apart, an auditory impression of finer graduations of formant pitch can be obtained by varying the relative intensities of the three contiguous harmonics (of the 120 Hz fundamental) that comprise the formant. In this study the intensities of the two outlying harmonics of a formant were sometimes intentionally unbalanced in an attempt to produce closer approximations to correct vowel color. The unbalancing is accomplished by varying the extent to which the white paint covers the 'channel' corresponding to a particular harmonic. Wherever this procedure has been used, we have estimated the equivalent center frequency of the formant by the relative widths of the painted lines.
5. With the vowels /ɛ/, /a/ and /ɔ/, the first-formant transitions started at a point 360 Hz below the steady-state level of the first formant. For /i/, /e/, /o/ and /u/, the transitions of the first formant were necessarily smaller, since the steady-state levels of the first formants of these vowels are all less than 360 Hz above the lowest frequency (120 Hz) produced by the playback; in these cases the first-formant transitions started at 240 Hz below the steady-state level for /e/ and /o/, and at 120 Hz below the steady state for /i/ and /u/.
6. We did not wish to add the burst because it not only produces an impression of the class of unvoiced stops, but, as was shown in an earlier experiment (Liberman et al., 1952), it also serves, by its position on the frequency scale, to differentiate the stops within that class. We should note here that the frequency position of the burst can probably be used as a cue for distinguishing among the voiced stops also. This will, of course, require the addition of certain 'voicing' constants.

There were, then, two sets of stimuli that were identical in all respects, except that in one set the minus transition of the first formant was relatively large and in the other very small.

Presentation of stimuli. A total of 77 stimuli (11 transitions times 7 schematic vowels) was used for each of the two sets of test patterns (voiced and unvoiced). These 77 stimuli were recorded from the playback onto magnetic tape, and then spliced into a random order, subject to the restrictions that in each successive group of 11 sounds each transition appears once and only once, and that each vowel appears at least once in each group but never more than twice and never in immediate succession.

In the final test tape the sound stimuli were arranged in such a way that each stimulus would be presented and then repeated after an interval of 0·9 s, with an interval of 6 s between successive pairs of identical stimuli. The latter interval provided sufficient time for the subject to make and record his judgment of one stimulus before being presented with the next. A rest period of 15 s was interpolated between successive groups of 11 stimuli.

The 'voiced' patterns, i.e. those with large transitions of the first formant, were presented to one group of 33 subjects for judgment as /b/, /d/ or /g/; the 'unvoiced' patterns, i.e. those with small transitions of the first formant, were presented to a second group of 33 subjects for judgment as /p/, /t/ or /k/. Then, to exhaust all combinations of the two kinds of first-formant transitions and the two kinds of judgment, we recruited two additional groups of 33 subjects each and asked one of these groups to judge the patterns with the large first-formant transitions as /p/, /t/ or /k/, and the other to judge the patterns with the small transitions of the first formant as /b/, /d/ or /g/.

In all cases the subject was asked to make an identification of each stimulus, even when he felt that his judgment was only a guess. The range of identifications permitted was limited to /p/, /t/ or /k/ for two groups of subjects and to /b/, /d/ or /g/ for the other two groups.

The entire stimulus series was presented twice for each subject. Thus, each subject made a total of 154 judgments.

Before subjects began to record their judgments, they were asked to listen to the first group of 11 stimuli in order that they might become somewhat acquainted with the nature of the sounds and the format of the experiment. For all subjects the opportunity to hear these 11 stimuli constituted the sum of their experience with the sounds produced by the pattern playback prior to their participation in this experiment.

Subjects. A total of 132 subjects (33 in each of the four conditions) served in the experiment. All were volunteers from undergraduate and graduate courses at the University of Connecticut.

Results. Before considering the particular responses that were made to the various second-formant transitions, we ought, first, to note in Figures 2 and 3 the similarities and differences in the general pattern of responses obtained with the two types of first formant (large and small minus transitions)

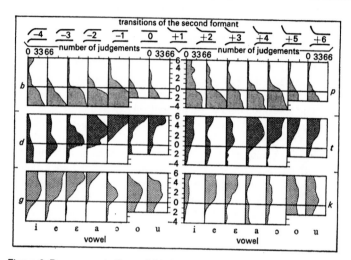

Figure 2 Responses to the variable transitions of the second formant obtained with large transitions of the first formant

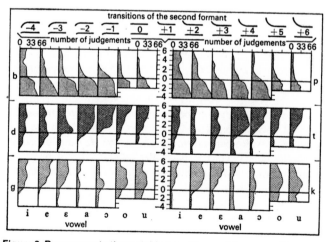

Figure 3 Responses to the variable transitions of the second formant obtained with small transitions of the first formant

and the two types of judgment (voiced and unvoiced). By comparing Figures 2 and 3, we see that the amount of agreement among subjects is somewhat greater when the first formant has the larger minus transition. It will be remembered in this connection that we had adopted the relatively straight first formant in an attempt to reduce the impression of voicing; that is, to make the synthetic stops sound less like /b-gd/ and somewhat more like /p-t-k/. Clearly, we did not succeed by this means in increasing the amount of agreement among subjects who tried to identify these stimuli as /p-t-k/. The data are displayed so that within each small rectangle, the number of times a stimulus was judged as /b/, /d/ or /g/ (or as /p/, /t/ or /k/) is plotted on the horizontal axis as a function of the direction and extent of the second-formant transition (shown on the vertical axis and illustrated at the top of the figure). The data were obtained from two groups of thirty-three subjects each. One group judged the stimuli as /b/, /d/ or /g/, the other as /p/, /t/ or /k/. Each subject made two judgments of each stimulus. The vowels with which the second-formant transition were paired are arranged along an articulatory continuum of tongue position from front to back. Because of the close proximity of the first and second formants of /o/ and /u/, the minus transitions for these vowels were not extended beyond a value of two.

We have noted earlier that it was not the purpose of this study to find the cues that distinguish voiced from unvoiced stops, and it should be emphasized here that we have not yet investigated this matter, except cursorily and in a few isolated cases. On the basis of such evidence as is now available, however, we believe that the voiced-voiceless distinction is more easily made if one is free, as we were not in this particular experiment, to use both burst and transition. The proper combination of burst and transition tends to produce an impression of the general class of unvoiced stops, the particular identity of the stop, i.e., /p/, /t/ or /k/, being determined both by the frequency position of the burst and the nature of the transition. It will presumably be possible, then, to obtain the voiced counterparts by making certain constant changes in the pattern, as, for example, by varying the time interval between burst and transition, or by adding constant 'markers', such as a 'voice bar' (a tone of 120 or 240 Hz sounding simultaneously with the burst). Thus, a particular combination of burst and second-formant transition would, with any given vowel, be used for the synthesis of either /p/ or /b/, a second such combination would be used for /t/ or /d/, and a third for /k/ or /g/; one could expect to shift back and forth between the voiced and voiceless stops without making significant changes in the frequency position of the burst or in the direction and extent of the second-formant transition.

With large or with small transitions of the first formant (Figure 2 or 3) we see that the amount of agreement is, in general, slightly greater when subjects are trying to identify the sounds as /b-d-g/. (This is not surprising, perhaps, in view of the fact that all of the stimuli sounded quite voiced.) It is nonetheless clear that the various second-formant transitions produce the same general pattern of responses, whether the stimuli that contain them are judged as /b-d-g/ or as /p-t-k/. For the purposes of this paper, then, we shall consider that the second-formant transitions have essentially the same effect within each of the two classes (voiced and unvoiced) of stop consonants, and we shall treat the results as if each of the pairs, /p-b/, /t-d/ and /k-g/, were a single sound.

The response distributions of Figures 2 and 3 show, in general, that /b/ (or /p/) was heard when the second formants of the vowels had minus transitions, i.e. transitions that extend into a frequency region lower than the frequency of the steady-state portion of the formant. When these minus transitions were presented with the vowels /i/, /e/, /ε/, /a/ and /ɔ/, there was considerable, and in some cases complete, agreement among subjects in identifying the sounds as /b-p/. With the vowels /o/ and /u/, on the other hand, these same transitions elicited few responses of /b-p/ (in relation to /g-k/ and /d-t/), but there is, nevertheless, a significant similarity in the pattern of judgments as between /o-u/ and /i-e-ε-a-ɔ/ in that the bulk of /b-p/ judgments occurs, for all these vowels, within the range of minus transitions.

The distributions of /d-t/ judgments center at different positions on the scale of transitions, depending on the vowel with which the transition was paired. In the case of /i/ the /d-t/ distributions are rather flat and low; indeed, there is for this vowel no value of transition at which the /d-t/ response was dominant. For the remaining vowels, however, there is a rather strong preference for identifying /d/ (or /t/) within some relatively narrow range of transitions, starting in the vicinity of a zero transition for the vowels /e/ and /ε/, and progressing to larger plus transitions through the vowel series /a-ɔ-o-u/.

The distributions of /g-k/ judgments would appear, for all plus transitions at least, to be the inverse of the /d-t/ distributions; that is, the /g-k/ judgments occur wherever the /d-t/ judgments do not. Considered in their own right, the distributions of /g-k/ responses show that the extreme plus transitions were heard as /g-k/ in the vowel series /i/ to /a/. The smaller plus transitions were also heard as /g-k/ with /i/ and /e/, but at /ε/ only the transitions of $+4$, $+5$ and $+6$ were judged very often as /g/ or /k/, and at /a/ such /g-k/ responses as did occur were made, for the most part, to the extreme transition of $+6$. With /ɔ/ the /g-k/ responses center at the small positive transitions and the distribution of /g-k/ responses seems then simply to grow in height and width through /o/ and /u/.

Alvin M. Liberman, *et al.* 323

With the vowels /ɔ/ and /ɛ/ relatively good /d/s and /t/s were produced by transitions of zero, or near zero, extent. This suggests that /d/ and /t/ have a characteristic second-formant position, or locus, somewhere near the level of the second formant of /e/ or /ɛ/, from which point transitions might be expected to fall or rise to the second formants of other vowels.[7] This possibility is consistent with our finding that the /d-t/ responses occurred primarily to progressively larger plus transitions as the frequency level of the second formant of the vowel became lower in the series /a/ through /u/. We have evidence from experiments now in progress that adds support to the assumption of fixed consonant loci for /d-t/, and suggests that there may be comparable loci for /b-p/ and for /g-k/, also. The establishment of these consonant loci would, of course, provide the basis for a greatly simplified description of the data of the present experiment.

It may be noted here that a consonant will be heard with the second formant at zero transition only when the first formant has some degree of minus transition. When both formants are straight, one hears nothing but the vowel.

Figure 4, which is intended to be a broader and less detailed representation of the results, is derived from the data in the left half of Figure 2 (stimulus patterns with the large transitions of the first formant, judged as /b-d-g/). For the purposes of Figure 4, a particular response was taken as

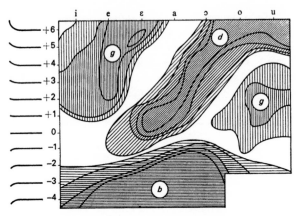

Figure 4 Map of the regions in which the judgments /b/, /d/ or /g/ were dominant

7. Potter, Kopp and Green (1947, pp. 81–103) have inferred from spectrograms the existence of a 'hub' or second formant, for each of the stop consonants. They assume that the frequency position of this hub is fixed for /p/ and /t/, being always at a relatively low frequency for /p/ and a relatively high frequency for /t/. The hub of /k/ is assumed to vary according to the following vowel.

'dominant' when (for any stimulus) the difference in the number of judgments between the most numerous and the next most numerous response exceeded 20 per cent of the sum of all responses. This constitutes the lowest degree of dominance, and is indicated in the figure by the lightest shading. The three darker shadings of Figure 4 correspond to increasing degrees of dominance (40, 60 and 80 per cent, respectively).

The results of this experiment show that the direction and degree of second-formant transitions can serve as cues for the aurally perceived distinctions among the stop consonants.[8] In judging some of the stimuli, all, or almost all, subjects made the same identifications. In other cases, the amount of agreement was considerably less than complete, but still sufficient to indicate that the second-formant transition has considerable cue value. However, certain cases remain in which the second-formant transition does not appear to provide an adequate basis for identifying the stop; with /i/, for example, we do not get, with any transition, a clearly dominant /t/ or /d/ response.

There is evidence from preliminary investigations that an increase in the identifiability of the synthetic stops will result from the inclusion of appropriate transitions of the *third* formant. It is quite clear, however, that the third-formant transitions are, in general, considerably less important for the perception of the stop consonant than are transitions of the second formant.

We have prepared and listened to a series of patterns in which, for each of the seven schematic vowels (/i/, /e/, /ɛ/, /ɑ/, /ɔ/, /o/ and /u/), third-formant transitions of −3, 0 and +3 were added to each of nine second-formant transitions (from −4, through 0, to +4). When −3 transitions of the third formant are added to minus transitions of the second formant, /b/ is heard with all vowels. The addition of the −3 transition in the third formant seems in these cases to improve the /b/, particularly with the back vowels /o/ and /u/, where, according to the data of Figures 2 and 3, the /b/ produced without third-formant transition is relatively poor. Adding a −3 transition of the third formant to plus transitions of the second formant

8. It appears that the *duration* of transition is also a cue for distinguishing among speech sounds, not within the class of stop consonants, but between this class and others. Thus, increasing the transition time beyond the largest value (0·08 s) used in the present experiment causes some of the stop consonants to be transformed first into semivowels and then, with further increases in duration of transition, into vowels of changing color. In the case of a +6 transition with /ɛ/, for example, the sound will be heard as /gɛ/, then /jɛ/, and, finally, as /iɛ/, as the duration of the transition is progressively lengthened. If the transition time is reduced below the lowest value used in the present experiment (0·04 s), a point is reached, eventually, at which the perception begins to change in various and complex ways; these changes are probably attributable to the fact that at very short durations the transitions are so abrupt as to be, in effect, bursts.

produces, in general, a /g/ impression, and in the case of those plus transitions of the second formant that were heard as /g/ in the two-formant patterns, the identifiability of the /g/ is somewhat improved. As might be expected, the addition of a third formant with zero transition does not appreciably change the sound; one hears essentially what was heard with the two-formant version. The addition of a +3 transition of the third formant tends in general to produce an impression of /d/. Combining this third-formant transition with the appropriate second-formant transition creates a /d/ that seems significantly better than the best that could be produced with first- and second-formant transitions alone.

Reference to the results of the earlier study on bursts will show that bursts are often effective just where the second-formant transitions alone fail. We should expect, then, that adding an appropriate burst to the transitions will further reduce the number of cases in which the response is equivocal.

Experiment 2: nasal consonants

Procedure. The stimuli of Experiment 2 were identical with those of Experiment 1, except that (a) the transitions were placed at the ends of the syllables rather than at the beginnings, (b) neutral, constant resonances were added after the transitions, and (c) the first formants had no transitions, instead of the constant minus transitions of Experiment 1. It was considered advisable to put the nasal consonants (/m/, /n/, /ŋ/) at the ends of the syllables because /ŋ/ does not occur in the initial position in English. The purpose of the neutral resonance was to add to all the sounds the nasal quality characteristic of /m/, /n/, /ŋ/ as a class. A straight first formant was used throughout because it has seemed in exploratory work that the best nasal consonants were produced in this way.

It will be seen in the patterns of Figure 5 that the nasal resonance consists of three formants, centered at 240 Hz, 1020 Hz and 2460 Hz, and, also, that the formants of the nasal resonance are somewhat less intense than those used to produce the synthetic vowels. The particular frequency positions and intensities of these nasal 'markers' were selected on the basis of exploratory experimentation, and were judged by the authors to produce rather indifferently the nasality of /m/, /n/ or /ŋ/.[9]

The procedure for presenting the stimuli was identical with that of Ex-

9. It is possible that the frequency positions of the 'nasal' formants are, in actual speech' characteristically different for /m/, /n/ and /ŋ/; if so, the synthetic sounds, will presumably be improved when these differences are included in the patterns. We have tried here simply to find a particular position of the formants that would produce a general nasal quality without strongly biasing the sound toward any one of the three nasal phones.

periment 1. The instructions to subjects were also exactly as they were in Experiment 1, except, of course, that they were asked in Experiment 2 to identify the sounds as /m/, /n/ or /ŋ/.

Subjects. A total of 33 undergraduate and graduate students at the University of Connecticut judged the stimulus patterns. All subjects were

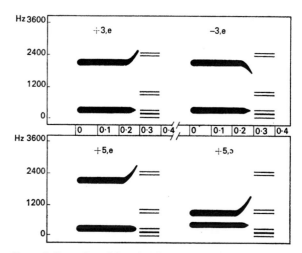

Figure 5 Examples of the stimuli used in Experiment 2

without prior experience in judging or listening to the synthetic speech sounds produced by the playback.

Results. The response distributions of Figure 6 show how the stimulus patterns of Experiment 2, which contained the second-formant transitions of Experiment 1 plus a nasal resonance, were identified as /m/, /n/ or /ŋ/. To provide a ready comparison between the results of Experiments 1 and 2 we have reproduced in Figure 6 the left half of Figure 3, showing how the /b-d-g/ judgments varied as a function of variations in the second-formant transitions (when the first formants had the small minus transitions that most closely approximate the straight first formants of Experiment 2).

The minus transitions that were heard in the first experiment as /p/ (or /b/) are heard here as /m/. The major difference between the stop and nasal consonants as cued by these minus transitions of the second formant would appear to be that the response to the stops is relatively strong, i.e., there is considerable agreement among subjects in identifying the minus transitions as /p-b/, for the vowels, /i/, /e/, /ɛ/, /a/, /ɔ/ and relatively weak for /o/ and /u/, while for the nasals the /m/ response is relatively weak with /i/, /e/, and strong with /ɛ/, /a/, /ɔ/, /o/, and /u/.

Alvin M. Liberman, *et al.* 327

The distributions of /n/ responses are quite flat for /i/ and /e/; for the remaining vowels, the /n/ responses clearly fall in the region of plus transitions and the bulk of the /n/ responses tend to move toward higher values of plus transition from /ɛ/ through /u/. As can be seen by comparison with the results of Experiment 1, the distributions of /n/ responses are very similar to those obtained for /d/ (or /t/).

The distributions of /ŋ/ responses are relatively flat and low for all the vowels – it is only with /i/ and /e/ that any transition is judged more often as

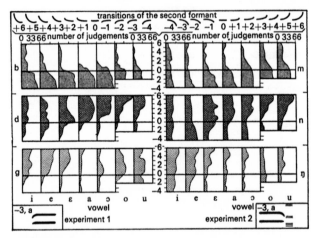

Figure 6 Distributions of /m/, /n/ and /ŋ/ judgments (Experiment 2) and /b/, /d/, /g/ judgments (Experiment 1)

/ŋ/ than as /m/ or /n/ – but one sees nevertheless that the /ŋ/ responses correspond to the /k-g/ responses of Experiment 1 in that they occur primarily in the region of plus transitions. One can also see, perhaps, that there is a tendency, roughly comparable to that seen in the /k-g/ distributions, for the bulk of the /ŋ/ responses to be displaced progressively toward the higher plus transitions for the vowels from /i/ through /a/; beyond /a/ the number of /ŋ/ responses is too few and the distributions are too nearly rectangular to permit detailed comparisons with /k-g/.

It is clear that the variable second-formant transitions can be cues for the perceived distinctions among /m/, /n/ and /ŋ/. A comparison with the results of Experiment 1, however, shows that the second-formant transitions were probably somewhat less effective as cues for the nasals than they were in providing a basis for distinguishing among the stops.

We do not conclude from the superiority of the stimuli of Experiment 1 that the transitions are necessarily less important for the perception of the nasals than for the stops. It is at least possible that changes in certain constant aspects of the stimulus patterns, such as the frequency positions of the formants that comprise the nasal resonance, might raise the amount of agreement in the /m-n-ŋ/ judgments, and it may be that the nasals are simply less identifiable than the stops in actual speech. One must consider also that the transitions were presented in the initial position in the syllable when they were judged as /b-d-g/, but in the terminal position for judgment as /m-n-ŋ/. By reversing the magnetic tape recordings that contain the stimuli for the first experiment (on the perception of /b-d-g/) we have been able to determine how the second-formant transitions are identified when the transitions (and hence the stops) are in the terminal position in the syllable. Under this condition we obtain response distributions that have patterns very similar to those of Experiments 1 and 2, but the amount of agreement among subjects is lower even than that which we have found for /m-n-ŋ/.[10] One might suppose, then, that greater agreement would have been obtained in the /m-n-ŋ/ experiment had the transitions been presented at the beginning of the syllables. We have obtained judgments under this condition (by reversing the magnetic tape of Experiment 2), but in this case we find no very large difference in the responses, either in regard to pattern or to amount of agreement. (The interpretation of this result is, of course, somewhat complicated by the fact that English-speaking subjects are not accustomed to hearing /ŋ/ in the initial position.)

For the purposes of this study the difference in the amount of agreement among subjects between Experiments 1 and 2 is less important, perhaps, than the very apparent similarities in the patterns of the response distributions. One finds in these distributions that a single second-formant transition can serve for /p/, /b/ and /m/, another for /t/, /d/ and /n/ and a third for /k/, /g/ and /ŋ/. Thus, three transitions are sufficient to classify nine speech sounds into three categories of three sounds each, and to enable a listener, with some degree of reliability, to distinguish among the categories. This arrangement of the sounds corresponds to a commonly accepted linguistic classification according to the place of articulation, in terms of which /p-b-m/ are bilabial, /t-d-n/ are linguo-alveolar and /k-g-ŋ/ are linguo-velar.

10. It may be noted that the effect of reversing the magnetic tape recordings of the stimuli is to convert a rising transition in initial position to a falling transition in terminal position, although both are minus transitions in the terminology of this paper and both are identified (with more or less agreement) as the same consonant.

We have not yet explored the possibility that the terminal transitions must be somewhat different from initials, in intensity or rate of change, for example, if they are to be maximally effective.

If a listener is to identify each of the nine sounds uniquely, he will need, in addition to the cues for place of articulation, some basis for determining whether a given sound belongs in the class of unvoiced stops (/p-t-k/), voiced stops (/b-d-g/), or nasal consonants (/m-n-ŋ/). It is possible that the distinctions among these three classes are effectively cued by a limited number of acoustic markers, such as voice bar and nasal resonance, each of which is constant within its class and characteristic of a manner, rather than a place, of articulation. The experiments reported here were not designed to test this possibility.

Summary

Spectrograms of stop consonant-plus-vowel syllables characteristically show rapid transitional movements (frequency shifts) of the formants at the vowel onset. To determine whether the transitions (particularly those of the second formant) are cues for the perceived distinctions among the stop consonants, two series of simplified, hand-painted spectrograms of transition-plus-vowel were prepared, then converted into sound by a special purpose playback and presented to naïve listeners for judgment as /b/, /d/ or /g/ and, separately, as /p/, /t/ or /k/. In terms of the extent of frequency shift, from the beginning of the syllable to the steady-state level of the second formant of the vowel, the transitions were varied in steps of 120 Hz from a point 480 Hz below the second formant ('minus' transitions) to a point 720 Hz above that formant ('plus' transitions).

Minus transitions were, in general, heard as /p/ or /b/. Plus transitions were heard as /t-d/ or /g-k/, depending on the size of the transition and the vowel with which it was paired. The amount of agreement among subjects indicated that the second-formant transitions can be important cues for distinguishing among either the voiceless stops (/p-t-k/) or the voiced stops (/b-d-g/).

A second experiment was performed to determine whether or not these same transitions of the second formant would serve to distinguish among the nasal consonants (/m-n-ŋ/), which are related to the stops in that the buccal occlusion is bilabial for /m-b-p/, linguo-alveolar for /n-t-d/, and linguo-velar for /ŋ-k-g/. The stimulus patterns of the second experiment were identical in all important respects to those of the first, except that a constant nasal resonance was added to each pattern and that the transitions were placed at the ends of the syllables.

There was in general somewhat less agreement among subjects in the second experiment than there had been in the first. Otherwise the results of the two experiments were quite similar: the transitions that had served for /p/ and /b/ were heard as /m/, those for /t/ and /d/ were heard as /n/, and those for /k/ and /g/ were heard as /ŋ/.

References

COOPER, F. S. (1950), 'Spectrum analysis', *J. acoust. Soc. Amer.*, vol. 22, pp. 761–2.

COOPER, F S., DELATTRE, P. C., LIBERMAN, A. M., BORST, J. M., and GERSTMAN, L. J. (1952), 'Some experiments on the perception of synthetic speech sounds', *J. acoust. Soc. Amer.*, vol. 24, pp. 597–606. Reprinted here, pp. 258–72.

COOPER, F. S., LIBERMAN, A. M., and BORST, J. M. (1951), 'The interconversion of audible and visible patterns as a basis for research in the perception of speech', *Proc. nat. Acad. Sci.*, vol. 37, pp. 318–25. Excerpt reprinted here, pp. 204–7.

DELATTRE, P. C., LIBERMAN, A. M., COOPER, F. S., and GERSTMAN, L. J. (1952), 'An experimental study of the acoustic determinants of vowel color; observations on one- and two-formant vowels synthesized from spectrographic patterns', *Word*, vol. 8, pp. 195–210. Reprinted here, pp. 221–37.

JOOS, M. (1948), *Acoustic Phonetics*, Language Monograph, no. 23, Baltimore.

LIBERMAN, A. M., DELARRRE, P. C., and COOPER, F. S. (1952), 'The role of selected stimulus-variables in the perception of the unvoiced stop consonants' *Amer. J. Psychol.*, vol. 65, pp. 497–516.

POTTER, R. K., KOPP, G. A., and GREEN, H. C. (1947), *Visible Speech*, Van Nostrand.

Perception and Linguistic Categories

It has long been clear to those working in linguistic phonetics that our perception of speech sounds is itself the fruit of the language learning process; the fact was indeed formulated by Sweet many years ago. An interesting and important development of the work on acoustic cues has been the experimental demonstration of the truth of this and of some of the relations between perception and the phonological system. In addition to the research on the recognition and identification of synthetic sounds described in the previous sections, there have been a large number of experiments designed to measure listeners' ability to discriminate between sounds related in some cue dimension. The measurements show that, with regard to certain types of cue, ability to discriminate fluctuates and perception tends to be rather sharply categorical; that is to say, certain ranges of the stimuli group themselves into categories corresponding to the phonological classes. For stimuli falling within the groups, discrimination is relatively poor but subjects are able to discriminate smaller differences in the regions between the groups, that is at the phoneme boundaries. It has also been shown that subjects with different mother tongues group the same range of stimuli differently and in a manner in keeping with the phonemic classes of their language.

These discoveries are of very considerable importance because they point to the possibility of establishing basic linguistic systems through the observations and measurement of the behaviour of language users.

22 Alvin M. Liberman, Katherine S. Harris, Howard S. Hoffman and Belver C. Griffith

The Discrimination of Speech Sounds Within and Across Phoneme Boundaries[1]

Alvin M. Liberman, Katherine S. Harris, Howard S. Hoffman and Belver C. Griffith, 'The discrimination of speech sounds within and across phoneme boundaries', *Journal of Experimental Psychology*, vol. 54 (1957), pp. 358–68.

In listening to speech, one typically reduces the number and variety of the many sounds with which one is bombarded by casting them into one or other of the phoneme[2] categories that his language allows. Thus, a listener will identify as /b/, for example, quite a large number of acoustically different sounds. Although these differences are likely to be many and various, some of them will occur along an acoustic continuum that contains cues for a different phoneme, such as /d/. This is important for the present study because it provides a basis for the question to be examined here: whether or not, with similar acoustic differences, a listener can better discriminate between sounds that lie on opposite sides of a phoneme boundary than he can between sounds that fall within the same phoneme category.

There are grounds for expecting an affirmative answer to this question. The most obvious, perhaps, are to be found in the common experience that in learning a new language one often has difficulty in making all the appropriate sound discriminations. The evidence for this is impressionistic in the extreme, and there is little information that would permit a definition of the more specific aspects of the difficulty. In whatever degree this difficulty exists, however, a reasonable assumption is that some part of it arises from the fact that a person who is newly exposed to the sounds of a strange language finds it necessary to categorize familiar acoustic continua in unfamiliar ways. If his discriminations have, by previous training, been sharpened and dulled according to the position of the phoneme boundaries of his native language, and if the acoustic continua of the old language are

1. This research was supported in part by the Carnegie Corporation of New York and in part by the Department of Defense in connection with Contract DA49-170-sc-1642.
2. The phoneme is most often taken to be the smallest unit of speech that can, by itself, distinguish one utterance from another as to meaning. Thus, the existence of the two words *bill* and *dill* makes it clear that /b/ and /d/ are different phonemes in English. It should be emphasized that the phoneme is not a single sound, but is, rather, a class which can and usually does include a great many sounds that differ from each other in various ways without causing any change in meaning.

categorized differently by the new one, then the learner might be expected to have difficulty perceiving the sounds of the new language until he had mastered some new discriminations and, perhaps, unlearned some old ones.

In more explicit psychological terms, an affirmative answer is to be expected on the basis that the situations being considered here clearly meet the conditions for acquired similarity and acquired distinctiveness. If either or both of these processes do, in fact, occur, then two speech sounds which a listener normally lumps into the same phoneme class would come to be less discriminable than sounds to which he habitually attaches different phoneme labels. Indeed, one might conceivably find in language some very common and easily accessible cases in which the effects of such processes as acquired similarity and acquired distinctiveness are as great as many years of practice can make them.

The present experiment was designed to investigate the relation between phonemic labelling and discrimination in one language and within one group of phonemes. For this purpose a synthesizer was used to generate speech-like sounds and to vary them in small steps along an acoustic continuum known to contain important cues for the perception of the voiced stops, /b/, /d/ and /g/. When listeners are asked to label these sounds as /b/, /d/ or /g/, they normally tend by their responses to divide the continuum into three sharply defined phoneme categories, the shifts from one response, or phoneme label, to another being very abrupt. It was the purpose of this experiment to determine how well these same sounds can be discriminated, and, in particular, to see whether the discrimination functions have sharp inflections that correspond in position to the abrupt shifts, i.e. phoneme boundaries, in the labelling responses. In addition, an attempt has been made to determine to what extent the relation between discrimination and labelling has here been reduced to its theoretical limit. For that purpose, the obtained discriminations have been compared with a function that is computed from the labelling data on the extreme assumption that the listener cannot hear any differences among these sounds beyond those that are revealed by his use of the phonemic labels.

Method

Apparatus. A special-purpose instrument, called a pattern playback, was used to generate the stimuli of this experiment. This instrument, which has been described in earlier papers (Cooper 1950, 1953; Cooper *et al.*, 1951), converts hand-painted spectrograms into sound, thus making it possible to synthesize speech-like auditory patterns and to control the various aspects of the pattern quite precisely.

Stimuli. Figure 1 illustrates the spectrograms used to produce the stimuli. The stimulus variable is the direction and extent of the second-formant transition, this variable having been found previously (Liberman *et al.*, 1954) to be important for the perceived distinctions among /b/, /d/ and /g/. In the stimulus pattern at the extreme left of the top row of the figure, the

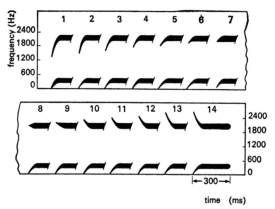

Figure 1

second formant rises from a point 840 Hz below its steady-state level, and in the pattern at the extreme right of the bottom row it falls from a point 720 Hz above the steady state. Between these two extremes, the starting point of the transition varies in steps of 120 Hz. For convenience these stimuli will be referred to by number, from 1 through 14, as indicated in Figure 1. Pattern 14, at the lower right, is complete in all respects.

The rising transition of the first formant had been found previously to be a marker for the class of voiced stops (Delattre *et al.*, 1955), and, as can be seen in Figure 1, this first-formant transition is constant in all the stimuli. In the steady-state part of the pattern the first formant centers at 360 Hz and the second at 2160 Hz. Formants at these frequencies produce a synthetic approximation to the vowel /e/ (as in *gate*).

The spectrograms were converted into sound on the pattern playback and recorded on magnetic tape. By copying, cutting and splicing the magnetic tape, all the stimulus arrangements described below were made.

Stimulus presentation and subjects. The stimuli were presented to subjects in two ways; singly, to determine how subjects would label them as /b/, /d/ or /g/, and in ABX arrangement to determine to what extent they could discriminate them on any basis at all.

For the labelling part of the experiment, six magnetic tapes were prepared, each of which contained a different randomization of the entire series of 14 stimuli. There was a 6 s interval between stimuli. These tapes were presented to subjects with instructions to judge each stimulus as /b/, /d/ or /g/.

To test discrimination by the ABX procedure, the stimuli were arranged in triads, each of which consisted of an A stimulus, a B stimulus, and a third stimulus, X, which was identical either to A or to B. The subjects were instructed to determine whether X was the same as A or the same as B. It was strongly emphasized to each subject, that he was to make his judgment on the basis of any cues he could hear. The measure of discriminability is, of course, the percentage of the time that the X stimulus is correctly matched to A or to B.

It was not the purpose of this experiment to obtain actual DLs, but only to measure relative discriminability at every step on the continuum. For that purpose, the A and B stimuli of the ABX triad were made up by pairing each stimulus with the stimulus one step, two steps, and three steps removed from it. Each stimulus was paired in this fashion with the stimuli lying to its right on the continuum shown in Figure 1. Thus, Stimulus 1 was paired with Stimulus 2 to form the A and B stimuli, respectively, of one ABX triad. Stimulus 1 was paired with Stimulus 3 in another triad, and with Stimulus 4 in a third. Similarly, Stimulus 2 was paired with Stimulus 3, with Stimulus 4, and with Stimulus 5, and so on for the remaining stimuli on the continuum. There was no stimulus one step to the right of Stimulus 14, so 14 does not appear as an A stimulus in the one-step series. For analogous reasons, Stimuli 13 and 14 do not appear as A stimuli in the two-step series, and Stimuli 12, 13 and 14 are missing from the three-step series.

From the above discussion, it follows that the number of A and B combinations was 36. For each combination of A and B stimuli, there were two triads – one in which X was identical to A and one in which X was identical to B. The total number of triads was 72. These triads were arranged into six tapes of 12 triads each. Within each ABX triad, the stimuli were spaced at 1 s intervals; successive triads were separated by 10 s.

There were two groups of subjects in the experiment. Since the procedures for the two groups were slightly different they will be described separately. Group 1 consisted of five paid volunteers, all undergraduate students at the University of Connecticut, who had never heard any synthetic speech prior to this experiment. For the first 17 sessions, subjects were given only the ABX discrimination task to do, without being told that these were synthetic speech sounds. Beginning with Session 18, they were informed that the sounds on the discrimination tapes were synthetic approximations to speech. At this point the labelling tapes were introduced, and for the next three sessions subjects were given four labelling tapes per session with instructions to identify each stimulus as a speech sound. During this period they were given no discrimination task. At Session 22 and thereafter subjects were asked to identify the stimuli on the labelling tapes as /b/, /d/ or /g/, and the discrimination task was resumed. In these sessions, the discrimination task was always undertaken after subjects had finished judging the stimuli on the labelling tapes.

For several reasons the discrimination data obtained before and after the introduction of the labelling tapes have been combined. First, an examination of the results showed that there was no obvious change in the discrimination judgments following the introduction of the labelling tapes and the instruction to judge the stimuli on those tapes as /b/, /d/ or /g/. Second, in the sessions in which the labelling tapes were first introduced, subjects reported that they had previously heard the sounds on the discrimination tapes as speech. Moreover, when they were asked to identify the speech sounds they heard, they responded mostly with /b/, /d/ and /g/.

When the discrimination data are combined, there are, for each subject in Group 1, a total of 21 judgments of each ABX triad. Since there were two triads for each combination of A and B stimuli, the total number of judgments of each A and B combination by each subject was 42. For each of the stimuli on the labelling tapes there are, for each subject, 32 judgments. All of the labelling judgments were obtained after Session 21 – i.e. after subjects had been asked specifically to identify the stimuli on the labelling tapes as /b/, /d/ or /g/.

Two of the five subjects in Group 1 were eliminated because they failed to apply the phoneme labels consistently. Since they did not clearly divide the stimulus continuum into phoneme categories, one cannot compare their discrimination of speech sounds within and across phoneme boundaries. It should be noted here that the stimuli of this experiment have previously been presented to large groups of listeners, and that it is quite unusual to find as many as two out of five who are as unreliable in their responses as the two subjects who were eliminated from this experiment.

Group 2 consisted of four workers at the Haskins Laboratories. These subjects had previously had extensive experience in listening to synthetic speech sounds. The procedure for Group 2 was like the procedure for Group 1 after Session 21. Thus, in each session, subjects identified the stimuli on one labelling tape, and then judged three of the discrimination tapes – a total of 36 ABX triads. (This plan could not be followed exactly in the last few sessions due to scheduling difficulties.) In all, each subject identified each of the stimuli on the labelling tapes 25 times, and he judged each ABX triad a total of 13 times. Since there were two triads for each A and B combination, each subject judged each A-B combination a total of 26 times.

Alvin M. Liberman, *et al.* 337

Of those subjects whose data will be shown individually in the following section on results, CD and R V are from Group 1, while L G and K H are from Group 2.

Results

In order to describe the method of presenting the data, and also to indicate in general terms the outcome of this study, the results that were obtained with one subject, CD, will be presented first. At the upper left of Figure 2 are plotted the labelling responses made by this subject when the

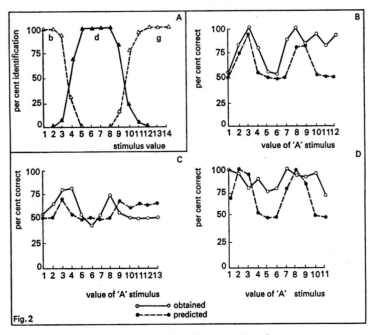

Figure 2 A: labelling data; B: two-step discrimination; C: one-step discrimination; D: three-step discrimination

14 stimuli were presented to him one at a time and in random order for judgment as /b/, /d/ or /g/. The values given on the ordinates in percentages are based on 32 and 42 judgments for the labelling and discrimination data respectively. It can be seen that Stimuli 1, 2 and 3 were identified primarily as /b/, Stimuli 5, 6, 7, 8 and 9 as /d/, and Stimuli 11, 12, 13 and 14 as /g/. The shifts from one response to another are very abrupt which is to say that the phoneme boundaries for this subject are very sharp and stable.

The discrimination data obtained with the same subject, CD, are also shown in Figure 2. Only the 'obtained' data points indicated by open circles and connected by solid lines will be considered at this time. Each point represents the percentage of correct responses for all ABX presentations (both ABA and ABB) when the A stimulus had the value shown on the abscissa and the B stimulus was one, two or three steps removed (for the one-, two- and three-step curves, respectively). Thus, for example, the first point on the one-step curve shows that this subject correctly discriminated Stimulus 1 and Stimulus 2 (one step higher on our stimulus scale) 54 per cent of the time.

A comparison of the discrimination functions with the labelling functions indicates that, other things equal, this subject does, indeed, discriminate better between stimuli that lie on either side of a phoneme boundary than he does between stimuli that fall within the same phoneme category. For example, it can be seen from the labelling curves that Stimuli 1 and 3 were both identified as /b/ almost all of the time, and the two-step discrimination curves show that this subject correctly discriminated these stimuli only 55 per cent of the time. Two steps beyond Stimulus 3, which was almost always identified as /b/, is Stimulus 5, which was always identified as /d/. The discrimination curves show that these two stimuli, consistently labelled as different phonemes, were correctly discriminated 100 per cent of the time.

It must, of course, be supposed that if a listener can always identify two stimuli as different (as in the case of Stimulus 3 and Stimulus 5), he will surely be able to discriminate them. On the other hand, it does not necessarily follow from the fact that he identifies two stimuli as the same phoneme (as with Stimulus 1 and Stimulus 3) that he cannot discriminate them. One might think that he would hear *two* types of /b/ – i.e. that he would hear what the linguist calls allophonic variations. In the example cited, the subject does not.

Clearly, the data obtained with this subject are not all so neat and striking as the particular examples chosen, and some of the other subjects were more variable, especially in their responses to the discrimination task, than the one subject, CD, whose responses have been shown in Figure 2. It is, nevertheless, reasonably apparent from an inspection of the data of all subjects that the discriminations tend to be relatively more acute in the vicinity of phoneme boundaries than in the middle of phoneme categories. Before presenting these other data, however, it is desirable to provide a basis on which all the results can be evaluated. For that purpose the working hypothesis will be stretched to a theoretical limit and its quantitative implications will be developed.

Make the extreme assumption that the subject can discriminate the stimuli only to the extent that he can identify them as different phonemes. Then suppose that in the discrimination task – i.e. when he is presented with the stimuli in ABX fashion and asked to say whether X is like A or like B – he can only assign the phonemic labels /b/, /d/ and /g/ to the individual stimuli, and that he has no other basis for discriminating among the stimulus members of the various ABX triads. One can, then, use his responses in the phonemic labelling part of the experiment as a basis for calculating the frequency with which he will correctly discriminate in any given ABX arrangement of the stimuli. To do this, one must first refer to the labelling part of the experiment and take account of the relative frequency with which the subject identified each of the 14 stimuli as /b/, /d/ or /g/. It is, of course, possible to go from these data to calculations of the probabilities that a given ABX triad will be heard as any one of the possible sequences of the three phonemes. One then needs only to determine for each triad which of the possible phonemic sequences will lead to responses that would be counted as correct discriminations.

By reference to the phonemic labelling part of the experiment we first determine for each A and B stimulus of the various ABX triads the relative frequency with which it was identified as /b/, as /d/ and as /g/. These relative frequencies will be used as estimates of the probabilities of hearing the various stimuli of the ABX triads as /b/, as /d/ and as /g/. Let us call the probabilities of hearing these phones p_b, p_d and p_g in the case of an A stimulus and p_b', p_d' and p_g' in the case of a B stimulus. We assume next that the various stimuli within each triad are perceived independently of each other. It follows, then, that the probability (for a given ABA triad) of hearing a particular sequence, such as /b/, /d/, /g/, is $p_b\, p_d'\, p_g$. Since there are three alternative responses, there are $3 \times 3 \times 3$, or 27, such phoneme sequences possible.

For any given triad the 27 possible phonemic sequences can be divided into three classes according to whether they lead the subject to make responses that would be counted as correct discriminations, as incorrect discriminations, or as discriminations that would on the average be correct half of the time and incorrect half of the time. In the case of any ABA type of triad, for example, the subject will be correct for any sequence in which the first and third stimulus members of the triad are heard as the same phoneme and the second member is heard as a different phoneme. He will be incorrect (again for the ABA type of triad) whenever the second and third members are heard as the same phoneme and the first is heard as a different phoneme. He will be correct half of the time and incorrect half of the time with two types of phoneme sequences: (a) all those in which he hears the first and second stimuli as the same phoneme and (b) those sequences in which he hears three different phonemes.[3]

These considerations can be expressed quantitatively in the following way. Let $P\ Corr_{(ABA)}$ be the proportion of the time that the listener is correct on a number of presentations of the same ABA sequence, P_R be the proportion of the time that the listener heard a sequence which would lead to correct discrimination, P_W be the proportion of the time that the listener heard a sequence which would lead to incorrect discrimination, and P_I be the proportion of the time that the listener heard a sequence which would, with equal likelihood, lead to correct and incorrect discriminations. Then

$$P\ Corr_{(ABA)} = 1P_R + 0P_W + 0 \cdot 5P_I.$$

If the probabilities of the particular sequences described above are substituted appropriately for the general expressions P_R, P_W and P_I, and if the resulting equation is then manipulated algebraically, we obtain

$$P\ Corr_{(ABA)} = 0 \cdot 5 + \frac{p_b^2 + p_d^2 + p_g^2 - p_b p_b' - p_d p_d' - p_g p_g'}{2}.$$

So far, we have been concerned only with the case in which the presented sequence is ABA; analogous considerations lead to a similar equation for ABB, although the particular sequences which are correct and incorrect are different.

$$P\ Corr_{(ABB)} = 0 \cdot 5 + \frac{p_b'^2 + p_d'^2 + p_g'^2 - p_b p_b' - p_d p_d' - p_g p_g'}{2}.$$

The ABA and ABB sequences were presented equally often; therefore, an average $P\ Corr$ is given by

$$P\ Corr = 0 \cdot 5 + \frac{(p_b - p_b')^2 + (p_d - p_d')^2 + (p_g - p_g')^2}{4}.$$

The solid points connected by dashed lines in Figure 2 represent the discrimination values derived from CD's labelling curves on the assumptions outlined above. It is seen in the case of this subject that the predicted functions do indeed take care of some, although by no means all, of the variations in the obtained discriminations. The assumptions predict the

3. When the subject hears a sequence of three different phonemes, he can be expected to make the correct discrimination half of the time only if we assume that he perceives each phoneme as equally like the other two. It is possible that the typical listener does not perceive /b/, /d/ and /g/ in precisely this way. However, the labelling data of this experiment are such as to produce essentially zero probabilities of hearing such sequences in the ABX triads. We have, therefore, not yet attempted to determine how the similarities among /b/, /d/ and /g/ are perceived, because a correction, no matter how large, would have negligible effect on the results being reported here.

points of high and low discrimination reasonably well, but they lead one to expect a general level of discrimination slightly lower than that obtained.

In Figure 3 are data obtained with three other subjects, R V, L G and K H. Each of the obtained values is based on 42 judgments in the case of R V, and on 26 judgments for L G and K H. The top row represents two-step discriminations and the bottom row represents three-step discriminations.

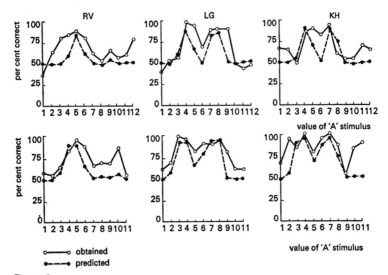

Figure 3

These data are not presented as a way of indicating the results for all subjects but only to show additional details of the results, including in particular a sample of the individual differences among subjects. It is seen that the position and number of the peaks in the predicted discrimination functions vary somewhat from one subject to another, reflecting differences in the way they had assigned phoneme labels to the stimuli when they were presented for identification. It is also apparent that the obtained discriminations follow the inter-subject differences in the predicted functions fairly well.

The simplest way to summarize the data for all subjects is to make a scatter plot of obtained values against predicted values. Such plots are shown in Figures 4, 5 and 6, for one-, two-, and three-step discriminations, respectively.[4] The small numerals on the three graphs indicate, where

4. It should be noted here that the reliabilities of all points in the scatter plots are not equal, since, as was pointed out under the section on procedure, the two groups of subjects made different numbers of judgments of the various A B X triads.

necessary, the number of values that occupy the same position of the coordinates. For the two- and three-step data, regression lines have been fitted by the method of least squares, and these are shown for each set of points. The regression for the one-step data has not been determined because so few predicted points lie above 50 per cent that a meaningful fit

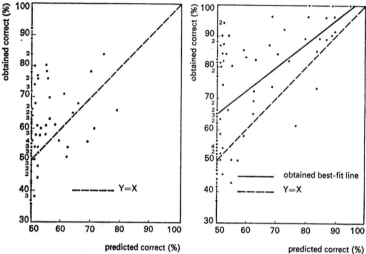

Figure 4 One-step discrimination   Figure 5 Two-step discrimination

cannot be obtained. The one-step data do not, therefore, provide a good test of our assumptions. For the two-and three-step data we should, of course, suppose that if the obtained data were essentially as predicted, give or take a little experimental error, the regression lines would be described by the equation '$x = y$'.

The relationship between predicted and obtained values has been measured by computing tau,[5] a nonparametric measure of correlation. The correlations are $+0.14$, $+0.43$, and $+0.43$ for the one-, two-, and three-step discriminations, respectively. Significance levels, in the same order, are $P = < 0.08$, $P = < 0.001$, and $P = < 0.001$. Thus, it is seen that the correlations are highly significant for the two- and three-step discriminations, but in the case of the one-step discrimination the relationship could have arisen by chance. The failure to obtain significance for the one-step discrimination is not surprising since, as was pointed out earlier, most of the one-step points are predicted to lie at 50 per cent.

5. We have used a nonparametric measure because our data fail to meet the assumption of homoscedasticity. For a description of tau, see Kendall (1948).

Although there is a significant relationship between obtained and predicted points for the two- and three-step discrimination data, it is apparent in both cases that the lines of best fit are systematically displaced upward. This indicates that while the assumptions predict fairly well the occurrence

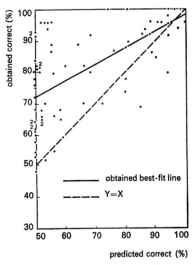

Figure 6 Three-step discrimination

and location of the inflections in the discrimination curves, they apparently lead to an underestimation of the general level of discrimination. This was previously noted in the data of the individual subjects as shown in Figures 2 and 3, where it was seen that the obtained discrimination functions tended to fit quite well with the predicted curves except that they were in general at a slightly higher level.

It is difficult on the basis of the data now available to make an unequivocal interpretation of the difference in level between obtained and predicted discrimination functions. One possibility, of course, is that this discrepancy represents a margin of 'true' discrimination – i.e., an ability of subjects to distinguish the speech sounds, not solely on the basis of the phonemic labels, but also more directly by the essential acoustic differences among the patterns. A very different possibility is that the discrepancy between obtained and predicted is the result of certain detailed aspects of the experimental procedure. For example, irrelevant discriminable aspects of the stimuli, such as accidental stray noise, could have provided subjects with an extraneous basis for deciding, in regard to the ABX triads, whether X was A or B. Such additional stimuli would, of course, have had no effect on the subjects' responses in the phonemic labelling part of the experiment. The result would have been, then, to make the obtained discriminations somewhat better than one would have expected them to be. In general, the procedures of this experiment were not such as to control most effectively for these irrelevant discriminanda. It will be possible in future research to take greater precautions against their occurrence, and then to determine whether and to what extent the discrepancy between obtained and predicted is reduced.

Within the data of the present experiment, however, there is some evidence that the discrepancy between obtained and predicted discrimination functions is due, at least in part, to 'true' discrimination. This evidence is to be found in the fact that the discrepancy would appear to be greater for the three-step than for the two-step function. One might expect to obtain this difference if each subject was truly discriminating the stimuli on the basis of their essential acoustic characteristics, since one would then presumably find as between the two- and three-step discriminations that the three-step discrimination was the easier. Other factors, such as the irrelevant discriminanda discussed in the preceding paragraph, would have affected the two- and three-step conditions equally, and would not have caused the departure from predicted values to be greater in the three- than in the two-step data.

Discussion

The results of this experiment cannot be assumed unequivocally to reflect the effects of learning on discrimination. There is, of course, the possibility that the inflections in the discrimination function are given innately, and that the phoneme boundaries have been placed so as to coincide with these discontinuities. This begins to seem unlikely when one considers that other languages have put phoneme boundaries at different places along the /b-d-g/ continuum. In itself, this would appear to reduce the probability that the sharp inflections in the discrimination functions are innately given. One would have far more compelling evidence, however, if it were found that native speakers of such languages have their points of maximal and minimal differential sensitivity displaced along the continuum to correspond with the phoneme boundaries of their respective languages. Research to test this possibility is feasible.

In order to find out whether the effects here described represent acquired similarity, acquired distinctiveness, or a combination of both, it will, of course, be appropriate to obtain discrimination data on non-speech stimuli that are otherwise identical with the synthetic approximations to speech. Complete identity is obviously impossible, unless one can get subjects to hear the same sounds sometimes as speech and sometimes not. One can, however, reasonably expect to make revealing comparisons between discrimination data obtained with speech and non-speech stimuli that vary along the same, simple stimulus dimensions. Sheer temporal duration, for example, is sometimes a cue for distinguishing speech sounds. (Duration of transitions distinguishes stop consonant from semivowel; duration of fricative noise is a cue for distinguishing among the classes fricative, affricate and stop.) It will be possible to obtain discrimination functions for variations in duration when those variations cue the perceived differences among phonemes, and to obtain comparable data for variations in duration of non-speech sounds. We should suppose that a comparison of discrimination functions such as these would help greatly to determine whether the typical listener's long training in speech perception has served selectively to sharpen or to dull his discrimination of speech sounds, or whether, perhaps, it has done both.

Summary

This experiment was designed to measure the relation between subjects' phonemic identifications (as /b/, /d/, /g/) of certain synthetic speech sounds and the extent to which they can discriminate the sounds as being different in any way. The stimuli were two-formant approximations to consonant-vowel syllables. They varied in the extent and direction of the second-formant transitions, this variable having previously been found to be an important cue for the perceived distinctions among /b/, /d/ and /g/.

In one part of the experiment these sounds were presented singly and in random order for identification as /b/, /d/ or /g/. The responses obtained in this way tended, with most listeners, to divide the stimulus continuum into three sharply bounded phonemic categories, indicating that the perceived shifts from one phoneme to another were rather abrupt.

In a second part of the experiment an ABX procedure was used to measure subjects' ability to discriminate these sounds. The results indicated that discrimination was better at the phoneme boundaries than in the middle of the phoneme category. That is, with acoustic differences equal, subjects discriminated better between speech sounds to which they habitually attach different phonemic labels than they did between sounds which they normally put into the same phoneme class. To obtain a more nearly precise evaluation of this effect, the obtained discrimination curves were compared with those that would be predicted from the phoneme identification curves on a most extreme assumption: namely, that each subject can only hear those differences that are revealed by the way in which he attached phonemic labels to the stimuli. The discrimination curves that were produced on this assumption predicted fairly well the occurrence and location of points of high and low discriminability in the obtained functions, but subjects tended in general to discriminate the stimuli somewhat better than expected from the extreme assumption.

References

COOPER, F. S. (1950), 'Spectrum analysis', *J. acoust. Soc. Amer.*, vol. 22, pp. 761–2.

COOPER, F. S. (1953), 'Some instrumental aids to research on speech', in *Report of the Fourth Annual Round Table Meeting on Linguistics and Language Teaching*, Institute of Languages and Linguistics, Georgetown University, Washington, DC, pp. 46–53.

COOPER, F. S., LIBERMAN, A. M., and BORST, J. M. (1951), 'The interconversion of audible and visible patterns as a basis for research in the perception of speech', *Proc. nat. Acad. Sci.*, vol. 37, pp. 318–25. Excerpt reprinted here, pp. 204–7.

DELATTRE, P. C., LIBERMAN, A. M., and COOPER, F. S. (1955), 'Acoustic loci and transitional cues for consonants', *J. acoust. Soc. Amer.*, vol. 27, pp. 769–73. Reprinted here, pp. 273–83.

KENDALL, M. G. (1948), *Rank Correlation Methods*, Griffin.

LIBERMAN, A. M., DELATTRE, P. C., COOPER, F. S., and GERSTMAN, L. J. (1954), 'The role of consonant–vowel transitions in the perception of the stop and nasal consonants', *Psychol. Mongr.*, vol. 68, no. 8. Reprinted here, pp. 315–31.

23 Leigh Lisker and Arthur S. Abramson

The Voicing Dimension: Some Experiments in Comparative Phonetics[1]

Leigh Lisker and Arthur S. Abramson, 'The voicing dimension: some experiments in comparative phonetics', in B. Hála, M. Romportl and P. Janota (eds.), *Proceedings of the 6th International Congress of Phonetic Sciences*, Academia, Prague, 1970, pp. 563–7.

Speech synthesis has made it possible to produce controlled variations along acoustic dimensions to test their perceptual relevance for phonemic distinctions. Zones of perceptual ambiguity are compared with boundaries between ranges of acoustic values measured in speech. We are interested in doing this in cross-language comparisons. For each of the languages we want to know the number of phonological categories along a dimension used in common. For languages with the same number of categories the boundaries need not be the same.

Our research has led us to believe that in many languages some phoneme categories are distinguished by the timing of glottal adjustments relative to supraglottal articulation, and that this timing relation determines not only the voicing state as narrowly defined, but the degree of aspiration and certain features associated with the so-called force of articulation as well. For word-initial stops in non-whispered speech, this relation is realized acoustically by what we have called voice onset time (VOT), i.e. the interval between the release burst and the onset of laryngeal pulsing (Lisker and Abramson, 1964, 1965). A recent pilot study with synthetic speech demonstrated the distinctive power of VOT (Abramson and Lisker, 1965; Liberman, Delattre and Cooper, 1958). The present study takes a closer look at its perceptual relevance in three languages, English, Spanish and Thai. The resulting data also furnish a basis for discrimination experiments.

We used the Haskins Laboratories parallel resonance synthesizer, which has three formant generators with variable frequencies and amplitudes, a choice of buzz or hiss excitation, or a mixture of the two, and control of the overall amplitude and fundamental frequency.

Our basic pattern was built on three steady-state formants for a vowel of the type [a]. Labial, apical and velar stops were made by adding appropriate release bursts and formant transitions to the beginning. We synthesized 37 VOT variants, ranging from 150 ms before the release to 150 ms

1. This research was supported by the National Institute of Child Health and Human Development of the National Institutes of Health and the Information Systems Branch of the Office of Naval Research.

after it. For voicing before the release (voicing lead), we used only low-frequency harmonics of the buzz source. For voice onset after release (voicing lag), the interval between burst and onset of pulsing was excited by hiss alone, with suppression of the first formant to simulate the effects of an open glottis. Calling the release zero time, we gave negative numbers to

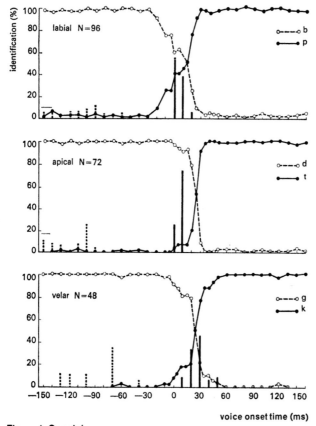

Figure 1 Spanish

voicing lead and positive numbers to lag. The stimuli varied in 10 ms steps, except for the range from −10 to +50, where we made them in 5 ms steps. Each variant had a fundamental frequency of 114 Hz, with a drop toward the end. The 37 variants were recorded in eight random orders, with two occurrences of each on each tape. The test subjects were five native speakers of Latin American Spanish, twelve of American English, and eight of Thai.

Leigh Lisker and Arthur S. Abramson 349

Using their own orthographies, the subjects identified the stimuli with their stop phonemes.

Figures 1–3 give the identification curves as functions of VOT values. The bars show frequency distributions of VOT values measured in speech. All the expected categories emerge, but the perceptual crossover zones do

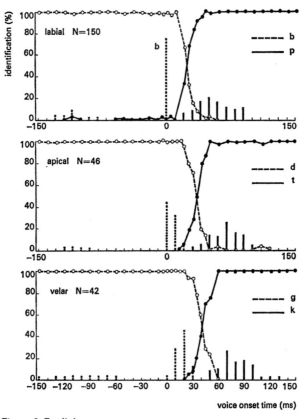

Figure 2 English

not always match very well the zones between the ranges of measured values. In Spanish (Figure 1), /bdg/ are produced with voicing lead, while /ptk/ have zero VOT or short lag. The three perceptual crossovers occur to the right of these boundaries, suggesting that some other features, perhaps burst and hiss intensities or formant transitions, were not optimally set. In Figure 2 the productions of English /bdg/ show a small scattering of lead values but a concentration at zero or just after it, while /ptk/ all show lag. The boundaries between ranges match the perceptual crossovers well, although there are slight discrepancies in the labials and apicals. For all three places of articulation the English perceptual crossovers have higher

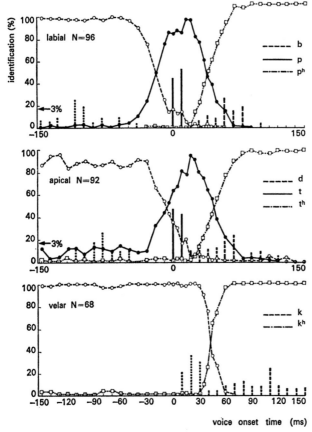

Figure 3 Thai

VOT values than the Spanish, though the differences are less than expected. Thai was chosen because for two of its places of closure it has three categories, usually called voiced, voiceless unaspirated and voiceless aspirated; the velars have only the latter two. The categories lie in the regions of voicing lead, zero VOT or short lag, and long lag respectively. The match between speech and perception (Figure 3) is good for the left-hand boundary for the labials and apicals, showing great sensitivity to voicing lead: the right-hand boundary, however, shows the same kind of mismatch as the Spanish and English. For the velars, nevertheless, the match is perfect.

For all three languages the stop categories occupy distinct ranges along the VOT dimension. To be sure, the match between our production and labelling data is somewhat less than perfect, but this is scarcely surprising in view of the severely restricted number of variables involved in the experiment. However, despite the likelihood that other acoustic features play a role in fixing the category boundaries studied, it seems quite clear that the timing of voice onset is a major factor in determining the location of those boundaries in languages as diverse phonetically as Spanish, English and Thai.

References

ABRAMSON, A. S., and LISKER, L. (1965), 'Voice onset time in stop consonants: acoustic analysis and synthesis', in D. E. Commins (ed.), *Proceedings of the 5th International Congress on Acoustics*, vol. 1A, paper A51, Liège.

LIBERMAN, A. M., DELATTRE, P. C., and COOPER, F. S. (1958), 'Some cues for the distinction between voiced and voiceless stops in initial position', *Language and Speech*, vol. 1, pp. 153–66.

LISKER, L., and ABRAMSON, A. S. (1964), 'A cross-language study of voicing in initial stops: acoustical measurements', *Word*, vol. 20, pp. 384–422.

LISKER, L., and ABRAMSON, A. S. (1965), 'Stop categorization and voice onset time', in E. Zwirner and W. Bethge (eds.), *Proceedings of the 5th International Congress of Phonetic Sciences*, pp. 389–91, Basel.

Part Four
Investigation of Prosodic Features

In the preceding sections the emphasis has been on the investigation of phonological systems. The next two sections present corresponding information about prosodic features and the methods and the rationale parallel those already dealt with. Analysis is again used in order to discover the acoustic correlates of prosodic features and to reveal the possible cues, and the perceptual experiments make use of synthesized stimuli in order to explore the influence of cues upon listeners' judgments. In certain cases it has been possible to throw some light on the hierarchical arrangement of cues and on the relative weight assigned to them by subjects, a stage which has not as yet been reached with regard to cues for phonemic judgments.

24 Ilse Lehiste and Gordon E. Peterson

Vowel Amplitude and Phonemic Stress in American English[1]

Ilse Lehiste and Gordon E. Peterson, 'Vowel amplitude and phonemic stress in American English', *Journal of the Acoustical Society of America*, vol. 31 (1959), pp. 428–35.

Since the beginning of the transmission of spoken messages by wire, the measurement of speech levels has been an enduring problem confronting communications engineers. The necessity of the measurement lies in the fact that communication systems are inherently noisy, and that they have limited power capacity. Thus, there is a basic problem of fitting the speech signal within the power capacity limitations of the system and above the noise level.

Speech, however, is not a uniform time function and its spectrum spreads throughout much of the audio-frequency range. As a result, it is necessary to be arbitrary in stating a single number to indicate speech level, and a multitude of instrumental procedures for deriving such a number have been employed.

There are at least three different ways in which amplitude information regarding speech can be derived and recorded.

1 Perhaps the least useful for research analysis is the meter reading. Because of its convenience, however, the volume indicator, first described in a standard form by Chinn, Gannett, and Morris (1940), has probably been used more extensively than any other type of device in monitoring speech and in estimating speech levels in research studies (such as intelligibility measures).

2 A number of continuous writing devices have been employed for measuring speech amplitudes. Pen recording instruments and the cathode-ray oscilloscope with associated camera fall within this general category. In general, ink writing devices employ an integrating time constant and usually respond to some function of the power levels of the signal rather than to linear amplitudes. An earlier review of this type of instrumentation was prepared by Stevens, Egan and Miller (1947).

3 An interesting and basic approach to obtaining statistical information about energy distributions in speech was developed by Dunn and White

1. This research was supported by the Information Systems Branch of the Office of Naval Research of the US Navy, under contract Nonr 1224 (22), NR 049–122.

Ilse Lehiste and Gordon E. Peterson 355

(1940), and a more recent instrumental method has been described by Benson and Hirsh (1953). Devices of the latter type employ discrete counting techniques which indicate the percentage of time during which certain amplitude or power values are exceeded in the speech wave.

Linguistically significant stress

It is a fundamental assumption of the present paper that the physical properties of speech are organized into a symbolic code. There are several components of this code and these components may be analysed and described at the physiological, the acoustical or the perceptual level. It is the intermediate acoustical signal which is primarily available for study. There are, in effect, two directions in which we might go in attempting to interpret this signal. One procedure would be to transform the signal to a series of auditory correlates such as pitch, loudness and duration. It is not immediately obvious that the psychophysical scales developed for simple stimuli such as pure tones would apply to the interpretation of such a signal. An inverse procedure would be to attempt to derive information about the processes of speech production from the acoustical signal. It is our belief that this latter procedure will provide information which more directly corresponds to the judgments of the listener about speech; i.e. the listener interprets speech according to the properties of the speech production mechanism rather than according to the psychophysical principles of the perception of abstract sounds.

Thus, in the present paper we take the philosophy that the primary information source of speech is the physiological mechanism, and that speech is structured basically in terms of the capabilities and limitations of this system (see Peterson, 1955). We assume the acoustical signal to be a representation of the positions and movements of the physiological mechanism relative to the distribution of air pressures within the mechanism. It is easy to show that there is not a complete, one-to-one correspondence between the physiological production and the acoustical result. We assume a further reduction from acoustical patterns to auditory analyses. It is our belief that the interpretation of the speech signal by a listener is based on a very complicated set of auditory parameters by means of which he makes an interpretation of the speech production.

Thus we seek to describe speech in terms of such factors as:

physiological effort
rate of vocal fold vibration
mode of laryngeal vibration
pharyngeal and oral articulation
palatopharyngeal closure
duration

While these factors are difficult to quantify, related perceptual terms, such as:

stress
pitch
vocal quality
segmental phonemes
nasality
quantity

are even less clearly defined.

Some factors are correlated in the code of any particular language, but the relationships may differ markedly from one language to another. The present paper is primarily concerned with a consideration of those parameters which contribute to the judgment of what has often been called stress in English. These parameters form an important aspect of the code of English, and may form the essential distinction between words or utterances which have very different meanings. Thus they are of considerable interest in research on automatic speech recognition. It is our conclusion that stress is actually physiological stress, and that in English it is reflected in at least four acoustical parameters: speech power, fundamental voice frequency, phonetic quality and duration. The relative effects of two of these parameters, amplitude and duration, have previously been studied in synthesized speech by Fry (1955). The present paper is primarily concerned with the intereffects of amplitude and phonetic quality.

We suggest that a listener will interpret sounds produced with equal effort as being in some respects similar with regard to stress. In everyday linguistic experience, the words *convict* (noun) and *convict* (verb) appear stressed either on the first syllable (noun) or second syllable (verb), and the degree of stress on the stressed syllable is subjectively felt to be the same. If the acoustical anergy of the syllabic sounds is measured, however, the first syllable appears to have considerably more energy in both instances. There must, then, be other factors besides energy which influence our judgments about stress in English. The research of Fry emphasized the effect of duration, and we should like to consider the influence of phonetic quality upon judgments of linguistically significant stress.

Fairbanks (1950) and others have previously observed that phonetic changes normally affect vowel amplitudes. Since the human vocal tract is a variable acoustical tube, with a variable radiating orifice, one would not expect to obtain the same pressure or power outputs for identical physiological input energies. Changes of amplitude of the sound wave may thus be caused by two major factors; first, if the phonetic quality of the vowel is held constant, a change in the amount of (input) power used to produce the sound may result in a change in output; second, if input energy is kept constant, a change in the phonetic quality of the vowel may result in a change in the output amplitude. It seems reasonable that in the production of speech, amplitude changes due to changes in phonetic quality should not significantly influence the perception of phonemic stress.

These observations suggest that the listener associates a certain intrinsic relative amplitude (or perhaps average power) with each vowel spectrum, and applies a corresponding 'correction factor' to the incoming signal. Assuming that duration and fundamental voice frequency are held constant, this procedure would enable a listener to identify a stressed syllable, even if the average or peak power of that syllable were less than that of an adjacent unstressed syllable containing a more open vowel. If such perceptual corrections are made, an automatic device for identifying linguistically stressed syllables should contain a set of such built-in correction factors.

Measurement of amplitude

The measurement of speech amplitude which will be most closely correlated with physiological effort is not immediately obvious. One of the simplest measurements, of course, is the instantaneous representation of the amplitude of the speech wave as produced on an ordinary cathode-ray oscilloscope. This wave can readily be reduced to instantaneous acoustical power by full wave rectification and the transformation of the wave to a logarithmic scale. Since phase effects within the vocal mechanism may affect the actual amplitudes appearing in the speech wave, there is some question as to whether instantaneous power measurements actually reflect the energy per unit time introduced into the production of speech.

This fact is perhaps the basic reason why integrating circuits of some type have generally been employed in the measurement of average speech powers. If one integrates the area under the instantaneous power curve, the total energy represented by the wave is obtained. In a continuous recording of integrated speech power, some time constant of integration is required, so that one may obtain, for example, a continuous trace of 'average speech power' as a function of time

$$\bar{p}(t) \approx \int_{t_1}^{t_2} \frac{e^2(t)dt}{T},$$

where $T = t_2 - t_1$.

We may assume that the physiological effort employed in the production of a sustained vowel is essentially constant. Thus power variations within the fundamental period do not reflect changes in vocal effort and may be eliminated. Since energy variations within the syllable may be of interest, a minimum desirable integrating time is of the order of the fundamental voice period (such as 0·01 s).

Measurements on sustained vowels

Data about the relative intensities of English vowels have been reported by several investigators (House and Fairbanks, 1953). In most of the studies, several speakers have been employed to pronounce test words (or nonsense syllables). In such studies the data are usually collected under controlled conditions, but without the use of monitoring meters, since they obviously would defeat the purpose of the experiment.

Our interests are in understanding the linguistic systems of specific dialects and of specific speakers; thus in order to limit the number of variables in this initial experiment it was decided to study the speech levels produced by one particular speaker. In order to obtain a basic set of data for reference without consonant influences, 20 lists of sustained vowels and diphthongs were recorded by G E P. Each list consisted of the following 15 syllable nuclei of English, arranged in random order:

/i ɪ eɪ ɛ æ ə ɑ ɔ oʊ ʊ u ɔɪ aʊ aɪ r/.

The lists were read into a condenser microphone placed 30 cm from the lips of the speaker in an anechoic chamber. The equipment was calibrated so that the amplitudes could be expressed in decibels relative to 0·0002 dyn/cm². Twelve lists were recorded on one day (late in the afternoon); eight lists were recorded four days later (in the morning). Each vowel was uttered three times in succession. The pitch was kept constant at 145 Hz by using a reference pulse which the speaker heard through a headphone and tried to imitate. Two additional lists were recorded with a masking noise of 130 dB in the ears of the speaker. The tapes were then reproduced and the values were read from a V U meter. The levels relative to 0·0002 dyn/cm² were computed, and the results are presented in Table 1. The sound pressure level equivalence is simply the rms value of a pure tone (in S P L) at the diaphragm of the microphone which would cause the same V U meter deflection as that due to the vowel. As it appears from the table, the average difference between the meter readings for the first day and the second day was 0·13 dB, which falls well within the range of error probable with this type of procedure.

In Table 1, row A contains the average values for one recording day on which 12 lists of 15 syllable nuclei each were recorded. Since every sound in each list was uttered three times, the values in this row represent the averages for 36 utterances. Row B contains the average values for the eigh- lists which were recorded four days later; these values represent the avert ages for 24 utterances. Row C contains the average for two lists, six utterances for each value, recorded with a masking noise of 130 dB in the ears of the speaker. The relative values shown in Table 1 are of the same order of magnitude and are approximately similar in distribution to those reported by Fairbanks, House, and Stevens (1950) and by Black (1949).

Table 1 Average values for one speaker of V U meter readings for sustained vowels relative to 0·0002 dyn/cm²

	i	ɪ	eɪ	ɛ	æ	ə	ɑ	ɔ	oʊ	ʊ	u	aʊ	aɪ	ɔɪ	r	Average for all vowels
A[a]	80·2	81·4	81·1	82·9	83·1	85·0	85·5	84·8	83·4	83·4	80·2	84·8	82·7	83·7	81·4	82·91
B[b]	80·0	81·1	81·1	84·1	82·8	83·7	86·0	86·8	83·6	83·2	80·8	83·9	82·3	84·7	81·5	83·04
C[c]	80·1	81·3	81·1	83·4	83·0	84·5	85·7	85·6	83·5	83·3	80·4	84·4	82·5	84·1	81·4	83·0
D[d]	78·8	81·3	81·5	82·0	84·0	85·7	86·0	85·2	83·8	82·3	78·3	85·0	84·2	83·8	80·9	82·85
E[e]	75·1	78·1	78·6	79·3	79·4	79·7	80·2	80·6	79·7	78·4	78·2	80·1	80·2	80·9	79·0	79·0

[a] Averages for twelve lists recorded on one day
[b] Averages for eight lists recorded four days later
[c] Averages for all twenty lists
[d] Averages for two lists recorded with 130 dB masking noise in the ears of the speaker
[e] Averages for each vowel for 1263 monosyllables of the C N C type

In listening casually to the recorded vowels, they appear to be about equally loud. This observation doubtless represents a confusion in perceptual judgment, however, for the equivalence is probably in physiological stress, not loudness. From what is known about the loudness of sinusoidal complexes, it seems very improbable that the vowels would appear equally loud if judged on that basis (see Howes, 1950).

A preliminary attempt was made to check the casual observation of loudness of the vowels. Another series of lists of randomized vowels was recorded; this time the speaker watched a V U meter in the recording room and produced all vowels at the same V U level. Some vowels required considerably greater effort than others. A tape was then prepared, in which various vowels produced with equal effort were mixed at random with vowels produced with unequal effort but which were equal in pressure level as measured by the V U meter. The vowels were arranged in random pairs and were presented to listeners, who were asked to judge the relative loudness of the two paired vowels. The listeners were specifically asked to judge the relative *loudness* of the vowels rather than their relative stress or accentuation. Almost invariably, the listeners identified the vowels that were produced with a greater amount of effort (such as /i/ and /u/ recorded at zero V U) as louder than vowels having greater intrinsic amplitude, but produced with normal effort (such as /ɑ/ and /ɔ/). The results appeared to confirm the basic assumption of this paper.

The listeners often reported changes in vowel quality on those sounds that had been produced with greater subjective effort; the vowels were described as 'tense' or 'harsh'. Thus, it appears that vocal quality may also be a factor in the judgments. From this limited study we cannot determine, of course, whether vocal quality changes have a significant influence upon judgments of stress in American English, but obviously vowel amplitude and vowel quality have a much more predominant influence.

Syllable amplitudes

The study of vowel amplitudes within actual speech presents many problems beyond those involved in the study of the amplitudes of sustained vowels. The next case in degree of complexity are the amplitudes of monosyllables. Since, by definition, nonsense syllables do not have certain of the distributional properties of actual speech, monosyllabic English words were chosen having the same vowel nuclei as indicated previously. The words were selected from the Thorndike and Lorge (1952) list and were all of the

Table 2 Distribution of the initial-final combinations (C—C, vowels pooled) in the list of 1263 CNC words. The initial consonant is shown in the column at the left; the final in the row across the top

	p	b	t	d	k	g	m	n	ŋ	f	v	θ	ð	s	z	ʃ	ʒ	r	l	č	ǰ	Total
p	8	1	10	3	8	3	1	7	1	1	1	2	-	5	4	1	-	6	10	7	2	81
b	-	3	12	8	8	6	4	10	1	2	-	5	1	5	2	1	1	5	7	2	-	83
t	5	3	8	3	7	2	8	8	2	2	-	2	1	2	1	1	-	7	9	2	-	73
d	3	3	6	5	6	3	8	10	1	2	2	3	-	3	3	2	-	4	7	1	3	75
k	7	4	10	7	6	2	5	10	1	4	3	-	-	4	1	1	-	3	10	4	1	83
g	2	-	8	6	-	2	2	4	2	1	2	1	-	4	4	3	-	2	8	-	2	53
m	3	2	8	8	5	2	2	7	-	1	2	4	-	9	1	3	-	6	7	2	2	74
n	3	1	10	5	5	1	3	7	-	1	2	-	-	4	3	1	-	2	6	2	1	57
f	-	1	6	5	2	3	3	9	1	2	1	1	-	3	1	1	-	5	12	1	1	58
v	-	1	2	1	-	2	-	3	-	-	1	-	-	3	2	-	-	1	5	1	1	23
θ	-	-	1	2	1	-	3	2	2	1	1	-	-	-	-	-	-	1	-	1	-	15
ð	-	-	1	-	-	-	1	3	-	-	-	-	-	2	2	-	-	1	-	-	-	10
s	7	2	8	6	7	1	5	8	4	2	4	2	2	4	2	1	-	5	8	2	4	84
z	-	-	-	-	-	-	-	1	-	-	-	-	-	1	-	-	-	1	1	-	-	4
ʃ	4	-	6	5	7	1	2	5	-	2	2	1	1	-	-	-	6	5	-	-	47
r	6	4	10	8	7	4	6	6	4	4	2	4	2	3	5	2	1	3	6	4	2	93
č	6	1	7	8	10	5	6	8	3	4	5	2	3	8	2	3	1	5	2	3	1	93
l	5	1	3	2	6	1	2	3	-	3	-	-	-	3	4	-	-	4	2	1	-	40
ǰ	1	4	4	1	3	4	4	8	-	1	1	-	-	2	1	1	-	2	4	-	1	42
h	6	1	9	8	6	3	6	2	2	2	4	1	-	3	6	2	-	4	8	2	1	76
w	2	1	5	7	6	2	2	6	1	3	3	1	1	1	2	2	-	4	7	2	2	60
hw	1	-	5	-	1	1	1	2	-	1	-	-	-	-	2	-	-	1	4	1	-	20
y	2	-	1	-	1	-	1	4	1	-	-	1	-	2	1	-	..	-	3	2	-	19
total	71	33	140	98	102	48	75	133	26	39	36	30	11	71	49	25	3	81	130	38	24	1263

CNC type. Both phonetic and phonemic considerations were involved in determining the initial and final Cs and the Ns. A total of 1263 such words were selected. The consonant distribution is shown in Table 2. Since the word list has been described elsewhere, further details of its composition will not be reviewed here (Lehiste and Peterson, 1959).

These monosyllabic words were placed in a constant frame (carrier sentence), 'say the word . . . again', where each word would normally receive the same degree of linguistic stress.

These sentences were recorded in the anechoic chamber with the same apparatus as employed for the sustained vowels; as before, the microphone was at a distance of 30 cm. In the recordings the same intonation contour was applied to each sentence.

The recordings were played into a VU meter and the values for the syllables were tabulated; the readings were recorded to the nearest decimal; repeated readings showed a very high reliability. The meter readings were referred to 0·0002 dyn/cm² at the microphone, as were the data for the sustained vowels. The resulting sound pressure levels based on the VU meter readings, are shown in Tables 3 and 4. Table 3 is for each of the initial

Table 3 Average amplitudes of syllable nuclei following each initial consonant phoneme (final consonants pooled)

Initial consonant	i	ɪ	eɪ	ɛ	æ	ə	ɑ	ɔ	oʊ	ʊ	u	aʊ	aɪ	ɔɪ	ɝ	Average
p	71·3	76·8	77·3	76·5	77·8	77·0	79·5	80·7	78·4	77·5	76·0	78·3	78·5	82·0	77·9	77·3
b	74·9	79·3	78·5	79·9	81·2	80·6	81·0	81·8	80·5	79·4	79·0	82·0	80·5	82·5	79·8	79·7
t	72·2	76·7	77·1	78·2	78·7	78·1	79·3	79·1	77·8	76·6	76·5	80·2	78·3	81·3	78·0	77·7
d	75·3	78·7	79·2	79·3	80·4	80·6	80·4	81·6	79·9	–	79·7	80·3	80·7	–	79·4	79·7
k	74·0	76·4	76·4	78·9	78·3	77·2	79·3	80·0	77·9	76·9	77·5	77·8	78·6	81·0	78·3	77·9
g	71·7	78·2	78·2	78·8	80·3	80·1	80·9	81·2	80·1	80·1	77·5	80·2	81·4	–	80·1	79·7
m	78·1	77·9	78·8	78·4	79·0	80·8	79·8	80·5	79·9	78·5	79·1	80·5	80·9	–	79·0	79·4
n	78·1	76·6	78·8	78·9	78·6	80·2	80·4	79·2	80·0	78·5	79·5	80·1	79·5	80·1	78·0	79·1
f	73·3	78·4	78·4	79·8	80·1	79·8	81·9	80·1	79·7	–	77·7	80·9	80·2	81·3	79·6	79·0
v	74·7	80·7	78·9	–	79·7	–	–	–	79·4	–	–	80·6	80·8	80·5	80·2	79·9
θ	76·9	76·8	77·4	–	78·2	80·5	–	79·0	–	–	–	–	78·7	–	80·7	78·3
ð	75·5	77·5	–	78·9	78·7	80·8	–	–	81·5	77·5	–	–	81·7	–	–	79·1
s	74·7	77·7	78·1	79·2	79·5	79·3	80·1	79·4	79·4	–	76·5	80·2	80·0	78·6	79·1	78·3
z	77·1	–	–	–	–	81·5	–	78·5	–	76·5	–	–	–	–	–	78·4
ʃ	73·7	77·6	77·8	79·5	79·7	79·3	79·7	79·6	79·3	79·1	77·5	79·7	79·4	–	77·9	78·2
r	77·3	80·1	80·2	80·2	81·0	81·6	82·4	81·1	81·4	79·1	80·0	81·8	81·0	83·1	–	80·5
l	77·2	79·7	80·2	81·3	80·5	81·5	81·3	82·1	80·5	79·2	80·5	81·5	81·2	79·6	79·9	80·2
č	73·4	77·3	78·2	78·7	78·7	79·1	79·5	79·3	78·8	–	75·0	–	78·6	81·4	77·7	77·7
ǰ	75·4	78·3	78·2	78·6	79·5	80·0	81·1	81·1	78·9	–	76·6	80·3	81·3	80·1	79·0	79·2
h	73·5	77·2	77·4	79·4	78·4	78·5	77·8	81·4	79·5	77·2	76·8	78·6	79·0	–	78·8	78·1
w	76·4	79·3	80·2	80·7	81·3	81·4	81·4	81·0	79·3	80·4	78·6	–	81·5	–	79·6	79·5
hw	74·1	78·1	81·5	80·2	78·9	–	79·5	–	–	–	–	–	80·7	–	81·1	78·6
y	–	77·7	78·9	79·7	79·4	81·5	79·2	80·7	78·5	80·9	75·2	–	–	–	79·4	79·0
average	75·1	78·1	78·6	79·3	79·4	79·7	80·2	80·6	79·7	78·4	78·2	80·1	80·2	80·9	79·0	79·0

consonants and each vowel nucleus (followed by any final consonant); Table 4 is for each vowel nucleus (preceded by any initial consonant), followed by each final consonant. These data are summarized in Table 5, which shows the initial and final consonants arranged according to the average sound

Table 4 Average amplitudes of syllable nuclei preceding each final consonant phoneme (initial consonants pooled)

Final consonant	i	ɪ	eɪ	ɛ	æ	ə	ɑ	ɔ	oʊ	ʊ	u	aʊ	aɪ	ɔɪ	r	Average
p	72·9	77·0	77·4	76·8	79·7	76·5	79·3	–	79·2	76·3	77·1	–	78·7	–	78·1	77·4
b	–	80·1	–	80·5	79·6	80·1	81·4	81·6	81·0	–	77·3	–	81·3	–	79·7	80·3
t	72·8	76·5	78·0	78·7	78·6	77·3	79·5	78·9	78·9	76·7	76·9	80·4	78·9	–	78·1	77·8
d	75·8	79·0	79·6	80·1	80·4	80·8	80·5	82·1	80·8	79·9	79·6	82·7	80·9	81·0	80·1	79·8
k	74·5	75·9	77·8	77·9	79·1	78·3	79·7	79·8	78·9	77·5	78·1	–	80·1	–	78·3	78·0
g	79·1	78·7	79·1	79·5	80·8	80·4	78·9	81·1	80·5	–	–	–	–	–	80·3	80·1
m	76·9	78·4	77·8	78·9	79·0	80·4	80·3	–	78·8	–	78·5	–	79·7	–	79·4	78·9
n	77·2	77·3	77·9	78·8	79·0	79·9	80·0	80·5	79·1	–	79·6	80·1	80·2	79·7	78·7	79·0
ŋ	–	77·5	–	–	78·8	80·6	–	80·0	–	–	–	–	–	–	–	79·1
f	75·5	78·3	78·9	79·4	79·3	79·7	–	80·2	81·8	–	78·3	–	80·7	81·3	79·1	78·9
v	76·9	80·6	79·5	–	81·3	81·1	–	81·5	80·9	–	80·1	–	80·4	–	78·6	79·8
θ	74·7	76·8	77·1	78·9	80·0	79·9	–	81·9	79·6	–	76·5	81·1	–	–	78·5	78·5
ð	76·0	79·5	80·0	–	–	–	–	81·1	–	77·3	–	79·8	–	–	78·7
s	73·3	77·1	78·3	79·7	80·6	79·5	–	80·8	–	76·1	77·6	79·5	81·0	80·9	78·3	78·8
z	74·2	79·5	78·7	–	79·5	81·4	82·1	81·1	80·2	–	79·4	81·4	81·1	81·0	78·9	79·2
ʃ	75·5	77·5	–	80·2	80·2	79·5	81·0	80·9	–	77·8	–	–	–	–	–	79·4
ʒ	77·1	–	79·2	–	–	–	–	–	–	–	79·7	–	–	–	–	78·7
r	–	79·5	81·3	79·3	–	81·0	80·6	–	78·8	79·2	80·2	80·3	–	–	80·0
l	76·5	79·8	79·5	80·6	79·6	81·0	80·8	81·1	80·3	80·4	78·1	80·3	81·0	81·3	80·6	79·9
č	73·7	77·5	–	79·0	77·5	78·6	80·5	–	78·2	–	75·5	78·1	–	–	78·6	77·5
ǰ	75·5	80·0	79·3	80·2	–	80·5	80·3	–	80·5	–	–	79·4	–	–	79·7	79·7
average	75·1	78·1	78·6	79·3	79·4	79·7	80·2	80·6	79·7	78·4	78·2	80·1	80·2	80·9	79·0	79·0

pressure levels (measured by a V U meter) of the vowel nuclei. It appears to the authors to be significant that just as great a decibel range on the vowel nuclei is associated with the initial consonants as with the final consonants. The essential order from strong to weak is (a) semivowels and voiced plosives, (b) glides, nasals and voiced fricatives, (c) voiceless fricatives, and (d) voiceless plosives.

A matrix was constructed for each syllable nucleus which shows the distribution of pressure levels according to the initial and final consonants. The average value for each syllable nucleus is shown in row E of Table 1. A comparison of the total data for sustained vowels and for the 1263 monosyllabic words is shown in Figure 1. While the speaker employed an average level of approximately 3 dB less for the vowel nuclei in syllables, it will be noted also that there are some significant shifts in relative level.

Table 5 Influence of initial and final consonants on the average amplitudes of all vowels

Amplitude of vowels	Initial consonant	Amplitude of vowels	Final consonant
80·5	r	80·3	b
80·2	l	80·1	g
79·9	v	80·0	r
79·7	b d g	79·9	l
79·5	w	79·8	d v
79·4	m	79·7	j
79·2	j	79·4	ʃ
79·1	ð n	79·2	z
79·0	y f	79·1	ŋ
78·6	w h	79·0	n
78·4	z	78·9	m f
78·3	θ s	78·8	s t
78·2	ʃ	78·7	ð ʒ
78·1	h	78·5	θ
77·9	k	78·0	k
77·7	t č	77·5	č
77·3	p	77·4	p

Measurement problem

While V U meter readings on the sustained vowels are doubtless closely correlated with average power values, the use of a meter with such a time constant and the specification of syllable amplitudes in terms of a single number seems highly arbitrary. For comparison, the syllables (in their sentence contexts) were also processed through a Sound Apparatus H P L high-speed level recorder. Peak readings of the graphs were obtained for a large sample of the syllables and compared with the V U meter readings. Differences were evident, but in general they were slight, and we have no specific evidence that one number is any more significant than the other. In the past, single numbers have usually been derived from the peaks of such graphs. Since the initial and final levels of the vowel parts of syllables are often considerably influenced by the consonant closures, it seems reasonable that the peak levels (often near the center of the vowel nucleus) best represent the vocal input energy (as modified, of course, by the vowel quality). Relatively short time variations in the speech level become particularly significant, however, when they mark successive stresses within a single vowel; or they may be very significant in other languages such as Estonian where such level variations may mark successive syllable boundaries (Lehiste, 1966).

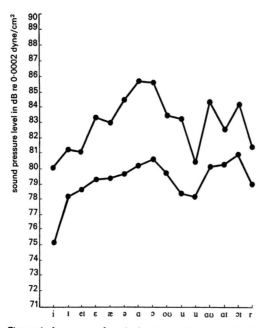

Figure 1 Averages of equivalent sound pressure levels (as observed with a V U meter) for sustained vowels and diphthongs, and for the vowel nuclei in monosyllables

As a practical procedure for speech power measurements, we are considering the use of a circuit which will integrate exactly over one or two fundamental voice frequency periods, with the reading to be taken from the maximum on each syllable nucleus. As a test of the basic hypothesis of this paper, we should like, of course, to correlate such data with physiological measurements. It seems likely that subglottal pressure measurements such as those developed by van den Berg (1956) should be most relevant. This hypothesis is based on the assumption that pressures, forces and muscle tensions are of primary significance in speech. Since speech production involves very small power levels, the actual work done or energy consumed seems secondary. Thus the tensions and forces applied as speech is produced seem to reflect best the degree of physiological effort, and should provide prominent cues in speech perception. Electromyographic techniques for measuring muscular activity in the larynx during phonation, such as those developed by Faaborg-Andersen (1957), might provide some further understanding of the influence of laryngeal quality upon judgments of stress.

The data which we have discussed would apply directly to only one condition of stress, the so-called primary stress, which according to one widely accepted theory forms one of four contrastive degrees of stress in English (Trager and Smith, 1951). There are very few data available on the relative amplitudes of the vowel nuclei of English in other stress conditions. In the opinion of the authors the concept of four phonemic levels of stress in English (as distinct from four intonation levels) needs a careful linguistic and experimental examination.

As a rough test of the above described influence of vowel quality upon stress in English, a series of words that distinguish between the two categories of noun and verb by means of contrastive stress placement were recorded.[2] The same frame as that used with the C N C words was employed, and an attempt was made to retain the same pitch contour. The recording instrumentation was that described in the foregoing. V U meter readings of the words show that in each case the primary stress can be identified by applying a correction factor from row E of Table 1.

Plate 47 presents sound spectrograms for two pairs of words from this latter set of recordings. The carrier sentence used is, 'Say the word . . . again.' In each pattern the upper spectrogram was made with a wide filter, so that the segmental phonemes may be identified easily; the middle spectrogram is a continuous amplitude display of the overall wave; and the lower spectrogram was made with a narrow analysing filter, so that the individual overtones are depicted (the pace is through the tenth harmonic). At the left of the figure is the pair *PERvert-perVERT*. As may be seen from the broad-band spectrograms, the segmental patterns are identical within the phonetic limits expected on successive utterances. The narrow-band spectrograms show the characteristic pitch curve associated with stressed syllables. At the right of the figure is the pair *INcline-inCLINE*. The segmental quality and the duration for the two pairs are approximately comparable; in fact, the unstressed [ɪ] in *inCLINE* appears longer than the stressed [ɪ] of *INcline*, although the opposite might be expected. Also shown in Plate 47 are continuous amplitude displays for each of these utterances. The amplitude scale is nonlinear; according to the calibration the difference for *PERvert-perVERT* is a little over 2 dB; the difference for the two syllables of *INcline* is approximately 0 dB. When correction factors for vowel quality are applied, the greater amplitude appears on the linguistically stressed syllable in each case.

2. The set of words which we examined is as follows: *conDUCT-COnduct, conVERSE-COnverse, conVICT-COnvict, conTENT-COntent, conVERT-COnvert, diGEST-DIgest, exPORT-EXport, imPORT-IMport, inCLINE-INcline, inCREASE-INcrease, perMIT-PERmit, perVERT-PERvert, preSENT-PREsent, proGRESS-PROgress, subJECT-SUBject.*

It will be evident from the narrow-band spectrograms that the intonations for these two pairs of words are not entirely comparable. We have been considering the hypothesis that phonetic variations in pitch level are due, to a considerable degree, to the intrinsic relative amplitude of the vowel to which the pitch is applied. Each phonemically significant pitch level can, of course, be manifested phonetically by a range of fundamental voice frequencies. The fact that fundamental voice frequency is correlated with vowel quality has been demonstrated by Fairbanks and House (1953), as well as others, in previous research. This rise in fundamental voice frequency for the vowels of higher tongue position has previously been somewhat of a mystery, since from a mechanical viewpoint, when the vocal cavities are more constricted the loading on the larynx should cause the fundamental to lower rather than to rise. It appears very probable that this phonetic variation in the pitch level associated with a certain phonemic stress may be influenced to a considerable extent by the intrinsic amplitude of the nucleus of the syllable carrying the stress, higher pitch compensating for lower intrinsic amplitude. These observations are made relative to English, of course; we have only some general impressions of how they might apply in other types of languages.

The authors hope to continue this preliminary research with a careful study of the correlations among relative power, vowel quality, fundamental voice frequency and duration as contributing factors to linguistically significant stress in English, and to extend the study to other speakers and to other degrees of stress beyond the primary stress which has been the topic of the present paper.

Summary

As a result of the considerations presented in this paper, it appears that perceptual judgments of linguistically significant stress may be based on speech power, fundamental voice frequency, vowel quality and duration; laryngeal quality may also make a very secondary contribution. The data presented in the present paper are based primarily on VU meter readings of vowels and syllables in a controlled context. The data suggest that 'correction factors' might be applied for the amplitudes of vowels according to vowel quality. Suggested correction factors are indicated for vowels within syllables. It seems reasonable that similar correction factors might actually be applied for pitch as well as for duration.

References

BENSON, R. W., and HIRSH, I. J. (1953), 'Some variables in audio spectrometry', *J. acoust. Soc. Amer.*, vol. 25, pp. 499–505.

BLACK, J. W. (1949), 'Natural frequency, duration and intensity of vowels in reading', *JSHD*, vol. 14, pp. 216–20.

CHINN, H. A., GANNETT, D. K., and MORRIS, R. M. (1940), 'A new standard volume indicator and reference level', *Bell System tech. J.*, no. 19, pp. 94–137.

DUNN, H. K., and WHITE, S. D. (1940), 'Statistical measurements on conversational speech', *Bell Telephone System tech. Pubns.*, Mongr. B–1206.

FAABORG-ANDERSEN, K. (1957), 'Electromyographic investigation of intrinsic laryngeal muscles in humans', *Acta Physiol. Scand.*, vol. 41, suppl. 140, pp. 7–148.

FAIRBANKS, G. (1950), 'A physiological correlative of vocal intensity', *Speech Mongr.*, vol. 17, pp. 390–95.

FAIRBANKS, G., HOUSE, A. S., and STEVENS, E. L. (1950), 'Experimental study of vowel intensities', *J. acoust. Soc. Amer.*, vol. 22, pp. 457–9.

FRY, D. B. (1955), 'Duration and intensity as physical correlates of linguistic stress', *J. acoust. Soc. Amer.*, vol. 27, pp. 765–8.

HOUSE, A. S., and FAIRBANKS, G. (1953), 'Influence of consonant environment upon the secondary acoustical characteristics of vowels', *J. acoust. Soc. Amer.*, vol. 25, pp. 105–13.

HOWES, D. H. (1950), 'The loudness of multicomponent tones', *Amer. J. Psychol.* vol. 63. pp. 1–30.

LEHISTE, I. (1966), 'Consonant quantity and phonological units in Estonian', in Indiana Univ. Publications, Uralic and Altaic Series, 65 (Bloomington).

LEHISTE, I., and PETERSON, G. E. (1959), 'Linguistic considerations in the study of speech intelligibility', *J. acoust. Soc. Amer.*, vol. 31, pp. 280–86.

FETERSON, G. E. (1955), 'An oral communication model', *Language*, vol. 31, pp. 414–27.

STEVENS, S. S., EGAN, J. P., and MILLER, G. A. (1947), 'Methods of measuring speech spectra', *J. acoust. Soc. Amer.*, vol. 19, pp. 771–80.

THORNDIKE, E. L., and LORGE, I. (1952), *The Teacher's Word Book of 30,000 Words*, Columbia University Press.

TRAGER, G. L., and SMITH, H. L. Jr (1951), 'An outline of English structure', *Studs. Ling. Occ. Paps.*, no. 3, Norman, Oklahoma.

VAN DEN BERG, J. W. (1956), 'Direct and indirect determination of the mean sub-glottic pressure, sound level, mean air flow, sub-glottic power and efficiency of a male voice for the vowel [a]', *Folia Phoniatr.*, vol. 8, pp. 1–24.

25 Arthur S. House

On Vowel Duration in English[1]

Arthur S. House, 'On vowel duration in English', *Journal of the Acoustical Society of America*, vol. 33 (1961), pp. 1174–8.

In conjunction with a more extensive program of speech analysis (House, Stevens and Fujisaki, 1960) a body of spoken material has been available for the measurement of the duration of various vowels of American English. The utterances provide an opportunity to describe the durational characteristics of vowels as a function of most of the phonetic attributes that might influence the length of vowels.

Materials and procedures

The speech materials are bisyllabic nonsense utterances of three adult males. Each nonsense word consists of an unstressed (carrier) syllable [hə], followed by a stressed syllable having the form consonant$_1$-vowel-consonant$_2$, where consonant$_1$ and consonant$_2$ represent the same phoneme. The twelve common vowels of American English and fourteen consonants that typically appear both initially and finally in American English syllables are used in the words. A number of consonants are not included to preserve the symmetry of the possible comparisons, namely, nasals are omitted because they have no voiceless cognates in English, etc.

The words were recorded in a quiet room using a high-quality magnetic tape recorder and an appropriate microphone. The talkers used a level of vocal effort best described as 'conversational' and maintained a fairly uniform pattern of stress and intonation. The word lists were randomized for each talker. During the recording procedures the talker and a trained observer evaluated the acceptability of each utterance paying particular attention to phonemic quality, stress and intonational pattern; the talker repeated those words that were not agreed upon. Before measurements were made the recorded words were evaluated again by three phonetically-sophisticated observers.

The recordings subsequently were used in preparing materials for a general analysis program that was performed on a digital computer. For

1. This work was supported in part by the U S Army Signal Corps, the Air Force Office of Scientific Research, and the Office of Naval Research, and in part by the Air Force Cambridge Research Laboratories under contract AF19(604)–6102.

this purpose it was necessary to sample the materials in time. The speech was recorded magnetically onto one track of a dual-track recorder and time-sampling pulses separated by 8·3 ms were recorded on the adjacent track. The dual-track recordings were used in making reference sound spectrograms. In this procedure, the sampling pulses were passed through an appropriate high-pass filter and appeared at the top of the sound spectrograms.

The durational measurements to be reported here were estimated from the time-sampling pulses on the sound spectrograms. The criteria used in determining the beginning and the end of a vowel are similar to those described in detail recently by Peterson and Lehiste (1960). In general, vowel

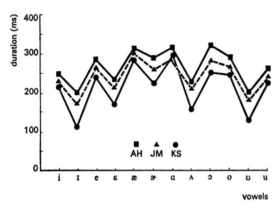

Figure 1 Average durations of twelve vowels of American English spoken by three male subjects

onset and offset criteria included the initiation and cessation of voicing, frication and formant structure; aspiration was not included as part of the vowel. The measurements, therefore, represent information pertinent to changes in source excitation during syllable articulation, but do not necessarily reveal the point at which a so-called vowel articulation *per se* began or ended.

Results

The data provided by the three talkers showed a consistent talker-to-talker variation; the vowel durations provided by each talker were characterized by highly similar vowel-to-vowel variations. Figure 1 shows the average duration of the twelve vowels for each talker; each point represents the average duration of the vowel occurring in fourteen different consonant environments and all vowels were uttered in the stressed syllable of a bisyllabic nonsense word. The curves show that, on the average, the same contrasts in duration were manifested in the speech of the three talkers. The talker with the shortest vowel durations on the average showed the greatest contrast from one vowel to another.

The same consistency is shown in Figure 2 where the durations of the twelve vowels are averaged for each consonant environment and plotted by talkers. The open symbols relate to the voiceless consonant environments identified at the bottom of the figure; the filled symbols relate to the voiced

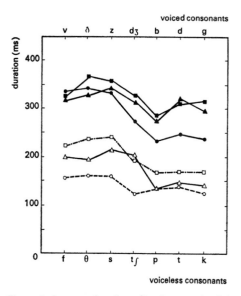

Figure 2 Average duration of twelve vowels of American English spoken by three male subjects. (Symbol key as in Figure 1)

consonant environments identified at the top of the figure. The curves demonstrate that the durations of the vowels of each talker varied from environment to environment in a similar manner. For convenience, therefore, in subsequent discussions the data for the three subjects will be pooled and averaged.

The durational measures of Figures 1 and 2 suggest that some fairly systematic and identifiable influences are operating to determine the actual length of a spoken vowel. Figure 2 is arranged, for example, to emphasize the fact that the average duration of vowels varies markedly as a function of the phonetic environment. The primary influence is contributed by the voicing characteristic of the consonant, whereas the manner of production of the consonant shows a smaller effect; the place of consonantal production is shown to have a negligible influence on the duration of the vowel.

Similarly, Figure 1 suggests that some of the vowels measured in this study can be divided into contrastive long-short pairs. The high-front vowels [i] and [ɪ] contrast in duration, as do the high-back vowels [u] and [ʊ], the mid-front vowels [e] and [ɛ], and the low-back vowels [ɑ] and [ʌ]. The four vowels [ɪ], [ɛ], [ʌ] and [ʊ], have been described many times before (Lehman and Heffner, 1940) as 'short' vowels, and they are in fact characterized by the shortest average durations of the vowels measured in this study. This type of contrast is sometimes called a tense-lax opposition. To facilitate discussion, the short vowels listed above will be referred to as lax and the other eight vowels will be called tense. This classification is open to question, however, particularly in the case of [æ] and [ɚ] in American English.

In Figure 3 the durations of the vowels are averaged for the three subjects and the curves are arranged to demonstrate the influence of various factors. The solid curve connects the so-called tense vowels and the dashed

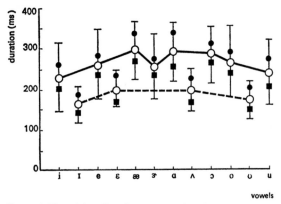

Figure 3 Vowel duration data arranged to demonstrate various contextual effects. The large unfilled circles are means for each vowel in fourteen contexts spoken by three subjects. The upper terminus of each vertical bar shows the average vowel duration in voiced contexts; the lower terminus is for voiceless contexts. The filled circle on each vertical bar shows the average vowel duration in fricative environments

curve connects the lax vowels; the average difference between these two categories approaches 100 ms. If [ɚ] is taken to be lax the symmetry of the figure increases. It could be argued also that the r coloring of this vowel tends to be an offglide that increases vowel length, suggesting that its present place in the figure is an overestimation of its duration.

The vertical bars associated with each vowel in Figure 3 demonstrate the influence of consonantal environment. The terminal values of the bars identify the average durations of the vowels in voiced consonant environments (the upper ends) and voiceless consonant environments (the lower ends), and the smaller points show vowel durations in fricative (solid) and stop (open) environments. As shown earlier the effect of the voicing characteristic is a major one, while the effect of manner of production is less pronounced. In general the range of variation of the lax vowels is less than that of the tense vowels.

It is clear that a number of parameters – most of which are specifiable in some articulatory or physiological sense – are active in determining the realized duration of a given vocalic sound. An indication of the range of durational variation and the strength of the various parameters, as well as the seeming lawfulness of the changes is shown in Figure 4. The figure shows the effect of four determinants of duration, two of which are labelled primary and two of which are labelled secondary. In addition, the mean durations for the three talkers are shown at the left to suggest the relative influence of individual talkers on vocalic duration.

Some obvious determinants of duration are not included in this analysis – those attributable to the individual talker, to rate of utterance, to the lexical stress pattern in which the vowel occurred and to the emphasis provided by connected discourse. Earlier investigators (Parmenter and Trevino, 1935) have reported data that show the average stressed vowel to be approximately 50 per cent longer than the average unstressed vowel. There also is evidence (Peterson and Lehiste, 1960) to suggest that as the rate of utterance increases, the change in the duration of unstressed syllabic nuclei is greater than the change in the duration of syllabic nuclei under stress.

The data in Figure 4 indicate that the voicing characteristic (or the effort) associated with the consonant environment – more strictly, the following consonant, as other research (Peterson and Lehiste, 1960; Lehman and Heffner, 1943; Bush, 1960) has demonstrated – changes the average duration of vowels markedly. Similarly, large changes are attributable to the characteristic tenseness (or closeness) of the vowel articulation itself. This opposition, of course, must be operative within a given articulatory class, that is, must operate to distinguish two kinds of high-front vowels like [i] and [ɪ].

When the data of the present experiment are arranged to show the effect of the two primary influences, it is seen in Figure 4 that the average duration of lax vowels in voiceless consonant environments (140 ms) is approximately 40 per cent of that of tense vowels in an environment consisting of voiced consonants (340 ms). The average durations in the two right-hand columns of Figure 4 demonstrate the effect of vowel openness (that is, ton-

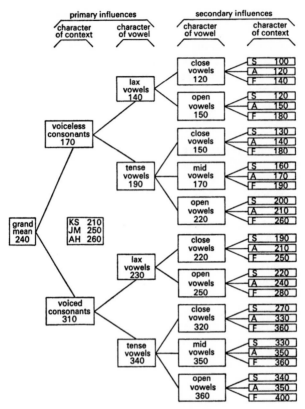

Figure 4 Demonstration of the magnitude of various influences on vowel duration. All numbers are mean vowel duration in ms, rounded to the nearest 10 ms. S = stop, A = affricative, F = fricative

gue height in the traditional phonetic sense) and the manner of production of the consonant environment. When, for example, the lax close vowels [ɪ] and [ʊ] in voiceless contexts are compared in duration to the lax open vowels [ε] and [ʌ] in similar contexts, the former are shorter than the latter by 30 ms on the average. Similarly, the average duration of lax close vowels in an environment of voiceless consonants varies from 100 ms when the consonants are stops to 140 ms when they are fricatives. The secondary influences are not great enough to eliminate overlap between all categories but, in general, there is a systematic progression from shortest to longest vowels shown in the right-hand column of Figure 4. The average values shown vary from 100 ms (close lax vowels in voiceless stop environments) to 400 ms (open tense vowels in voiced fricative environments). This range is extended still further when individual talker variation is included. For example, the average duration for the former category spoken by the talker with the shortest average durations (K S) is 70 ms, and the average duration for the latter category spoken by the talker with the longest average durations (A H) is 410 ms.

Discussion

Study of the four influences on vowel duration demonstrated in Figure 4 does not suggest any simple explanation of the durational behavior of vocalic sounds in American English. There are available to the theorist two extreme views – the durational variations are explicable in terms of the physiological process that produced the utterances and are inherent in the process, or, the variations in duration are part of the phonology of the language and are learned by persons who use this signalling system.

The first explanation is untenable as an overall explanation on two different grounds. The data show, for example, that the average duration of vowels increases with so-called vocalic tenseness and with vocalic openness. Tenseness, however, is a descriptive phonetic term that correlates with closeness when contrasting pairs such as [i]-[ɪ], [u]-[ʊ], etc. are compared. The secondary influence on duration shown in Figure 4 might more aptly be called tongue height with high (close) and low (open) contrasts. The two influences associated with the vowel articulation itself, then, are not explicable in the same articulatory terms since vowel duration increases as tongue height increases in one case and as tongue height decreases in the other.

The second piece of evidence against an overall inherently physiological explanation is provided by cross-linguistic study of vowel duration. It has been shown (Zimmerman and Sapon, 1958), for example, that the lengthening effect of a following voiced consonant on a stressed English vowel does not obtain in Spanish, suggesting that durational variations are, in part at least, learned by talkers of English and not employed by talkers of Spanish.

It is appealing, however, to speculate that some inherent articulatory influences on vowel duration do exist in general. The articulatory processes that seem to qualify are the manner of production of consonant contexts and the open-close dimension of vowel articulation (other things being constant). Many reports agree that vowels associated with stop consonants are slightly shorter than those associated with fricatives, and that duration varies inversely with tongue height as displayed in the traditional vowel diagram (particularly when tense and lax vowels are considered separately). It seems reasonable to hypothesize that the articulation of both close vowels and stop consonants may represent less muscular adjustment from a physiologic rest position of the vocal tract and may consequently require relatively less muscular effort than the production of sounds requiring more deviation from the rest position.

The *primary* influences operating on vowel duration in American English, however, do not lend themselves to such an explanation. Voiceless consonants in English are typically described as fortis or aspirated, a characteristic that suggests greater muscular effort during their production, when compared with voiced consonants. Nevertheless, vowels preceding voiceless consonants are shorter in duration than those before voiced consonants. Likewise, the primary influence on duration attributable directly to the vowel cannot be explained in articulatory terms alone. Although a given lax vowel is more open than its tense opposition, on the average lax vowels are shorter than tense vowels.

The measured diminution of duration associated with lax vowels, however, might be attributed to a reduction in the vocal effort expended in producing the vowels. There is one kind of indirect evidence that tends to support such a hypothesis. The overall relative amplitude of the lax vowels in tense-lax pairs is known to be less than that of their corresponding tense vowels, a finding contradictory to the prediction of an acoustic theory of speech production that assumes constant glottal excitation (Fant, 1960). Since the frequencies of the first formants of the lax vowels [ɪ], [ɛ], [ʌ] and [ʊ] are higher than those of [i], [e], [ɑ] and [u], respectively, the theory predicts they will have a higher overall level. The deviation of measured data (see Fairbanks, House and Stevens, 1950; Black, 1949) from this prediction can be interpreted as a change in the level of vocal effort during the production of lax vowels, and it seems reasonable to speculate that this diminution in effort is also shown in a reduction in duration.

The shortening of vowels preceding voiceless consonants must similarly be attributed to an articulatory activity arbitrarily imposed by the phonologic system of English that calls for the prolongation of vowels before voiced consonant sounds.

These considerations suggest strongly that the two primary influences described above are learned modes of articulation that are used to supplement the phonologic system of American English, and that the secondary influences described above are inherent in the production of speech and will appear in languages characterized by such contrastive processes.

A weakness in the analysis presented here has to do with the criteria used in defining the duration of the vowels. As indicated above, the vowel boundaries were defined primarily in terms of source characteristics, and the measurements, therefore, are not a precise description of the time-varying articulatory events. The present criteria, and possibly the materials as well, tend to magnify the apparent differences attributable to variations in consonantal context, particularly those produced by voiceless-voiced cognates. For example, the aspiration at the onset of a vowel following a stop consonant was not included in the measurement of the vowel. The average duration of this aspirated portion varies from 5–10 ms after voiced stops to 50–80 ms after voiceless stops, suggesting that the *articulation per se* varies less than does the voiced portion of the vocalic event. The appropriateness of such an interpretation is strengthened by measurements of lip activity and voicing onset during the production of syllables including bilabial stop consonants reported recently by Fujimura (1961). Such considerations suggest that when the duration of the articulatory vowel event is measured, the primary influence of the voicing characteristic of the consonantal context may be less than that reported here. In spite of these difficulties, it is highly probable that the data discussed above are a reasonably valid description of the durations of vowel articulations in natural utterances.

Acknowledgments

The participation of Kenneth N. Stevens in the experimental and interpretive portions of the study is acknowledged with gratitude, as is the criticism provided by Osamu Fujimura. A perceptive observation by Grant Fairbanks stimulated the writing of this note and has been incorporated into the discussion.

References

BLACK, J. W. (1949), 'Natural frequency, duration and intensity of vowels in reading', *JSHD*, vol. 14, pp. 216–20.

BUSH, C. N. (1960), 'The effect of phonetic environment upon the acoustic distinctive features of certain English consonants', unpublished Ph.D. dissertation, Stanford University.

FAIRBANKS, G., HOUSE, A. S., and STEVENS, E. L. (1950), 'An experimental study of vowel intensities', *J. acoust. Soc. Amer.*, vol. 22, p. 457–9.

FANT, C. G. M. (1960), *Acoustic Theory of Speech Production*, Mouton, The Hague.

FUJIMURA, O. (1961), 'Bilabial stop and nasal consonants: a motion picture study and its acoustical implications', *J. Speech Hearing Res.*, vol. 4, pp. 233–47.

HOUSE, A. S., STEVENS, K. N., and FUJISAKI, H. (1960), 'Automatic measurement of the formants of vowels in diverse consonantal environments', *J. acoust. Soc. Amer.*, vol. 32, p. 1517 (abstract).

LEHMAN, W. P., and HEFFNER, R. M. S. (1940), 'Notes on the length of vowels (III)', *Amer. Speech*, vol. 15, pp. 377–80.

LEHMAN, W. P., and HEFFNER, R. M. S. (1943), 'Notes on the length of vowels (VI)', *Amer. Speech*, vol. 18, pp. 208–15.

PARMENTER C. E., and TREVINO, S. N. (1935), 'The length of the sounds of a Middle Westerner', *Amer. Speech*, vol. 10, pp. 129–33.

PETERSON, G. E., and LEHISTE, I. (1960), 'Duration of syllable nuclei in English', *J. acoust. Soc. Amer.*, vol. 32, pp. 693–703.

ZIMMERMAN, S. A., and SAPON, S. M. (1958), 'Note on vowel duration seen cross-linguistically', *J. acoust. Soc. Amer.*, vol. 30, pp. 152–3.

26 Ilse Lehiste and Gordon E. Peterson

Some Basic Considerations in the Analysis of Intonation[1]

Ilse Lehiste and Gordon E. Peterson, 'Some basic considerations in the analysis of intonation', *Journal of the Acoustical Society of America*, vol. 33 (1961), pp. 419–25.

Introduction

In most languages, the fundamental frequency of the voice has a distinctive function. In so-called 'tone languages', pitch level or movement may contribute to lexical and morphological distinctions. In languages where pitch has no such function, levels or contours of pitch may in part determine the meaning of the message in which the contour appears. Some analyses of English postulate suprasegmental morphemes, consisting of pitches and terminal junctures, with differential meaning (Trager and Smith, 1957). According to two widely accepted analyses, American English has a system of four intonation levels (Pike, 1945; Wells, 1945). Both of these systems were formulated without the benefit of instrumental analysis. The present paper represents an attempt to analyse acoustically one intonation contour in American English, and to determine some of the factors that influence the phonetic realization of the intonation contour.

Material and method

The material analysed consists of the corpus of material described in a previous publication (Peterson and Lehiste, 1960). Briefly, there are two sets of utterances, a large set of 1263 utterances by one speaker, and a smaller set of 350 utterances by five speakers. It is assumed that a reasonable correspondence between the two sets of data indicates that the larger set may be considered representative, even though every item included in the larger set was not actually compared with data from several different speakers. The sets consist of the frame 'Say the word . . . again.' Primary stress and a change from highest to lowest intonation level occurred on the word that was in the commutation position. The speaker for the large corpus used 1263 CNC words[2] with the frame; the five speakers of the control group

1. This research was supported by the Information Systems Branch of the Office of Naval Research of the US Navy under contract.
2. The term 'CNC word' refers to monosyllabic words consisting of an initial consonant phoneme, one of the fifteen stressed syllable nuclei of American English, and a final consonant phoneme. Both the consonant phonemes and the syllable nuclei may be phonetically complex. The set of 1263 words is described in more detail by Lehiste and Peterson (1959b).

all read an identical set of 70 words in the same frame. All speakers used approximately the same stress and pitch pattern.

Various acoustic analyses were made of the recorded data; the measurements most relevant for the present paper were from 4 in. narrow-band spectrograms. The fundamental frequency could be determined from these spectrograms with an accuracy of approximately ±1 Hz.[3]

Intrinsic fundamental frequency

The average fundamental frequency that was associated with each stressed syllable nucleus was computed for both sets of data. The results appear in Table 1 and Figure 1. It will be noted that the fundamental frequency

Table 1 Average fundamental frequency associated with syllable nuclei

SN	Average for five speakers	GEP	Peterson-Barney
i	129	183	136
	130	173	135
eɪ	130	169	
ɛ	127	166	130
æ	125	162	127
ə	127	164	130
ɑ	120	163	124
ɔ	116	165	129
oʊ	122	170	
ʊ	133	171	137
u	134	182	141
ɑʊ	119	159	
ɑɪ	124	160	
ɔɪ	123	163	
ɝ	130	170	133

3. The fundamental frequency was derived by measuring the center frequency of selected higher harmonics on a 4 in. narrow-band spectrogram; the measured frequency was divided by the order number of the respective harmonic to obtain the fundamental frequency. Usually, both the 10th and the 20th harmonics were measured. On these spectrograms 0·1 in. represents about 88 Hz, and the individual harmonics are appreciably narrower. Calibration tones and repeated measurements show the accuracy to be within ±20 Hz, and in the region of the 20th harmonic this represents an accuracy of ±1 Hz. Rapid cycle-to-cycle fluctuations in fundamental frequency are smoothed by the analysing filter, of course, and are not represented in such measurements.

measures for the speaker of the CNC list are appreciably higher than those for the male speakers of the Peterson and Barney data (1952). This is probably the result of the fact that the measurements presented in Figure 1 were taken at the peak of the intonation contour, and that the speaker employed a relatively wide range of fundamental voice frequency. A different intonation pattern was associated with the utterances measured in the course of the Peterson-Barney study. It will be noted further from both Table 1 and Figure 1 that for any given speaker an intrinsic fundamental frequency is associated with each vowel. The two curves of Figure 1 resemble an acoustical vowel diagram, in which /i/ and /u/ are associated

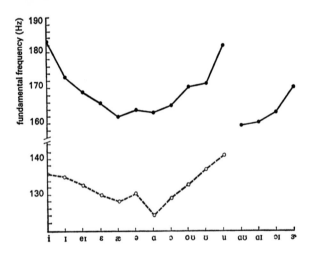

Figure 1 The points connected by the solid lines represent the average fundamental frequencies arranged according to syllable nuclei, that occurred at the peak of the intonation contour in the 1263 CNC words uttered by GEP; the points connected by the dashed lines represent average values from Peterson and Barney (1952)

with the highest intrinsic fundamental voice frequencies, the open vowels (in articulatory terms) are associated with the lowest fundamental frequencies, and the central vowels (such as /ə/ and /ɝ/) occur approximately in the middle of the frequency range. The peak of the intonation contour occurred on the first element of the diphthong, and the fundamental frequency associated with it was similar to that occurring on /ɑ/ and /ɔ/. This is not a new observation; reports have appeared previously in the literature describing similar findings (Peterson and Barney, 1952; House and Fairbanks, 1953). In the present set of data, however, the intrinsic fundamental frequency is related to a specific intonation contour in spoken American English. If a system of several levels is postulated, it appears significant that the same level is habitually associated with a variety of fundamental frequency values, varying in a manner which is influenced by the phonetic quality of the vowel. In linguistic terms, the selection of a particular pitch allophone is conditioned by the segmental quality of the syllable nucleus.

Initial and final consonants

Each syllable nucleus thus appears to be associated with a specific average fundamental frequency. Within each set of utterances containing the same stressed syllable nucleus, further regular variations were observed. The larger set of utterances contained several samples of the various vowel-consonant combinations, so that it was possible to study the influence of each initial and final consonant upon the fundamental frequency associated with each syllable nucleus. The smaller set contained only from three to five occurrences of each of fifteen syllable nuclei, and therefore it was not possible to compare the results, although the same general effects were observed in this limited set.

Table 2 and Figure 2 represent the influence of initial consonants upon the fundamental frequency associated with syllable nuclei. The table presents the average fundamental frequency for all occurrences of the syllable

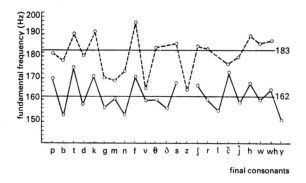

final consonants

Figure 2 The fundamental frequency is of two vowels from the C N C set uttered by G E P, presented as a function of the initial consonant. The points connected by the dashed line represent the values associated with /i/; the points connected by the solid line represent the respective values for /æ/. The top straight line shows the average for all occurrences of /i/; the bottom straight line presents the average value of /æ/

Ilse Lehiste and Gordon E. Peterson 381

nucleus preceded by each of the consonants listed.[4] Figure 2 presents two curves, showing the fundamental frequency of two vowels /i/ and /æ/ as a function of the initial consonant; these two vowels have the highest and the lowest intrinsic fundamental frequencies respectively in this set of data. The straight lines in Figure 2 represent the average fundamental frequencies for /i/ and /æ/, computed for 105 occurrences of /i/ and 131 occurrences of /æ/.

Table 2 Fundamental frequency of the peak of the intonation contour, in Hz, as influenced by the initial consonant of the test word

Syllable nucleus	i	ɪ	eɪ	ɛ	æ	ə	ɑ	ɔ	oʊ	ʊ	u	aʊ	aɪ	ɔɪ	ɚ
average peak	183	173	169	166	162	164	163	165	170	171	182	159	160	163	170
preceding consonant															
p	182	176	180	174	170	169	166	175	181	178	198	168	166	175	173
b	178	165	161	163	153	159	164	161	164	173	178	160	160	160	169
t	191	180	175	170	175	169	175	171	173	170	194	165	169	170	180
d	180	167	166	158	158	157	160	158	166		190	148	157		164
k	192	176	178	175	171	173	172	175	176	178	196	168	178	170	174
g	170	172	167	163	156	166	160	159	170	160	160	152	152		167
m	169	168	158	164	161	156	153	162	163		173	163	163		156
n	173	164	164	163	153	151	156	164	163	175	173	130	158	145	169
f	196	181	170	173	171	169	170	172	171	165	178	160	165	165	165
v	165	165	154		160			158				148	150	158	158
θ	184	177	170		160	165		173					160		180
ð	185	170		156	156	150			155				165		
s	186	177	175	173	168	175	173	168	175	155	183	177	164	170	170
z	165				160				165		190				
ʃ	185	180	175	173	167	171	168	168	175	165	185	148	170		175
r	183	167	168	159	160	162	156	156	168	180	181	158	160	165	
l	179	174	161	165	155	157	152	160	164	165	173	155	151	150	170
č	177	185	185	179	173	173	173	166	178		188		155	185	175
ǰ	180	169	163	151	159	162	160	165	160		172	145	165	130	158
h	190	182	182	172	168	170	164	171	174	165	189	173	160		173
w	186	176	171	164	160	168	149	158	170	165	180		159		169
wh	187	174	180	169	165		158						172		170
y		175	170	166	150	145	152	145	170	170	185				170

In general, higher fundamental frequencies occur after a voiceless consonant and considerably lower fundamental frequencies occur after a voiced consonant. This distinction is accompanied by a different distribution of the fundamental frequency movement over the test word: after a voiceless consonant, and particularly after a voiceless fricative, the highest peak occurs immediately after the consonant; whereas after a voiced consonant, especially a voiced resonant, the fundamental frequency rises slowly, and the peak occurs approximately in the middle of the test word (see Peterson and Lehiste, 1960).

4. The number of occurrences from which the value for each entry was computed may be found from the distribution charts of initial and final consonants and syllable nuclei in the C N C words, Lehiste and Peterson (1959b).

In these data, the final consonants have no such regular influence on the preceding syllable nuclei. Table 3 presents average values associated with each final consonant and syllable nucleus; Figure 3 shows the same material

Table 3 Fundamental frequency of the peak of the intonation contour, in Hz, as influenced by the final consonant of the test word

Syllable nucleus	i	ɪ	eɪ	ɛ	æ	ə	ɑ	ɔ	ou	ʊ	u	ɑʊ	aɪ	ɔ	ɝ
average peak following consonant	183	173	169	166	162	164	163	165	170	171	182	159	160	163	170
p	191	179	173	169	164	176	167		177	180	183		154		175
b		166		170	165	167	161	155	160		188		165		165
t	185	172	166	163	163	164	160	168	164	162	184	157	164		172
d	180	172	168	167	163	165	160	153	168	167	178	160	165	160	168
k	174	177	177	163	165	166	160	167	171	172	175		168		172
g	160	173	160	171	160	162	165	157	159						170
m	185	171	169	157	160	164	172		167		183		159		163
n	181	176	167	169	165	168	163	161	165		178	145	162	150	169
ŋ		171			166	159		162							
f	181	170	175	154	166	163		165	170		182		160	180	175
v	184	182	168		165	162		170	169		180		156		171
θ	187	173	160	167	160	155		151	165		184	170			172
ð	182	175	168						170		185		156		
s	184	172	176	164	156	163		163		180	176	161	160	175	172
z	184	193	168		153	155	160	164	174		179	160	160	160	160
ʃ	190	178		165	161	157	158	145		173					
ʒ	165		155								175				
r		173	153	170			166	169			174	172	165	156	
l	181	170	169	161	165	165	165	170	169	170	194	158	160	165	174
č	181	175		175	167	172	153		175		205	167			178
j	180	173	173	173		162	170		170			160			158

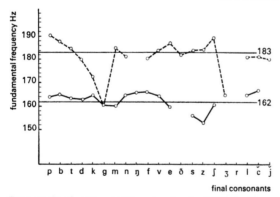

Figure 3 The fundamental frequencies for /i/ (dashed curve) and /æ/ (solid curve) for GEP as a function of the final consonant of the CNC sequence. The top straight line shows the average for all occurrences of /i/; the bottom straight line presents the average value for /æ/

graphically for the two vowels /i/ and /æ/. As in Figure 2, the straight lines represent the average fundamental frequencies for /i/ and /æ/, computed for 105 occurrences of /i/ and 131 occurrences of /æ/. It appears that the distance of the points from the straight lines is related to the number of occurrences of a particular syllable nucleus-final consonant sequence. The greater the number of occurrences, the closer is the value for a particular final consonant to the average value, and thus the smaller the distance of the point from the line representing the average value. The position of points representing single occurrences of a particular sequence may be influenced by the initial consonant, and may fall anywhere within the limits of fluctuation possible for a given syllable nucleus. It seems probable that in English the voiceless-voiced contrast of the final consonant has no significant influence on the fundamental frequency appearing in a preceding syllable nucleus. The two instances of greatest divergence from the average are the values associated with the sequences /ig/ and /iʒ/. Both points represent only one word each, *league* and *liege*, and it is likely that the initial /l/ has caused the low fundamental frequency on both words.

Table 4 and Figure 4 present the combined data for GEP for all initial and final consonants and all syllable nuclei. The solid curve presents the average values for all syllable nuclei associated with an initial consonant,

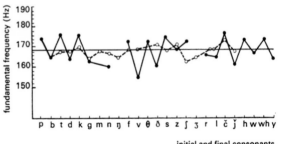

Figure 4 Average peak values of all fifteen syllable nuclei as functions of initial and final consonants. The averages were computed from the 1263 CNC words recorded by GEP

and the dashed curve shows the corresponding fundamental frequencies associated with each final consonant phoneme. The straight line represents the average fundamental frequency that occurred at the peak of the intonation contour in all 1263 utterances. It appears that the initial consonant influences the frequency associated with the syllable nucleus, and that voiceless initial consonants are associated with a higher fundamental frequency than are voiced initial consonants.

Table 4 Influence of initial and final consonants on the fundamental voice frequency at the peak of the intonation contour in CNC words

Consonant	Average for all vowels after initial consonant	Average for all vowels before final consonant
p	175	174
b	165	166
t	176	168
d	163	168
k	176	170
g	163	164
m	162	168
n	161	167
ŋ		165
f	173	169
v	155	169
θ	173	170
ð	161	171
s	175	169
z	169	171
ʃ	173	163
ʒ		165
r	166	168
l	164	169
č	177	174
j	161	168
h	174	
w	167	
wh	174	
y	164	
Average	169	169

Test word intonation contours

The foregoing analysis has shown that the phonetic quality of the syllable nucleus is one of the factors that determine the fundamental frequency at which the peak intonation level is realized. The next consideration is whether the lower level at which the downward movement terminates in a given CNC word also depends upon the phonetic quality of the syllable nucleus. If the lower intonation level shows fluctuations similar to those of the peak, the further implication should be considered that the movement from one intonation level to the next may involve a fixed ratio of frequencies, possibly corresponding to some musical interval. If this holds true, it is necessary to investigate whether different speakers use the same intervals when producing the same intonation contour.

The fundamental frequency on the final part of the test word, as well as the fundamental frequencies associated with the precontour 'say the word' and with the final word in the sentence, 'again', were measured for both sets of data. Table 5 presents these data for GEP, and Table 6 for the five

Table 5 Average fundamental frequencies at specified points within the sentences uttered by GEP

			Fundamental frequency				
			Test word		End of frame ('again')		
SN	Number of occurrences	Precontour ('word') end	Peak	End	Beg	Peak	End
i	105	129	183	94	115	132	87
ɪ	141	126	173	98	114	131	87
eɪ	119	130	169	98	116	131	91
ɛ	94	129	166	95	115	132	88
æ	131	126	162	92	112	130	87
ə	109	124	164	98	111	128	85
ɑ	75	127	163	93	113	128	88
ɔ	79	125	165	92	111	130	84
oʊ	93	126	170	93	113	130	84
ʊ	28	125	171	91	109	127	81
u	74	127	182	94	113	133	87
aʊ	35	127	159	93	113	127	86
aɪ	93	125	160	91	111	129	85
ɔɪ	16	128	163	93	111	129	84
ɝ	71	126	171	94	113	131	85
average		127	169	94	113	130	86
total	1263						

speakers of the smaller set of utterances. The first and second columns in these tables indicate the syllable nuclei and the number of occurrences of each in the two sets of material. The third column presents the average fundamental frequency of the first part of the frame sentence, 'say the word'. The following two columns show the average values of the peak that occurred during the test word, and the average values of the frequency at the end of the test word. The last three columns present three measure-

Table 6 Average fundamental frequencies at specified points within the sentences uttered by five speakers

SN	Number of occurrences	Precontour ('word') end	Fundamental frequency				
			Test word		End of frame ('again')		
			Peak	End	Beg	Peak	End
i	25	102	129	90	92	100	77
ɪ	20	104	130	91	93	99	78
eɪ	20	102	130	87	92	97	78
ɛ	20	105	127	91	95	101	81
æ	20	103	125	87	92	98	78
ə	20	105	127	90	92	99	77
ɑ	25	104	120	89	90	100	80
ɔ	20	100	116	83	90	96	77
oʊ	20	104	122	88	90	96	78
ʊ	15	101	133	90	96	97	78
u	20	103	134	88	93	97	77
aʊ	20	103	119	84	91	98	79
aɪ	20	101	124	85	89	96	79
ɔɪ	15	103	123	88	89	96	77
ɝ	20	104	130	86	92	96	78
average		103	126	88	92	98	78
total	300						

ments taken during the final word of the frame, 'again'; the measurements present the fundamental frequency that occurred on the unstressed first syllable, on the highest peak of the stressed second syllable, and at the end of the utterance. It appears that there is no significant connection between the average fundamental frequency of the peak, as determined by the phonetic value of the syllable nucleus, and the fundamental frequency pattern of the rest of the contour. The average values for the lower intonation levels on the test words show only negligible fluctuations. This indicates that no fixed ratios of frequencies are involved. As may be seen from Table 7, the interval range differs considerably with each speaker. The same intonation contour was habitually pronounced by one speaker with a downward movement in frequency with a frequency ratio between a major third and a pure fourth, whereas the speaker with the greatest voice inflection used a downward movement in frequency approximately equivalent to a major seventh. It may perhaps be concluded that the actual interval range is irrelevant in this intonation contour.

Table 7 also contains statistical information about the percentage of musically 'pure' intervals used by the different speakers.[5] The calculation is based on comparing the frequency ratios used by the different speakers

Table 7 Fundamental frequency ratios on the test words expressed as musical intervals

Speaker	Average frequency ratio on test word		Corresponding musical interval	Percentage of 'pure' intervals (3,4,5,6,8)
Bi	136/83	1·64	m6-M6	25
Br	126/99	1·27	M3-P4	27
Ch	120/82	1·46	D5-P5	22
He	136/97	1·40	P4-D5	30
Re	113/78	1·45	D5-P5	32
GEP (total set)	169/94	1·79	m7-M7	14
GEP /i/	183/94	1·95	M7-P8	14
GEP /æ/	162/92	1·76	m7-M7	14

with the ratios of successive harmonics of a complex tone. Several factors make this part of the table tentative. The accuracy of measurement is approximately ±1 Hz. This limitation of measurement accuracy affects the ratio in a different manner, depending on the ranges in which the measurements are taken. Little is known, however, about the fluctuation in fundamental frequency within which a listener may identify a pitch movement with a specific musical interval, particularly when this interval occurs in speech. It is at least a possibility that the fluctuation in fundamental frequency due to vowel quality has no corresponding effect on the perception of the pitch interval.

Word and frame contours

In the spectrographic analysis, the test word and the final word of the frame 'again', were always included. This often did not leave room for the complete frame preceding the test word, but a selected set of analyses showed that the

5. For the purposes of this study, a musically 'pure' interval was defined as the difference between two fundamental frequencies that can be expressed as a simple numerical ratio: 2/1 for an octave, 3/2 for a pure fifth, 4/3 for a pure fourth, 5/4 for a major third, 6/5 for a minor third, etc. We considered an intonation pattern to represent a 'pure' interval when the ratio between the two frequency values did not differ from that of a 'pure' interval by more than 1/100.

contour preceding the frame was approximately level for the various informants. Thus, only the average fundamental frequency on the part of the precontour immediately preceding the test word, i.e. on 'word', appears in column 3 of Tables 5 and 6. Both perceptually and physically (in terms of Hz) the precontour appears to form a middle intonation level compared to the highest and lowest levels that were observed on the test word. Since the segmental structure of the part of the utterance on which this middle intonation level occurred remained identical for all utterances, the data provide some information about the range of variations within one phonemic intonation level, unconditioned by differences in phonetic quality.

Table 8 shows that the syllable nucleus of the following test word has no essential influence on the fundamental frequency used on the last word

Table 8 Fundamental frequency ranges for 'word' in utterances preceding syllable nuclei /i/ and /ɑ/

Fundamental frequency ranges for 'word' (Hz)	Number of occurrences of 'word' preceding S N	
	i	ɑ
106–110		3
111–115	2	6
116–120	17	12
121–125	33	20
126–130	37	16
131–135	7	11
136–140	8	7
141–145	1	

of the precontour. The table presents the number of instances in which the fundamental frequency on 'word' fell within a particular frequency range preceding test words containing the syllable nuclei /i/ and /ɑ/. The frequency ranges are approximately the same for the fundamental frequency on 'word' preceding 105 occurrences of test words containing /i/ and 75 occurrences of test words containing /ɑ/ as syllable nucleus. Since the intrinsic fundamental frequency on /i/ is appreciably higher that that on /ɑ/, the rise in frequency from the precontour to the peak of the intonation contour is correspondingly different. The fundamental frequency on words with /i/ rises approximately 55 Hz from the end of the precontour, but only 36 Hz from the end of the precontour for /ɑ/. Table 9 shows the number of instances in which the rise in fundamental frequency from the end of the precontour to the peak of the test word fell within a particular range. Since

Table 9 Ranges of the rise of fundamental frequency from the end of the precontour to the peak occurring on syllable nuclei /i/ and /ɑ/

Difference between precontour and peak of SN (Hz)	Number of occurrences of SN i	ɑ
11–15		2
16–20		1
21–25		8
26–30	2	12
31–35	2	20
36–40	8	16
41–45	11	9
46–50	20	5
51–55	20	1
56–60	17	1
61–65	18	
66–70	3	
71–75	3	
76–80	1	

the values on the precontour remained relatively constant, a greater rise was associated with /i/ than /ɑ/. The actual value reached by the syllable nucleus depends partly on the initial consonant, as has been shown. Considerable overlap between the ranges of fundamental frequency for the different vowels may be expected; for example, the fundamental frequency of a vowel with high intrinsic fundamental frequency occurring in a word beginning with a consonant that has a lowering influence may overlap that of a vowel with a low intrinsic fundamental frequency preceded by a consonant that has a raising influence. Table 10 presents both the ranges for /i/ and /ɑ/ and the area of overlap between the two. In addition, the fundamental frequency occurring on a syllable nucleus may vary over a certain range in successive repetitions of the same word. Table 11 shows the percentage of instances in which the fundamental frequency on the 1263 occurrences of 'word' at the end of the precontour fell within a specified frequency range. Approximately 75 per cent of all occurrences were between 116 and 130 Hz, but the total range was from 105 to 145 Hz.

The contour applied to the last word in the frame is, in a sense, a smaller-scale repetition of the sequence of three levels that appeared on 'Say the word . . .' Here, too, we found three levels; from the point of

Table 10 Fundamental frequency ranges for test words containing syllable nuclei /i/ and /ɑ/

Fundamental frequency ranges for test word (Hz)	Number of occurrences of S N	
	i	ɑ
136–140		3
141–145		5
146–150	1	3
151–155	1	8
156–160	2	19
161–165	8	10
166–170	8	14
171–175	10	7
176–180	20	5
181–185	17	1
186–190	24	
191–195	6	
196–200	4	
201–205	3	
206–210		
211–215	1	

Table 11 Percentages of instances in which the fundamental frequencies associated with the 1263 utterances of 'word' fell within various ranges

Fundamental frequency ranges (Hz)	Percentage of occurrences
105–110	2·6
111–115	4·2
116–120	21·2
121–125	25·1
126–130	30·5
131–135	9·2
136–140	6·6
141–145	0·6

view of the item 'again' alone, these might be described as a sequence of middle, high and low intonation levels. However, the actual values that appeared as a manifestiation of these three levels differed considerably from those appearing on the first part of the contour. For GEP the *high* level on 'again' was consistently slightly higher than the *middle* level of the first part, but was very considerably lower than the *high* of the first part of the contour ('Say the word . . .'). For the five speakers of the smaller set, the *high* of the sequence of intonation levels on 'again' was lower than the *middle* of the first part of the contour. The *low* of 'again' was noticeably lower than the *low* that occurred on the test word. The drop from *high* to *low* in the contour on 'again' was always smaller than the comparable drop on the test word; expressed in musical intervals, the average drop was approximately equal to a pure fifth (*v.* a major seventh) for GEP and equal to a major third (*v.* a diminished fifth) for the five speakers. The physical data do not suggest any immediate technique for identifying the levels as they appeared on the word 'again' with any of the levels that occurred on the first part of the contour preceding the word 'again'.

We considered the hypothesis that the pitch peak on the word 'again' might be conditioned by the presence of secondary stress at the beginning of the second syllable, and that the intonation pattern on 'again' might thus involve only a sequence of *middle* intonation level followed by *low* intonation level. In the case of GEP, this appears plausible, as the average value of the fundamental frequency of the peak that appeared on 'again' was slightly higher than that occurring on the precontour. In the case of the five speakers, however, this hypothesis appears untenable. The peak on 'again' is lower than the level used on the precontour; there were actually a considerable number of instances where the fundamental frequency on the word 'again' was consistently falling, so that the frequency on the syllable with secondary stress was lower than the frequency on the unstressed first syllable. In Table 6, it may be seen that the average difference between the values that were measured on the unstressed and stressed syllables may differ by as little as 1 Hz (when 'again' followed words with the syllable nucleus /ʊ/), with a maximum average difference of 10 Hz (on 'again' following /ɑ/). The difference between the averages on the unstressed and stressed syllables in 'again' is approximately 6 Hz, which may be compared with the differences that occurred on different repetitions of the last word in the precontour, where the differences between the averages amounted to a maximum of 5 Hz. In all instances, however, subjective listening made it possible to identify the stress on the second syllable of 'again'. It appears from the analysis of this part of the intonation contour that differences in stress are not necessarily represented by conditioned differences in the phonetic realization of intonation levels.

Conclusion

The investigation reported in this paper indicates a number of problems involved in the instrumental analysis of intonation. A linguistically significant intonation level may have a wide range of phonetic manifestations. Some factors that influence the selection of a particular pitch allophone have been described. It appears that the phonetic quality of the syllabic sound has an influence on the fundamental frequency at which the intonation level is produced. Further, the initial consonant in a consonant-vowel sequence may influence the fundamental frequency appearing on the vowel following the consonant. The variations in fundamental frequency, however, that may occur when the same intonation level is repeatedly produced on the same word, may be greater than the variations associated with changes in segmental quality; the differences can only be established when a sufficient number of utterances are compared. The influence of stress upon the manifestation of a particular intonation level needs to be explored more fully; the data reported here suggest that, at least in some instances, lower fundamental frequency may occur on a stressed syllable than on a preceding unstressed syllable. The problem of relating contour-like movements to musical intervals seems to be less relevant for a study of English than for a study of tone languages; it appears from our data that the intonation contours of American English are not based on recurring musical intervals. Most of the data presented illustrate the realization of a single intonation level occurring under sentence-maximum stress; the question of contrastive intonation levels and their relation to contrastive degree of stress remains to be considered. The instrumental analysis of intonation emerges as a problem of great complexity.

References

HOUSE, A. S., and FAIRBANKS, G. (1953), 'The influence of consonant environment upon the secondary acoustical characteristics of vowels', *J. acoust. Soc. Amer.*, vol. 25, pp. 105–13.

LEHISTE, I., and PETERSON, G. E. (1959a), 'Linguistic considerations in the study of speech intelligibility', *J. acoust. Soc. Amer.*, vol. 31, pp. 280–86.

LEHISTE, I., and PETERSON, G. E. (1959b), 'Studies of syllable nuclei, Part 1', *Report no.* 3, University of Michigan Speech Research Laboratory, November.

PETERSON, G. E., and BARNEY, H. L. (1952), 'Control methods used in a study of the vowels', *J. acoust. Soc. Amer.*, vol. 24, pp. 175–84. Reprinted here, pp. 104–22.

PETERSON, G. E., and LEHISTE, I. (1960), 'Duration of syllable nuclei in English', *J. acoust. Soc. Amer.*, vol. 332, pp. 693–703.

PIKE, K. L. (1945), *The Intonation of American English*, University of Michigan Press.

TRAGER, G. L., and SMITH, H. L. Jr (1957), 'An outline of English structure': *Studies in Linguistics: Occasional Papers*, No. 3, Norman, Oklahoma, pp. 44–52, 65–77.

WELLS, R. S. (1945), 'The pitch phonemes of English', *Language*, vol. 21, pp. 27–39.

27 Philip Lieberman

Some Acoustic Correlates of Word Stress in American English

Philip Lieberman, 'Some acoustic correlates of word stress in American English', *Journal of the Acoustical Society of America*, vol. 32 (1960), pp. 451–4.

The object of this experiment was to investigate the relevance of changes in the fundamental frequency, envelope amplitude and duration to mechanical recognition of the stressed syllable in English stress pairs.

Procedure

The stress pairs used in this experiment are listed in context in Table 1. They are of the type in which a word may be either a noun or a verb, the primary difference being in the stress pattern.

Table 1 Nou–nverb stress pairs

---

1 We had a *contract*.
2 Grandfather was a *rebel*.
3 The dam will *overflow*.
4 George has one good *attribute*.
5 That war was a great *conflict*.
6 Don't *conflict* with his policy.
7 *Conduct* Josephine there.
8 We will *compress* the channel.
9 Let's *contest* the will.
10 *Rebel* from your state of misery.
11 Put a cold *compress* on his head.
12 What a horrible *contrast*.
13 Let us not *torment* their souls.
14 He's often an *absent* scholar.
15 *Compact* this bale of hay.
16 There may be an *overflow* if you close the drain.
17 Don't *contract* the flu.
18 To what would he *attribute* this sensation.
19 His *conduct* was lamentable.
20 First National is having a *contest*.
21 Let's *contrast* their policies.
22 It has an *uplift*.
23 You may be in *torment* eternally.

24 That's an *escort* destroyer.
25 Look at that *incline*.
26 Roads should not *incline*.
27 Don't *insult* him.
28 Don't *object* to him.
29 Let's *record* this.
30 The Reader's *Digest* is here.
31 We will *convert* this machine to scrap.
32 George once made a *convert*.
33 We need an *export*.
34 My *object* all sublime.
35 Kinsey made a *survey*.
36 That's an *insult*.
37 *Escort* this patron outside.
38 Let's *export* grass.
39 I can't *digest* inner tubes.
40 What a *minute* cut of meat.
41 *Minute* steak is on the menu.
42 This is a *compact* car.
43 Let's *survey* the field.
44 I bought a new *record*.
45 Let us *uplift* their souls.
46 Don't *absent* yourself now.
47 It's a *compound* fracture.
48 Let us *compound* a brew.
49 Let us *perfect* the art.
50 That's *perfect*.

Twenty-five pairs were recorded by six female and ten male native speakers of American English. Ten speakers were natives of New England, three of the Middle Atlantic area, one of the Southeast, one of the Midwest, and one of the Far West. Their educational level varied from high school to graduate school. The test words were presented in context in lists of sentences; each subject was instructed to read each sentence silently, reading only the italicized word aloud. 'Grandfather was a *rebel*' and '*Rebel* from your state of misery' are two sentences typical of the test material.

The lists were randomized to prevent 'sing song' patterns, and the subjects' responses were tape recorded after they had practised to their satisfaction. There was no attempt to teach a subject a stress form that was not in his normal speaking vocabulary.

Two observers listened to the tape recordings and judged the stressed syllable of each utterance twice. If all four judgments did not agree, the utterance was discarded. The stressed syllables of all the utterances accepted for processing could be clearly perceived.

The fundamental frequency of each utterance was determined and recorded by means of the pitch extractor shown in the block diagram of Figure 1. The mode of operation of this device[1] is analogous to the way in which voicing appears in the vertical striations of a wideband spectrogram.

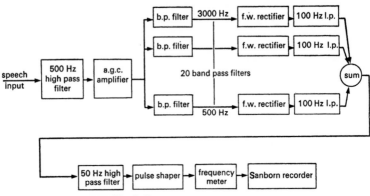

Figure 1 Pitch extractor block diagram

After the speech signal passes through the bank of filters and full wave rectifiers, only the glottal excitation rate is coherent in all the channels. When these channels are summed, the fundamental frequency can be reconstructed. The circuit values used in this working model are not necessarily optimum, but were found to give accurate pitch information over the frequency range of interest.

The envelope of each utterance was also recorded with full wave rectification and 5-ms smoothing on another track of the Sanborn recorder.

Results

The relation of the perceived syllable stress to the fundamental frequency, peak envelope amplitude, duration and integral of the amplitude with respect to time is shown in Table 2. Column 2 lists the numbers of utterances for each speaker that displayed clearly perceived stress patterns. Columns 3 to 5 list the number of times that the stressed syllable of a given utterance had a higher maximum fundamental frequency (when this maximum extended over at least two periods), a greater peak envelope amplitude, or a longer duration than the unstressed syllable of the same utter-

1. Caldwell P. Smith, US Patent no. 2 691 137, 'A device for extracting the excitation function from speech signals' (1954).

Table 2 Results of measurements

Speaker number	Number of words	Word basis			Pair basis		
		Frequency	Amplitude	Duration	Frequency	Amplitude	Duration
1	50	48	43	35	43	45	40
2	50	50	45	32	48	45	38
3	43	40	39	31	39	39	35
4	44	42	34	30	29	30	29
5	46	40	38	30	37	42	30
6	43	38	39	27	23	40	27
7	50	40	41	39	34	45	40
8	48	39	40	30	31	42	39
9	41	36	38	25	23	39	29
10	46	43	43	37	36	44	38
11	44	35	37	32	32	36	40
12	42	38	33	30	30	40	30
13	41	36	41	25	25	40	23
14	38	34	34	26	25	37	22
15	39	36	35	25	24	35	24
16	41	36	34	32	24	32	33

ance. Column 3 lists the number of times that the fundamental frequency of the stressed syllable was higher. Column 4 lists the number of times that the peak envelope of the stressed syllable was greater, while Column 5 lists the number of times that its duration was longer. Columns 6 to 8 make the same comparison for the stressed syllable of a given word and its unstressed counterpart in the other word of the stress pair; for example, the first syllable of *con'trast* compared with the first syllable of *contrast'*, or, for example, the second syllables of *overflow'* and *over'flow*. The syllable boundaries were determined by a simple amplitude threshold since a period of relative silence usually occurred between the syllables. Column 6 lists the number of times that the stressed syllable had a higher fundamental frequency, Column 7 the number of times that it had greater peak envelope amplitude, and Column 8 the number of times the stressed syllable was longer in duration.

The stressed syllable had a higher fundamental frequency than the unstressed syllable of the same utterance in 90 per cent of the cases, a higher peak envelope amplitude in 87 per cent, and a longer duration in 66 per cent. The stressed syllable compared with its unstressed counterpart in the other word of the stress pair had a higher fundamental frequency in 72 per cent of the cases, a higher peak envelope amplitude in 90 per cent, and a longer duration in 70 per cent.

The integrals of the amplitude with respect to time of the stressed and unstressed syllables of the same word were computed graphically over each syllable and then compared. In 92 per cent of the cases the integral of the stressed to unstressed syllables of each word was also divided by that of the unstressed to stressed syllables of the other stress form. In 99·9 per cent of the cases the resulting ratio was greater than 1.

In no case did the stressed syllable have both a lower amplitude and a lower fundamental frequency than the unstressed syllable. Moreover, the stressed syllable in all but two cases had either, or both, a greater integral of amplitude with respect to time (over the syllable's duration) or a longer duration than the unstressed syllable of the same utterance.

Figure 2 notes those utterances contained in Columns 3–5 of Table 2 in which either the higher fundamental frequency or peak envelope amplitude

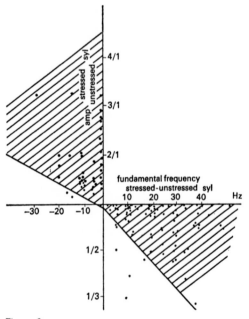

Figure 2

did not concur with the perceptual stress judgment. The difference in fundamental frequency between the stressed and unstressed syllables of the same utterance is plotted on the abscissa while the ratio of the peak amplitudes on the same stressed and unstressed syllables is plotted on the ordinate. The shaded area bounded by the two solid lines and the amplitude and frequency axis includes 97 per cent of the points where a 'trading effect' between the amplitude and pitch cues seems to occur. That is, changes in fundamental frequency coherent with the perceptual stress compensate for noncoherent changes in amplitude, or vice versa. The higher slope of the boundary line in the fourth quadrant tends to indicate that pitch is a somewhat 'stronger' cue than amplitude. However, the amplitude in this study has been simply normalized, and some correction factor should be included for cases where the stressed and unstressed syllables have vowels of differing intrinsic intensity (see Fant, 1952; Fairbanks, House and Stevens, 1950; Peterson and Barney, 1952).

Discussion

The data indicate that higher fundamental frequencies and envelope amplitudes are the most relevant of the unidimensional acoustic correlates of stressed syllables. The fundamental frequency seems most relevant, which concurs with the results reported by D. B. Fry for synthetic stress pairs (1955, 1958). However, in contrast to Fry's results the envelope amplitude seems more important than duration. The effects of the cases where the stressed and unstressed syllables had vowels of differing intrinsic intensities may, in part, account for this difference. The degree of correlation with perceptual stress judgments is not improved when a stressed syllable is compared to a similar, but unstressed, syllable. Some improvement does, however, occur when the integral of the amplitude with respect to time over the duration of the entire syllable is considered.

It is difficult to see how a relative judgment in which a listener must presumably hear both the stressed and unstressed forms of a particular syllable can be reconciled with the certainty with which such judgments can be made on hearing a single isolated utterance. The data presented in Figure 2

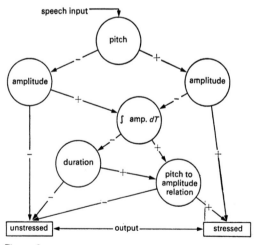

Figure 3

are pertinent to this discussion in that they indicate that stress judgments are made on a multiplicity of simple decisions involving several cues. A program for mechanically recognizing the stressed syllables in stress pairs is presented in Figure 3.

The first step of this program is to note the syllable that has the higher fundamental frequency. This is indicated on the diagram by the positive arrow. If the amplitude of this syllable is also higher, then it is the stressed syllable. If, however, the peak amplitude is lower, as indicated by the negative arrow, the integral of the amplitude with respect to time over the entire syllable is noted. If this is positive and the pitch difference and amplitude ratio between the stressed and unstressed syllables fall into the permissible area of Figure 2, then the syllable is stressed. Many other paths can be followed that all arrive at either a stressed or unstressed judgment. Judgments made on the basis of this scheme on the data were in agreement with the perceptual stress judgments 99·2 per cent of the time.

Conclusion

Since the array of acoustic events measured was by no means complete (for example, changes of vowel quality were ignored), no conclusions with regard to the most important single acoustic correlate of syllable stress can be made. However, it is clearly possible to make unequivocal stress judgments for many different speakers with a simple binary program that uses all the redundancies inherent in a restricted set of multi-dimensional acoustic events. It also seems likely that error-correcting 'trading' relationships exist within the set of acoustic correlates and that automatic recognition programs may function with increased certainty through their use.

References

FAIRBANKS, G., HOUSE, A. S., and STEVENS, E. L. (1950), 'An experimental study of vowel intensities', *J. acoust. Soc. Amer.*, vol. 22, pp. 457–9.

FANT, C. G. M. (1952), 'Transmission properties of the vocal tract with application to the acoustic specification of phonemes', *Technical Report*, no. 12, Acoustic Laboratory, MIT, January.

FRY, D. B. (1955), 'Duration and intensity as physical correlates of linguistic stress', *J. acoust. Soc. Amer.*, vol. 27, pp. 765–8.

FRY, D. B. (1958), 'Experiments in the perception of stress', *Language and Speech*, vol. 1, p. 126–52. Reprinted here, pp. 401–24.

PETERSON, G. E., and BARNEY, A. L. (1952), 'Control methods used in a study of the vowels', *J. acoust. Soc. Amer.*, vol. 24, pp. 175–84. Reprinted here, pp. 104–22.

28 Dennis B. Fry

Experiments in the Perception of Stress

Dennis B. Fry, 'Experiments in the perception of stress', *Language and Speech*, vol. 1 (1958), pp. 126–52.

Stress as a term in a descriptive system

A number of the terms used in descriptive linguistics refer to events that occur at different levels and at different stages in the process of speech communication. One such term is 'stress' which generally denotes both an aspect of the articulatory or motor side of speech and also a feature of the sounds perceived by a listener. Part of the usefulness of the term to linguistic description lies in the very fact that it spans both the transmission and the reception phase of speech, but its use sometimes forms the basis for the unjustifiable assumption of a one-to-one correlation between transmission and reception in this particular domain. Writers on phonetics and linguistics generally use 'stress' to denote either 'the degree of force with which a syllable is uttered' (Jones, 1949) or 'degree of loudness' (Bloch and Trager, 1942), but it is often implied or explicitly stated that these two things are completely correlated; Bloomfield (1933), for example, says that stress 'consists in speaking one of these syllables louder than the other or others'.

An experimental approach to the problem of stress requires somewhat more rigorous formulation of the uses of the term and of the types of event that are open to investigation. In the common usage, succeeding parts of an utterance are said to bear stronger or weaker stress in comparison with other parts of the utterance, and normally the parts so characterized are syllables. Hence stress is a term that refers to a relation between syllables and successive variations in this relation constitute the rhythmic pattern of an utterance just as successive variations in tone-relations make up the intonation pattern. The rhythmic pattern plays a very important role in English and the work reported in this paper deals only with examples drawn from this language.

Stress as a descriptive term may, then, on the one hand, refer to features of the skilled movements that constitute the transmission side of speech and it may be possible to devise experimental methods of measuring variations in the force of utterance during a speech sequence. If this were done, it is likely that the variations would be seen to be more closely connected with phonation than with articulation and it is unlikely that there would be an exact correlation between degrees of stress in the linguistic sense and measured force of utterance. On the other hand, stress may refer to the reception of speech and in this case it denotes a complex of perceptual dimensions.

A sound stimulus may be varied along several physical dimensions, and such variations, provided they fall within certain ranges, will give rise to changes in basic psychological dimensions: pitch, loudness, quality and length. These are basic dimensions in the sense of being independently variable. It is possible to present to a listener sounds which he will judge to be different in pitch but the same loudness, quality and length, or different in quality, but the same pitch, loudness and length, and so on. In addition to these basic perceptual dimensions, there are others which constitute in effect a complex of these first four. Thus in psycho-physical experiments on the 'volume' or on the 'density' of sounds, the listener operates with a complex of the simple dimensions.

Perception of the sounds of speech always involves a complex of these dimensions; the listener is never concerned exclusively with one of them. He takes in continuous variations along all of the basic dimensions and his linguistic judgments are determined by their interaction. This fact is only one more illustration of the redundant character of speech as a mode of communication. The listener, in normal conditions, has a number of cues that he can use as the basis of any single judgment and these cues are provided by variations in any and all of the perceptual dimensions. On the other hand, the listener may, for a specific judgment, be more dependent on one than on another: in establishing a phonemic sequence, he may depend very largely on succeeding variations in quality; in taking in an intonation pattern, he may commonly rely mainly on variations in pitch.

Perceptual factors in stress judgments

In the case of stress judgments, even in one particular language, all four dimensions may play a part and this accounts to some extent for the difficulty of defining the term and for the occurrence in descriptive linguistics of terms such as 'pitch accent', 'force accent', etc., which are used to denote the supremacy of one dimension over the others in specific circumstances. If we consider the stress patterns of English in perceptual terms, there are a number of factors that influence a judgment of stress. The listener relies on differences in:

the length of syllables;
the loudness of syllables;
the pitch of syllables;

the sound qualities occurring in the syllables;
the kinaesthetic memories associated with his own production of the syllables he is receiving.

These factors form a complex in which no one is independent of the others. Thus a stress judgment may be influenced by the length of a syllable, and particularly by the length of the vowel that it contains, but not independently of the vowel quality. In the English word /mo:bid/ the first syllable is perceived as stressed, partly because the first vowel is long. This vowel is, however, long in opposition to the first vowel of /mo:biditi/ and not in contrast with the second vowel /i/, for in the latter word, the first vowel is still long in contrast with the second, although the stress is now perceived to be on the second syllable.

Certain quality differences in English have particular significance in stress judgments. The substitution of the neutral vowel /ə/ for some other vowel, the reduction of a diphthong to a pure vowel, or the centralization of a vowel are all powerful cues in the judgment of stress. Some features of consonant quality, such as the strength of friction or aspiration and the sharpness of onset of the consonant sound may act in a similar way.

It has sometimes been denied that the listener's kinaesthetic memories of his own speech can play any part in the reception of speech. Experimental demonstration of the operation of this factor may indeed be difficult though it might possibly be achieved. The arguments generally advanced against this view are however largely irrelevant. Thus it is said that a listener may be able to understand speech in a language of which he cannot himself utter a word, and this is taken to 'prove' that kinaesthetic patterns contribute nothing to the reception of speech. This, however, is merely to assume an identity between two statements, (a) that kinaesthetic patterns contribute to the reception of speech, and (b) that kinaesthetic patterns are *essential* for the reception of speech. The second of these is, of course, quite unjustifiable and is indeed contrary to the whole character of speech as a mode of communication. The redundancy of speech has been demonstrated in a number of ways; it is important to realize that it is to be found at every level of speech activity and as a consequence there is scarcely any feature which can be said to be essential for speech communication. A system that is common to the speaker and the listener and a time pattern of change in the medium of communication are indeed the only two factors that can be regarded as essential. For the rest, speech consists of features that subserve these requirements and operate in combinations that depend upon the conditions of the moment. The purpose of experimental work is to explore these combinations and to study their relation to the conditions in which they occur. In ordinary working, and particularly in the case of a listener receiving his native language, it is probable that the listener's kinaesthetic memories play some part in his reception of speech. If this is so, it is likely that the contribution will be particularly strong in the case of stress judgments since rhythm of all kinds has a powerful motor component.

Physical correlates of the perceptual factors

In order to experiment with judgments of stress it is necessary first to determine the physical dimensions of the speech stimulus that we may expect to be closely correlated with the perceptual factors. We have already said that the influence of the listener's kinaesthetic images is not directly accessible to experimental investigation but the other four factors can be assigned physical correlates reliably from established experimental data. This does not, of course, mean that there is in any case a one-to-one correlation between the stimulus dimension and the perceptual effect.

The length of sounds will be closely correlated with the duration of given sections of the speech wave-form. Differences in loudness will be associated in part with the intensity of the speech wave-motions and this in turn will depend upon the frequency complex or formant structure of the sound. Pitch differences will depend mainly upon variations in fundamental frequency and quality differences on variations in formant structure.

The basic method of experimental study consists in presenting to a group of listeners speech sounds in which these physical dimensions can be varied independently and systematically, developing a method by which the listener's stress judgments can be recorded and determining by statistical treatment the influence of the physical variations. The experiments reported in this paper are concerned with the first three dimensions only, that is, with variations in the duration, intensity and fundamental frequency of the speech stimulus. One set of such experiments has already been reported in some detail (Fry, 1955).

Synthesis of the test material

The essence of this method is that the properties of the speech signals may be closely controlled. This is generally not possible in the case of live speech and only partially so in recorded speech, so that the most satisfactory method is to synthesize the required speech sounds in some way that will afford the necessary control over all the variables of the speech. The pattern playback equipment at the Haskins Laboratories was used for the purpose (see Liberman, Delattre and Cooper, 1952). In this machine, speech-like sounds are generated and controlled by means of a painted spectrogram, which can be made to resemble to any desired degree a spectrogram from live speech. As in the common type of speech spectrogram, the frequency composition of the sound (its formant structure) is related to the disposition of the pattern with respect to the vertical axis, the total intensity of the sound depends on both the area and the density of the traces, and the duration of any segment is associated with the extent of any configuration along the horizonal axis. The painted spectrogram forms the control system in the process of speech synthesis. The pattern playback equipment generates an extended range of harmonics of a single fundamental (120 Hz) and does not afford the possibility of changing the fundamental frequency of the synthesized sounds. The apparatus was used for the first series of experiments concerned with the duration and intensity of the synthesized syllables; in these, the fundamental frequency was kept constant at 120 Hz. The second series was concerned with the effect of varying the fundamental frequency, and for this purpose a modification of the Vocoder (the Voback) was used (Borst and Cooper, 1957). The same painted spectrograms in this case controlled the output of the channels of a Vocoder synthesizer unit, and additional tracks on the spectrogram controlled the switching on of the pseudo-larynx tone and the frequency of this tone (the larynx frequency).

Listeners' judgments of stress

The next problem in these experiments was to formulate the questions to be asked of the listeners. In all projects of this nature, it is an advantage if the subjects used can be induced to supply an operational response to the speech stimulus in conditions that do not differ too widely from those of normal speech communication. In experimenting with variations at the phonemic level, it is possible to achieve this satisfactorily by asking the subject to write down or to speak back what he hears. No special training in phonetic techniques is needed to enable the subject to show that he takes one stimulus to be *key* and another, *tea*. Reaction to differences of stress is in another category in the sense that orthography does not mark stress variations and the subject has no ready-made code in which to record them. As a consequence, the untrained subject is less aware of stress than of phonemic distinctions and it is correspondingly difficult to evoke an operational response to stress differences. There is in English, however, an association between stress pattern and grammatical function in certain classes of word; for most English speakers, the word /'sʌbdʒikt/, with trochaic rhythm is a noun, and the word /səb'dʒekt/, with iambic rhythm, a verb. It has been found that listeners with no phonetic training, on hearing an isolated word of this type, can judge whether they hear the noun or the verb form and in this way can register whether they hear the stress on the first or second syllable. The material used was confined to five pairs of words, all of this type: *subject, object, digest, contract, permit.*

The analytical basis of the test material

The next task was to synthesize material for listening tests in which variations in the chosen physical parameters could be made systematically. This involved a decision on three major points: the physical dimensions to be explored, the range of variation to be covered and the size of the steps within each range. The obvious basis for such decisions is to be found in analytical study of the type of material to be synthesized and spectrograms were made of utterances of the test words by a number of different speakers. An account of this work, together with some of the measurements obtained, is to be found in a previously published report (Fry, 1955), and it will be enough here to indicate the general method. The selected words, both nouns and verbs, were included in sentences and great care was taken to ensure a common context, as far as possible, for both the noun and the verb in each pair. Twelve speakers then recorded all the sentences and spectrograms were made from the recordings.

The physical parameters selected for the first series of experiments were duration and intensity and the spectrograms were examined and measured in order to establish the modes and range of variation which were associated with the two word classes, noun and verb. Several well-marked features emerged as a result of this analysis. First, the differences between a noun and a verb were carried almost entirely by the 'vowel' stretches of the wavemotions (see Fry, 1955) and it was evident that in synthesizing test material the whole range of variation might justifiably be made in the 'vowel' stretches. Second, the distribution of both durations and intensities showed a well-defined bimodality; that is to say the noun/verb opposition was reflected in the physical data and in fact there was very little overlapping of the values for the members of each pair of words.

This effect was even more apparent when the ratio of one vowel to another was plotted rather than the absolute value for either duration or intensity. This agrees with the linguistic description of stress as a relation between syllables and is very much to be expected at the physical level since stress relations survive changes in the rate of utterance (involving changes in absolute durations) and also changes in the mean intensity level of the speech. Hence the synthesis of test material was carried out having regard to suitable ratios of duration and intensity and the range of variation was established in similar terms.

The third feature of the analytical data was that the distribution of duration and intensity ratios showed certain differences. Figure 1 shows that the measurements fall into two groups with a well-defined cross-over point from noun to verb values; in the case of intensity, this fell approximately in the middle of the range for all the five pairs of words. That is to say, the range of intensity ratios covered by the twelve speakers was approximately

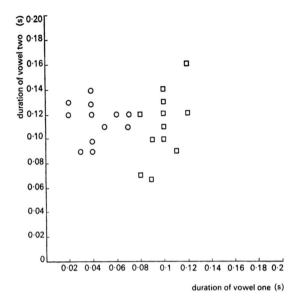

Figure 1a Measured vowel durations for the word-pair *subject*

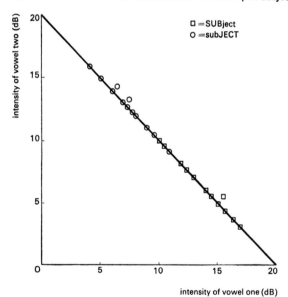

Figure 1b Measured intensities for the word-pair *subject*. In the plotting of intensity, the overall intensity level is brought to the same value for all speakers

the same in the noun as in the verb; for *subject*, the ratio V1/V2 was 14 dB in the noun and −14 dB in the verb, with the cross-over point at equal intensity for the two vowels. In the case of duration ratio, each pair of words had its own pattern of variation; the range and the cross-over value were different for each of the five pairs of words. For *contract*, for example, the range of duration ratios was from 0·1 to 1·06 and the cross-over value 0·50, while for *digest* the range was from 0·53 to 2·87, and the cross-over at 1·25.

In selecting values of duration and intensity for synthesizing the test words, the chief object was to cover as nearly as possible the total range of observed values and at the same time to make certain of exploring the part of the range close to the cross-over value from noun to verb. On the basis of the analytical data, it was decided to adopt an intensity range of ±10 dB for all the five pairs of words and to use a different range of duration ratios for each pair.

The number of steps to be used in each range was partly determined by the length of the listening test that subjects could be asked to undergo and it was found that, from this point of view, five steps in each dimension was a suitable number. In both duration and intensity, the two extreme values were chosen to be near the ends of the observed range, the middle value was approximately at the cross-over value from noun to verb and the intervening values were chosen with the object of exploring the uncertainty range between noun and verb. In the case of *subject*, for example, the observed duration ratios (V1/V2) ranged from 0·15 to 1·28, with the cross-over at 0·66, and the chosen experimental values were 0·25, 0·40, 0·60, 1·00 and 1·25. For all pairs of words, the intensity ratios (V1/V2) were −10, −5, 0, 5 and 10 dB.

The combination of physical cues

It has been pointed out already that judgments of stress depend upon a complex of perceptual factors which are interdependent. It follows that the effects of the physical correlates of these perceptual factors are also likely to be interrelated. In any speech sequence presented to a listener, the duration, intensity, fundamental frequency and formant structure all act as cues which determine the listener's stress judgments and there is no method of rendering any of these physical dimensions inoperative. The clearest example of this is to be found, perhaps, in the formant structure of the speech sounds. In the verb /səb'dʒekt/ the first syllable contains the vowel /ə/ and the second /e/, and formant structure typical of these sounds is an important factor in determining the listener's stress judgment. A modification of formant structure, in the direction of /ʌ/ in the first vowel or in the direction of /i/ in the second, would at once bias the stress judgments towards the trochaic or noun form. In synthesizing these words, therefore, whatever the formant structure may be, it is bound to exert a biasing effect. Hence in experiments with synthesized speech, we may decide to vary any one of the four physical dimensions and to keep the other three constant, but the chosen values for the latter will none the less contribute to the listeners' stress judgments.

The duration and intensity test

In the first series of experiments, it was decided to maintain constant values for formant structure and for fundamental frequency and to vary duration and intensity. Fundamental frequency for all the voiced sounds was kept constant at 120 Hz. The formant structure during the vowel stretches gave a vowel quality corresponding to the stressed vowel in every case; that is, the first vowel in all versions of *subject* sounded like /ʌ/ and the second vowel, like /e/, and similarly for all the other word-pairs. Hence the biasing effect of the formant structure would tend in the opposite direction in the first and second syllables of a word and would thus be partially cancelled out. Another consideration was that the test was first made with a large group of American listeners. In American speech, it happens quite commonly that there is little or no opposition of vowel quality in such noun and verb pairs and hence the biasing effect would be rather less considerable. It turned out, in practice, that there was no marked difference between the responses of the American subjects and those of a small group of English subjects.

The variations in duration and intensity ratio covered the required ranges in five steps, as has been already indicated. In order to economize in test material the two sets of variations were combined together in one set of test items. For each of the five word-pairs, versions were synthesized which covered the five steps of duration ratio and the five steps of intensity ratio, each value of duration being combined with each value of intensity. This gave a listening test of 125 items, which appeared to be about the longest test that listeners could comfortably manage on one testing occasion. All versions of the test word-pairs were recorded and assembled in random order. Each test item was inserted in a carrier sentence (also synthesized) and was heard in the context 'Where is the accent in – ?' Listeners were asked to make a response to every item and to register this on a test sheet where the appropriate word-pair was printed for each test-item in this form: SUBject: subJECT, CONtract: conTRACT, and so on. They were asked to underline the form that they heard.

Results of the duration and intensity test

This test was carried out by 118 subjects; the effect of variation in the physical cues was measured in terms of the proportion of these listeners who judged a given stimulus to be a noun or verb, that is to have trochaic or iambic rhythm. Since all subjects made a judgment about every test item, the number of noun judgments for one item is equal to 118– (the number of verb judgments). For simplicity, therefore, all results of the test are given as the number of noun judgments, usually presented as a percentage of the total number of subjects.

In the case of all five word-pairs, the total range of stimuli was enough to cause a complete swing of the listener's judgments from noun to verb; one version in each set produced a noun judgment from 97–100 per cent of the listeners, and at the other end of the range, one version produced less than 10 per cent of noun judgments, with the exception of *permit* in which the lowest value was 13 per cent. The change in judgments followed the expected trend: where V1 was long in proportion to V2, there was a majority of noun judgments, and similarly where V1 was more intense than V2. The effect was reinforced in versions where V1 was both longer and more intense than V2. The disagreement amongst subjects was greater, that is the percentage of noun judgments was nearest to 50 per cent, when the duration and intensity cues were opposed to each other, as for example in versions where V1 was longer but of lower intensity than V2.

The relative strength of the duration and the intensity cue

There is no doubt from the experimental results that in the English word-pairs used in the test, both duration and intensity ratio have a marked influence in determining stress judgments. An interesting question that one might try to answer on the basis of these results concerns the relative strength of the two cues. Information on this point can be abstracted from the results by summing the noun judgments for all intensity ratios at each duration ratio, i.e. by taking the mean of the column values in the matrix of results. This gives the effect of changing duration ratio, and similarly summing for each intensity ratio, i.e. taking the row averages, gives the effect of changing intensity. The total taken for all five word-pairs showed that the total change in noun judgments due to duration was from 12 per cent to 92 per cent, and that due to intensity ratio was from 40 per cent to 82 per cent.

In order to establish the significance of this relation, we need to make a quantitative comparison of the duration and intensity ratios used in the experiment. Since the range of values was approximately equal to those found in the analytical data, that is in natural speech, the range of duration change can be regarded as at least in this sense equivalent to the range of intensity change. In Figure 2, the aggregate of noun judgments for each duration and intensity ratio is plotted. This is a formal representation of the results in which the abscissae are simply succeeding steps of duration or intensity change and not points on a quantitative scale. It is evident from the experimental results that an extension of the duration range would not lead to any major change in noun judgments since these already cover nearly the whole range 0–100 per cent. Whether extension of the intensity range would give judgment values near to 0 or to 100 per cent could be determined by experiment, but it was in fact clear from the preliminary syntheses

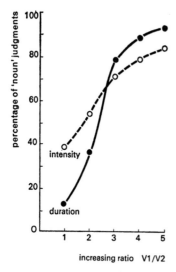

Figure 2 Percentage of listeners' 'noun' judgments for all test words as a function of (a) vowel duration ratio and (b) vowel intensity ratio

that preceded the final test that extreme steps of intensity change from V1 to V2 served only to make the stimulus sound very unnatural without increasing the impression of strong stress. Such an experiment would, further, leave unresolved the question of equivalence between duration range and intensity range and it seemed therefore worthwhile to seek an alternative method of treating the existing results in order to reach some conclusion concerning the relative strength of the duration and intensity cues.

As we have already said, the response to any stimulus in the test is made up of four factors: the response due to duration, that due to intensity, to fundamental frequency and to formant structure. The force of any of these factors could be more reliably abstracted from the data if the degree of agreement amongst subjects were expressed on a scale which was not artificially compressed by the barriers of 0 and 100 per cent. Such a measure is provided by taking the logit number for each test item instead of the percentage of noun judgments. The subjects were able to make one of two responses to each item. If p = proportion of noun judgments, and $q = (1-p)$ = proportion of verb judgments, then logit $p = \log_e p/q$. The range of logit values will be $\pm\infty$, the smallest degree of agreement (50 per cent) will have the logit 0; positive values of logit p will indicate agreement in a noun judgment and negative values agreement in a verb judgment. The logit response for each test item will represent a factor due to duration and a factor due to intensity and these factors can then be abstracted as before by taking the row and column averages of the matrix of results. An inspection of the crude data made it clear that they would not yield an exact fit with this type of treatment since there were several irregularities in the pattern. A difficulty arises with values of 0 per cent and 100 per cent, which would theoretically give logits of $-\infty$ and $+\infty$; it seemed good enough for our purposes to consider them crudely as $\frac{1}{2}$ per cent (logit $= -5\cdot293$) and $99\frac{1}{2}$ per cent (logit $= 5\cdot293$) since the irregularities in the pattern make it impossible to use the most refined statistical methods.

The procedure was to calculate the logit values for all percentages occurring in the results and to tabulate these for each of the word-pairs used in the test. The common logit for each duration ratio was obtained by taking the column averages and for each intensity ratio by taking the row averages. The supposition is that the logit for any combination of duration and intensity can be expressed as a sum of a duration effect and an intensity effect: one may reasonably expect this to be approximately true although, as we have said, the irregularities in the distribution make it impossible to test the hypothesis with any exactness. We can only measure relative effects: since both the column and the row averages may be considered to contain the general average, we have subtracted this general average from all column (i.e. duration) averages to avoid counting it twice over. The logits for each word-pair were plotted separately as a function of duration and intensity ratio and a typical result (for the word-pair *subject*) is given in Figure 3.

It will be seen that the logits both for duration and for intensity lie approximately on a straight line. We may conclude from this that succeeding steps of duration change produce equal changes in the logit and the same is true for intensity changes. This means that the ratio p/q, i.e. noun/verb, is multiplied by nearly the same factor for equal changes in duration and intensity and thus rises in a geometrical progression. Since this is so, we may now compare the effect of duration and intensity by comparing the slope of the two lines. In the case of *subject*, the whole range of intensity change of 20 dB produces a logit rise of $2\cdot5$. On the duration line, a change in the logit of $2\cdot5$ is effected by a change in duration ratio of approximately $0\cdot6$. Similar calculations in the case of the other word pairs give the following

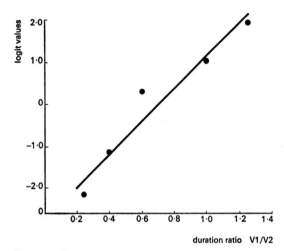

Figure 3a Common logit values for duration ratio from the results for the word-pair *subject*

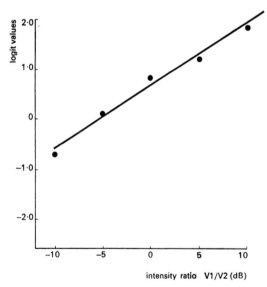

Figure 3b Common logit values for intensity ratio from the results for the word-pair *subject*

results: *object*, 20 dB is approximately equivalent to a duration ratio change of 0·4, *digest*, 0·16, *contract*, 0·35 and *permit* 0·9. This method of treating the data therefore affords a means of making a quantitative comparison of the duration and intensity cues and their influence on stress judgments.

Stress judgments and variation in fundamental frequency

A second series of experiments was undertaken to explore the role of fundamental frequency variations in determining stress judgments. It is clear that such variations will affect the intonation pattern perceived by the listener, and in English speech, the perception of a rhythmic pattern is very closely bound up with the perception of intonation. In the case of the word-pairs used in the previous experiment, in many contexts the sentence intonation pattern would have an over-riding influence on the decision as to whether the noun or verb form had occurred. This factor complicates the problem of examining the part played by fundamental frequency variation in stress judgments since the resulting pitch changes will not only contribute to the perception of stress but will tend to impose upon the stimulus sequence a sentence intonation which may be decisive for the stress judgment.

The purpose of this set of experiments was to study the effect of fundamental frequency variation in conditions where the influence of sentence intonation is reduced to a minimum. It is generally true that in English the functionally most important parts of a sentence intonation pattern are syllables in which the pitch changes in the course of the syllable. Syllables with level tone are the nearest one can get to units that are neutral with respect to sentence intonation, though it is obviously not possible to make sentence intonation inoperative. These experiments were made, therefore, by synthesizing sequences in which fundamental frequency remained constant throughout a syllable and any change of frequency was made between syllables.

The material was confined to the word-pair *subject*. Versions of this were synthesized in which a change of fundamental frequency was effected at the junction between the first and second syllable. It has been already said that this synthesis was carried out with the Voback (Borst and Cooper, 1957), a device in which hand-painted spectrograms are used to control the synthesizer action of an 18-channel Vocoder. The duration, intensity and formant structure of the synthesized sounds were controlled in a manner similar to that used in the previous experiments (though the sound produced by the Vocoder is of a different character) and additional sections of the painted pattern served to control the switching of the buzz and hiss generators and the frequency of the fundamental during the buzz sequences. This frequency was measured by means of a General Electric audio-frequency meter connected across the buzz generator.

As in the previous test, two physical dimensions were explored at the same time; the duration ratios already used in *subject* were used in the new test and were combined with step-changes of frequency ranging from 5 Hz to 90 Hz. The intensity ratio was constant at equal intensity for V1 and V2 and the formant structure was the same as in the first test.

The choice of fundamental frequencies for this test involved a number of considerations that should be briefly mentioned. The listeners were to hear a series of sense-groups, each containing two syllables, and to make a judgment about the stress pattern. The effect of sentence intonation was to be minimized, but apart from this it was desirable that the stimuli should be as natural as possible since this was likely to make the judgments more consistent. In English speech there is a strong tendency for a sense group to be spoken in one key and for musical modulation to take place between groups. This effect of key depends largely upon the occurrence in the group of some reference pitch, of which the speaker is unaware, but which regulates the pitch of all the syllables in the group. In the test items it was therefore decided to adopt a reference frequency which would occur in every item, and in order to limit the number of variables in the test, the same reference was used throughout the test. The synthesized speech was intended to sound like that of a male speaker, and the selected reference frequency of 97 Hz gave this effect successfully.

The range of variation in fundamental frequency was decided on similar grounds. In the intonation patterns heard from most English speakers changes in pitch of more than one octave are infrequent and are not often met with in successive syllables, even from the most excitable speakers. Preliminary syntheses showed in fact that a change of 90 Hz on 97 Hz (approximately a semi-tone less than one octave) produced stimuli that sounded rather unnatural and hence this upper limit was adopted as being likely to show up the maximum effect of frequency change without introducing very unnatural stimuli which would perhaps make listeners respond in a random manner.

The relation between the reference frequency and that of the other syllable was found to be important for the naturalness of the stimulus. Each syllable was on one tone, that is of constant frequency, and if the relation between the syllables was such as to make the impression of an exact musical interval, the test word appeared to be sung and listeners found it difficult to make a stress judgment. Care was taken therefore to avoid this effect as far as possible and this was one reason for the fixing of the reference frequency at 97 Hz. In preliminary experiments a reference frequency of 100 Hz with frequency intervals of multiples of 5 Hz was used. Many of the stimuli then had much too musical an effect which was eliminated by the change of the reference frequency to 97 Hz. Frequency changes as small as 3 Hz were used in the first experiments but listeners' responses to these items were very inconsistent and were disregarded in the final test. The frequency steps ultimately selected were designed to explore adequately the range of variation up to 90 Hz and the experimental values were 5, 10, 15, 20, 30, 40, 60 and 90 Hz.

It was expected that an important factor in determining stress judgments would be the direction of frequency change in the course of the stimulus word and it was necessary therefore to make the step-change of frequency in both directions, that is in one case with the first vowel on a higher frequency than the second, in the other case with the first vowel lower. In all cases the lower vowel was at the reference frequency of 97 Hz. The total of frequency changes was therefore 16, each of the 8 intervals used in two directions. The 5 duration ratios were combined with each of the frequency changes, giving a total of 80 test items. In this test the items were not inserted in a carrier sentence since this would tend to increase rather than to minimize the influence of sentence intonation on the results. Subjects were asked to register their responses in the same way as in the previous test.

Results of the fundamental frequency test

The effect of pitch on the perception of stress is generally held to be that a higher pitch produces an impression of greater stress. This experiment was designed to test first the hypothesis that, if two syllables differ in fundamental frequency, the syllable having the higher frequency is more likely to be judged as stressed. It was intended also to determine whether this principle, if it operates at all, is subject to modification through the effect of duration ratio, which was shown by the first experiment to be an important factor in stress judgments. Last, the experiment was intended to show whether the size of a frequency step between syllables has a marked effect on stress judgments.

If a syllable of higher fundamental frequency tends to be judged stressed then in this test the step-down change of fundamental would lead listeners to perceive the stress on the first syllable of the test word, that is, it would tend to increase the number of noun judgments, and the step-up change would decrease the number of noun judgments. In all, 41 subjects carried out this test; they included a group of American and a group of English speakers. Figure 4 gives the results of the test as percentage noun judgments for each duration ratio, with the step-down and step-up changes plotted separately.

The effect of changing duration ratio reappears clearly in the results of this test and the shape of the curves is similar to those obtained in the first experiment, but there is good evidence of the effect of fundamental frequency change suggested by the hypothesis. The step-up change of frequency moves the whole curve in the direction of fewer noun judgments and the step-down change displaces it in the direction of more noun judgments. The difference between means for step-up and step-down change is significant at the 1 per cent level for all duration ratios.

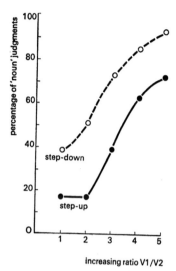

Figure 4 The effect of step changes of fundamental frequency on 'noun' judgments for the word-pair *subject*

Effect of the size of the step-change in frequency

In the case of both duration and intensity ratio it has been shown that progressive increase in these quantities is reflected in increasing noun judgments by the subjects. The next question to be asked with regard to fundamental frequency is whether increase in the frequency ratio of V1 to V2 would have a similar effect, or whether fundamental frequency change, unlike duration and intensity change, tends to produce an all-or-none effect.

The effects of frequency change were abstracted from the data by combining all duration ratios for each step change of frequency. In order to detect any possible trend in the results, the logit response for each frequency was calculated and the values are shown in Figure 5. The first important feature of these results is the discontinuity in logit response between the values -5 and 5 Hz, that is at the cross-over from a step-up to a step-down change in fundamental frequency. This confirms the conclusion already reached by inspecting the results for duration ratio in this experiment. Increase in the size of the frequency step appears to produce no marked trend in the results, however. The logit values for the step changes lie approximately on a horizontal line, indicating that the size of the change is having no appreciable effect. For the step-up change, if there is any trend, it is in

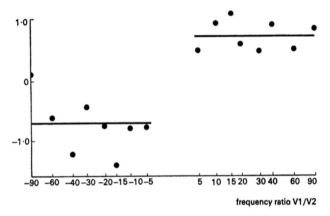

Figure 5 Logit response for step change of fundamental frequency. Frequencies are plotted on a logarithmic scale

the direction opposite to the expected one. An increase in the size of the step-up gives a slight increase in noun judgments, rather than the expected decrease. This effect is contributed largely by the 90 Hz change and it may well be that this large step-up appeared even more unnatural to the listeners than an equal step-down and thus caused greater uncertainty in the judgments.

These results provide good evidence for supposing that a step-change of fundamental frequency affects stress judgments in a specific way. It appears likely that so long as the resulting pitch change is easily perceptible to the listener, he tends to judge a higher syllable as more stressed, but the magnitude of the pitch change makes little contribution to his judgment. This would be consistent with the fact that a frequency change of 3 Hz led to a dispersion of the listeners' judgments; it may well have been too small to cause the all-or-none effect in the perception of stress.

Sentence intonation and stress judgments

The role of intonation in determining stress judgments has already been touched upon in connection with the previous experiment in which efforts were made to reduce the influence of sentence intonation. It is clear, however, that any account of the factors affecting stress judgments is incomplete without an attempt to answer certain questions about sentence intonation. The most important of these is the question whether, as one would expect, sentence intonation is so strong as to be capable of outweighing all other factors in stress judgments.

A third set of experiments was carried out to answer this question. As in the previous experiments, these were designed to explore a range of variation in physical cues and to determine the effect of this variation on stress judgments in the same way as before. The important variable was again fundamental frequency, but this time the variations were chosen to allow sentence intonation the maximum effect.

It was said earlier that, broadly speaking, a syllable containing a pitch change is functionally more important in English intonation than a level syllable, and for this third test versions of the word-pair *subject* were synthesized in which fundamental frequency changed in the course of one vowel stretch. It should be made clear, however, that the purpose was not to reproduce faithfully certain English intonations, but rather to cover a wide range of patterns of fundamental frequency variation and to study the effect of these.

The syllable inflection test

Again the intensity ratio of the two vowels in each version was kept constant at equal intensity and the same formant structure was used as before. The five duration ratios were combined with the fundamental frequency variations. In order to reduce the number of variables, the frequency range over which the fundamental varied within one vowel was kept constant throughout the test. A reference frequency of 97 Hz was again used, that is at some time during the stimulus word the fundamental reached this minimum value. The highest frequency used was 130 Hz and when frequency changed in the course of a syllable it covered the whole of this range from 97 to 130 Hz. A number of stimulus words included one level syllable and the fundamental frequency for such syllables was either 97 or 130 Hz.

Two types of frequency change within the syllable were used. In the first type, the frequency changed continuously throughout the vowel, and in the second, the frequency change occupied only half the vowel duration. Figure 6 shows the graph of frequency change with time for the types of syllable used in the test. It will be seen that the rate of change of frequency was allowed to vary with the duration of the vowel. Stimulus words were synthesized which covered a range of sixteen patterns, each combined with five duration ratios. The different patterns are listed in Table 1 where the frequency variation for each word is shown symbolically and the letters serve to identify the patterns in discussing the results.

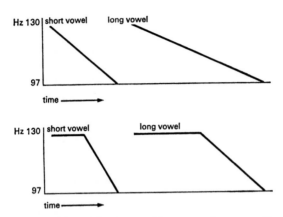

Figure 6 Types of fundamental frequency change used in the syllable inflection test

Table 1

	Frequency pattern	Range of noun judgments (%)	Mean
A	＼＿	57–95	80
B	＿＼	12–38	24
C	＿＼	38–83	59
D	＿／	3–74	39
E	／＿	50–95	74
F	／＿	42–96	70
G	＼＼	8–66	32
H	／＼	41–88	70
I	＼／	12–82	53
J	＾＼＿	49–95	79
K	＾＼／	38–87	63
L	＿＾＼	13–59	34
M	＿＾＼	3–49	24
N	＼＾＼	8–37	17
O	＿＿／	16–74	51
P	＿＿／	8–61	34

Results of the syllable inflection test

Responses to this test were obtained from 76 subjects, including both American and English speakers. The first important consideration in examining the results is that the frequency variations cannot in this case be placed on a quantitative scale; the test was designed to show up an all-or-none effect and it is for this that we have to look in the data from the test. It is to be expected, and the data indeed show once more, that increasing duration ratio will have the effect of increasing the number of noun judgments, but the first question is whether any patterns of frequency variation override the duration cue. In the absence of a fundamental frequency cue, for example when the five duration ratios are combined with equal intensity in the two vowels, on a monotone, then the smallest duration ratio produces a majority of verb judgments, and the largest ratio gives a majority of nouns. A simple criterion might be applied first of all to the data from

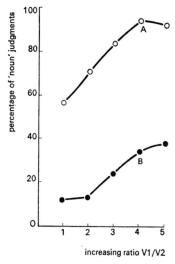

Figure 7 The effect on 'noun' judgments of two patterns of fundamental frequency change (see Table 1)

the syllable inflection test and we might look for any frequency pattern for which the number of noun judgments either never falls below or never reaches 50 per cent, that is for cases in which the whole curve is transposed above or below the 50 per cent level. Such cases are to be found in the results and Figure 7 gives the curves for two such patterns, A and B. For pattern A, even with the smallest duration ratio, there is a majority of noun judgments and for pattern B, the greatest duration ratio still produces a substantial majority of verb judgments. These two frequency patterns will, obviously, sound to the listener like two common English intonation patterns in which the fall normally occurs in the stressed syllable and it is not surprising that they should influence stress judgments so strongly. A similar effect is to be found for patterns J and M, which are functionally similar to A and B. The range and the mean of noun judgments for all patterns are given in Table 1, and it will be seen that the range for J is 49–95 per cent, that for M is 3–49. The influence of fundamental frequency change is not, however, confined to patterns giving rise to a familiar intonation. Both E and F produced an un-English intonation but nonetheless evoked a large majority of noun judgments because of the inflection in the first syllable.

The effect of different types of frequency pattern

A wide variety of patterns was used in this experiment in the hope of answering certain questions concerning the effectiveness of different types of fundamental frequency variation in determining stress judgments. The stimulus words contained three kinds of syllable: level syllables, syllables with a linear change of frequency and syllables with a curvilinear change. These syllables occurred sometimes as the first and sometimes as the second syllable of a stimulus word and it was possible by grouping the results to obtain some information on the relative power of these syllabic patterns to influence stress judgments. If we compare patterns A and B, for example, a noun judgment for A means that the subject heard a linear change of frequency as stressed in contrast to a level syllable. In B, a verb judgment means the same thing. But a verb judgment for A or a noun judgment for B means that the subject heard a level syllable as stressed in contrast to a linear change. Provided that the five duration ratios are equally represented in the samples, we can group sets of data together in this way and obtain some indication of the association between types of syllable and the judgment that the syllable is stressed. The first contrast treated in this way was that between inflected and level syllables. In all patterns that contained both a level and an inflected syllable 66 per cent of all inflected syllables were judged stressed and 33 per cent of level syllables. This difference was highly significant at the 1 per cent level.

The two types of inflected syllable were compared in a similar way. For example, patterns A and J contain an inflected first syllable, in the one case a linear and in the other a curvilinear inflection. By comparing the number of noun judgments in this and in similar cases we gain a measure of the relative effectiveness of the two types of syllable. Of all syllables with linear frequency change, 62 per cent were judged stressed, whilst 72 per cent of the syllables with curvilinear change were heard as stressed. This difference is not significant.

The last comparison made in this way was between rising and falling inflections. The intonation patterns of English involve both rising and falling tones and the word-pairs used in these experiments could certainly occur in contexts where noun and verb might both be required by the sentence intonation pattern to bear a rising or a falling tone. It would appear, therefore, that this stress judgment should be independent of the difference between rising and falling changes in fundamental frequency. The result obtained by grouping the data was that 61 per cent of rising syllables were judged stressed and 64 per cent of falling syllables, a difference that was not significant.

A final comment is necessary on this experiment with frequency patterns. The variations in frequency indicated in Table 1 should not be simply equated with English intonation patterns. Whilst it is true that many items appeared to have a fairly natural intonation, it cannot be assumed that this intonation was necessarily the one suggested by the frequency pattern. A preliminary attempt has been made to correlate the intonation pattern with the frequency pattern by asking several trained listeners to note the intonation they heard in each item. It is clear from these judgments that a number of the vowels are so short that a change of fundamental frequency is not perceived and the syllable is judged to have a level tone. Other effects of this sort may appear as a result of further investigation on these lines.

Conclusions

The experiments reported in this paper represent an attempt to explore three physical dimensions which appear to be important in determining stress judgments in English: duration, intensity and fundamental frequency. The importance of the duration ratio is confirmed by the fresh data presented here; it seems that in English, in a considerable variety of conditions, changes of vowel duration ratio can swing listeners' perception of strong stress from the first to the second syllable in the type of disyllable that has been considered. There seems no reason to doubt that this factor operates in stress judgments in other rhythmic contexts. Intensity ratio has a similar influence but it is somewhat less marked. The data show no case in which change of intensity ratio caused a complete shift of the stress judgment from first to second syllable.

Change in fundamental frequency differs from change of duration and intensity in that it tends to produce an all-or-none effect, that is to say the magnitude of the frequency change seems to be relatively unimportant while the fact that a frequency change has taken place is all-important. The experiments with a step-change of frequency show that a higher syllable is more likely to be perceived as stressed; the experiments with more complex patterns of fundamental frequency change suggest that sentence intonation is an overriding factor in determining the perception of stress and that in this sense the fundamental frequency cue may outweigh the duration cue.

In conclusion, it may be necessary to reiterate that all judgments of stress in natural speech depend on the complicated interaction of a number of cues. Experiments such as those described above require a drastic simplification of the conditions in which the judgment is made and even so there are still a number of factors which cannot be controlled until further work has been done in this field. The formant structure cue still remains to be investigated and it is quite probable that for English listeners, at least, the changes in vowel quality introduced by variations in formant structure may prove one of the most powerful factors in determining stress.

The author wishes to thank Dr F. S. Cooper and the staff of the Haskins Laboratories for their help in carrying out some of these experiments and Dr C. A. B. Smith for suggesting methods of treating the data.

References

BLOCH, B., and TRAGER, G. L. (1942), *Outline of Linguistic Analysis*, Waverley Press, Baltimore.

BLOOMFIELD, L. (1933) *Language*, Holt, Rinehart & Winston.

BORST, J. M., and COOPER, F. S. (1957), 'Speech research devices based on a channel Vocoder', *J. acoust. Soc. Amer.*, vol. 29, p. 777 (abstract).

FRY, D. B. (1955), 'Duration and intensity as physical correlates of linguistic stress', *J. acoust. Soc. Amer.*, vol. 27, pp. 765–8 .

JONES, D. (1949), *An Outline of English Phonetics*, Heffer, Cambridge.

LIBERMAN, A. M., DELATTRE, P. C., and COOPER, F. S. (1932), 'The role of selected stimulus variables in the perception of the unvoiced stop consonants', *Amer. J. Psychol.*, vol. 65, pp. 497–516.

29 Dennis B. Fry

The Dependence of Stress Judgments on Vowel Formant Structure

Dennis B. Fry, 'The dependence of stress judgments on vowel formant structure',
in E. Zwirner and W. Bethge (eds.), *Proceedings of the 6th International Congress of
Phonetic Sciences*, Karger, 1965, pp. 306–11.

The experiments reported in this paper attempted to explore the part played by vowel quality in stress judgments obtained from English listeners. Versions of the word-pairs *object, contract, subject* and *digest* were synthesized in which there was systematic variation of the frequency of the first and second formants in the first syllable of *object, contract* and *digest* and the second syllable of *object* and *subject*. Variations in vowel duration ratio were introduced in the same stimuli in order to provide a means of estimating the weight to be assigned to the changes in formant structure. The specification of the test stimuli is contained in the information shown in Table 1. The fundamental frequency of the periodic sounds was kept constant at 120 Hz throughout. The overall intensity of syllables was regulated so that the maximum intensity in the two syllables of a test word was equal and a constant difference of 6 dB between formant 1 and formant 2 was maintained throughout. In Table 1, f1, f2 and f3 refer to frequencies used in the first syllable of *object, contract* and *digest*, f4, f5 and f6 to those in the second syllable of *object* and *subject*; f1 and f4 are the formant arrangements likely to give the lowest number of 'noun' judgments. Duration ratios are labelled d1, d2 and d3; d1 indicates the duration ratio likely to give the lowest number of 'noun' judgments.

The stimuli were made into a listening test in which each stimulus occurred once. They were in random order and were preceded by five practice items. Stimuli succeeded each other at intervals of 2 s with a gap of 10 s after each set of 10 items. No carrier sentence or number announcement was used. Stress judgments were obtained from one hundred subjects who were all young speakers of Southern English, nearly all brought up in the south or in the Midlands.

In presenting the results of these experiments, a recurring difficulty is the problem of comparing the scale of variation in the two dimensions. In the present case, it can be said that the range of variation in F1/F2 was as wide as it could be without introducing a marked unnaturalness in the vowels which provided the end-point of each range; that is to say that in the first syllable of *object* and *contract*, for example, the F1/F2 values at the ends of the range gave as clear an [o] and as clear an [ə] as could be obtained. It has been shown in an earlier paper that context must be expected to play a considerable part in any judgments based on vowel quality. In previous experiments, it has been found consistently that this context effect works in

Table 1 Experimental duration ratios (V1/V2)

	d1	d2	d3
object	0·45	0·66	1·33
contract	0·2	0·53	0·8
digest	0·63	1·0	1·3
subject	0·25	0·6	1·0

Experimental F1/F2 values (Hz)

		First syllable				Second syllable		
		F1	F2	F1	F2	F1	F2	F3
object	f 1	570	1380			570	1980	
	f 2	600	1260			570	1980	
	f 3	600	1020			570	1980	
contract	f 1	570	1380			720	1800	2520
	f 2	600	1260			720	1800	2520
	f 3	600	1020			720	1800	2520
digest	f 1	480	2040			570	1980	
	f 2	840	1440 →	570	1800	570	1980	
	f 3	840	1440 →	480	2040	570	1980	
object	f 4	600	1020			570	1980	
	f 5	600	1020			540	2160	
	f 6	600	1020			400	2280	
subject	f 4	720	1320			570	1980	
	f 5	720	1320			540	2160	
	f 6	720	1320			400	2280	

the direction of contrast, that is to say that the perceptual difference between vowels is increased by their juxtaposition (Fry, Abramson, Eimas and Liberman, 1962). If we assume that the same tendency holds good with regard to the stimuli in the present experiments, this would mean that an [o], f3, would sound more back and more open when it followed the corresponding f2 or f1, and an [ə], f1, would sound more central when it followed the corresponding f2 or f3. The effect would therefore be to force the judgments at one end of the scale further in the direction of 'noun' and at the other end, further in the direction of 'verb', thereby increasing the apparent effect of the variation in F 1/F2. That some influence of this kind was at work is suggested by the rather anomalous results obtained with the middle F1/F2 value in some word-pairs, where in one case f2 produced slightly more 'nouns' than f3 and in two other cases the same number of 'nouns' as f1.

The relative effect of the formant changes and the duration changes can be judged from the range of percentage 'noun' judgments given in Table 2.

Table 2

	Percentage 'nouns'	
	f 1–3	d 1–3
object	45–62	32–72
contract	35–52	12–72
digest	33–56	14–76
	f 4–6	d 1–3
object	60–65	39–84
subject	57–63	31–82

In every case the increase in 'noun' judgments produced by the change in duration ratio is greatly in excess of that produced by the change in formant frequencies. There is no doubt that in the conditions of this experiment, the weight of the duration cue is very considerably greater than that of the formant structure cue. This fact is expressed in Figure 1 where the 'noun' scores for all word-pairs are pooled and the effect of the three steps of duration change and three steps of formant change are abstracted. The difficulty of comparing or equating the two scales has already been pointed out; here the steps of change are set off arbitrarily on the horizontal scale as though they were equal, with the duration and formant values giving the greatest number of 'verb' judgments nearest the origin. In the case of the formant values, f1 and 4, f2 and 5, and f3 and 6 are pooled.

It seemed clear from preliminary experiments that there was a certain asymmetry with respect to the effect of formant change in the first and the second syllables of the words: vowel change in the first syllable had a greater effect on the judgments than change in the second syllable. This fact is shown in Figure 2 where the effects of f1–3 and of f4–6 are plotted separately. This difference might be explained simply by the fact that in the particular words employed in the test the formant change in the second

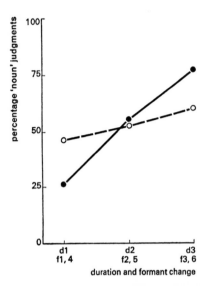

Figure 1 The effect of changes in duration ratio and FI/F2 plot on the percentage of 'noun' judgments, scores for all word-pairs and all subjects pooled. The continuous curve refers to duration ratio and the dotted curve to formant structure

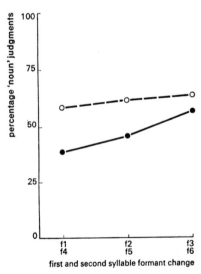

Figure 2 The effect of changes in formant structure in the first and second syllable. The continuous curve refers to change in the first syllable, and the dotted curve to change in the second

syllables was smaller than that in the first, judged either phonetically or by the crude test of the difference between F1 and F2 in hertz. The change from [o] to [ə] would probably strike many people as being perceptually greater than the change from [e] to [i]; in the stimuli used in the test, the frequency difference between F1 and F2 changed in the first progression from 420 to 810 Hz and in the second from 1410 to 1880 Hz, a much smaller proportional change. When listening to the synthetic stimuli, however, it is difficult to resist the impression that there is something in the situation which renders vowel change in the second syllable really less effective than change in the first syllable. It is not easy to see how this can be checked further by experiment except perhaps by synthesizing a series in which the vowel quality in the second syllable of such word-pairs as *subject* and *object* varied from [e] to [ə]. The latter pronunciation has a certain regional flavour but it might be possible to find out whether the effect could be enhanced in this way.

The relative weight of formant structure and duration ratio

The difficulty of arriving at any quantitative estimate of the relative weights of stress cues is aggravated in the case of formant changes by the fundamental problem of formulating a reasonable method of quantizing distances in the F1/F2 space. Any arrangement of scales chosen for this purpose is necessarily somewhat arbitrary and, in the absence of much fundamental work on the perceptual scales relevant to speech, is not likely to be very closely related to impressions of quality. In the present experiments, an attempt to arrive at some notion of the relations between the duration and the formant cues has been made by using the method outlined in a previous paper (Fry, 1958) of plotting the logit values for percentages resulting from changes in duration ratio and in F1/F2 plot. In this way it is possible to find out approximately what change in duration ratio has an effect on the stress judgments equal to that produced by the total change of formants used experimentally in any word-pair. These computations show that the swing in listeners' judgments due to the whole range of formant shift in the first syllable of *object* and of *digest* could be effected by a change in duration ratio of about 0·4 in the same words; for the first syllable of *contract*, the equivalent duration ratio change is about 0·16 and for the second syllable of both *object* and *subject*, about 0·1. If these ratios are compared with the ranges shown in Table 1, it will be seen that they constitute a small proportion of the total ranges used experimentally. Values given previously as a basis for comparing the effects of duration and intensity in the same word-pairs were as follows: a difference of 20 dB between the two syllables of the stimulus was about equivalent to a difference in duration ratio of 0·4 for *object*, 0·16 for *digest*, 0·35 for *contract* and 0·6 for *subject*. A difference of 20 dB is rather large, and also it must be remembered that the stimuli in the two experiments were not identical, but a comparison of the two sets of figures suggests at least that the formant structure cue for stress may in fact be less effective than the intensity cue. A firmer conclusion on this point should, however, await the results of a direct experimental comparison of the two kinds of cue in action.

References

FRY, D. B. (1958), 'Experiments in the perception of stress', *Language and Speech*, vol. 1, pp. 126–52. Reprinted here, pp. 401–24.

FRY, D. B., ABRAMSON, A. S., EIMAS, P. D., and LIBERMAN, A. M. (1962), 'The identification and discrimination of synthetic vowels', *Language and Speech*, vol. 5 pp. 171–89.

30 Kerstin Hadding-Koch and Michael Studdert-Kennedy

An Experimental Study of Some Intonation Contours

Kerstin Hadding-Koch and Michael Studdert-Kennedy, 'An experimental study of some intonation contours', *Phonetica*, vol. 11 (1964), pp. 175–85.

Introduction

Questions[1] are often said to be distinguished from statements by a terminal rise in fundamental frequency (f_0) as against a terminal fall. However, questions may also be distinguished by a comparatively high f_0 throughout the utterance (Hermann, 1942). Spectrographic analyses of Swedish speech have shown that, in this language, questions tend to be spoken on a higher f_0 than statements, usually ending in a moderate rise (Hadding-Koch, 1961). If four f_0 levels are postulated in the description, with arrows showing the direction of the terminal glide, the intonation contour[2] of a Swedish question, with a precontour marked before the stress, and the stress being indicated by two figures, could be described as 3 42 ↑ [3] (the superscript 3 indicates the terminal level of the glide), or, if less 'interested', as 2 32 ↑ [3]. A typical statement, on the other hand, could be described as 2 31 ↓ or 2 21 ↓.

Similarly, a typical American English question is said to display a continuously rising contour that may be notated, for example, 2 23 ↑ or 2 23 ↑ [4] (Pike, 1945; Bronstein, 1960). A typical American English statement may be notated exactly as in Swedish 2 31 ↓.

However, polite statements in Swedish, though spoken on a lower frequency level than questions, quite often end with a rise. In American English also, terminal rises are reported to occur in statements (Uldall, 1962). In fact Uldall, using synthetic speech, demonstrated that an utterance could have quite a large terminal rise and still be heard as a statement, if the rise was preceded by a high fall. If there was no pitch higher than the

---

1. 'Question' refers throughout to so-called yes–no questions.
2. The acoustic correlates of intonation are said to be changes in one or more of three variables: fundamental frequency, intensity and duration, with fundamental frequency being the strongest single cue (Bolinger, 1958; Denes, 1959; Denes and Milton-Williams, 1962). The present study is concerned with only one of these variables, fundamental frequency, and the term 'intonation contour' refers to contours of fundamental frequency.

end point of the terminal rise, the utterance tended to be heard as a question.

These facts concerning both Swedish and American English suggest that not only the direction and range of the terminal glide, but the shape and level of the entire contour affect listeners' judgments (Gårding and Abramson, 1960; Hadding-Koch, 1961). The present experiment was designed to explore this notion in more detail by means of synthetic intonation contours, and to compare for Swedish and American listeners their preferred question and statement contours. In addition, as a partial check on the degree to which listeners could actually hear the detailed tonal movements involved, some purely psychophysical data were collected.

Method

The utterance *För Jane* [foe 'Jein] = *for Jane*, spoken on a monotone and in such a way as to be acceptable as Swedish to Swedes, as American to Americans was recorded on magnetic tape. From this recording forty-two different fundamental frequency contours, simulating Swedish intonation, were prepared by a procedure described below. The f_0 values were based on detailed spectrographic analyses of a long sample of the Swedish speaker's natural speech. The correspondences between level notation and fundamental frequency derived from this analysis are given in Table 1. As poles,

Table 1 Correspondences between level notation and fundamental frequency (from Hadding-Koch, 1961)

Level	Fundamental frequency (Hz)
4	370 and above
3	260–370
2	175–260
1	175 and below

a Swedish question contour, 2 42 ↑ ⁴, and statement contour, 2 31 ↓, were used. In this present experiment the first number represents the level of the precontour on *För*, the second number the level of the intonation 'peak', the third number the level of the 'turning point' (Gårding, 1960) before the terminal glide. Between the poles of ideal question and statement, various f_0 values at peak, turning point and end were introduced. Diagrams of the contours are reproduced above Figures 1 and 2. All contours started at a fundamental frequency of 250 Hz, sustained for 140 ms over *För*. They then rose to a peak of either 370 Hz (the *S*, or super high series of contours) or 310 Hz (the *H*, or high, series), dropped to one of three turning points:

130 Hz (*S1* and *H1* series), 175 Hz (*S2* and *H2* series), or 220 Hz (*S3* and *H3* series), and then proceeded to one of seven end points between 130 Hz and 370 Hz. The rise and fall on either side of the peak lasted for 300 ms, the terminal rise or fall, from turning point to end point, lasted 200 ms. The actual contours were rounded at peak and turning point rather than pointed as in the schematic contours above the figures.

The intonation was varied by means of the Intonator connected with the Vocoder at Haskins Laboratories, New York. The Vocoder first analyses a speech sample in a bank of filters and then reconstitutes it in a simplified form on the basis of information obtained from the analysis (Dudley, 1939; Borst and Cooper, 1957). The fundamental frequency of the output is controlled by the Intonator, and may be varied independently of other characteristics of the speech sample. Thus, the same utterance may be given any desired number of different fundamental frequency patterns. Instructions to the Intonator are transmitted through photoelectric tubes responding to light reflected from a contour painted on an acetate loop. Also attached to the loop is a strip of adhesive magnetic tape bearing the speech sample to be processed. The loop is reeled past the photoelectric tubes of the Intonator and the magnetic input heads of the Vocoder. The outputs of the synthesizer in the present experiment were the forty-two stimuli previously described. These were recorded on magnetic tape and spliced into five different random orders, with a 5-second interval between stimuli and a 10-second pause after every tenth stimulus. They were presented to 25 Swedish and 24 American undergraduates in two counterbalanced sessions. In each session all five test orders were presented with a short pause between orders. In one session subjects were instructed to indicate for each stimulus whether it would be better characterized as a statement or a question (semantic judgment). In another session subjects were instructed to indicate for each stimulus whether it ended with a rising or a falling pitch (psychophysical judgment). Approximately half the subjects in each group (Swedish and American) made their psychophysical judgments first.

Results

In the semantic test, responses varied as a function of the fundamental frequency at all three of the variable points of the contours: peak, turning point and end point.

Figure 1 presents the semantic data for the Swedish subjects (above) and American subjects (below) on the *S* series of contours (peak at 370 Hz). Against the ordinate are plotted the percentages of question and statement responses. Against the abscissa are plotted the values of the terminal rise or fall of fundamental frequency (end point minus turning point): a

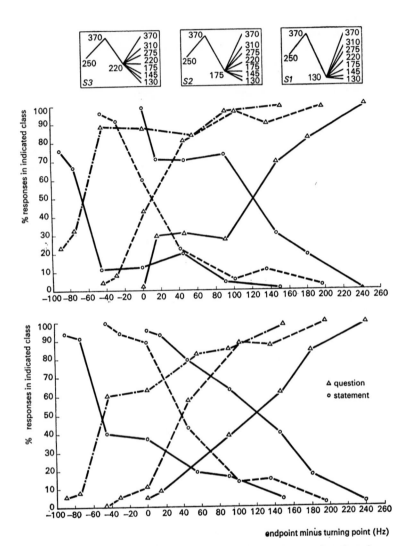

Figure 1 Percentage of statement and question responses as a function of the terminal rise (positive) or fall (negative) of f_0 (endpoint f_0 minus turning point f_0)

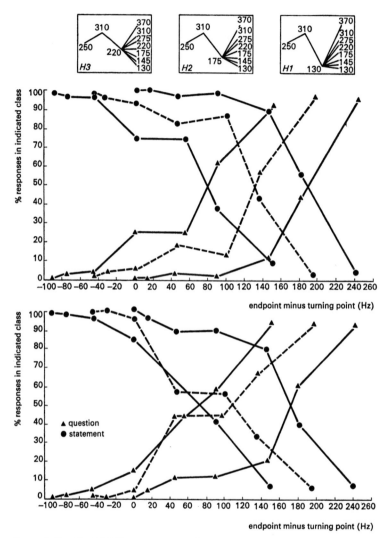

Figure 2 Peak f_o at 310 Hz: percentage of statement and question responses as a function of the terminal rise (positive) or fall (negative) of f_o (endpoint f_o minus turning point f_o)

negative value indicates a terminal fall, a positive value a terminal rise. Parameters of the curves are peak f_0 (370 Hz) and turning point f_0 (130 Hz for $S1$, 175 Hz for $S2$, 220 Hz for $S3$).

The effect of the terminal rise or fall is immediately obvious and very much as expected: for all three series the higher the terminal rise, the higher the percentage of question responses. Equally obvious is the effect of the fundamental frequency at the turning point. For purposes of comparison we may consider the so-called points of subjective equality, that is, the indifference points at which subjects' responses cross over from predominantly statements to predominantly questions. For the Swedish subjects we find the crossover in the $S1$ series at a final rise of 120 Hz, in the $S2$ series at a final rise of 12 Hz, and in the $S3$ series at a final fall of 65 Hz. Thus, the f_0 value of the turning point may quite override the effect of the terminal rise or fall. For example, a terminal fall of 45 Hz is heard as a statement 96 per cent of the time when the turning point is at 175 Hz, but as a question 89 per cent of the time when the turning point is at 220 Hz. Similar effects are present in the American data. But the Americans display some preference for statements over questions. As compared with the Swedes they require somewhat smaller terminal falls to be sure they hear statements, somewhat larger terminal rises to be sure they hear questions.

In the H series (peak f_0:310 Hz) the number of questions heard again increases with the f_0 value at the turning point, although less markedly. Figure 2 presents the data for the Swedish subjects (above) and the American subjects (below). Here the groups differ little in their question curves. But the Swedes display a preference for statements, particularly in the $H2$ and $H3$ series.

If the S and H series are compared (Figures 1 and 2), it appears that more questions are heard in the S series and more statements in the H series. In other words, a rise in f_0 at the peak – exactly as a rise in f_0 at the turning point – is accompanied by an increase in the number of questions heard. Figure 3 facilitates this comparison by displaying the Swedish data for the $S2$ and $H2$ series on the same axes. For example, a stimulus with a final rise of 100 Hz is heard as a question 96 per cent of the time when the peak is at 370 Hz (S), but as a statement 89 per cent of the time when the peak is at 310 Hz (H). In other words, the lowered peak overrides the effects of a substantial final rise, and induces a virtual reversal of the response distributions.

Turning, finally, to the results of the psychophysical tests, in which subjects were asked to indicate whether the contours ended with a rising or a falling pitch, we find greater subject uncertainty but the same general effects as have been described for the semantic tests. Figure 4 compares the Ameri-

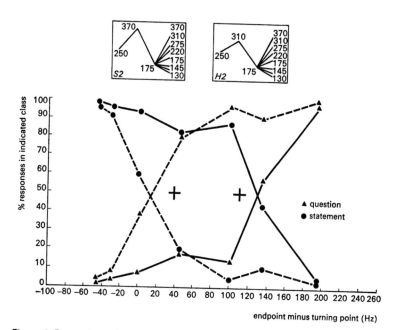

Figure 3 Percentage of statement and question responses as a function of the
terminal rise (positive) or fall (negative) of f_0 for Swedish subjects. The curves
for the two values of peak f_0 (370 Hz (S) and 310 Hz (H), with turning point f_0
constant at 175 Hz, are compared. The crosses indicate the points of subjective
equality for the US subjects in the S2 (left) and H2 (right) series

can psychophysical and semantic data for the H1 series of contours: the
two sets of data are nearly identical. Contours identified as statements tend
to be heard as having a terminal fall (even when, in fact, the final contour is
rising), while contours identified as questions tend to be heard as having a
terminal rise. On other series, the agreement is not always so marked. For
example, Figure 5 displays the American psychophysical and semantic
data from the S3 series. Here, as is generally true, the psychophysical
judgments are more uncertain than the semantic – particularly for the
contours displaying terminal falls. Nonetheless, there is still remarkable
agreement between the two sets of curves.

Discussion

The results confirm what naturalistic observation and some previous experiments have already suggested: that listeners may make use of the entire
f_0 contour in identifying questions and statements. Not only terminal rise

or fall, but also preceding peak and turning point are relevant. These three variables interact in a manner that cannot be easily described. But, in general, for a given f_0 at the other two points, an increase in f_0 at the third point leads to an increase in the number of questions heard.

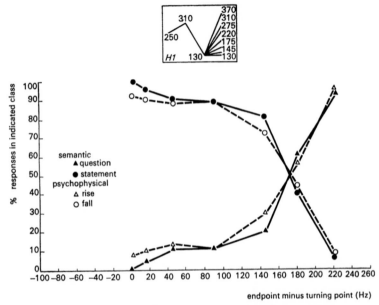

Figure 4 Percentage of statement and question responses (semantic: solid line) and of rise and fall responses (psychophysical: hatched line) as a function of terminal rise (positive) or fall (negative) of f_0 (American Subjects)

As to the actual f_0 values preferred by listeners for the question and statement contours, the Swedish results agree with the predictions based on spectrographic analysis. The contours yielding the greatest proportion of question responses (S2) had a peak at 370 Hz and a turning point at 220 Hz. This contour yielded a high proportion of question responses even when there was a moderate terminal fall. But the preferred question contour was 2 42 plus a final rise. Similarly, the contours yielding the greatest proportion of statements (H1) had a peak at 310 Hz and a turning point at 130 Hz. Here, a large proportion of statement responses occurred even when there was a considerable terminal rise (cf. Introduction). But the preferred statement contour was 2 31. Since the turning point f_0 (130 Hz) was the lowest f_0 in the experiment, no final fall could occur with the H1 contour.

As was stated earlier, Swedish and American English are said to have similar typical statement contours, but different typical question contours. As to questions, the data of the present experiment do not contradict this. For, although both groups selected a typical Swedish question (*S3*, 2 42 ↑) as their preferred question contour, the Americans did require a higher terminal rise to reach complete agreement on their question responses than the Swedes: lacking the typical continuously rising question

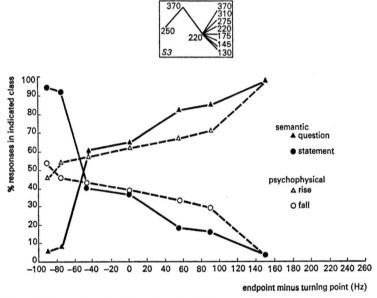

Figure 5 Percentage of statement and question responses (semantic: solid line) and of rise and fall responses (psychophysical: hatched line) as a function of terminal rise (positive) or fall (negative) of f_0 (American Subjects)

of American English (2 23 ↓), they gave more weight to the terminal glides than did the Swedes. However, they also gave more weight to the terminal glides in the preferred statement series (*H1*). This suggests that the two groups may differ in their preferred statement as well as in their preferred question contours. Further experiments designed to examine in more detail the differences between the two groups are in progress.

Finally, the psychophysical data perhaps throw some light on the process by which the f_0 values at peak and turning point exert their influence on listeners' semantic judgments. These data show that listeners were unable to follow the terminal glide with anything like the precision that might have been predicted from simple pure tone pitch discrimination (Stevens and Davis, 1938): psychophysical judgments were influenced by peak and turning point f_0 very much as semantic judgments. Insofar as semantic and psychophysical judgments agree (as in Figure 4), it would seem that listeners may have been using the *perceived* direction of the terminal glide rather than its physically measured direction to make their semantic decisions. The role of peak and turning point f_0 would then seem to lie in their effect on the perception of the terminal glide. On the other hand, insofar as the psychophysical data display greater uncertainty than the semantic (as in Figure 5), the peak and turning point f_0 values would seem to exert an independent influence on the semantic judgment, presumably in some weighted combination with the perceived terminal glide. Further experiments, including a study of the perception of non-speech control signals, have been designed to study these relations more fully and are now in progress.[3]

Summary

The intonation contour of a single utterance was systematically varied and presented for judgment to Swedish and American subjects. In counterbalanced sessions, subjects were asked to classify the contours as (a) questions or statements (semantic judgment), (b) having terminal rises or falls (psychophysical judgment). The data from the two groups of subjects and from the two types of judgments are described and compared.

3. We should like to acknowledge that the research reported here was supported in part by a grant from the National Science Foundation, Washington, D C.

References

BOLINGER, D. L. (1958), 'A theory of pitch accent in English', *Word*, vol. 14, pp. 109–49.

BORST, J. M., and COOPER, F. S. (1957), 'Speech research devices based on a channel Vocoder', *J. acoust. Soc. Amer.*, vol. 29, p. 777.

BRONSTEIN, A. J. (1960), *The Pronunciation of American English: An Introduction to Phonetics*, Appleton-Century-Crofts.

DENES, P. (1959), 'A preliminary investigation of certain aspects of intonation' *Language and Speech*, vol. 2, pp. 106–22.

DENES, P., and MILTON-WILLIAMS, J. (1962), 'Further studies in intonation', *Language and Speech*, vol. 5, pp. 1–14.

DUDLEY, H. (1939), 'Remaking speech', *J. acoust. Soc. Amer.*, vol. 11, pp. 169–75.

GÅRDING, E. (1960), 'A study of the perception of some American English intonation contours', Paper read before 75th Meeting Mod. Lang. Ass. Amer., Philadelphia, 28 December.

GÅRDING, E., and ABRAMSON, A. S. (1960), 'A study of the perception of some American English intonation contours', *Haskins Labs. Quarterly Progress Report 34*.

HADDING-KOCH, K. (1961), *Acoustic-phonetic Studies in the Intonation of Southern Swedish*, Gleerups, Lund.

HERMANN, E. (1942), 'Probleme der Frage', *Nachrichten von der Akademie der Wissenschaften in Göttingen*, pp. 3–4.

PIKE, K. L. (1945), *The Intonation of American English*, University of Michigan, Ann Arbor.

STEVENS, S. S., and DAVIS, H. (1938), *Hearing, its Psychology and Physiology*, Wiley.

ULDALL, E. T. (1960), 'Attitudinal meanings conveyed by intonation contours', *Language and Speech*, vol. 3, pp. 223–34.

ULDALL, E. T. (1962), 'Ambiguity: question or statement? or "Are you asking me or telling me?" ', *Proc. IV Int. Congr. Phon. Sci.*, pp. 779–83, Mouton, The Hague.

Part Five
Speech Synthesis by Rule

A considerable proportion of the experimental work described in this book was originally stimulated by practical aims and all of it could be applied to such aims. It would be almost true to say that in this early period of the computer age speech communication forms a technological bottleneck in the sense that for many purposes men need to talk to machines and to have machines talk to them. With the developments in artificial intelligence which must lie in the future, this need will become greater. In all advances of this kind a major contribution is made by increase in our understanding of how the human machine works and papers reprinted here represent such an increase with respect to speech. Machines do not of course have to mimic human operation but a study of the latter often determines the goals which are set for machines. We are at present a very long way from having at our disposal a machine which can recognize and process speech sounds like a human being and for this reason this book includes no material on automatic speech recognition. The lack of such a device is an effective obstacle in the path of man–machine communication by speech. The complementary operation, speech from machine to man is however well within our grasp. If our knowledge of the acoustic cues used, say, in English were complete, including naturally all those referring to prosodic features, then it would be possible to draw up rules which would enable a computer to instruct a speech synthesizer in such a way as to produce intelligible running speech on the basis of a text roughly in the form of a phonemic transcription. The last paper in the book gives an idea of the form which such rules would take and of some of the considerations which are involved in the solution of this problem.

31 Alvin M. Liberman, Frances Ingemann, Leigh Lisker, Pierre C. Delattre and Franklin S. Cooper

Minimal Rules for Synthesizing Speech[1]

Alvin M. Liberman, Frances Ingemann, Leigh Lisker, Pierre C. Delattre and Franklin S. Cooper, 'Minimal rules for synthesizing speech', *Journal of the Acoustical Society of America*, vol. 31 (1959), pp. 1490–99.

Introduction

During the past ten years a series of studies has been carried out at Haskins Laboratories in an attempt to uncover the acoustic cues that underlie the perception of speech. Many different aspects of the problem have been investigated. Some of the results have been published in acoustical, linguistic and psychological journals, and some have been quietly entombed in the files of the Laboratory. A few members of the staff have been close to all stages of the work, and so, with all the published and unpublished information quite literally at their fingertips, they have been able for some time to paint spectrographic patterns appropriate for the synthesis of almost any utterance. That is, they can paint to order, as it were, simple, schematized spectrograms which, when run through the Pattern Playback or the Voback,[2] produce speech at rather respectable levels of intelligibility. These spectrograms are prepared largely on the basis of research results and without looking at a real speech spectrogram of the utterance being synthesized. To that extent we have for a rather long time now been synthesizing speech by rule. At least in a sense. But not in the sense that the phrase 'rules for synthesizing speech' is used in the title of this paper. In the ideal case, and that is what we want to talk about here, the rules would be together in one place, written down for all to see, and they would be perfectly explicit in all particulars, so that a person with no knowledge of speech or spectrograms could, by reference to the rules, synthesize speech as well as anyone else.

1. This paper was read by invitation before the fifty-sixth meeting of the Acoustical Society of America in November 1958. The work described here was supported in part by the Carnegie Corporation of New York, in part by the Prosthetic and Sensory Aids Service of the Veterans Administration in connection with Contract No. V1005M1253, and in part by the Department of Defense in connection with Contract No. DA49-170-sc-2564.
2. For accounts of these research tools, see Cooper (1950); Cooper, Liberman and Borst (1951); Borst and Cooper (1957).

Recently, one of the authors of this paper, Frances Ingemann, undertook to prepare just such a set of rules. For this purpose she combed, winnowed, refined and distilled the material in our files. Her first set of rules for synthesis was described to this Society at the Ann Arbor meeting (1957) and recorded samples of the results were played.

We do not propose in this paper to set forth all of the rules in detail or to consider the improvements that have been made since Dr Ingemann's earlier report to the Society. Rather, we intend to talk about rules for synthesis in relation to some general aspects of the processes of speech production and perception. We shall try, then, to organize some relatively familiar data and concepts in terms of their relevance to a somewhat less familiar problem.

It may help in setting the problem to think in terms of a machine that will process a discrete phonemic input in such a way as to produce a speech output. We shall suppose that the information available at the input is in the form of a succession of phonemes such as would result from an analysis of a series of utterances by a competent linguist. Fortunately, we need not be concerned here with the precise nature of the phonemic system that was assumed in making this analysis. For our present purposes it is sufficient to know that these phonemes represent discrete elements of the kind everyone knows as consonants and vowels. So far as the output is concerned, we ask simply that it be easily intelligible at normal rates of production.

This exercise may be considered to have any one or all of several purposes. On the one hand it may be practical. One thinks, for example, of the synthesizer end of a speech-recognizer band width compression system or, perhaps, of a reading machine for the blind. On the other hand, the aim may be quite academic, and, in a rather specific sense, not too different from that which motivates the linguist. Given that we know something about the acoustic cues for the various phonemes, we should like to systematize the data by deriving from them an orderly set of rules for synthesis, and, ideally, we should like to produce rules that are few in number, simple in structure and susceptible of mechanization.

Synthesis from prerecorded elements

For the purposes of this paper it will be helpful to begin by assuming that we know nothing about the acoustic patterns that underlie language, and that we are going to try nevertheless to convert a phonemic input to speech. In that case we are likely to consider, as the simplest solution, a system in which an inventory of prerecorded sounds is assigned in one-to-one fashion to the phonemic signals at the input end. In this system the incoming phonemes simply key the prerecorded sounds. If we instrument such an arrangement, we will almost surely find it quite unsatisfactory. Of all the various difficulties that one will ultimately experience with this system, the most immediately obvious will be a noticeable bumpiness and roughness in the output. One thinks, then, of setting up various smoothing operations, and, indeed, it is surely possible to improve the output by such means. But no amount of smoothing will solve what is here a very fundamental, and, by now, familiar problem. One has only to look at spectrograms to see that speech tends to vary more or less continuously over stretches of greater than phonemic length. The patterns rarely break at what might be considered to be phoneme boundaries, and those who have tried to find the acoustic limits of the phoneme have come to know this as the problem of segmentation.

Now none of this should be taken to deny the existence of the phoneme, either as a convenient linguistic abstraction or as a perceptual unit. It indicates merely that the perceptually and linguistically discrete phonemes are often combined and, indeed, in some cases encoded, into units that are more than one phoneme in length. They are not strung together like beads on a string. It is for this reason that one encounters difficulties when he tries to snip phonemes out of a magnetic tape recording, or when, conversely, he tries to synthesize speech from prerecorded phonemic elements.[3]

If one insists, nevertheless, on trying to produce speech from prerecorded phonemes, he is likely to be forced into one of two undesirable courses. One possibility is to employ different recordings, or allophonic variants, of most of the phonemes for most of the combinations in which they occur. This obviously requires a formidable inventory of prerecorded elements. The number of elements can be reduced by creating classes of variants, each class being represented by a single typical form. But this reduction in the number of items is only to be had by severely compromising the quality of the output; in short, the rougher the approximation to proper junctions, the rougher and less intelligible the speech.

An alternative is to try to record, or recover, the speech sounds in very brief form as, for example, in a rapid recitation of the alphabet (plus a baker's dozen of additional sounds). The difficulty, of course, is that the phonemes have now become syllables and the intended synthetic speech has become a kind of 'spelling bee'. Nor is this difficulty avoidable: a shift from spelling to phonetic pronunciation only shortens and centralizes the vowel that clings to almost every consonant; indeed, it is difficult to imagine how a voiced stop, for example, could possibly be produced or heard with-

3. For the purposes of this discussion it does not matter greatly whether the elements are pronounced and recorded in isolation or, alternatively, cut out of recordings of connected speech and then reassembled into new combinations. Some of the difficulties that arise in connection with the latter procedure are illustrated in Harris' account of his attempt to isolate the 'building blocks of speech'. See Harris (1952).

out some vowel-like sound preceding or following it. Thus, we see that this alternative does violence to the speech process; moreover, it has but limited practical utility, since the spelling-bee output will not be so readily or rapidly comprehended as ordinary speech with its phonemes in syllabic combination.

What has been said so far does not mean that one cannot work from prerecorded elements. Rather, it suggests that if one wants by this technique to produce speech rather than spelling, and if one prefers not to deal with allophonic variants, then among the prerecorded elements has to be included a number of units which exceed one phoneme in length. An inevitable result is that the inventory must be very large (as it was found, above, to be for the method of allophonic variants when high-quality speech was desired). Thus, in a recent attempt to synthesize speech from discrete segments, Peterson, Wang and Sivertsen (1958) have used what they call 'dyads', a dyad being a segment which contains 'parts of two phones with their mutual influence in the middle of the segment'. To produce one idiolect by this technique Peterson, Wang and Sivertsen estimate that some 8000 dyads are necessary. (It should be noted that this number includes provision for three levels of intonation for many of the dyads.) For some purposes such a system may well represent a practical solution. It is not the only solution, however, and from one standpoint not the most interesting. We have in mind here that one may quite properly regard a set of rules for synthesis as a description of the acoustic basis for the perception of language.[4] If so, it must be concluded that discrete segments provide an uneconomical description, since, as has been seen, the number of segments or entries in the system is extremely large.[5]

Synthesis by phonemic rules

Although it is very difficult to produce speech from prerecorded phonemic segments, it is nevertheless possible to generate speech from discrete phonemic instructions. That is, rules for synthesis *can* be written which make it possible to go from phonemic units to speech, and thus reduce by a very large factor the total number of rules needed.[6] This can be done by taking advantage of what is known about the cues for speech perception.

4. We are here concerned only with those aspects of the acoustic pattern that carry the linguistic information.
5. A description of the acoustic basis of language in these terms is, of course, also incomplete unless the patterns present in each segment are fully described in acoustic terms.
6. As used in this paper a 'rule' will refer to all the statements that must be made in order to specify whatever unit (e.g., phoneme, subphonemic feature, syllable) of the language is being used as a basis for synthesis.

The patterns of Figure 1 illustrate some of these cues and also point to one of the reasons why it is so very difficult to cut and reassemble phonemic segments. When converted into sound by the Pattern Playback, the hand-drawn spectrograms seen in the figure produce reasonably close approximations to the consonant-vowel syllables indicated. All that we can say

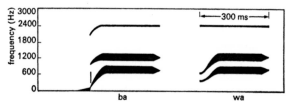

Figure 1 Hand drawn spectrographic patterns illustrating some of the acoustic cues for the stop consonant /b/ and the semivowel /w/

about these particular spectrograms that is relevant to the present discussion has been said at other times in talks before this Society and in published papers. (See Cooper *et al.*, 1952; Liberman *et al.*, 1954, 1956; O'Connor *et al.*, 1957.) Therefore, we ask the indulgence of the reader and, in return, promise to be brief.

Research with patterns such as those shown in Figure 1 has shown that a primary cue for the perception of these and certain other consonants is the relatively rapid shift in the formant frequencies seen at the left of each pattern. These shifts have been named 'transitions', which is unfortunate because this designation implies that they are mere incidents in the process of going from phoneme to phoneme. Far from being incidental links between phonemes, these transitions are themselves among the most important cues to the perception of many of the consonants. It cannot be too strongly emphasized that the perceptual function of the transitions is not to avoid clicks and thumps, but rather to provide important and sometimes essential information for phoneme identification. This is to say that the essential perceptual cue is sometimes given by information concerning the change from one frequency position to another. For the consonant phonemes of Figure 1, and for others too, it is unqualifiedly true that there is no position in the pattern that will be perceived as the intended consonant, or, indeed, as any consonant when it is in steady state. Sounding the initial steady-state portion of /w/ will cause the listener to hear the vowel /u/. Every point on the transition leading into the steady-state vowel will, if prolonged, produce a vowel-like sound.[7] The listener will perceive

7. It was found in an earlier study (see O'Connor *et al.*, 1957) that in the case of /w/ in initial position a brief steady-state segment at the onset helps to avoid a stop consonant effect, but it is not really essential. One must be careful, however, not to

Alvin M. Liberman, *et al.* 449

/w/ only if he is given information about where the formant begins, where it ends, and how long it takes to move from the one frequency to the other. Normally, this information is conveyed continuously by the transitions. It is always possible, of course, to degrade the patterns to some degree, as for example by erasing parts of the transitions, without utterly destroying the phoneme as perceived. Indeed, in the case of /w/ one can synthesize it reasonably well by moving from the initial steady state to the steady state of the vowel without actually sounding the transition at all, provided the normal time relationships are preserved.[8] This is a rather extreme case – one cannot remove nearly so much of the transition for the /b/ of Figure 1, or, indeed, for any of the stop or nasal consonants – and even so it is clear that some indication of the /w/ transitions, as given by the abrupt shift from the initial steady state to the vowel, is a necessary condition for the perception of the /w/ phoneme. These considerations lead us to disagree with an assumption that Peterson, Wang and Sivertsen (1958) took as basic to their segmentation technique, namely, that 'the intelligibility of speech is carried by the more sustained or target positions of the vowels, consonants, and other phonetic features'. We would rather say that for many of the consonants an important and sometimes necessary condition for intelligibility is that the listener be provided with information concerning the direction, extent and duration of formant 'movement'. When we consider that this information is normally present in formant transitions, and that it cannot really be dispensed with, we see one of the reasons why it is so difficult, starting with recorded utterances, to isolate and recombine phonemic segments.

Now to arrive at 'phonemic' rules for the generation of syllables like those of Figure 1, we begin by taking into account that all the transitions for a given consonant have a common feature. This is illustrated in Figure

---

have the steady-state segment exceed about 30 ms, because at longer durations the listener hears a vowel preceding the /w/. It is not always clear in spectrograms of real speech whether or not there is an initial steady-state segment, and, if so, how long the segment is. With the Pattern Playback it is possible to stop the pattern at any point and determine what that part of the pattern sounds like in steady state.

8. For the purposes of producing speech by recombining prerecorded phonemic segments, one might take advantage of this possibility with /w/ by isolating something approximating the initial steady state of /w/ which, when spliced in the proper temporal relationship to any of several vowels would, perhaps, produce a fair impression of /w/ plus vowel. This technique would almost certainly not work nearly so well with other consonants, and it will in any case probably be harder to do with real speech than with the idealized, schematized, hand-drawn patterns described in the text. In general, we should expect the application of this technique to be somewhat limited and to produce something less than ideal results, for at best it represents a way to force speech into a wholly unnatural mould.

2, where we see in the bottom row that, although the extent and direction of the transitions are different for /d/ before different vowels, it is nevertheless clear that the transitions have originated from approximately the same place. This common origin has been called the locus,[9] and it has been possible to define characteristic loci for essentially all the consonants.

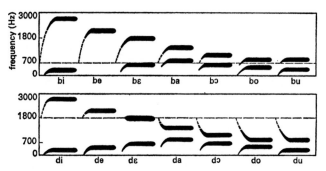

Figure 2 Second-formant transitions appropriate for /b/ and /d/ before various vowels

Knowing the first-, second-, and third-formant loci for all the consonants is the key that unlocks the syllable and makes it feasible to write rules at the phoneme level. For example, we may say of /d/ that its second formant should start at about 1800 Hz and proceed then at a certain rate to the steady-state level appropriate for the second formant of the following vowel. If, alternatively, we want to synthesize a syllable consisting of /b/ plus vowel, we see from the patterns in the top row of the figure that we should start the second formant at about 700 Hz and proceed to the vowel level from there. In fact, the situation is somewhat more complicated than this in several ways. For example, the stops must not actually start at the loci – rather, they should only 'point' to them. In the patterns of the figure the dashed lines represent non-explicit portions of the complete transition specified by the locus hypothesis. This characteristic of the locus is one of the class markers for the stops, as it is also for the nasals. For these and other classes of consonants it is, of course, necessary to add other acoustic cues, such as the noises that occur with stops, affricates, and fricatives,[10] and

9. For a detailed treatment of the 'locus', see Delattre, Liberman and Cooper (1955); Harris, Hoffman, Liberman, Delattre and Cooper (1958). A rationalization in terms of articulatory-acoustic considerations is contained in a paper by Stevens and House (1956). In certain ways the locus is similar to the 'hub' (see Potter, Kopp and Green, 1947).
10. Liberman, Delattre and Cooper (1952); Schatz (1954); Hughes and Halle (1956); Halle, Hughes and Radley (1957); Harris (1958).

the relatively brief steady-state resonances that mark the nasals, liquids, and semivowels.

At a different level of complication it is, as we have already implied, necessary that the application of a phoneme rule be made in relation to the phonemes on either side. Thus, in the example used, the second-formant transition for /d/ led to the second-formant level appropriate for the next vowel, wherever that might have been. This means that contextual information must be used in *applying* the rules for successive phonemes, but only to the extent that one must know – as he must in any case – the appropriate formant levels for the next phoneme so that the transitions may be properly connected. Given that the situation is even approximately this simple, we can see how, in principle, the number of rules can approximate the number of phonemes.

Synthesis by subphonemic rules

But if economy in terms of number of rules is our aim – and it would appear to be a reasonable one – we can go further by setting up the rules in terms of subphonemic dimensions. Figure 3 contains hand-drawn spectrographic

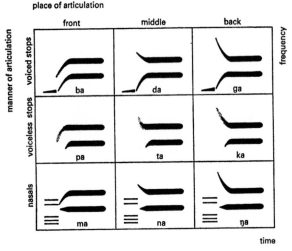

Figure 3 Patterns illustrating some of the acoustic cues for the stop and nasal consonants

patterns that illustrate how this can be done. Here we see hand-painted spectrograms that will produce reasonable approximations to the syllables /ba, da, ga, pa, ta, ka, ma, na, ŋa/. All the sounds having the same place of articulation – that is, all the sounds in a given column – have the same second-formant transition. Similarly, all the sounds having the same manner of articulation – that is, those in a given row – have the same first-formant transition, and in some cases, additional markers, as for the nasality of /m, n, ŋ/. Thus, it is possible to set up a rule for a front place of articulation, a middle place of articulation and a back place of articulation. Similarly, there is a rule for the class of voiced stops, one for the voiceless stops, and one for nasality. In this way we obtain nine phonemes with six rules.

It should be noted here that when the rules are written at a subphonemic level, arrangements must be made for simultaneous (as well as sequential) combination. Thus, for the consonant phoneme of a syllable, for example, we must put together, at the very least, the appropriate rule for place of articulation and the appropriate rule for manner; these, in turn, must be 'meshed' with the rules for the vowel or other consonants of the syllable.

As we have seen, the number of rules is considerably reduced by operating at a subphonemic level. In the ideal case we would, of course, have only as many rules as there are subphonemic features, and this would be in the neighborhood of ten. However, for reasons which will be given below, it is not possible to achieve this ideal.

Additional rules for position

One complication at either the phonemic or subphonemic level is that we must sometimes make special provision for positional variations. The few simple examples so far have been of consonants in initial position. Now in most cases it is possible to produce patterns suitable for other positions

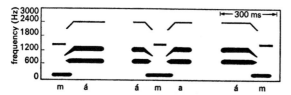

Figure 4 Patterns illustrating some of the cues for /m/ in different positions

from the same basic rules (Lisker, 1957a, 1957b). That is, it is usually possible to frame a basic rule for a phoneme or a subphonemic dimension and then derive the particular patterns for each of several positions. As an example, let us take the patterns for the nasal labial consonant /m/ in initial, intervocalic, and final positions, as shown in Figure 4. The basic rules for /m/ require that there be steady-state formants of specified duration, intensities and frequencies. Furthermore, they require that any adjacent formants have transitions of a specified duration which are discontinuous with the nasal formants and which point to certain locus frequencies. As we see from Figure 4, the differences among the initial, intervocalic and final patterns for /m/ involve only the presence or absence of transitions on either side of the nasal formants. Whether or not a transition is to be drawn depends on whether adjacent formants are specified, and that depends, of course, on the rules appropriate for the immediate neighbors of /m/ in the sequence of input phonemes. In other words, before we can have a transition we must have, at the input, two contiguous phonemes both of whose rules call for this acoustic feature.

The preceding example illustrates the most common type of positional variation that must be accommodated by our rules of synthesis. As we have elected to handle them, such positional variations follow from the different ways in which rules for adjacent phonemes 'mesh' to specify the transitional portions of our patterns; therefore, additional 'connection' rules are not necessary.

In certain cases, however, it is not possible to derive a desired pattern entirely from the basic rules for the constituent phonemes, although we are never forced to the extreme of having to write an entirely new rule for such a case. Rather, we find that an appropriate pattern can be produced simply by applying a qualification or 'position modifier' to the basic rule. An example of this is the pattern for the syllable /glu/ shown in Figure 5. The

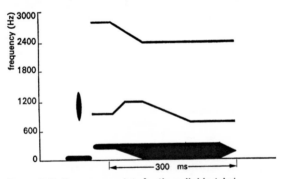

Figure 5 Pattern appropriate for the syllable /glu/

basic rule for /g/ calls for an interval that is silent except for a voice bar, followed by a burst, and it further stipulates that adjacent formants have transitions which point to particular locus frequencies. The rule for /l/ calls for steady-state formants of a certain duration and specified intensities and frequencies, and it further requires that these /l/ formants be continuous with transitions to any adjacent formants. The rule for the vowel /u/

specifies the duration, intensity and frequency of each of three formants which are steady state, except as rules for neighboring phonemes prescribe transitions. Now a rigid application of the basic rules for the phonemes constituting the syllable /glu/ yields an ultimate acoustic output of less than tolerable intelligibility. A marked improvement is achieved if the basic rule for each phoneme is modified as follows: /g/ before /l/ requires only a burst of specified frequency; /l/ before /u/ has the frequency of its second formant lowered somewhat; /u/ following /l/ has a second formant which first rises from the second-formant frequency of /l/, and then, after a specified duration, shifts at a given rate to the normal steady-state frequency for /u/. At this point it should be remarked that these position modifiers operate on classes of phonemes; thus, the modification for /g/ applies also to the other stops, the modifier for /l/ applies also to /w, r, j/, and the modifier for /u/ applies also to /o/ and /ɔ/. In other words, the kind of economy gained by going from phoneme rules to subphonemic rules extends to the position modifiers as well.

Similar problems occur and similarly general solutions are found for other positional variations, as, for example, in the neighborhood of juncture.

Linguistic digression

We should like to digress here to discuss briefly the implications of what has been said for the problem of how to define the phoneme. As you remember, we began by referring to a machine that would process a discrete phonemic input so as to produce a speech-like output. The phonemic input would be furnished by linguistic analysis. We might soon discover on consulting several equally competent linguists that they were of divided opinion on two subjects at least. First, they might have different ideas on the best way to define the phoneme; and second, they would not agree entirely on what the phonemes of a particular language are. Now the first point may be dismissed as a bit of academic quibbling, for we observe that two linguists with conflicting definitions of the phoneme can come out with phonemic analyses that are remarkably alike. It is of interest, nevertheless, that at least one linguist, Zellig Harris (1951), has proposed an operational definition of the phoneme which would require for its application that we synthesize speech from prerecorded utterances cut up into segments of phoneme length. For example, if the question were whether two sounds in different environments were or were not the same phoneme, one would interchange the appropriate snippets of tape, play back, and listen to determine whether the resulting utterance, as perceived, was reasonably satisfactory. Now we know that in many cases this operation cannot really be performed satisfactorily, and therefore has very little utility as a tool for phonemic analysis. However, the linguist may be able to do a roughly equivalent thing in terms of our rules and their modifiers. For the case of the sounds in different environments, the question would be whether one could satisfactorily synthesize them by using the same rule in both cases, provided only he applied the appropriate positional modifier.

The second point of dispute among the linguists is more important to us, since it actually affects what is to go into the input of the synthesizer. For example, one linguist will transcribe the vocalic part of the word *cake* with a single symbol where another will write it as a sequence of two. Then again, they may have differences of opinion about where to put the phonemes that sometimes mark boundaries between words. Instead of waiting for the linguists to resolve these conflicts among themselves, we might try each of the alternative analyses they provide, and then select that one which yields the most intelligible and natural-sounding speech output. Of course, if two alternatives yield the same kind of results by this test, then we may conclude that the problem is phonetically irrelevant and hand it back to the linguists.

Additional rules for stress and syllabic encoding

Before this digression into linguistics, we were considering the necessity of adding rules beyond the ideal minimum and had discussed the matter of positional variations.

There remain two other types of complication that deserve mention. The first of these arises in connection with prosodic features, particularly stress.[11] We might have supposed that the basic rules, derived as they are largely from experiments with isolated syllables, would, if anything, yield connected speech that is 'over-intelligible' to the point of sounding stilted. Now the speech we get certainly sounds stilted if differences in stress are not provided for, but it is also often markedly less intelligible than would be predicted from the levels of intelligibility achieved for its constituent vowels and consonants when these are tested in nonsense syllables. The quality of the synthetic speech is significantly improved, both in intelligibility and in naturalness, if at least two degrees of stress are provided for in the rules. The stress differences can be specified by one or more acoustic features, such as fundamental frequency, intensity and duration. (Fundamental frequency is also, of course, the basis for variations in intonation, but no attempt has yet been made to include this feature in the rules.) At the present time only duration is actually being used in the rules for stress.

In order to achieve the greatest gain from adjusting vowel durations for two degrees of stress it is necessary to reduce the durations of some vowels,

11. Fry (1955); Bolinger and Gerstman (1957); Bolinger (1958a, b); Fry (1958); Lisker (1957b).

specifically those in medial unstressed syllables, to such an extent that no steady-state remains. By the rules for stressed syllables, a simple consonant-vowel-consonant pattern consists at the very least of an initial transition, a steady-state segment, and a final transition. The steady-state segment has formant frequencies characteristic of the vowel alone; the transitions have durations and end points fixed according to the place and manner rules for the consonants. To convert such a syllable into a form appropriate for the unstressed conditions, we must effectively omit the steady-state segment, as pointed out above. This means that the second and third formants are in

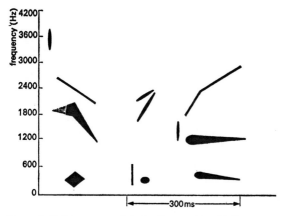

Figure 6 Pattern appropriate for the word 'typical'

fact drawn as straight lines connecting the end-point frequencies given by the place rules for the adjacent consonants. (It is necessary that the second formant pass through the 1000–2000 Hz region. Where the straight line rule would violate this restriction – as, for example, in the case of a vowel between two labials – the second formant must be curved to bring it up or down into the required frequency range.) The configuration of the first formant will depend on whether the adjacent consonants are voiced or voiceless: if voiced, the first formant will move from its initial frequency to 500 Hz and then to its final frequency; if voiceless, it will remain at a steady-state frequency of 500 Hz. In Figure 6 the pattern for the word 'typical' shows an unstressed vowel between voiceless stops drawn according to this rule.

The other kind of complication is infrequent enough to be of no great practical consequence, perhaps, but is of some interest nevertheless. This difficulty arises because there is occasionally a rather complex relation between the phoneme as a perceptual unit and the sound that elicits it. An example is given in Figure 7. Here we see a single locus for /g/ before the vowels /i, e, ɛ, a/, but between /a/ and /ɔ/ there is a large and sudden jump to a new locus. It is of more than passing interest that there is no corresponding break in the articulation of the consonant. Between /a/ and /ɔ/ there is a change from unrounded to rounded in the articulation of the vowel, and we may suppose that some rounding of the vowel concomitant with consonant articulation produces the sudden shift in consonant locus.

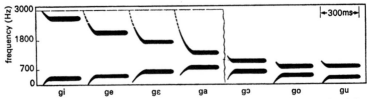

Figure 7 Patterns illustrating second-formant transitions appropriate for /g/ before various vowels

It remains true, however, that so far as the consonant articulation itself is concerned, there is no discontinuity. This is to say, then, that the relation between articulation and phoneme is more nearly one-to-one than that between phoneme and sound. We have in other papers discussed the reason for and the possible significance of this fact (see Liberman, Delattre and Cooper, 1952; Liberman, 1957). Here we will simply note, first, that this requires an addition to the acoustic rules; second, that it must occasionally wreak havoc with attempts to work from prerecorded phonemic segments; and third, that this complication would not affect the rules of synthesis for an articulatory model. We should also stress the point, so clearly evident in this instance, that very often phonemes are literally *encoded* into syllables at the acoustic level; in such cases the syllable becomes, in a very real sense, the irreducible acoustic unit.

Complexity v. number of rules; resultant intelligibility

We have so far talked about the number of rules required to do the job as if the matter of number were the only significant dimension of this problem. It is not. Obviously, we must consider not only the number of rules but also their simplicity. A rule, as we have been using the term, includes all the statements that must be made in order to specify a given unit of the system. Thus, at the subphonemic level, a rule includes all the specifications for a bilabial place of production, for example, or a stop-consonant manner. A given rule may require many specifications or only a few. Simplicity or complexity is largely independent of the number of rules, and becomes, therefore, a separate consideration.

In the discussion so far we have also, perhaps, given the impression that there is a single, ideal and final set of rules. It is, we suppose, obvious that beyond a certain point, reduction in the number of rules, or an increase in their simplicity, will be accomplished only at the cost of naturalness and intelligibility. It remains to be determined just how and within what limits intelligibility and naturalness will vary as a function of the number of rules. In this paper we have more or less implicitly assumed some particular and reasonable level of intelligibility, and have considered the *minimum* set of rules for that level. At present there are nine rules for place of consonant articulation, five for manner of consonant articulation, and three rules for voicing. For the vowels we have two manner and twelve place rules. In addition, we have one stress modifier and about twelve position modifiers. We should emphasize that there is nothing hard and fast about the numbers cited; they serve only to indicate roughly how large an inventory we are currently dealing with.

We have made no comprehensive attempt as yet to measure the intelligibility of the speech produced by such rules. This is not because we are uninterested in intelligibility, but rather because the rules have been changing rapidly, and the data on a really long test are likely to be out of date by the time they have been tabulated. We think it is safe to say that the intelligibility is of a fairly high order. In a few short and rather informal tests, sentence intelligibility has ranged between 60 per cent and 100 per cent depending on the nature of the sentences and the extent to which the listeners are accustomed to hearing this kind of synthetic speech.

Example of the rules and their application

To illustrate just how the various categories of rules are combined to specify a pattern let us derive the pattern for the word 'labs' as shown in Figure 8. This word is represented in the input language by the sequence of phonemes: /læbz/.

/l/ The first phoneme is a member of the class of resonant consonants, i.e., /w, r, l, j/. The *manner* rule for the resonants calls for three formants to be maintained (with specified intensities) at appropriate locus frequencies for 30 ms. The manner rule further specifies that adjacent formants shall have transitions of 75 ms drawn so as to be continuous with the locus formants. (This manner characteristic is referred to in the table of Figure 8 as an 'explicit locus'.) The manner rule for the resonants also fixes the first-formant locus at 360 Hz. Lastly, the resonant manner rule specifies a sound of the harmonic or 'buzz' type. The *place* rule for /l/ specifies locus frequencies of 360, 1260 and 2880 Hz.

/æ/ The next phoneme of the input is a member of the class of long vowels. The manner rule for this class calls for three formants of the buzz variety,

Synthesis by rules: læbz

Manner			
Resonants /wrlj/: periodic sound (buzz); formant intensities and durations are specified; F1 locus is high; formants have explicit loci	*Long vowels* /ieæeaɔo/: periodic sound (buzz); formant intensities and durations are specified	*Stops* /pbtdkg/: no sound at formant frequencies, i.e. 'silence'; burst of specified frequency and band width follows 'silence'; F1 locus is low; F2 and F3 have virtual loci	*Fricatives* /fvθðsz∫ʒ/: a periodic sound (hiss); intensity and band width are specified; F1 locus is intermediate; F2 and F3 have virtual loci
Place			
/l/: F2 and F3 loci are specified	/æ/: formant frequencies specified	*Labials* /pbfvm/: F2 and F3 loci are specified; frequencies of buzz and hiss are specified	*Alveolars* /tdsz/: F2 and F3 loci are specified; frequencies of buzz and hiss are specified
Voicing			
(the voicing rules are only applied to those phonemes for which the condition of voicing has differential value. For the resonants and vowels, which are invariably voiced, the acoustic features correlated with voicing are specified under *Manner*		*Voiced* /bdg/: voice bar; duration of 'silence' is specified; F1 onset is not delayed	*Voiced* /vðzʒ/: voice bar; duration of hiss is specified; F1 onset is not delayed
Position			
vowels in final syllable; duration is double that specified under *Manner*			

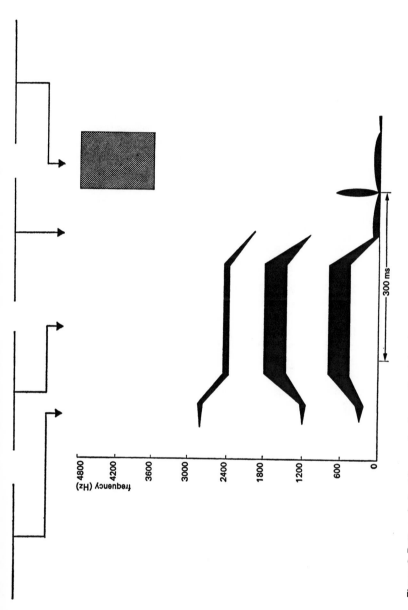

Figure 8 Pattern derived from rules for synthesizing the word /læbz/

Alvin M. Liberman, *et al.* 461

having a duration of 150 ms. The place rule for /æ/ fixes formant frequencies at 750, 1650 and 2460 Hz, and also specifies formant intensities.

/b/ The next phoneme shares its manner rule with all the other stops, /b, d, g, p, t, k/; this rule calls for an interval of 'silence' (an interval devoid of acoustic energy at all frequencies above the fundamental of the buzz) followed by a burst, and further specifies that adjacent formants have 50 ms transitions pointing toward locus frequencies given by the place rule appropriate to the particular stop. ('Pointing to' means that the end-point frequencies of the actual transitions are midway between the locus frequencies and the formant frequencies of the next phoneme. This characteristic of the stop consonant manner is referred to in the table of Figure 8 as a 'virtual locus'.) The manner rule also fixes the locus of the first formant at the frequency of the voice bar. The labial place rule, which serves equally for /b, p, m, f, v/, specifies that adjacent second- and third-formant transitions point to frequencies of 720 and 2100 Hz, respectively. The *voicing* rule for stops (applicable equally to /b, d, g/) requires that the duration of the 'silent' interval be 70 ms and that this interval be filled by a 'voice bar', that is, acoustic energy at the buzz fundamental frequency.

/z/ For the final phoneme, the manner rule is that appropriate for the fricatives, /f, v, θ, ð, s, z, ʃ, ʒ/, and it calls for an interval of band-limited noise (that is, a 'hiss' rather than a buzz sound). The fricative manner rule also specifies that adjacent formants have 50 ms transitions pointing toward virtual loci given by the place rule for the particular fricative; further by the manner rule, the first-formant locus is at 240 Hz. The alveolar place rule for either /z/ or /s/ specifies that the noise (required by the fricative manner rule) have a lower cut-off frequency of 3600 Hz, and that adjacent second- and third-formant transitions point to frequencies of 1800 and 2700 Hz, respectively. The voicing rule states that the noise should be of low intensity, have a duration of 100 ms and be accompanied by a voice bar.

Finally, we apply a *position modifier* for syllables immediately before silence or juncture which doubles the duration of the vowel, making the overall duration of /æ/ 300 ms. At this point we have completely specified a pattern that is directly convertible to an acoustic stimulus which the naïve listener will readily identify as the word 'labs'.

Rules *v*. prerecorded elements: further discussion

Instead of trying now merely to summarize what has already been said, we would rather try to bring into the open a few considerations that have been only implicit in the discussion so far. In particular we should like to call attention to the fact that we have casually mixed two rather different aspects of the problem. The first has to do with the size of the unit in terms of which the rules are written, the second, with the difference between assembling prerecorded elements on the one hand and the real honest-to-goodness fabrication of speech on the other. When we introduced the matter of prerecorded elements earlier, it was primarily to make a point about speech. This was somewhat unfair. Although the use of prerecorded elements is synthesis only in the most sweeping sense of the word,[12] it is sufficiently interesting both in practice and in principle that we ought to deal with it in its own right. The practical advantages of such a system are obvious enough. The difficulty, as we tried to point out earlier, is largely in the matter of linkage. As we have seen, linkage presents great difficulties at the level of phonemes. Indeed, the difficulties are likely to be so great that one will be driven to use elements which are of essentially syllabic dimensions, and even here problems will occur in the matter of joining the syllables. With units the size of words one will, of course, have much less difficulty about linkages, though he may not, even so, be completely out of the woods.

If we have seemed earlier in this discussion to be unenthusiastic about synthesis from prerecorded elements, we should say now that we have been sufficiently interested ourselves to have begun to explore the possibilities of such a system, at least at the level of words (Liberman et al., 1956). We have been particularly interested in trying to find the minimum number of versions of each word which will produce appropriate stresses and intonations when the words are arranged in various combinations. This has proved to be a challenging and interesting problem in the sense that its solution will either depend on the application of already known linguistic principles, or, alternatively, will provide information basic to the formulation of such principles.

To return to the point about linkages, the obvious generalization is that the problem grows less severe as the size of the prerecorded unit increases. There is, presumably, a function relating intelligibility or maximum speed of communication to size of the prerecorded units, and this function must certainly rise, though at an ever decreasing rate, as we go from smaller to larger units. At present, we know that with prerecorded phoneme units we are way down on the intelligibility or speed scale, if indeed, we are on it at all. With prerecorded words we may be within shouting distance of the asymptote. We strongly suspect, without benefit of evidence, that syllables will be marginally useful if we want to communicate at normal speech rates.

12. The speech sounds in the prerecorded elements are of course produced by human articulatory apparatus and recorded just as any other utterances can be. The synthetic aspect of this process consists only of entering these elements into combinations different from those in which they were originally recorded.

It may well be that, for some purposes, prerecorded elements will turn out to be the method of choice. In principle, the system is interesting because when the units are of phonemic dimensions the difficulties one encounters illustrate some important truths about speech, and when the units are the size of words, we encounter some partially soluble and therefore challenging problems of stress and intonation – as well as of instrumentation.

We have already dealt at length with true synthesis as opposed to the use of prerecorded elements. With true synthesis the linkage problem is soluble at all levels, and has to a large extent been solved. The rules for synthesis can be written at various levels. Indeed, this system is inherently flexible in all respects. Its limits are set primarily by the limits of our knowledge about speech and, from a practical standpoint, by the difficulties of instrumenting true synthesis rather than random access.

We saw that with prerecorded elements the total inventory of segments (or rules) will likely approximate the number of syllables at the very least. By using true synthesis we can considerably reduce the number of rules by writing them either at the phoneme or subphoneme level. In either case some rules must be added to take care of positional variations, essential prosodic features, and the special cases in which the acoustic encoding of the phonemes into syllables makes it impossible to get along with only one rule for a single phoneme or subphonemic feature. When the rules are written at the phoneme level there must, of course, be provision for connecting the formant transitions or formants of successive phonemes, and at the subphonemic level additional arrangements must be made for simultaneous combination of the rules pertaining to the several features that constitute the phoneme.

Exactly how and where one might wish to make practical use of the rules for true synthesis depends on a large number of considerations that lie far outside the scope of this paper. In this account, we have been interested in such rules primarily because they constitute a description of the acoustic basis of speech perception. The kind of information contained in that description will, we think, prove useful for a variety of practical and theoretical purposes.

References

BOLINGER, D. L. (1958a), 'On intensity as a qualitative improvement of pitch accent', *Lingua*, vol. 7, pp. 175–82.

BOLINGER, D. L. (1958b), 'A theory of pitch accent in English', *Word*, vol. 14, pp. 109–49.

BOLINGER, D. L., and GERSTMAN, L. J. (1957), 'Disjuncture as a cue to constructs', *Word*, vol. 13, pp. 246–55.

BORST, J. M., and COOPER, F. S. (1957), 'Speech research devices based on a channel Vocoder', *J. acoust. Soc. Amer.*, vol. 29, p. 777 (abstract).

COOPER, F. S. (1950), 'Spectrum analysis', *J. acoust. Soc. Amer.*, vol. 22, pp. 761-2.

COOPER, F. S., LIBERMAN, A. M., and BORST, J. M. (1951), 'The interconversion of audible and visible patterns as a basis for research in the perception of speech', *Proc. nat. Acad. Sci.*, vol. 37, pp. 318-25. Excerpt reprinted here, pp. 204-7.

COOPER, F. S., DELATTRE, P. C., LIBERMAN, A. M., BORST, J. M., and GERSTMAN, L. J. (1952), 'Some experiments on the perception of synthetic speech sounds', *J. acoust. Soc. Amer.*, vol. 24, pp. 597-606. Reprinted here, pp. 258-72.

DELATTRE, P. C., LIBERMAN, A. M., and COOPER, F. S. (1955), 'Acoustic loci and transitional cues for consonants', *J. acoust. Soc. Amer.*, vol. 27, pp. 769-73. Reprinted here, pp. 273-83.

FRY, D. B. (1955), 'Duration and intensity as physical correlates of linguistic stress', *J. acoust. Soc. Amer.*, vol. 27, pp. 765-8.

FRY, D. B. (1958), 'Experiments in the perception of stress', *Language and Speech*, vol. 1, pp. 126-52. Reprinted here, pp. 401-24.

HALLE, M., HUGHES, G. W., and RADLEY, J.-P. A. (1957), 'Acoustic properties of stop consonants', *J. acoust. Soc. Amer.*, vol. 29, pp. 107-16. Excerpt reprinted here, pp. 162-76.

HARRIS, C. M. (1952), 'A study of the building blocks in speech', *J. acoust. Soc. Amer.*, vol. 25, pp. 962-9.

HARRIS, K. S. (1958), 'Cues for the discrimination of American English fricatives in spoken syllables', *Language and Speech*, vol. 1, pp. 1-7. Reprinted here, pp. 284-97.

HARRIS, K. S., HOFFMAN, H. S., LIBERMAN, A. M., DELATTRE, P. C., and COOPER, F. S. (1958), 'Effect of third formant transitions on the perception of the voiced stop consonants', *J. acoust. Soc. Amer.*, vol. 30, pp. 122-6.

HARRIS, Z. S. (1951), *Methods in Structural Linguistics*, University of Chicago Press.

HUGHES, G. W., and HALLE, M. C. (1956), 'Spectral properties of fricative consonants', *J. acoust. Soc. Amer.*, vol. 28, pp. 303-10. Excerpt reprinted here, pp. 151-61.

INGEMANN, F. (1957), 'Speech synthesis by rule', *J. acoust. Soc. Amer.*, vol. 29, p. 1255 (abstract).

LIBERMAN, A. M. (1957), 'Some results of research on speech perception', *J. acoust. Soc. Amer.*, vol. 29, pp. 117-23.

LIBERMAN, A. M., DELATTRE, P. C., COOPER, F. S., and GERSTMAN, L. J. (1954), 'The role of consonant-vowel transitions in the perception of the stop and nasal consonants', *Psychol. Mongr.*, vol. 68, no. 8, pp. 1-13. Reprinted here, pp. 315-31.

LIBERMAN, A. M., DELATTRE, P. C., GERSTMAN, L. J., and COOPER, F. S. (1956), 'Tempo of frequency change as a cue for distinguishing classes of speech', *J. exp. Psychol.*, vol. 52, pp. 127-37.

LIBERMAN, A. M., DELATTRE, P. C., and COOPER, F. S. (1952), 'The role of selected stimulus variables in the perception of the unvoiced consonants', *Amer. J. Psychol.*, vol. 65, pp. 497-516.

LIBERMAN, A. M., INGEMANN, F., LISKER, L., DELATTRE, P. C., and COOPER, F. S. (1956), 'Summary of fourth technical session on reading machines for the blind', Veterans Administration, Washington DC, 23-24 August. Prepared by the Prosthetic and Sensory Aids Service, 252 Seventh Avenue, New York 1.

LISKER, L. (1957a) 'Minimal cues for separating /w, r, l, j/ in intervocalic position' *Word*, vol. 13, pp. 256-67.

LISKER, L. (1957b), 'Linguistic segments, acoustic segments and synthetic speech', *Language*, vol. 33, pp. 42–9.

O'CONNOR, J. D., GERSTMAN, L. J., LIBERMAN, A. M., DELATTRE, P. C., and COOPER, F. S. (1957), 'Acoustic cues for the perception of initial /w, j, r, l/ in English', *Word*, vol. 13, pp. 24–43. Reprinted here, pp. 298–314.

PETERSON, G. E., WANG, W. S.-Y., and SIVERTSEN, E. (1958), 'Segmentation techniques in speech synthesis', *J. acoust. Soc. Amer.*, vol., 30, pp. 739–42.

POTTER, R. K., KOPP, G. A., and GREEN, H. C. (1947), *Visible Speech*, Van Nostrand.

SCHATZ, C. (1954), 'The role of context in the perception of stops', *Language*, vol. 30, pp. 47–56.

STEVENS, K. N., and HOUSE, A. S. (1956), 'Studies of formant transitions using a vocal tract analog', *J. acoust. Soc. Amer.*, vol. 28, pp. 578–85.

Further Reading

C. G. M. FANT, *Acoustic Theory of Speech Production*, Mouton, The Hague, 1960.

J. L. FLANAGAN, *Speech Analysis, Synthesis and Perception*, Springer, Berlin, 2nd edn, 1972.

H. FLETCHER, *Speech and Hearing in Communication*, Van Nostrand, 1953.

M. JOOS, *Acoustic Phonetics*, Language Monographs, no. 23, Linguistic Society of America, Baltimore, 1948.

G. A. MILLER, *Language and Communication*, McGraw-Hill, 1951.

E. PULGRAM, *Introduction to the Spectrography of Speech*, Mouton, The Hague, 1959.

H. SWEET, *The Practical Study of Languages*, Oxford University Press, 1964.

Acknowledgements

Grateful acknowledgement is made to the individual authors who have kindly granted permission for the reprinting of their papers and to the following for permission to reproduce the material listed below:

Bell Telephone Laboratories	Reading 1
American Speech and Hearing Association	Readings 2 and 3
Acoustical Society of America	Readings 4, 6, 9, 10, 12, 17, 18, 24, 25, 26, 27, 31
International Phonetic Association	Reading 5
Mouton (The Hague)	Reading 7
Robert Draper (Teddington)	Readings 8, 16, 19, 28
Van Nostrand (New York)	Reading 11
National Academy of Sciences	Reading 13
Word	Readings 15 and 20
American Psychological Association	Readings 21 and 22
Academia (Prague)	Reading 23
Karger (Basel)	Readings 29 and 30

469